AFTER ARTEST

SUNY SERIES ON SPORT, CULTURE, AND SOCIAL RELATIONS
CL Cole and Michael A. Messner, editors

*A complete listing of the books in this series
appears in the back of the book*

AFTER ARTEST

The NBA and the Assault on Blackness

DAVID J. LEONARD

Cover image: © Djma / Dreamstime.com

Published by
State University of New York Press, Albany

For information, contact State University of New York Press, Albany, NY
www.sunypress.edu

Production by Diane Ganeles
Marketing by Michael Campochiaro

Library of Congress Cataloging in Publication Data

Leonard, David J.
  After Artest : the NBA and the assault on Blackness / David Leonard.
  p. cm. — (SUNY series on sport, culture, and social relations)
  Includes bibliographical references and index.
  ISBN 978-1-4384-4206-8 (pbk. : alk. paper)
  ISBN 978-1-4384-4205-1 (hardcover : alk. paper)
  1. Basketball—United States—Sociological aspects. 2. African
American basketball players—Social conditions. 3. Basketball
fans—United States—Social conditions. 4. Minorities in sports—United
States. 5. Discrimination in sports—United States. I. Title.
  GV889.26.L37 2012
  796.323'64—dc23
2011023207

10 9 8 7 6 5 4 3 2 1

received from Harry Edwards—have propelled this project forward. Whether as sources of education and knowledge regarding cultural studies, critical sports studies, race in America, and the history of the NBA, or just as willing and capable partners in trash-talking battles about basketball, many people deserve a lot of love here. I thank Kofi Hadjor, Douglas Daniels, Oliver Wang, Dylan Rodriguez, Jared Sexton, Lea Redmond, Mark Anthony Neal, and Liz Lee, each of whom has pushed me in significant ways to grow into an NBA/cultural studies scholar and, more importantly, to transform myself from a fan into a scholar (who remains a fan). I also have to thank my many high school friends for the hours we spent together on the basketball court during our teenage years and for their analyses of the NBA, which, after irritating and infuriating me, often inspired me to engage in deeper analysis and reflection. I also must thank Todd Boyd, Dave Zirin, William Rhoden, Scoop Jackson, and the many other voices within the popular sporting discourse who continue to offer the challenging and provocative analysis that is sometimes so hard to find. Special thanks to Dave Zirin for suggesting the book's title.

Many intellectual influences (Robin D.G. Kelley, Grant Farred, David Andrews, Joel Rosen, Michael Giardina, Kyle Kusz, Mary McDonald, Dwight McBride, Michael Giardina, Herman Gray, and Patricia Hill Collins)—some of whom I have had the opportunity to learn from directly and others whose words and insight I have only encountered through reading their works—have shaped my understanding of race and sports and deserve a lot of credit for my completion of this project. Big thanks to Rod Murray and Stacey Lorenz for their assistance with source material and inspiring research. Likewise, Nancy Ellengate, my initial editor at State University of New York, and Larin McLaughlin, my second editor, and Andrew Kenyon, my final editor, as well as the rest of the staff at State University of New York Press (particularly Diane Ganeles and Michael Campochiaro), deserve much credit for their constant support and patience. Much thanks also needs to go to C. Richard King, Lisa Guerrero, Carmen Lugo-Lugo, Jose Alamillo, Mary Bloodsworth-Lugo, Kim Christen, Paula Groves-Price, and Rory Ong who form my current intellectual and pedagogical community, not only directly encouraging and assisting me in the completion of this monograph, but inspiring me through their own work and commitment to social justice.

Special thanks need to go to Rich King: Each and every project I work on, especially those in the realm of sports studies, are a testament to your guidance, knowledge, and support. Hopefully this monograph will be as good as Derek Fisher's .04 shot against the San Antonio Spurs, which would mean you are a hall-a-famer like Phil Jackson—someone who inspires, encourages, and facilitates my best.

ACKNOWLEDGMENTS

As with the execution of the perfect play, the design of a lockdown defense on LeBron or Kobe, the sweetness of a 3-on-2 break, and an alley-oop to Shaq, a block shot by Dwight Howard, a baby hook from Magic, MJ's fall-a-way jumper, Kareem's sky hook, A.I.'s crossover, and, of course, the Worm's masterful defense, this monograph reflects the influences of many individuals whose passion, commitment to racial justice and transformative cultural studies, love for and questions about the NBA and the surrounding culture, intellectual curiosity, and talents have greatly benefited me.

It reflects and builds on numerous conversations, experiences, and classes; it represents the coming together of the many things I have learned from others.

Although this book formally began to take shape following several conversations with Nancy Jackson and subsequent support from C.L. Cole—a wonderful mentor and someone I am honored to call a colleague—and Nancy Ellengate, its origin dates back to my childhood, when I was encouraged to read against the grain and challenge assumptions. I was taught that being a contrarian was not necessarily a bad thing. Of course, the hours in front of TV watching Magic dominate Bird, and then Showtime versus the Bad Boys, as well as those early trips to the Great Western Forum in anticipation of a Coop-a-loop, or to the Sports Arena to watch whoever was playing the Clippers, established in me a passion, if not love, for the NBA, and provided a critical foundation for examining the racial battles of the NBA.

My parents and siblings, who for some reason don't share my passion for the NBA/the Lakers, instilled in me not just a love of sport, but also a certain level of popular culture literacy that made this project possible. Subsequent experiences—from my Black Studies seminar on the black athlete at the University of California, Santa Barbara with Otis Madison (who knew you could study sport) and my undergraduate thesis project on the black college athlete under the guidance of Cedric Robinson, to the support and mentoring I have

CONTENTS

To Sophie Nicole Leonard whose life, even in death, taught me about myself, the labors of love, and life's true challenge; I miss and love you

To my father, James M. Leonard, who taught me that indeed it is not whether you win or lose but how you play the game, especially when, in this game, the opponent, the referee, the rules of the game, and even the fans are working against you

Less obvious, but no less important, have been the all-too-often invisible efforts of the faculty, students, and staff of the Department of Comparative Ethnic Studies at Washington State University. Whether through posing questions that led me to rethink things in class discussion, these individuals have dramatically impacted my work. This book would look much different, would undoubtedly be inferior, without you. In particular, I wish to thank Sanford Richmond (I wait to hear your counterarguments), Marc Robinson, Robert Zachary Williams, Bruce Lee Hazelwood, Cameron Moody, Martin Boston, Cameron Sparks (KB8/24), Stephen Norris, Pete Caster, Lupe Contreras, and countless others. To Kelvin Monroe, my man, my teammate, who inspires, teaches, and just loves with such grace and ease. Love and respect.

Many thanks (big props) to Jessica Hulst, who served as a research assistant, copy editor, motivational speaker, and spiritual advisor at the inception of this project. Much love and thanks to Amanda Leonard, whose editorial talents and support assisted in the completion of this project. Thanks also to the College of Liberal Arts at Washington State University for financial support.

To my family, I owe a special and significant debt of gratitude that these words can only begin to repay. Their love, support, tolerance, and patience have meant more to me than they know. The years working on this book were tough, but its completion is a testament to our strength and determination to move forward. To Rea Jadyn Leonard, all my love and respect for bringing the joys of life to me each and every day with your intelligence, your thoughtful questions, smiles, and kisses—and, of course, for being a Lakers fan like her Dad. To Sam Holden Leonard, you complete me, because of your energy, your challenging spirit, your silliness, and your love for Kobe and the Lakers. And finally, to Anna Chow, thanks for the encouragement, the love, the respect, the daily insights, and for not complaining about the TV remaining fixed on all things NBA for the past few years. You are both the MVP and the coach of the year for this project.

1

AFTER ARTEST

The NBA and the Assault on Blackness

The real question, how does it feel to be a problem.
—W.E.B. DuBois, 1903 (Quoted in Jackson 2006, p. 9)

Ron Artest more than likely will be suspended, but so should Kobe.
(Resnick 2009)

Kobe vs. Artest: Proof Artest Will Kill Your Team
(2009)

NBA Bad Boy Ron Artest of L.A. Lakers Admits He Had A Problem: Drinking During Games!
(Douglas 2009)

Trevor Ariza loses shoe, Ron Artest tosses it into the stands.
(2009)

Artest, who's trying to put his bad-boy image behind him, said he could simply display his ring in his living room or he could wear it. But I think it'll be more important to give back to something I believe in, which is providing kids with someone to talk to because it's so expensive. I pay for parenting counseling, marriage counseling and anger management, and it's very expensive. This will be for children of all demographics, rich or poor—preferably the rich can pay for their own psychologists—but it'll be a great way to help kids who don't know where they're going in their life at this point. ("Ron Artest Plans" 2010)

INTRODUCTION

At first glance, the above headlines point to the fact that Ron Artest's personal history, and especially his association with the Palace Brawl, continues to determine the public narrative assigned to him by the dominant media and broader public discourse. Even those instances of praise and celebratory redemption does so in relationship to his past indiscretions. Despite the banality of his exchange with Kobe and his tossing of another player's shoe off the court (his sportsmanship was questioned by an announcer), and notwithstanding his efforts to admit to a past drinking problem[1] or shed light on the issue of mental health, each in varying degrees have been the read through the lens of the Palace Brawl.

In 2009, Ron Artest admitted to drinking alcohol at halftime while he was a member of the Chicago Bulls. Hoping to teach kids by sharing his past mistakes, Artest's admission, not surprisingly, prompted much media and public debate. Although some people questioned the truthfulness of his admission, others used this moment as an opportunity to speculate about whether Artest was indeed drunk when he entered the stands in 2004. Likewise, his tossing of Trevor Ariza's shoe into the stands, along with his physical and verbal altercations with Kobe Bryant, were given amplified meaning and importance considering his role. In all four instances, Artest's past and his character are used as points of reference.

Often invoking his involvement in the 2004 Palace Brawl, the dominant frame that facilitates his representations is not only constrained by Artest's personal and professional histories, but by the prism of race and blackness. He is consistently imagined as a problem. The nature of these representations point to the ways in which blackness overdetermines not only the meaning of Artest, but of all black NBA players in a post-Brawl context. Post-Artest, blackness is the hegemonic point of reference for both the commentaries and the policy shifts within the NBA, demonstrating that the Palace Brawl changed the racial meaning of the NBA and thus changed the regulatory practices governing the league.

The purpose of *After Artest* is threefold:

1. To examine the changing racial landscape of the NBA following the November 22, 2004, Palace Brawl, which involved Ron Artest, several Detroit Piston fans, and several other Pacer (and Pistons) players.
2. To think about how race (particularly anti-black racism), ideas of colorblindness, and white racial frames colored the conversations and resulting policy shifts within the NBA.
3. To reflect on the broader significance and meaning of a post–Palace Brawl NBA that at one level mirrors hegemonic

notions of/about blackness, and yet at another level functions as
a privileged (or exceptional) space for the criminalization (and
consumption) of black bodies in the perpetuation and denial of
dominant white racial frames.

In fulfilling these three goals, *After Artest* offers a rather simple argument: Highlighting the league's blackness, the Palace Brawl mandated the
transformation of NBA policy regarding the governance of black bodies.
Negating the two-decade long project of David Stern, the Palace Brawl
belied the popular narrative, dominated by the figure of Michael Jordan, in
which race within the NBA was seen as insignificant. The Palace Brawl was
the culmination of the recoloring of the NBA. It represented a moment when
the blackness of the league was irrefutable and thus needed to be managed,
controlled, and, if necessary, destroyed. *After Artest* argues that the Palace
Brawl served as that "aha moment" in which blackness displaced the racially
transcendent signifier of Michael Jordan. This blackness, and its representative threat, were undeniable and, as such, necessitated intervention, termed as
an *assault* within this book's title. Not surprisingly, anti-black racist/white
racial frames have anchored the debates and policies that have followed
Artest; frames based on racial transcendence or colorblindness remain in the
background. In this sense, Artest mandated a reversal wherein race/blackness
had to be noticed (and controlled/destroyed), leading to public articulations
of the white racial frame instead of denials of racial significance. Finally, *After
Artest* argues that the debates and struggles over racial meaning within the
NBA are not isolated; instead they coexist alongside and are in dialogue with
those narratives, ideologies and discursive articulations about the criminal justice system, education, and countless other institutions.

GUIDING FRAMEWORKS

Before further identifying and reflecting on the book's argument and point of
entry, it will be useful to highlight three of the guiding frameworks that serve
as foundation for my discussion here: (1) new racism; (2) white racial framing; and (3) anti-black racism.

New Racism[2]

In recent years, it has become increasingly popular to describe America's current racial moment as an era of "colorblind racism," "new racism," or even
"racism 2.0" (Wise 2009; Duster 2003; Doane, 2003; Eduardo Bonilla-Silva,
2003). The implication here is that although it's often difficult to define and

locate in the absence of Klan rallies and Jim Crow signs, race and racism remain defining features of American life. According to Patricia Hill Collins, new racism "reflects a situation of permanence and change" (2004, p. 33). Many of the outcomes and much of the societal inequality of today mirror the circumstances of 1896, 1919, and 1968, yet the cultural practices, institutional organization, political/policy formation, and geographic orientation have all changed. Peter Teo, in an essay analyzing racial discourse within Australian newspapers, identifies new racism as a "form of racism that is much more subtle, covert, and hence insidious" (2000, p. 8). Notwithstanding the vast amount of statistical data illustrating the persistence of racial inequality, new racism is defined by processes wherein "whites explain the apparent contradiction between professed color blindness, and the United States' color-coded inequality" (Bonilla-Silva 2003, p. 2). Embracing a variety of lenses and rhetorical strategies, whites are able to rework America's contemporary racial reality to legitimize notions of colorblindness, freedom, equality, democracy, and America.

In this vein, Bonilla-Silva argues that colorblind racism functions as a mechanism for keeping blacks and other minorities "at the bottom of the well" (2003, pp. 2–3). Colorblind racism is subtle, institutional, and composed of "apparently nonracial" practices, yet it enables inequality, segregation, and white privilege to remain intact. For example, whereas Jim Crow segregation was enforced through overtly racist signs, restrictive covenants, and violence, today's practices include landlords not showing units or advertising vacant properties, denying vacancy, and quoting higher prices to minority applicants. The tactics of each era are different, but the results remain the same. Bonilla-Silva describes the shift within racism as follows:

> Yet this new ideology has become a formidable political tool for the maintenance of the racial order. Much as Jim Crow racism served as the glue for defending a brutal and overt system of racial oppression in the pre–Civil Rights era, color-blind racism serves today as the ideological armor for a covert and institutionalized system in the post–Civil Rights era. And the beauty of this new ideology is that it aids the maintenance of white privilege without fanfare, without naming who it subjects and those who it rewards. (2003, p. 3)

As evident here, the prominence of colorblindness and the use of implicitly racial language appear to reflect the newest form of an old system by which white privilege has long been maintained through the ideological/institutional justifications of white supremacy. Similarly, Collins identifies new racism as "the juxtaposition of old and new, in some cases a continuation of long-standing practices of racial rule and, in other cases the development of something original" (Collins 2004, pp. 54–55). Henry Giroux also argues that new racism is not defined by the declining significance of race, but rather its fluidity, its contradictions, its metamorphoses, and by the ubiquity of the denials voiced regarding the importance of race after the civil rights movement. "The importance of race and the enduring fact of racism are relegated to the dustbin of history at a time in American life when the discourses of race and the spectacle of racial representation saturate the dominant media and public life" writes Giroux. "The politics of the color line and representations of race have become far more subtle and complicated than they were in the Jim Crow era (2003, p. 192). More broadly, Giroux defines the specific dimensions of new racism in the following way:

> Unlike the old racism, which defined racial difference in terms of fixed biological categories organized hierarchically, the new racism operates in various guises proclaiming among other things race neutrality, asserting culture as a market of racial difference, or making race as a private matter. Unlike the crude racism with its biological referents and pseudoscientific legitimizations, buttressing its appeal to white racial superiority, the new racism cynically recodes itself within the vocabulary of the civil rights movement. (2003, p. 192)

Amy Elizabeth Ansell similarly focus on the ways in which cultural differences mark and rationalize the existence of inequality:

> It is a form of racism that utilizes themes related to culture and nation as a replacement for the now discredited biological referents of the old racism. It is concerned less with notions of racial superiority in the narrow sense than with the alleged "threat" people of color pose—either because of their mere presence or because of their demand for "special privileges"—to economic, socio-political, and cultural vitality of the dominant (White) society. It is, in short, a new form of racism that operates with the category of "race." It is a new form of exclusionary politics that operates indirectly and in stealth via the rhetorical inclusion of people of color and the sanitized nature of its racist appeal. (1997, pp. 20–21)

Bonilla-Silva identifies four central frames of colorblind racism—abstract liberalism, naturalization, cultural racism, and minimization of racism—which together define the new racist discourse. The two latter frames are particularly useful in understanding contemporary sporting culture and the approach offered in *After Artest*, given that the NBA functions as an important site for the denial of contemporary racism and the demonization and exclusion of racialized bodies through cultural argumentation and discourse. "Cultural racism is a frame that relies on culturally-based arguments," Bonilla-Silva explains (Bonilla-Silva 2003, p. 28). According to Carrington and McDonald, "cultural racism posits that although different ethnic groups or 'races' may not exist in a hierarchical biological relationship, they are nevertheless culturally distinct, each group having their own incompatible lifestyles, customs and ways of seeing the world" (2001, p. 1). Similarly, Spencer concludes, "cultural racism is thus predicated on an understanding of culture as a whole way of life and has implications for racism in sport" (2004, p. 121).

Instead of basing exclusion and inequality on purely biological explanations, dominant racial discourses locate social problems in the cultural deficiencies of the African American community. Rather than circulating evidence of the biological inferiority of black men and women, a common practice in the United States was evident in the exclusion of bodies of color from American sports teams through the first half of the twentieth century. Contemporary (new racist) racial discourse (including the narratives circulating about blackness and the NBA) focuses on cultural and class differences as the predominant narrative to explain persistent inequality. By repeating those narratives that celebrate racial progress and the availability of the American Dream to many African Americans, amid a focus on the black underclass, new racism demonizes and blames those who continue to live in their own nightmares because of personal failures and deficiencies all while denying the importance of race. "The clock has been turned back on racial progress in American, though scarcely anyone seems to notice," argues Michelle Alexander in *New Jim Crow: Mass Incarceration in an Era of Colorblindness*. "All eyes are fixed on people like Barack Obama and Oprah Winfrey, who have defied the odds and risen to power, fame, and fortune" (2010, p. 175). Narratives of success and those exceptional exceptions are used as evidence of a post-racial America.

A second frame, which both dominates contemporary racial discourses and infects our understanding of the representations and media discourse surrounding the NBA, minimizes the continued importance of racism. This minimization of the racism frame "suggests that discrimination is no longer a central factor affecting minorities' life chances" (Bonilla-Silva 2003, p. 29). Teo describes this defining element in a similar fashion, detailing the ways in which the dominant racial discourse generates "discursive strategies that *blame* the victims for their circumstances on their own social, economic, and even cultural disadvantage" (2000, p. 8). Dismissing hate crimes, police brutality, racial profiling, continued inequality and individual prejudice, new racist discourse frequently accuses people of color of using race as a "crutch," being overly sensitive when it comes to racism, or deploying the "race card" (Bonilla-Silva 2003, p. 29), while they simultaneously deny the existence of racism, instead blaming the cultural deficiencies of people of color for any instance of inequality.

The realities of new racism are clearly part and parcel of an NBA discourse, even after Artest, so there are certain limitations to thinking about the NBA through this lens given both the centrality of the racial discourse and the continued deployment of historical white racial frames.

White Racial Frame

According to Joe Feagin, "the socially inherited racial frame is a comprehensive orienting structure, a 'tool kit' that whites and others have long used to understand, interpret, and act in social settings" (Feagin 2009, p. 13). This tool kit contains stereotypes, which Picca and Feagin describe as "filters, straining out information inconsistent with the dominant racial frame" (2007, p. 10) and "'big picture' narratives that connect frame elements into historically oriented stories with morals that are especially important to white Americans" (Feagin 2009, p. 13). My efforts here seek to illustrate how, within a post-Artest NBA discourse, these stereotypes and "big picture narratives" literally play out on players' bodies, elucidating how the dominant racial frame guides both the consumption and demonization of black athletes which, in turn, "structures [white] events and performances" (Feagin 2009, p. 12) outside the arena of sports. Joe Feagin describes the white racial frame as a "master frame," "that has routinely defined a way of being, a broad perspective on life" (2009, p. 11; 2009, p. 13; Feagin 2008). Frames encompass a "conceptual and interpretative scheme that shapes and channels assessments of everyday events and encounters with people" (Feagin 2006, p. 26). Focusing on tropes of hard work or ideas of superiority, highlighting narratives that legitimize meritocracy and the prospects of rags-to-riches, dominant racial frames "make powerful use of stereotypes [and] images, provid[ing] the language and interpretations that help structure, normalize, and make sense out of society" (2009, p. 11). Feagin notes further that a dominant white racial frame "not only explains and interprets the everyday world but also implies or offers actions in line with the frame's explanatory perspective" (2006, p. 26). In summary, Feagin describes the interface between dominant white racial frames and the daily/institutional structuring of society in the following way:

> From the beginning the white racial frame has not only rationalized the exploitative structure of racial oppression, but also played a central role in *actually structuring* this society on a daily basis by

providing important understandings, images, narratives, emotions, and operational norms that determine a great array of individual and group actions within all major societal sectors. The dominant white racial frame is active and directing; it is learned at parent's knee, in school, and from the media; and once learned, it both guides and rationalizes discriminatory behavior. (2009, pp. 15–16)

Eduardo Bonilla-Silva also identifies frames as representations used "to explain how the world is or ought to be," in the establishment of racial ideology (Bonilla-Silva 2010, p. 10). Based on and in "hierarchy and domination," the dominant white racial frame function as "building blocks for manufacturing versions of actions, self, and social structures" (Weatherell and Potter quoted in Bonilla-Silva 2010, p. 10). In other words, white frames are "the central component of any dominant racial ideology," establishing the "paths for interpreting information" (Bonilla-Silva 2010, p. 26). They exist "as cul-de-sacs because after people filter issues through them, they explain racial phenomena following a predictable route" (Bonilla-Silva 2003, p. 26). While predictable, they are powerful precisely because they "misrepresent the world," thereby "provid[ing] the intellectual road map used by rulers to navigate the always rocky road of domination" (Bonilla-Silva 2010, p. 26). Both Bonilla-Silva and Feagin see white racial frames as akin to Omi and Wimant's idea of a racial project, described as "simultaneously an interpretation, representation, or explanation of racial dynamics, and an effort to reorganize and redistribute resources along particular racial lines" (1994, p. 56).

Whereas Joe Feagin and Eduardo Bonilla-Silva use the descriptor of white racial frames, Ronald Jackson utilizes the idea of scripts to explain the ways in which black bodies are infused with meaning. "Black bodies were inscribed with a set of meanings, which helped to perpetuate the scripter's racial ideology. Through these scripts, race gradually became its own corporeal politics," he writes. "Mass-mediated culture practices," thus, "redistribute and recycle" a myriad of "racially xenophobic tendencies" that are "scripted [on] the black body" (2006, p. 9). Similarly, Wiegman (1995) focuses on gaze to describe the ways in which whites look at black bodies and their experiences: "Gaze is a specular event, a tool for examining sites of obsessive desire that admit the visibility of difference but remain troubled by it" (Jackson 2006, p. 10). Although the gaze itself can "be impartial or non-obligatory," racial signifiers "evoke feelings, thoughts, perhaps anxieties" (Jackson 2006, p. 10). The gaze and the perquisite frames "suggest that there must be the presence of an Other" (Jackson 2006, p. 10). In this regard, dominant white racial frames or scripts emphasize the Otherness of/in black bodies. Frames, like "stereotypes, are a crude set of mental representations of the world" that "perpetuate a needed sense of difference between 'self' and the 'object,' which becomes the Other" (Gillman 1985, pp. 17–18; Quoted in Andrews 2001c, p. 110). Both in stereotype, and through narrative, blackness as the Other becomes a perpetual threat that requires control, if not annihilation.

I proceed to demonstrate how a white racial frame guided the media and public discourses[3] that arose in response to the Palace Brawl and how, furthermore, long-standing narratives, stereotypes, and frames have infected and affected the NBA. My object here is not to isolate the NBA, to highlight the ways in which stereotypes and dominant racial frames inform a post-Artest NBA narrative, but rather to elucidate the dialectics and exchanges that take place/exist between the racialized and racializing world of the NBA and the broader cultural, social, and political landscape that informs and is informed by the happenings in the NBA. My focus is, thus, to reflect on white racial frames within the NBA that ubiquitously give voice to and are guided by an ideology of anti-blackness. The recognition of the blackness of the NBA and the fallacy of racial transcendence compelled discursive and policy shifts based on/in these frames and an ideology of anti-blackness.

ANTI-BLACK RACISM AND THE NBA

Todd Boyd argues that the NBA "remains one of the few places in American society where there is a consistent racial discourse," where race, whether directly or indirectly, is the subject of conversation at all times (Boyd 2000, p. 60). In 1984, David Stern began his tenure as the NBA's commissioner. Even more so than the MLB or the NFL, the NBA had been plagued by criticism that the league was too black, a criticism that didn't simply refer to the demographics of the league, but also the aesthetics, styles, and transparent blackness of its bodies. According to David Stern, "sponsors were flocking out of the NBA because it was perceived as a bunch of high-salaried, drug-sniffing black guys" (Quoted in Hughes 2004, p. 164). At this moment, perceptions of race and anti-black sentiment were leading the NBA down a path of failure. A *Boston Globe* reporter told Stern that "nobody wants to watch ten black guys in short pants running up and down the court" (Quoted in Wynter 2002, p. 99). Boyd describes the situation facing the NBA in the 1970s and early 1980s in the following way: "The league was on one hand becoming increasingly Black, not only in terms of population but in style of play and in its overall aesthetic." He further notes that a "proliferation of cocaine in the NBA" during this period contributed to "the looming cloud of racially based perception that informed the population shift. As far as the public was concerned, these players were criminals and not indulgent artists. . . . Thus, the NBA came to be thought of as simply another example of Black criminality, not unlike those Black criminals represented in other aspects of society across the news media" (Boyd 2003, p. 39). Not surprisingly, Stern's early tenure was marked/characterized/defined by accusations against the players of selfishness, criminality, and drug use; lamentations about the disconnect between fans and players; and an overall contempt for the NBA's product (Hughes 2004; Boyd 2003; Tucker 2003; Denzin 2001; Boyd 2000; Cole and Andrews 1996a). Beyond instituting policy changes, some of which remain in place, that emphasize "managing player behavior" (Hughes 2004, p. 164) and sought to police, discipline, and control hyper–black bodies, the NBA and its marketing partners have long de-emphasized the blackness of the NBA baller. To counteract race-based contempt, Stern and the NBA have focused on deracializing the league, on facilitating colorblindness, which they have considered key to the success of the NBA.[4]

Magic Johnson, Larry Bird, and David Stern's NBA enterprise were able to expand the popularity of the NBA during the 1980s and simultaneously counter the negative associations of drugs, violence, and dysfunction (blackness) so prominent during that era, but Jordan took this to a new level. Reflecting the creativity, style, spontaneity, and sense of individuality (Boyd 2003, pp. 103–104) associated with hip-hop culture specifically and black culture in general, Jordan was able to capitalize on the emerging cultural popularity of hip-hop while still concealing his blackness from fans; he was able to decouple hip-hop and blackness within the white imagination. Jordan provided a blackness of a different color;[5] he provided a racial reassurance and pleasure, which today's players cannot because of their performed racial identities. As noted by David Andrews, "Jordan's carefully scripted televisual adventures on the corporate playground were designed to substantiate an all-American (which in Manning Marable's terms means white) hard bodied identity (Jeffords 1994) which would appeal to the racially sensitive sensibilities of the American mass market" (Andrews 2000, p. 174). Likewise, in his $3,000 suit, with his dominance both on and off the court and his refusal to talk about race or politics, Jordan "allow[ed] us to believe what we wish to believe: that in this country, have-nots can still become haves; that the American dream is still working" (Ken Naughton, quoted in Andrews 2000, p. 175). David Falk, Jordan's agent, linked together his marketing possibilities/success, his overall popularity, and his racial identity in illustrative ways:

> When players of color become stars they are no longer perceived as being of color. The color sort of vanishes. I don't think people look at Michael Jordan anymore and say he's a black superstar. They say he's a superstar. They totally accepted him into the mainstream. Before he got there he might have been African American, but once he arrived, he had such a high level of acceptance that I think that description goes away. (Quoted in Rhoden 2006, p. 204)

To understand Falk's construction of Jordan, and the associated narrative frame that guided his position within the cultural landscape, it is important to reflect on the meaning of racial transcendence. As Jordan was "cast as a spectacular talent, midsized, well-spoken, attractive, accessible, old-time values, wholesome, clean, natural, not too goody-two shoes, without a bit of deviltry in him" (Falk quoted in Andrews 2001c, p. 125), his representation was not race neutral but wrapped up in the racial stereotypes and frames associated with whiteness and blackness (Ammons 1997). Read as the embodiment of "personal drive, responsibility, integrity, and success," as opposed to "the stereotypical representations of deviant, promiscuous, and irresponsible black males," Jordan's racially transcendent, colorblind-driven, raceless image was always tied to racial language. He represented the possibility of acceptance by whites (racial transcendence), which meant he was able to "transcend his own race" (Rhoden 2006, p. 204), or better said, the overdetermining and limiting stains of blackness. Yet, the illusion persisted that his success and popularity marked a paradigm shift for the NBA, in the marketing of African American sports stars, and for the nation as a whole, where "you could look at him [and] really not see his color. Like O.J. Simpson, Jordan was racially and politically neutral" (Rhoden 2006, p. 203), at least according to the dominant white racial frame.

David Stern, answering questions about the persistence of a race problem in the NBA, encapsulates the NBA's mission of colorblindness: "By and large the majority of the sport public is colorblind. I do not believe they care if Julius Erving or Carl Lewis or Mark Breland is black. They're great champions, and the people will respond to them, regardless of race" (Quoted in Wynter 2002, p. 99). Taking this a step further, Falk concludes that not only do black NBA stars have the potential to occupy newly racialized/raceless bodies upon securing all-star status, their popularity and that of the NBA game depends upon such a racial transformation. "Celebrities aren't black. People don't look at Michael as being black. They accept that he's different because he is a celebrity" (Quoted in Gates 1998, p. 54). Notwithstanding the efforts of the NBA to obscure or mediate racial difference—to deny or minimize the existence of racism both inside and outside its arenas—race and dominant white racial frames continue to impact the NBA's organization and reception. Whether in terms of the stereotypes that imagine black NBA players as violent, dysfunctional criminals, or the public/media demands for conformity and discipline, the NBA is defined by elements of both the old and the new, of both culturally and racially based arguments concerning social difference. That is, in spite of purported paradigm shifts, the idea of colorblindness, as with the racial landscape after Artest, is guided by the dominant white racial frames and the ideology of anti-blackness.

According to Elizabeth Alexander, the history of American racism has always been defined by practices where black bodies are put on display "for public consumption," whether in the form of "public rapes, beatings, and lynchings" or in "the gladiatorial arenas of basketball and boxing" (1994, p. 92). Similarly, Jonathan Markowitz describes the ways in which the sports media contributes to the widespread criminalization of the black body: "The bodies of African American athletes from a variety of sports have been at the center of a number of mass media spectacles in recent years, most notably involving Mike Tyson and O.J. Simpson, but NBA players have been particularly likely to occupy center stage in American racial discourse" (2006, p. 401). Thus, especially after Artest, the discourse surrounding the NBA—even amid the hyper-commodification and celebrity of a handful of black NBA stars—has worked to circulate and legitimize dominant discourses about pathological and abhorrent black bodies. "Black male bodies are increasingly admired and commodified in rap, hip hop, and certain sports, but at the same time they continue to be used to invoke fear. Black men are both held in contempt and valued as entertainment" (Collins 2005; Leonard 2004), writes Abby Ferber. "Yet this is really nothing new. Black men have been defined as a threat throughout American history while being accepted in roles that serve and entertain White people, where they can ostensibly be controlled and made to appear nonthreatening" (Ferber 2007, p. 12). *After Artest* gives voice to the ways in which the decisions guiding the NBA in the wake of the Palace Brawl, along with the reactions expressed by the media and public, reflected long-standing efforts to control black male bodies.

It is important to understand that the NBA, like sports in general, generates competing images of blackness. On the one hand there are the "'bad boy Black athletes" (Collins 2005, p. 153) who are consistently depicted as "overly physical, out of control, prone to violence, driven by instinct, and hypersexual"—they are "unruly and disrespectful," "inherently dangerous," and "in need of civilizing" (Ferber 2007, p. 20). At the other end of the spectrum are the NBA stars, black athletes, who "are perceived as controlled by White males" (Ferber 2007, p. 20) and are "defined as the 'good Blacks'" (Ferber 2007, p. 20). An awareness of this dialectic between good and bad is crucial for understanding both the role race has played in the NBA historically and within the media and public discourses in wake of the Palace Brawl, illustrating the impetus for regimes of regulation, surveillance, and discipline in a post-Artest moment. The visibility of blackness—and its badness—mandated regulatory transformation. "The negative depiction of bad boys works to reinforce efforts to tame their 'out of control' nature" (Ferber 2007, p. 20). These representations contribute to what Alice Walker dubs a "prison of image, whereby stereotypes function not as errors, but rather forms of social control" (Quoted in Asante 2008, p. 16). Illustrating the ways in which race and racial meaning have functioned within the NBA after Artest, I argue the centrality of racism here, as "a gaze that insists upon the power to make others conform, to perform endlessly in the prison of prior expectation" (Williams 1997, p. 74).

The NBA black body has become a stand-in for a broader discussion about race in American society; in a sense, the black NBA baller has come to embody the essentialized black subject within the white imagination. Discussing the media coverage of Latrell Sprewell's conflict with then coach P.J. Carleisimo, Linda Tucker argues that the media consistently "represented the incident in ways that vilified Sprewell through the use of derogatory images of black men" (2003, p. 401). Moreover, Sarah Banet-Weiser concludes that the "NBA exploits and makes exotic the racist discourse of the Black menace even as it domesticates this cultural figure (1999, p. 406). Predictably, much of the existing literature dealing with race and sports focuses on basketball (Markovitz 2006; Leonard 2006; Hughes 2004; Leonard, 2004; Boyd 2003; Andrews 2001b; Andrews 2001c; Cole 2001; Denzin 2001; Boyd 2000; Banet-Wiser 1999; Boyd 1997, Andrews 1996; Cole and Andrews 1996; Cole 1996; Denzin 1996). For example, Tucker argues that it is not surprising that race/blackness is central to the NBA discourse, and more revealingly, she describes the relationship between the NBA's racialized discourse and broader discussions about race both inside and outside of sporting cultures. "In ways absent from other sports, the Blackness, sexuality, and the physical and emotional vulnerability of the majority of players are stamped on the face of the game of basketball" (2003, p. 313). Similarly, Markovitz, in his discussion of the Kobe Bryant rape case, concludes that "because NBA players are always already at the center of an eroticized and racialized mass-media spectacle, it is not surprising that allegations of sexual misconduct on the part of an NBA superstar should be immediately seized on and scrutinized for larger lessons about celebrity, gender, and racial conflict in American society" (2006, p. 401).

THE NBA BEYOND ARTEST

After Artest pushes the discussion of race and the NBA beyond the press box, beyond what happens in the arenas, and even beyond commodification and consumption, toward a consideration of the dialectics that exist between the NBA/its discourse and an ongoing history of racialized violence. Much of the literature focuses almost exclusively on the ways in which dominant racial frames, stereotypes, and representations of black men impact media coverage and fan reception. Specifically, the majority of the literature focusing on race or blackness in the NBA examines how racial ideologies impact the representation and reception of particular black NBA players, such as Michael Jordan (Andrews 2001a; Andrews 2001b; Andrews 2001c; Andrews 2000d; Andrews

2000; Cole 2001), Allen Iverson (Boyd 2003; Platt 2003), Latrell Sprewell (Shropshire 2000; Boyd 2000b), Kobe Bryant (Mipuri 2011; Markovitz 2006; Leonard 2004), LeBron James (Guerrero 2011), nd countless other players. Likewise, the literature, with some exceptions (e.g., Guerrero 2011; Mipuri 2011; Cole 2001; King and Springwood 2001; McDonald 2001; Andrews 2000) tends to focus on how broader racial ideologies have infected the basketball court, in terms of its cultural, aesthetic, and social development. Although there have been a number of monographs and edited collections dedicated to examining issues of race and the experiences of African Americans within the NBA, these works mainly focus on (1) the historical contributions made by African Americans to the evolution of basketball and the NBA; or (2) the racial tensions and constructions of blackness evident both in the media and fan reactions to a myriad of events, including Latrell Sprewell choking his coach and the 1999 lockout.

To a certain extent, the existing literature has dealt with race and blackness while ignoring the larger implications of white racial framing within an NBA discourse. For example, Todd Boyd, with *Young Black Rich and Famous: The Rise of the NBA, The Hip Hop Invasion and the Transformation of American Culture* explores the ways in which African Americans, through hip-hop culture, have transformed the NBA. Arguing that this cultural shift has not been easy or without conflict or resistance, Boyd provides an important historical treatment of the evolution of the NBA's aesthetics and cultural significance. Likewise, Boyd's and Kenneth L. Shropshire's edited collection, *Basketball Jones: America Above the Rim*, brings together essays by a number of scholars who reflect on the cultural significance and meaning of the American basketball culture, a space defined by and saturated with black bodies and cultural styles. "While baseball remains the key vessel of sports nostalgia and tradition, it is basketball that currently saturates popular culture and permeates our national identity" (Boyd and Shropshire 2000, p. 5). Reflecting on the importance of the NBA beyond wins and losses, Boyd and Shropshire conclude that, "Basketball assumes a larger place than either [football and baseball] in the lexicon of popular culture throughout the world. This may not be the New World Order that Bush was referring to, but when you consider that a sport once dismissed as a black man's sport has come to represent America worldwide, then it is obvious that, if nothing else, the old order has been replaced" (Boyd and Shropshire 2000, p. 11). Like Boyd and Shropshire, much of the other literature focuses on the cultural impact of basketball culture and both the meaning and tensions that arise from the blackness associated with contemporary basketball. For example, Wertham (2005) and Platt (2002) both focus on the transformation of the game of basketball and the ways in which shifts within the NBA often impact the broader culture.

Much of the literature has focused on how the cultural shifts outside the NBA (specifically hip-hop) have transformed the league in terms of its cultural and racial meaning, its aesthetics and on-the-court play, and its overall significance within the American and transnational cultures. Others, like Brooks (2009), May (2008), McLaughlin (2008), Smith (2007), and McNutt (2002), highlight the ways in which basketball intersects with identity formation, personal aspirations, community development, and cultural practices. These works highlight the impact of the popularity of basketball on a spectrum of communities, particularly black youth, theorizing about not only the cultural impact but also the political, social, and economic imprint.

These themes certainly play a role in *After Artest*, but the focus here is less on the interface between broader cultural happenings and the transformation of the NBA and more on the connections between the NBA discourse and the broader discourse of anti-black racism. Instead of focusing solely on the court, this monograph attempts to examine the ways in which racial ideologies, dominant white racial frames, and racializing culture wars infect not only the discursive field surrounding the NBA, but also the dialectic between the NBA arena and society at large.

So, whereas much of the literature focuses on how the NBA has transformed American culture or the black community, this text looks at how American culture, in the form of racial ideologies and dominant white racial frames, has constrained and contained the NBA and, in particular, its black bodies. Highlighting the shared structure, values, and ideologies of nations and sporting culture, Gamel Abdel-Shehid, in *Who Da Man? Black Masculinities and Sporting Cultures*, illustrates the importance of looking to sports in an effort to understand the larger processes associated with social difference, social structures, and race-based repression. Discussing "both nations and sporting cultures," Abdel-Shehid argues that "Social difference haunts these institutions, given that [it] . . . often threatens to undo the cohesion of nations and sporting cultures at every turn" (2005, p. 3). As such, he concludes that,

> Both structures, by virtue of their overdetermining and repressive demand for sameness, are troubled or "haunted" by the reality and complexity of social difference. As such, nations and sporting cultures by and large act as repressive or normalizing structures that, by virtue of an inability to tolerate discord, constantly attempt to produce conformity and sameness, and disavow difference and inequality.
>
> The repressive nature of sporting cultures and nationalism result in the need for social difference to be constantly managed. Those marked as "different" are encouraged or rather expected to,

assimilate, or fit into the existing frameworks of team or nation. (2005, pp. 3–4)

After Artest takes a similar approach, highlighting the shared discursive and ideological qualities of the NBA and larger national narratives, emphasizing how the NBA and its surrounding discourse does a lot of the racializing, disciplining, and punishing purportedly needed to mediate social difference. I emphasize how, in the wake of the Palace Brawl, a moment that highlighted social and cultural differences, which are simultaneously feared and commodified, the NBA undertook a series of policy shifts and rhetorical campaigns that attempted to mediate these potentially harmful differences through demands for assimilation, disciplinarity, and conformity. This book is not simply an examination of the policy shifts by which the NBA sought to mediate these differences, it is also an examination of the important role the sports media (a partner of the NBA) played in this process. However, as in the work of Abdel-Shehid—along with that of Andrews, Cole, King, and others—the discussion is not limited to the state of conditions in the NBA after Artest, but also considers how the NBA's efforts to mediate/erase social difference, to demand conformity through calls for disciplinarity and surveillance, both impact and reflect larger discussions/formations about race and nation. In other words, I use this cultural moment to examine the post-Artest discourse, which includes the structure of the NBA and the surrounding media discourse, to reflect on the "new racism" the culture wars, and oft-employed racial frames and narratives regarding black criminality, the American Dream, and post–civil rights America.

In this sense, this monograph builds on the tradition of critical sports scholars (Gamal Abdel-Shehid, David Andrews, C.L. Cole, Susan Birrell, Mary McDonald, C. Richard King) and other scholars interested in race and popular culture (Mark Anthony Neal, Patricia Hill Collins, S. Craig Watkins, Herman Gray) who have illustrated the usefulness of the examination of sporting cultures (and other cultural projects) as a "vehicle for developing progressive understandings of the *broader* social, economic, political, and technological concerns that frame contemporary culture" (Andrews 2001b, p. xv). Writing about Michael Jordan and describing the collection of essays that appear in *Michael Jordan, Inc.: Corporate Sport, Media Culture, and Late Modern America*, Andrews argues for scholarship that "makes sense of a celebrated figure, whose public existence graphically exteriorizes a late capitalist order defined by the convergence of corporate and media interests" (2001b, p. xv). This collection explored the cultural, political, economic, racial, and social landscapes through an examination of Michael Jordan.

In fact, much of this segment of the literature focuses on the ways in which particular NBA figures have been used as ideological tools for the benefit of larger national narratives. NBA stars, and sports stars of color in general, are commodified as evidence of a race neutral or post-racial America wherein all Americans have the same opportunities to succeed and be accepted (Andrews 2001a; Andrews and Jackson 2001; Cole and Andrews 2001; Denzin 2001; King and Springwood 2001). The success of black athletes, and the supposed adoration America feels for black NBA stars, is posited as evidence for racial progress and colorblindness (McDonald and Andrews 2001, p. 26). Mary McDonald and David L. Andrews—writing about Michael Jordan in the context of the New Right and the rise of Reagan conservativism during the 1980s and early 1990s—conclude that not only was Jordan "portrayed as the moral obverse of the masses of African Americans vilified by the New Right for allegedly lacking the (new) right stuff" (2001, p. 26), but that his success was seen/employed as evidence that all Americans can potentially secure the American Dream, that achievement in the U.S. is fundamentally merit-based, and that America has transcended the stains of racism and attained a state wherein everyone has an equal chance to succeed in life. "Jordan is thus aligned with other African Americans stars of this era such as Bill Cosby, Whoopi Goldberg, and Oprah Winfrey whose high-profile success stories further condemned the struggling African American masses for lacking . . . personal resolution" write McDonald and Andrews. "Reaganism's doctrine of rugged individualism and color-blind bigotry, was all that was required to achieve in American society" (2001, p. 27). Such discursive practice remains prominent today, as contemporary athletes (e.g., LeBron James, Dwight Howard, Dwyane Wade, Kobe Bryant), like Jordan, not exist as floating signifiers of the American Dream, the opportunity available to those who follow the right path, but also as symbols of a post-racial America. These *black* athletes are not just accepted—they are celebrated and praised. They function as "the moral obverse" of those NBA stars who are condemned, vilified, and policed both inside and outside of sports. Under such racial binaries, the condemnation of Allen Iverson, Ron Artest, Rasheed Wallace, and Carmelo Anthony is not and cannot be racial, given the love and praise with which black athletes are lavished by society and the media; rather, the criticism directed toward these athletes has been prompted/elicited by their own cultural and moral failings.

The importance of these works rests with their ability to highlight the broader significance of the discursive articulations and representational offerings within the world of basketball/sports and interface between the narratives and media representation surrounding the NBA and larger political narratives about post-racialness, the American Dream, the Protestant work ethnic, and meritocracy. Similarly, C.L. Cole, using the term "American Jordan" as a strategic device for emphasizing Jordan's "position as a 'representative character' of America's political culture," highlights the ways in which the culture of the NBA and representations of Jordan interfaced with 1980s racial politics, particularly those processes that have imagined the "Criminal-BlackMan" (Russell 1998, p. 3) as a perpetual threat to the nation.

Understanding Jordan's position in the national culture, and the implications of his being embodied in the fantasies and anxieties that dominated America in the 1980s and 1990s, requires that we consider "how the multiple desires and pleasures mobilized through identification with Michael Jordan are deeply implicated in racially coded deviance and its affective solicitations, especially the 'revenge' underlying the contemporary 'will to punish'" (Cole 2001a, p. 71).

My task here is thus to examine "the *broader* social, economic, political, and technological concerns that frame contemporary culture" subsequent to the Palace Brawl. The NBA, as evident both in the representations/experiences of a number of players—including Michael Jordan, Kobe Bryant, Ron Artest, and countless others—and the occurrence of several incidents, functions as a "cultural product 'constituted with and constituted of a larger context of relations'" (Grossberg 1997, p. 57) characteristic of the American condition at the turn of the century" (Andrews 2001b, p. xv). Like the works of Andrews and Cole, this book heeds the call and adopts the methodological approach articulated by Susan Birrell and Mary G. McDonald, who defined "the methodology of 'reading' sport" as "finding the cultural meanings that circulate within narratives of particular incidents or celebrities" (Birrell and McDonald 2000, p. 11). Noting the importance of examining "the ways that sexuality, race, gender, and class privileges" operates within sporting cultures, Birrell and McDonald highlight the potential utility of critical sport intervention: "Reading sport critically can be used as a methodology for uncovering, foregrounding, and producing counternarratives, that is alternative accounts of particular events and celebrities that have been decentered, obscured, and dismissed by hegemonic forces" (p. 11). Elsewhere, Birrell and McDonald (1999) describe this methodological and theoretical approach to sporting cultures in the following way:

> [It provides] vantage points from which to observe, critique, and intervene in the complex and contradictory interactions of the power lines of ability, age, race, class, nationality, gender, and sexuality. [It] provides interventions into the dynamics of power, revealing what might have been obscured, while placing events and celebrities within their particular historical and political contexts. (Quoted in Andrews 2000b, pp. xv–xvi)

In this vein, this book represents an effort to look not only at how the Palace Brawl ushered in a new era within the NBA given its elucidation of the league's blackness, but how hegemonic constructions of blackness have overdetermined the interpretations of and reactions to this fight, as is evident in the post-brawl commentaries and the NBA's subsequent policy shifts. The task of this book is to use a post-Artest NBA discourse to understand the manner in which blackness is imagined and framed within and beyond the NBA. *After Artest* accepts the methodological challenge articulated by Birrell and McDonald, but rather than exclusively offering a counternarrative for the Palace Brawl, the age debate, and the NBA's imposed dress code, this monograph provides a broader counternarrative centering on race and power in the era after Artest.

THIS BOOK

Examining the "social and cultural antagonisms" (Watkins 1998, p. 22) of the NBA and its surrounding media discourse – along with the "specific motifs" (Watkins 1998, p. 22), racial tropes, and rhetorical devices that have been employed within the discourse—this monograph focuses on the ideological field of the NBA. According to Watkins, "the ideological field—defined here as the terrain where ideas, signs, representations, and other symbolic materials circulate and inform public discourses about the social world—functions as a battleground for the clash between competing political players and their views of the world" (Watkins 1998, p. 26).

At the core of this project is a desire to look at the ways in which racial meaning ("common sense") has affected NBA policy and media engagement after Artest. Precisely, I am concerned with describing a post-Artest NBA racial landscape, highlighting the cultural and policy shifts that came about as the blackness of the league became increasingly evident (and troubling) in wake of the Palace Brawl; moreover, I am concerned with exploring the dialects that exist between the white racial frames and narratives that are commonplace within the NBA and the larger structures, discourses, and cultural debates that color and are colored by what is happening in the NBA.

After Artest builds on the tradition of critical discourse analysis,[6] which looks "beyond the description of [the] discourse to an explanation of how and why particular discourses are produced (Teo 2000, p. 11). My analysis of race and the NBA not only includes an examination of how the discourse guides or "reflects social processes and structures," but also how it "affirms, consolidates, and in this way reproduces existing social structures" (Teo 2000, p. 11). *After Artest*, looks at how the racialized and racializing common sense of the current moment guides and infects the post-brawl discourse. Yet, at the same, my focus is on how the racialized and racializing common sense generated by the NBA (the discourse) "sustains and reinforces dominant social structures and relations"—how it contributes to hegemony.

While examining the shifting racial landscape that follows the Palace Brawl, *After Artest* also analyzes how the NBA and the media/popular discourse function as racial spectacle. "Th[is] spectacle is not a collection of images; rather it is a social relationship that is mediated by images." It is "both the outcome and the goal of the dominant model of production" (Guy Debord quoted in Abdel-Shehid 2005, p. 8). According to Douglas Kellner, "spectacles are those phenomena of media, culture, and society that embody the society's basic values." They "serve to enculturate individuals into this way of life and dramatize the society's conflicts and models of conflict resolution" (Quoted in King and Springwood 2001, p. 11). *After Artest* concerns itself with "those spectacles" that contain and are defined by interrelated images and commodities "that transform" a post-brawl NBA "into a broader field of public culture where race is quite literally practice as an allegory play and performance" (King and Springwood 2001, p. 11). Through the consideration of critical discourse analysis and racial spectacle, I provide a textual reading of a series of commentaries about the NBA and the debates and policy shifts that occurred after Artest, not simply as a methodological attempt to examine the ideological field of the NBA, but in order to access the broader issues and themes surrounding anti-black racism, both within and beyond America's basketball arenas. Reflecting on the Palace Brawl (chapter 2), the debates concerning straight out of high school NBA players (chapter 3) and the NBA dress code (chapter 4) within a larger cultural, racial, ideological and discursive context (Collins 2004; Gray 2004; Neal 2005), this work specifically examines the racial text of a post-Artest NBA landscape and its broader context. This monograph provides a space for analyzing the meaning, context, and nature of contemporary racism, utilizing the NBA, which—despite the number and popularity of its black players and the financial perks it provides to once poor inner-city children[7]—is rife with discourses and relations reflective of contemporary anti-black racism. Unlike the work of my distinguished peers, this monograph does not limit the discussion to the basketball world, but offers a bridge between and across discourses and institutions.

After Artest examines the centrality of race after Artest within the NBA. The Palace Brawl put the illusion of racial transcendance to rest, mandating an assault on blackness. Arguing that the culture and policies of the NBA in wake of the Palace Brawl have been defined by demonization, surveillance, and a systematic assault on blackness, *After Artest* highlights league efforts and media narratives that have simultaneously pathologized blackness and deracialized the players in the minds' of fans. While examining the tropes, narratives, rhetorical devices, and representational offerings since "the Malice at the Palace," *After Artest* does not focus exclusively on race and basketball but also looks at the interface between the white racial framing/anti-blackness that guides the NBA and broader historic and contemporary racial meanings, practices, and discourses. In other words, as basketball is more than a game, the policies, representations, and narratives articulated through and about the NBA (and its black players) have a larger place, meaning, and significance in our society. This effort is to highlight the dialects here, elucidating that after Artest the NBA has changed and in doing so these changes have contributed to, and are reflective of, broader social, racial, and political forces. As such, it does not just look at how stereotypes "mold media coverage and popular appreciation" (King and Springwood 2001, p. 11) of the NBA, it argues that the spectacle of the NBA—the racialized and racializing common sense articulated through the NBA—"dramatizes our conflicts, celebrates our values, and projects our deepest hopes and fears" (Kellner quoted in King and Springwood 2001, p. 11), all while contributing to a racial hegemony that exists inside and outside America's arenas.

2

"I Went to a Basketball Game and a Vibe Awards Broke Out"[1] or "Negroes Gone Wild"[2]

The Palace Melee and the Racialized Culture War

Ron Artest of the Indiana Pacers has been suspended for the rest of the season by the NBA for brawling with the fans. The good news is he's been named to host next year's Vibe Awards.
—David Letterman, November 22, 2004

Do you really want to go there? Do I have to? I think it's fair to say that the NBA was the first sport that was widely viewed as a black sport. And whatever the numbers ultimately are for other the other sports, the NBA will always be treated a certain way because of that. Our players are so visible that if they have Afros or cornrows or tattoos—white or black—our consumers pick it up. So, I think there are always some elements of race involved that affect judgments about the NBA.
—David Stern (Quoted in Lee 2004)

I think Fallujah is safer than Detroit Michigan these days.
(Freelove 2004)

INTRODUCTION

On November 19, 2004, a fight (pushing and shoving to be exact) between Ron Artest and Ben Wallace escalated into a melee. Before the last punch was thrown and the final cup of beer was dumped on a player's head, the alarms had been sounded concerning not only what this incident

23

meant for the future of the league, but the problems symbolized and/or embodied by this fight—the influx of selfish, bling-bling, hip-hop, thug ball players. Described as a "riot" (Bulpett 2004; Lawrence 2004; Mushnick 2004; Smith 2004a), "a watershed moment for the league" (Marc Ganis quoted in Lawrence 2005), a moment confirming the NBA was indeed the "National Brawlers Association" (Quoted in Lee 2005), an example of "Negroes gone wild" (Page 2004; Quoted in Lee 2005), an instance where "mayhem rule[d]" (Lage 2004), "a rainbow riot" (Rhoden 2004a) and "the malice at the Palace" (Burwell 2004a; Fuchs 2004), the almost fight between Ron Artest and Ben Wallace, which turned into a confrontation between members of the Indiana Pacers and individuals presumed to be Detroit Pistons fans, prompted panic, outrage, and debate from a spectrum of cultural spaces.

With 15 seconds remaining and the outcome already decided, Ron Artest gave Ben Wallace a hard foul. Wallace responded by shoving Artest. Rather than retaliating, Artest retreated, lying prone on the scorer's table, a fact that Grant Farred described as particularly important. "The black body at rest is conceptually unassimilable within the discourse of the NBA because of the offense it gives (white fans) . . ." (2007). In "The Event of the Black Body at Rest," he argues that, "Artest's resting, even the performance of being at rest, makes it a powerful moment in NBA time—the time of racialized American history, the actual time with which the NBA clock so intent on providing its white audience with a culturally hip yet still sufficiently sanitized black prod-uct, is out of sync" (2007). After a few seconds of lying motionless on the scorer's table, Artest was hit by a flying cup, which prompted him to quickly ascend into the stands and culminated in altercations between him and his teammates and several fans in the stands and on the court. In subsequent weeks, the Palace Brawl would elicit mass hysteria, debate, panic, and subse-quent changes to the racial meaning and governing of the NBA. Grant Farred describes the event and its aftermath in these powerful terms:

> The event in question can be, as it has been in the media, distilled to a name: Ron Artest. . . . Supine on the scorer's table, Pistons fans, some of them inebriated, most of them white and male and unhappy at Artest's "showboating" in their building (the Palace at Auburn Hills, on the outskirts of the "Motor City"), inserted them-selves into the event. They transformed a player-on-player incident into—and initiated—the event by throwing beer on the black male's body. A tough player, Artest responded by charging into the stands to find the offending fans; second later, he was joined by his teammates Jermaine O'Neal and Stephen Jackson, Pacer players intent on protecting their colleague. A melee ensured as players and fans tussled, as officials found themselves unable to reimpose order

on the game. This event provoked, as Stuart Hall might have it, a wide-ranging "moral crisis" in the media—a "crisis" about sport, about sportsmanship, about player salaries and their concomitant privileges, and race. All of which produced, in a predictable convergence of these factors, an opportunistic attack on the culture of hiphop and its influence on the NBA. (2007, pp. 60–61)

The fact that Artest wasn't a "good sport" and resorted to violence, elicited a great deal of criticism from many facets of the media. Not surprisingly, the burden of guilt for the melee was placed squarely on Artest's shoulders by numerous commentators, who used the incident as evidence that the NBA was indeed too hip-hop[3], too out-of-control, too dangerous—it was a league that was simply too black.

The Palace Brawl not only generated widespread media coverage and commentary, but also ubiquitous online chatter. For example, in the days following, the following reactions, questions, and explanations were offered on fuckedupsports.com:

- "Did the Jiggaboo need to blindly attack the first fan he saw" (Milton, November 22, 2004).
- "The NBA is full of Niggers. I am sick of them and additutdes [sic] they carry. I would bitch slap Artest in a second. I would steal that mutha fuckas pride" (Joe Nigger, November 20, 2004).[4]
- "Its like I always say, 'you ca take the NBA player out of the jungle but. . . ." (Louie Faraconvict, November 20, 2004).
- "What do you expect from a bunch of Niggers? Nigger Basketball Association. I won't ever spent a dime on those million dollar felons" (Shocked and Awed, November 21, 2004).
- "I felt as if I was watching a fracas at the city zoo when I turned into ESPN on Friday Night. It was as if a spectator at the show threw a banana peel at an unsuspecting monkey who then charged into the crowd and attacked the superior species out of pure animal instinct" (Muhammed, November 2, 2004).
- "Aint nothing butta Detroit party Y'all" (Wealthy white man, November 22, 2004).

On freerepublic.com, a conversation similarly broke out concerning "why athletes behave like criminals":

- "I personally haven't watched an NBA games [sic] since the millionaire morons began smashing backboards, hanging from

hoops like apes, thumping their chests and behaving like
bohemian teenagers on drugs" (The Crusader, November 22,
2004).

- "Daddies. Too many don't know theirs." (ApesForEvolution,
November 22, 2004).

Although these rhetorical utterances might be dismissed as those of extrem-
ists and, therefore, not reflective of the mainstream discourse and debate that
followed the Palace Brawl, the racial logics, ideologies, frames, tropes, and
discursive formulations that are evident here are the same ones that guide the
commentaries, debates, and mainstream media framing of this event. As such,
this chapter examines the post-Brawl discourse in the context of the NBA's
larger racialized culture war and the broader assault on blackness. Seeking to
contextualize both this discourse and the resulting "moral crisis" (Farred
2006, p. 61) within the broader social, racial, cultural and political landscapes
of both the NBA and society at large, I argue not only that events surrounding the "Motown Melee" ushered in a new era for the NBA defined by a need
to control the undeniable blackness of the league and the illusion of racial
transcendence,[5] but also that the spectacle of this moment of violence and the
resulting panics reflected and built on long-standing discursive and ideological formulations of blackness.

Given the importance of this event, and the central themes of this
monograph, the discussion of this recent event will establish a foundation for
examining race, anti-black racism, the NBA and America's new culture wars,
as well as the predominant themes of both this ideological battle and this
work: hip-hop, ghetto/thug influences on the league, values, morality, colorblind rhetoric, generational divide, money, and race. According to the media
discourse, while a problem in itself, the Palace Brawl also signified a larger
issue: the growing power and influence of the hip-hop generation as represented by a group of millionaire, ghetto-raised, gangsta ballers, who not only
brought the crossover, trash-talking and high-flying dunks into the league,
but also ego, excess, and violence. They threatened the financial viability of
the league, along with the connections between fan and player. It demonstrated that hip-hop as cultural style, as swagger, as signifier of coolness,
wasn't compatible with all NBA fans. The elusive goal of racial transcendence
would be impossible should the relationship with hip-hop continue because
of the imagined links between hip-hop and blackness. Blackness was always
just beneath the surface, a powder-keg waiting to explode the NBA's bubble
of racial neutrality. With the Palace Brawl, Artest popped the bubble; with
his body lying on the scorer's table or his (and others) fighting in the stands,
blackness was in full view, requiring efforts to control and manage their
racialized bodies.

Examining the textual implications of the fight itself (in terms of the historical implications of a predominantly white fan base gazing at black bodies that are forbidden to look back), the spoken and unspoken reactions and the larger context of meaning, this chapter not only seeks to understand this particular spectacle, but also establish a context for understanding the various issues raised throughout the monograph, such as the assault on teenaged NBA ballers and hip-hop clothing.

At the core of the racialized culture war that came into public view both during and after the Palace Brawl was a battle about the influence and presence of blackness in the NBA and the realm of popular culture. Within the context of a larger and long-standing reactionary cultural and ideologically based project that blames black culture, black bodies, and blackness for the pollution, corruption, and denigration of American life, the argument that hip-hop sowed the seeds of the Brawl is a predictable one. From the perspective of this argument, the fact that Artest attacked those "poor" fans and others responded with aggression was not surprising given the importance of blackness within the league. The fight demonstrated the dangers of too many black bodies and too much black cultural influences on the league and its fans, calling for efforts to rid the league of the purported cultural expressions of blackness and if necessary purge those bodies whose racial existence threatened the league and its pleasure to white owners, fans, and media commentators.

OPENING UP THE WOUNDS:
FAN-PLAYER TENSIONS AND DIVISIONS

The guiding theme of the post–Palace Brawl discourse was that of player-fan division. The perception underlying this discourse was that the specifics of the incident or the variables in operation—Artest's erratic personality, the close proximity of fans at NBA games, the failures of security and even alcohol consumption by fans—were superfluous to the more difficult and important questions and issues concerning the division and tensions between the NBA's players and its fans (Adande 2004; Canzano 2004; Downey 2004; Elmore 2004; Jenkins 2004; Justice 2004; Keown 2004; Litke 2004; Nolan 2004; Plaschke 2004; Reynolds 2004; Rhoden 2004a; Rhoden 2004b; Smith 2004b; Whitlock 2004; Wilbon 2004a; Wilbon 2004c; Wilstein 2004a). According to Phil Taylor of *Sports Illustrated*, "The Pistons-Pacers fight wasn't just the result of a few fans having about a dozen too many, and it wasn't just about Artest looking for trouble and finding it again. The Brawl came about because of far deeper, more complicated problems that can't be completely remedied with more security or more sobriety. The tensions that led to the melee won't go away overnight" (2004). It came about because "they don't like each other, they don't respect each other, and they don't understand each other" (Plaschke 2004); because "deep down, player America and fan America are on different wavelengths, with different opinions on just about every issue" (Keown 2004). According to the broader media discourse, the tensions predated the fight, resulting from increased and exorbitant player salaries, poor play, and image problems stemming from high profile incidents (e.g., the Kobe Bryant case; Latrell Sprewell choking his coach and, years later, lamenting that his $14.6 million salary might not be sufficient because he too "needed to feed his family") (Armour 2004; Robbins 2004a), and countless other problems (Adande 2004; Armour 2004; Canzano 2004; Clay 2004; Elmore 2004). "Maybe the Detroit fight was part of the crash," suggested Richard Justice. "Too many fans see the NBA, not as the league of Tim Duncan and Kevin Garnett but as the league of Allen Iverson and Kobe Bryant, of the Dream Team's embarrassment in Athens, and of a perception that players care more about endorsements and lifestyle than winning" (2004). The problems facing the league resulted from fans imagining the league through those bodies associated with hip-hop and criminal misconduct and not those who racially transcending "good negroes."

Bill Reynolds, in "Shocking Brawl a Telltale Sign of the Great Divide," describes the context of the melee as follows:

> How did an incident between two teams, one we've seen so many times before, escalate into something so ugly?
>
> I suspect it's several things, none the least being the growing disconnect that exists between fans and players. Many players have come to be viewed by fans as spoiled, overpaid princes, whose sense of entitlement too often seems as large as their paychecks. It's a gulf only increased by the fact that, in the NBA anyway, the overwhelming majority of the players is black and the overwhelming majority of the fans is white.
>
> Whatever the reasons, the disconnect is there, one that only seems to widen as both the salaries and ticket prices get bigger, the money coloring everything. (2004)

Similarly, in "A Disconnect between NBA players and Fans," Steve Wilstein argues that "the self-inflicted image crisis" (Lawrence 2004), resulting from the Brawl was not "an aberration," but rather reflected the existence of a pre-existing gulf between fans and players. Noting that the number of whites who purported to dislike or hate the NBA rose from 21 percent in 1993 to 30 percent 10 years later, while at the same time this sentiment declined among blacks from 4.3 percent to 2.9 percent,[6] Wilstein identifies the Palace

Brawl as a predictable consequence of the fan-player disconnect and the "self-destructive path" (Wilstein 2004a) the NBA was following via its relationship with hip-hop:

> There is a growing disconnect between many fans and the NBA, whose American players, perhaps more than those in any other sport, are perceived as arrogant, selfish and overpaid. Those images were reinforced this summer by the U.S. team at the Athens Olympics.
>
> Though there are surely many players, perhaps the majority, who don't fit that characterization, the attention drawn by the likes of Latrell Sprewell, Allen Iverson, Ron Artest and, during the past year, Kobe Bryant, have weighed heavily on the league.
>
> The subject no one wants to talk about, the one that makes everyone edgy, is race and its relevance to the NBA's problem. (2004)

In this sense, the specifics—Artest's foul, Wallace shoving Artest; his lying on the table; a fan throwing a cup of beer at Artest; his charging into the stands—merely ignited a powder keg that had been building over the years. "The antagonism between the two sides is like a ruse and the cup of beer thrown was just the latest match causing the biggest explosion we've witnessed so far" (Taylor 2004).

Given the underlying tensions, divisions, and animosity, the discourse ultimately concludes that the actions of Artest and the other players, along with those of the fans to a lesser degree, forced the NBA "To look in the mirror" (Araton 2004a) and see the problems it faced once "the walls came down" (Plaschke 2004). The fight merely exposed the deep-seated problems, which had long been eroding the power and profitability of the league. Tony Kornheiser explains: "From the emails I have received, from the comments I have heard personally and from what I have seen on television, it is clear to me—and should be clear to anyone—that the non-stop replays of this incident, this riot, brought out deep-seated feelings of resentment toward the NBA and its players" (Kornheiser 2004). Kornheiser further notes that "The era of good feelings we saw with Magic, Michael, and Larry" were gone. "Stern doesn't need a weatherman to know which way the wind blows. It's blowing hot and angry from the general public. And it's blowing right at his league" (Kornheiser 2004).

Likewise, Charles Elmore concludes that the fist of Ron Artest didn't simply enact punishment against those Pistons fans, it broke an "invisible barrier" (Jorge Bargioni quoted in Elmore 2004), challenging a culture of denial that plagued the league:

The boundary between fans and players shattered in a brawl of Pacers, Pistons, and patrons. Something else cracked too. The NBA's image already straining under falling TV ratings, the Kobe Bryant trial and a growing rap sheet of player misbehavior, has become the biggest repair order in professional sports.

Until the Brawl, thing things that made some fans question the product were, while not particularly helpful at the box office, at least safely under glass—a rape or shooting trial here, a suspension for choking a coach there, the refusal of some NBA stars to play in the Olympics and the disappointing player of those who did go. It happened in the window of a TV screen, or inside the transparent bubble surrounding the court.

The knuckles of Ron Artest, striking out into the stands, broke the bubble. (Elmore 2004)

As in much of the discourse, the focus of the general public, although often generic and nondescript, underscored white-and-red-state America's opposition to and contempt for the primarily black NBA. Moreover, the focus on hip-hop, attitudes, and criminality as the driving forces behind the player-fan gulf elucidated the racial dimensions of this discourse.

Although a small element of the discourse constructs tensions as dialectical (Araton 2004a; Boyd 2004b; Dwyre 2004; Keown 2004; Kornheiser 2004; Plaschke 2004; Rhoden 2004a; Wilstein 2004a), emphasizing the role of fan behavior and attitudes, little insight is provided into the ways in which generation (Boyd 2004b; Zirin 2004), class (Boyd 2004b; Wherry 2004; Zirin 2004), race (Boyd 2004b; Downey 2004; Reynolds 2004; Wherry 2004; Whitlock 2004; Wilstein 2004a; Zirin 2004), racism, and power (Boyd 2004b; Zirin 2004) informed this culturally contested moment. Instead, the bulk of the media discourse source the tensions, divisions and animosity to hip-hop driven criminal behavior and values, or to the failures of the players themselves. The implication was that while the tension may have been mutual, the players were responsible for that tension. The Palace Brawl "leaves the NBA facing the question of what in the world to do about . . . the deteriorating relationship between players and paying customers," notes Michael Wilbon in "Friday Fracas was Criminal at Every Level." The Brawl brought into focus "the increasing perception that the league is full of young, underachieving, unprofessional, richer-than-ever, thug divas unable to maintain the level of play established by the previous generation's stars" (Wilbon 2004c). William Rhoden concludes that "the melee was caused by fans, drunken fans, riotous fans" (although Ron Artest was "the villain of this drama"). Yet, he also argues that this "rainbow riot" provides a window into the broader problems facing the NBA. "Commissioner David Stern's larger problem is that the NBA image is changing before his eyes," he asserted. "A league once defined by nonthreatening figures like Michael Jordan, Magic Johnson, and Larry Bird before him, is becoming younger, and more aggressive and more concerned about being real than making fans, sponsors, and even the commissioner comfortable" (2004a). The selfishness, the performed hip-hop identities, and the blackness of the players were thus the reasons for the tension and, therefore, comprised the fundamental cause spurring this culminating fight.

THUGS AND CRIMINALS[7]

As the media deconstructed the Palace Brawl as both an outgrowth and a snapshot representation of a divided NBA nation, much of the coverage imagined this division as one between law-abiding (notwithstanding the few misbehaving) fans and criminally minded players (Armour 2004; Clay 2004). For example, Nancy Armour, in an Associated Press commentary, contextualizes the November 19 Brawl in the following terms: "Nowadays there are enough mug shots out there to spawn a new trading card industry. Players are doing and saying things that defy common sense, annoying their high-priced whines" (2004). Likewise, Harvey Araton critiques the post-Brawl commentary, saying, "Frankly, I've already heard too many diatribes begin with 'These guys,' which always sounds to be like 'These black thugs with tattoos and cornnrows'" (2004b). Similarly, Bob Cook describes the hyperbolic arguments employed in those post-game commentaries as such: "So the brawl becomes a flashpoint for anyone who wants to argue. With thinly veiled racial references that the NBA is nothing but thugs . . ." (Cook 2004). The discursive articulations surrounding the Brawl, thus, became a site for the rehashing and rehearsing of dominant ideologies concerning black criminality.

Criminalization reflects the process of extending criminal meaning to a previously legally unclassified social practice, body, or group. For example, black male bodies throughout history have come to represent that which is deviant, criminal, and threatening. Writing about the war on drugs and America's racial caste system, Michelle Alexander argues that, "the stigma of race was once the shame of the slave . . . today the stigma of race is the shame of the criminal" (2010, p. 193). Resulting from the white racial framing promulgated "by political and media elite" (Alexander 2010, p. 193), "the era of mass incarceration" has reduced "what it means to be criminal in our collective consciousness to what it means to be black." In other words, "the term black criminal is nearly redundant. . . . To be a black man is to be thought of as a criminal, and to be a black criminal is to be despicable—a social pariah" (Alexander 2010, p. 193). Herman Gray argues further, "The black other occupies a complex site, a place where fears, desires, and repressed dreams are lodged. The black is a site of spectacle, in which whites imagine blackness as a potential measure of evil and menace" (Gray 1995, p. 165). Blackness within dominant society and within the world of sports represents a sign of "social decay," disorder and "danger" (Andrews 2001b, p. 117). Connecting this process to the ongoing culture wars, the Reagan revolution, deindustrialization, and the continuously expanding American prison system, S. Craig Watkins argues in *Representing* that the criminalized black body functions as a powerful marker of social decay, pathology, and danger, thus necessitating state control and intervention.

> The criminalization of black youth and inner city communities was necessary to legitimate the crisis. Legitimation is the process by which the state secures consent from society by giving the illusion that it is acting in the common interest of society. . . . Law and order appeals bind the nation together at the same time they divide and polarize society along lines of race and class. The merger of the criminal, the lower and the dangerous classes promotes the commonsense notion that most pernicious threats to a harmonious society come from the bottom of the social and economic hierarchy. In this sense, then the war on drugs deflects the anxiety and discontent of ordinary Americans and their resentment away from corporate and political elite and against the poor. (1998, pp. 37–38)

The trope of black criminality has been central to a white racial frame in that this danger and deviance has been used to justify inequality, to rationalize high rates of incarceration, and to sanction various forms of institutional violence.

While a post–civil rights context has seen a shift away from explicit racial explanations of criminality, racially coded cultural explanations justify surveillance, hyper-policing, and the mass incarceration of African Americans. In the absence of codified anti-black racism, the tenets of colorblind racism, with its cultural and biological components, assumes that "these innately physical males (black athletes) would be misbehaving" without sports (Andrews 2000, p. 182). "In this racism, the other's identity warrants its very annihilation because it is seen as impure, evil, and inferior," notes Henry Giroux. "Moreover, whiteness represents itself as a universal marker for being civilized and in doing so posits the Other within the language of pathology, fear, madness, and degeneration" (Giroux 1994, p. 75).

The increased cultural importance of sports, coupled with the fact that a disproportionate number of African Americans are involved in major collegiate and professional sports, fuels the attention paid to the alleged criminal misconduct of athletes. In the context of increased attention to "law-and-order" and the increased focus on the ghetto/hip-hop/blackness as a source of cultural pollution and criminal activity, media culture has come to conflate the "athlete, the gangster rapper, and the criminal into a single black male persona that the sports industry, the music industry, and the advertising industry have made into the predominant image of black masculinity" (Hoberman 1997, p. xviii). From the political pulpit to the multiplicity of articles written about the epidemic of crime within sports, the white imagination relates crime and bodies to fear within the black male population, while simultaneously exonerating whiteness of all societal transgressions. The criminalization of black youth through both the justice system and popular culture has relegated an entire generation of black youth to a criminal state within the white popular imagination. The lurking black male represents the ideologized body that lays the foundation and evidence for greater state power and surveillance (Cole 2001a, p. 68; Andrews 2001b, p. 114; Mauer 2001). "Public perceptions and media representations transform minor infractions into moral dramas and major trasngressions into scandals, often of national import," argue King and Springwood. "To be sure, popular attitude toward and coverage of illicit activities and wrongdoings of athletes regardless of race, have attained unprecidented importance; however, the particular history of blackness and the peculiar return of race in sociopolitical discourse imprint all African Americans as deviant, not simply those who break the law" (2001, pp. 116–117). Further articulating the importance of sporting cultures in this regard, Ferber argues, "The disproportionate media coverage focused on violent and sexual assault charges brought against Black male athletes compared to similar charges against White male athletes, reifies this stereotype of Black men as inherently dangerous in need of civilizing. The message is that all Black men are essentially bad boys but that some can become 'good guys' if tamed and controlled by White men" (Ferber 2007, p. 20).

The repeated references to Artest and the other players involved in the fight as having traded in their uniforms for "gang colors" and "gang styles" (Limbaugh 2004), as being "thugs" ("Basketball's Thugs" 2004; Clay 2004; Kindred 2004; Moore 2004b; "Rampaging Thugs" 2004; "Readers Express Little Sympathy for Players" 2004; "Sell Sport Not Thuggery" 2004; "Thugs, Sports, and Consequences" 2004; E. Smith 2004; Wiseman 2004), or as merely engaging in "thuggish violence" ("Basketball's Thugs" 2004) reflect the criminalization of the players, the NBA, and of black youth in general. "The commercialization of the thug image leads, perhaps inevitably, to the problematic assumption that black men, not just athletes are violent and dangerous," writes Jeffrey Lane, in *Under the Boards: The Cultural Revolution in Basketball*. "Moreover, too often the understanding that whites have of blacks is profoundly skewed by the simple fact that—as with the 'Prep-school Gangsters'—whites interact with blacks only indirectly, through the consumption of a very limited number of representations" (2007, p. 65). While failing to recognize the historic nature of the criminalization of black bodies, a process that predates hip-hop, or the integration of the NBA, Lane illustrates the ways in which a thug trope guides fan engagement with the NBA. Although establishing a binary that is in many ways contradicted by reality, Kobena Mercer reflects on the long-standing criminalization of black bodies as well:

> As a major public area, sport is a key site of white ambivalence, fear and fantasy. The spectacle of black bodies triumphant in rituals of masculine competition reinforces the fixed idea that black men are all "brawn and not brains," and yet because the white man is beaten at his own game—football, boxing, cricket, athletes—the Other is idolized to the point of envy. This schism is played out in the popular tabloid press. On the front page headlines black males become highly visible as a threat to white society, as muggers, rapists, terrorists, and guerrillas: their bodies become the imago of a savage and unstoppable capacity for destruction and violence. But turn to the back pages, the sports pages, and the black man's body is heroized and lionized. (Quoted in Andrews 2001b, p. 131)

What should become evident, however, in examining the Artest situation and the broader discourse surrounding the NBA is the convergence of the front and back pages, such that those athletes who Mercer describes as being "heroized and lionized" are instead demonized and feared, not just because of the physical manifestations of violence (i.e., criminality), but because of the cultural morals and values that they supposedly bring into the arena and onto America's cultural landscape.

Hamilton Nolan describes the incident as one "when athletes attack" (2004), recalling a contemporary headline, which read: "National Brawlers Association" (Quoted in Lee 2005). Michael Lee reports that one editorial described the Brawl and the broader culture of the NBA as "a halfway house for pampered self-indulgent millionaire athletes with minimally controlled tempers" (Quoted in Lee 2005). According to this argument, as a home to criminals, the NBA was little more than a halfway house.

Such rhetorical links that connected crime and criminality to the NBA were relatively commonplace after the Palace Brawl. George Neumayr in "Rap Sheets (Rhetorical Question of the Day): Why do our athletes Behave like Criminals?" offers the following assessment: "The sports sections of newspapers often double as crime sheets, itemizing the rapes, domestic beat-ings, strip-club melees, cocaine busts and so forth implicating professional athletes" (2004). Questioning the willingness of NBA officials to address the crime epidemic amongst its ranks, Neumayr sees the league's problems as not symbolic or perceptional but based in the criminality of its players. "Why, they wonder, are our athletes acting like criminals? Because many of your ath-letes are criminals. . . . The NBA increasingly looks like a glorified league for ex-cons" (2004). To substantiate his claim, Neumayr, like an editorial in the *Providence Journal* (2004), invokes the work of Jeff Benedict.

Benedict (Benedict 2004; Benedict and Yaeger 1999; Benedict 1999; Benedict, 1998), constructs the world of sports and the NBA specifically as an excessively criminal world. For example, in *Out of Bounds: Inside the NBA's Culture of Rape, Violence & Crime*, Benedict reports that 4 in 10 NBA players possess a police record involving a serious crime. His examination of the 2001–2002 NBA Season, found that 71 out of 177 had been "arrested or oth-erwise recommended by police to prosecuting attorneys for indictment for a serious crime" ("King Kaufman's sports daily"). Beyond the methodological shortcomings of a study that only examined 43 percent of its players (177 out of the 417 American-born players within the NBA), his failure to differenti-ate between a police investigation, arrest, prosecution, and conviction, not only demonstrates the severe limitations of his work but the ways in which black bodies are presumed to be guilty. As evident with his cited presence within post-Artest commentaries, Benedict's research provided "evidence" for the historically and racially based stereotype about the crime epidemic within the NBA (Lane 2007, p. xv).[8]

Benedict influences extend beyond his elucidating a crime problem within the NBA, but with his arguments about the cause of this problem: a permissive culture that doesn't hold NBA players accountable and the influ-ence of hip-hop on the league and its players. Accordingly, he argues:

> The long-standing logo of the NBA is a red, white, and blue sil-houette of a basketball player dribbling a ball.[9] The image symbol-izes Americana and the beauty of pure skill. But there is nothing admirable or beautiful about the emerging image of today's NBA player: diamond-studded ears, flesh plastered with offensive body tattoos, and nicknames like "The Answer" and "Big Dog." Instead of a place to showcase teamwork, courageous play, and selfless pass-ing, individual NBA players are converting the hardwood into a stage for hedonists to thumb their noses at rules, laws, and social norms accepted by a large segment of the NBA's traditional fan base. (2004, p. 193)

As evident here, post-Brawl commentaries consistently identified this moment of criminal misconduct as yet another example of the NBA crime epidemic.

Stern called the Detroit episode "shocking, repulsive, and inexcusable," but to others it was surely a fracas waiting to happen. As Jeff Benedict documented in his book *Out of Bounds: Inside the NBA's Culture of Rape, Violence, and Crime*, basketball has created a world for millionaire thugs where social norms no longer apply. Increasingly players are drafted right out of high school, without the maturation that college or the military or some other public service might provide ("NBA Cosseted Thugs" 2004).

The increasing numbers of players skipping college, many of whom come from "poverty stricken to lower class families that are uneducated" (comments from fuckedupsports.com), have been deprived of discipline and are bereft of proper values. This situation has not only led to Artest and his teammates violently attacking fans, but also to a league dominated by criminals. Nancy Armour seems to conclude that the league's criminal element is corrosive, destructive, and widespread: "Nowadays, there are enough mug shots out there to spawn a new trading card industry" (2004). Similarly, commenting on Neumayr's "Rap Sheets," respondents concluded that many (black) athletes, including Artest, behave like criminals because, essentially, they are criminals: "Maybe just perhaps because dey be gangstas to start, who jus' happen t'be fine at hittin' da J" (SAJ, freerepublic.com, 2004). Emphasizing the impact of a culture of poverty and commonly accepted dialectics between crime and the ghetto, other respondents concluded that the NBA (and sports in general) is dominated by criminals because a disproportionate number of ballers grew up in America's criminal-producing ghettos. According to this logic, America's ghettos produce athletes, rappers, welfare queens, crack babies, and criminals. "What do you suppose is the percentage of NBA players who learned their etiquette on the playground in 'the hood?' I think therein lies the problem" (MarineBrat, Freerepublic.com, 2004). "The real issue is whether single moms, who head most black households, are equipped to provide the proper academic atmosphere at home," writes Shaun Powell. Because so many single mothers work full-time jobs, "it's an effort to juggle the job and the household especially when many of these single mothers don't get home until dinnertime. How many have the energy to cope with the demands of family five exhausting days a week? And then there's the question of how many of those working mothers have an advanced education themselves" (Powell 2007, p. 73).

Gregory Clay similarly laments "a perception that the NBA is fostering and embracing a thug culture." More instructively, he writes that the Artest-induced Brawl was not an isolated incident, choosing to link it to a 1998

Sports Illustrated study about the NBA and children born "out of wedlock." To further illustrate the connection between the NBA's purported "sexual irresponsibility," the Artest Brawl and criminality, Clay concludes: "Because of that sexual irresponsibility, who is to say an NBA player won't end up like former Carolina Panthers wide receiver Rae Carruth, now serving an 18–20 year prison term for concocting the murder of his pregnant girlfriend" (2004). In other words, the criminality of the NBA's black players should surprise no one given how many children they supposedly have "out-of-wedlock." Just as the arrest of Kobe Bryant prompted media efforts[10] to link his arrest to broader trends within contemporary sports culture, the Palace Brawl was framed as a symptom of a larger problem that has resulted from the influence of urban/hip-hop culture (blackness).

Through a multitude of rhetorical devices and tropes, the discourse consistently pointed not simply to the criminal element of the NBA, as evidenced by the Ron Artest Brawl, but to the criminality, pathology, and threatening/violent behavior and values of the ghetto (geographically and culturally) itself. While the criminality and pathological values corrupting the NBA had bubbled up during the Palace Brawl, the essential threat remained present. The ultimate danger facing the league and its fans resided in the NBA halfway house. Lacking discipline and the influence of a father figure, and exposed to hip-hop and poverty, the NBA's black players, like their "non-ballin brthern," are destined to attack, rob, rape, and terrorize. "Many NBA players are actually nothing but thugs who are gifted physically to do one thing, and if not for that they would be in prison" ("Letters—Basketball Stars of Today Just Hoodlums with a Hoop" 2004). Artest, like many inside and outside of America's basketball arenas, have been "written off by society as pathological or useless" (Dyson 2007, p. 71).

The most emblematic example of the "hoodlum with a hoop" trope, which describes a player who in spite basketball and the class advantages that results from an NBA career, still supposedly commits crime, is Ron Artest. Within the media reporting, there was an effort to link crime to geography (the ghetto) through references to Artest's own personal history. According to Matt Marrone, Artest, despite numerous past suspensions "had a reputation for being a hothead since his high school days," a fact not surprising given that he "grew up in a Queensbridge housing project" (2004). Artest was imagined as an archetype of both the ghetto and hip-hop and, therefore, of the pathological and criminal corruption of the NBA. "Branded America's menace" (Wise and Jenkins 2004), a "child" who "must act on a whim" (Telander 2004) and who is prone to "tantrums" (Marrone 2004); a "historically troubled soul" (Moore 2004a) who "two years ago" "was in a perpetual paranoid rage" (Ryan 2004)[11]; "an extremely talented player who doesn't compute things upstairs"

(Windhorst 2004); "a crazed man with a history of crazed outbursts and rampages" (Wiseman 2004); someone with "anger issues" (Robbins 2004b); a "spoiled brat" with "mush for brains" (Mariotti 2004b); "a troubled young person" (Zirin 2004); a "punk" (Kindred 2004), "lunatic" (LeBatard 2004), and a "knucklehead" ("Artest Outburst Typical of Street-Stupid Culture" 2004) "who is in need of some serious help" (Rosenberg 2004), the efforts to not only criminalize, but also to psychologize Artest were ubiquitous. Artest didn't simply make a bad decision or even commit a crime; he was depicted as bad at his core, a criminal at heart, not surprising given his geographic origins. Regardless of behavior or context, Artest was fundamentally threatening and dangerous, as was evident on that fateful night.

Within a white supremacist imagination, he was an animal who could only be caged and controlled for so long. The Brawl was thus about Artest or, more broadly, the NBA's players and its culture, rather than being about race, racism, or the structural dimensions of contemporary sporting cultures. Just as "in discussions about crime and the rising population of incarcerated people," the Palace Brawl, along with the subsequent media response and the NBA's dolling out of punishment, was "treated as a contingency, at best as a product of a 'culture of poverty,' and at worst as proof of an assumed black monopoly of criminality" (Davis 1998b, p. 265). To understand the focus on Artest's criminal body is to understand the ways in which black men have always functioned within our white supremacist society as "figures, or symbols of something else: lust, violence, sexuality, degeneracy . . ." (Marriott 2000, pp. 43–44). Evident both in the media discourse concerning Artest and the NBA and in the aftermath of Hurricane Katrina, "black social death is characterized by the seemingly instantaneous social alienation of a delineated category of racially pathologized people whose formal status within the civic body is permanently marked b the irreconcilable—and socially defining—tension between centuries of racially formed, genocidal enslavement and the multiple historical *recodifications* of black subjection to institutionalized white supremacist violence" (Rodriguez 2007, p. 134).

Jason Diamos is emblematic of the essentializing process inherent in the pathologizing of Artest and the black community as a whole. In "For Artest Today's Trouble Took Root Years ago," he documents Artest's pattern of misbehavior stemming from his "hot temper." "Even as a high school freshman at Laselle Academy in Manhattan, he was benched for 13 games" (2004). In other words, Artest had a record and a history that point to his erratic and violent personality. Diamonds, like Jenkins, LeBatard, Marrone and Wise, makes note of the Artest family history, that is, his having grown up in the Queensbridge Housing Project in Long Island. In fact, LeBatard is very explicit with his conclusions in this regard, arguing, "Artest, straight street, comes from one of the roughest patches of pavement on our planet—Queensbridge in New York. He isn't going to get hit in the head, calmly point out the fan and immediately begin litigation that sues the fan for assault damages such as intimidation in the work place" (2004). Artest seems to agree with the hegemonic explanation for his various transgressions, one that locates violence and anger in his ghetto upbringing and imagines him as a "menace to society." "People say I'm a thug or whatever. But my cousin got life for killing someone. I have other cousins who sold cocaine and drugs. So what type of person am I supposed to be? Don't I deserve some credit for overcoming that? I didn't see a lot of nice stuff growing up, so really, who am I supposed to be?" (Quoted in Wise and Jenkins 2004). Wise and Jenkins also identify Artest's ghetto upbringing as an important factor not only in seeking to understand this man who charged into the stands one night, but also as a step toward complicating the accepted stereotypes of the ghetto, Artest, and the NBA player.

> The social centers of housing life, the basketball courts, are located in the building's courtyards. Scores of college-bound players learned to play there, including WNBA star Chamique Holdsclaw, who grew up in the nearby Astoria Houses. Artest and Holdsclaw played on the same Boys and Girls Club team. "Ron Ron," she called him, like everyone else in the neighborhood.
>
> Queensbridge Houses also is where some significant rappers have found their voices, including Nas, Mobb Deep and N.O.R.E. Music and basketball went hand in hand. There was crime, gunplay and empty vials on the streets, but also a very solid working-class ethic. Artest's mother, Sarah, was a bank teller, and his father, Ron Artest Sr., held several jobs over the years. He still works on a truck, delivering Snapple juice products.
>
> "I don't know one person in this building on welfare," says Jamaal Speede, 42, a housing consultant and longtime resident of Queensbridge who is close to the Artest family. "Everyone wakes up and has somewhere to go." (Wise and Jenkins 2004)

As the embodiment of a hegemonic ghettocentric imagination (Watkins 1997) that focuses on violence, the projects, welfare, and the personal demons that threaten the safety and harmony of society, the discussion about Artest relied on heavily utilized tropes and discourse. Likewise, Artest's personal relationship to hip-hop and the music industry (Clay 2004; Elmore 2004; Marrone 2004; Ryan 2004; Smith 2004b), along with that of the entire black NBA, became a focal point for the post-Brawl commentary.

HIP-HOP TO BLAME FOR PALACE BRAWL

Predictably, the abundant commentary focusing on what led to the fight seen around the world and why did not limit its attention to player-fan conflicts, or even to the criminality plaguing the NBA, but also honed in on the polluting impact of hip-hop's influence on the NBA. For example, George Blaha, a broadcaster for the Detroit Pistons, argues that the Brawl was both "fairly predictable" and "almost inevitable" given the NBA's relationship to the worlds of hip-hop and rap music, "where everything violent sells" (Quoted in Dwyre 2004). John Wooden identifies this fan-player fight as resulting from the mind-set and mentality of the "me generation," which appears to be the term he uses for the hip-hop generation (Quoted in Dwyre 2004).

According to David Hinckley, "Among all things that aren't clear, this much is: somehow a big chunk of blame will fall on rap music and hip-hop culture" (2004). Likewise, Cynthia Fuchs notes that the debate prompted by the "Motown Melee" would ultimately focus on the negative impact of hip-hop culture. "As journalists sought other ways to parse fan-player tensions, a framework emerges more nuanced than familiar black versus white standoff, such that Artest comes to embody a generational shift" (2004). To Fuchs and others (Boyd 2004b), the generational shifts and conflicts center on the meaning and visibility of hip-hop within both the NBA and the culture in general. Fuchs further notes that "specifically and unsurprisingly, this line of reason names his [Artest] hip-hop attitude and goes on to scold the NBA" for its decision to join forces with the destructive and dangerous hip-hop community. "The invocation of hip-hop indicts the players, of course, and not the fans engaged in the fight. Their aggression comes from elsewhere, perhaps their resentment that hip-hop and basketball play so well" (Fuchs 2004) or "perhaps the longstanding contempt and derision directed at black athletes" (Rhoden 2006). Equally evident, the fan contempt—akin to the media derision seen during those post-fight commentaries—reflected a disdain for and demonization of the values and cultural ethos professed within hip-hop culture, leaving commentators with both a scapegoat (Neal 2004; Wang 2004) and a raceless explanation for fan and media animosity toward the NBA and its primarily black players.

In the months following the Palace Brawl, social, political, and cultural commentators found themselves in constant conversation about this fight and its larger cultural meaning and significance. They took to the air to lament the influence of hip-hop (the "ghetto mentality"), warning of impending doom within the league if it didn't check its marriage to the hip-hop world (Celizic 2004; Limbaugh 2004; Taylor, 2004; Wilbon 2004a; Wilstein 2004a). Similar debates took place within classrooms, on the Internet, and presumably in local barbershops and in front of various water coolers and cappuccino machines. Regardless of location or the nature of the conversation, the reaction to this spectacle was nothing new, reflecting both the power of basketball and its importance as a cultural site of conversation regarding race, class, American values, and national identity.

Hip-hop culture was not perceived as the only reason for fan animosity and contempt for today's NBA, but its influence on the NBA was seen as contributing to the destructive and pathological values that bubbled over at the Palace of Auburn Hills. The NBA's longstanding efforts to embrace hip-hop culture as part of its marketing strategy, and to promote hip-hop ballers, resulted in both a systematic and sustained backlash by fans, who saw their fears confirmed when the realities of a pathological, hip-hop culture invaded the otherwise safe (suburban) confines of their basketball stands. Such logic and rhetorical argumentation guided the post-Brawl commentary.

Shortly after the Brawl, conservative commentator Rush Limbaugh took to the air to not only denounce Artest and the other players involved, but to place the incident within a broader context defined by the polluting impact of hip-hop culture. "This is the hip-hop culture on parade," notes Limbaugh. "This is gang behavior on parade minus the guns. That's the culture that the NBA has become" ("Limbaugh on NBA fight"). Limbaugh was not alone in the demonization of hip-hop through its conflation with criminality. George Neumayr also laments the ways in which hip-hop and the criminal presence within the NBA led to this specific fight. Not limiting his argument to crime, he quickly (and without any subtlety) moved his focus to hip-hop, demonstrating the essential link between hip-hop culture (blackness) and criminality. For Neumayr, the NBA courting hip-hop is tantamount to introducing criminals into the NBA, and vice-versa.

> The league has joined . . . to promote a culture of rebelliousness that has made them very rich while allowing them to pose as progressive. For reasons of raw business, they were willing to bring a culture of lawless behavior into the NBA, licensing NBA gear to hip-hop companies, presenting the vulgarity-spewing, showboating stunts of their stars to impressionable children not as bad behavior but as an authentic and "real" culture even as black parents, such as Bill Cosby, were trying to discourage their children from embracing this emptiness.
>
> Only now as the effects of that hip-hop culture become more vivid and startling to the public does the NBA take dramatic action. . . . The NBA increasingly looks like a glorified men's league for ex-cons. But as long as the bucks keep flowing its cynical organizers are happy to indulge these spoiled and dangerous stars. (Neumayr 2004)

Similarly, on the blog "The Conservative Revolution," the influence of hip-hop on the NBA was denounced in the days following the "Palace Melee." "The NBA has centered themselves around the hip-hop culture for the last 5 years in order to create a stronger fan base," argued this blogger. "The players buy into that and fans buy into that. Have you ever seen so many thugs as you do in the NBA? There are always fights in the NBA. . . . I think the real problem is the NBA is comprised of a couple hundred street bangers and the NBA think that is a good thing" ("Pacers-Pistons all out brawl" 2004). Like so many commentaries, Geoffrey Norman, with his "Gangstaball," explicates the links between hip-hop and the NBA/Ron Artest by making mention of Artest's own rap career. "The first of the basketball players to head into the stands in Detroit, seeking a fan to hit, was Ron Artest, who had earlier asked his team for a little time off to concentrate on his rap album. Artest is one of the NBA's 'troubled' stars" (Norman 2004). To Norman, Limbaugh, and countless other commentators, the Palace Brawl demonstrated that the influence of hip-hop had compromised the values of the NBA and led to a Brawl that exposed the problems facing the league.

At the core of the racialized culture war that came into public view during (and in the aftermath of) the Brawl was a battle over the influences of hip-hop on basketball, with headlines reading "hip-hop hoops feeding negative stereotypes," "hip-hop culture contributes to NBA's bad rap," and "NBA's problems are cultural, not racial" (Celizic 2004; Limbaugh 2004; Taylor, 2004; Wilbon 2004a). Lamenting the cost of hip-hop's intrusion into the NBA, where fans "like pro game, not the players" because of the league's "image problem" and its "punks and thugs," commentators called for action: reform to bring the league back to its glorious (white, and white-controlled) past (Elmore 2004; Kindred 2004; Whitlock 2004). "As the NBA tries to recapture some respectability in the aftermath of the fight seen 'round the world, it nervously dances around a misguided culture that's slowly suffocating the league," writes Shaun Powell. "Stern was the man who boldly rescued the NBA from an image of being too black in the late 1970s. Now he must contend with the image of the NBA being too black, in a different sense, in the new millennium" (Powell 2004). Powell not only calls for action—for an effort to rid the league of "the middle finger mentality" embraced by far too many young black players in the league—but emphasizes how this current image problem differs from those of years past, given the dominance of young, hip-hop influenced "angry black males" who don't understand what it means "to be professional and dignified black players." The anger, the poor behavior, the criminality, and, of course, the fan opposition were all consequences of the hyper-marketing of hip-hop-gangster-thug ballers. "Allen Iverson, Latrell Sprewell, Kobe Bryant, Dream Team failures, an embrace of all the negative aspects of the hip-hop culture and a horrid style of play have conspired to make the NBA easy to ignore" (Whitlock 2004). To *Kansas City Star* columnist, Jason Whitlock, the Brawl merely exposed the poisons slowly killing the NBA.

> American sports fans, particularly those who consistently shell out the hundreds of dollars it takes to attend a professional game, are fed up with black professional basketball players in particular and black professional athletes to a lesser degree.
>
> Yeah, let's cut through all the garbage and get to the real issue. The people paying the bills don't like the product, don't like the attitude, don't like the showboating and don't like the flamboyance. The NBA, which relies heavily on African-American players, is at the forefront of fan backlash. Stern realizes this, and that's why, spurred on by the Detroit brawl, he is reacting decisively.
>
> What the players must come to grips with is that just because race is an element in the backlash, that doesn't mean the backlash is fueled by racism (2004).

That is, the contempt and distaste for black ballers is understandable given their acceptance and promulgation of hip-hop culture. In a sense, the backlash against hip-hop within the NBA is logical and justifiable because of the destructiveness of this culture and the attitudes of the hip-hop player.

This is a frequent theme within the post-Brawl discourse: the intrusion of a criminally minded, hip-hop, black culture is not only to blame for Ron Artest, Jermaine O'Neal, Stephen Jackson, and others attacking fans, and the reasons behind white animosity against the overwhelming black league, but also a reason for the persistent failures within the black community. "Last week's ugliness wasn't the problem. It was the symptom" (Canzano 2004). To Canzano, the league's "whining, unsportsmanlike hyper entitled attitude," its promotion of "post-dunk celebrations," which "are usually taunts," and its cultivation of a culture that "thinks that embarrassing other players, showing them up with a stare, a chest bump, a double biceps pose or a Darius Miles 'horn rising ceremony'" is, while entertaining, symptomatic of the fact that the league has lost its way, with hip-hop serving as its guide toward criminality and waning fan support (Canzano 2004; McNulty 2004). The Palace Brawl was merely an outgrowth or a symptom of those pathological values that define the hip-hop nation. The hegemony of hip-hop has created a league of "pampered, multimillionaire athletes who imagine that no rules apply to them" ("Basketball's Thugs" 2004). Or, as Mark Bartlestein, Ron Artest's former agent, described the situation: "Players are not competing, they're trying to embarrass the person they're playing against. . . . After a touchdown, or a dunk, you're proving your manhood. It's a culture that is all about embarrassing someone or calling attention to yourself or of just competing. It's incredible" (Quoted in Telander 2004). While rarely linking such cultural attributes directly to blackness or even hip-hop, the associations made assumed to exist between ego, "trash talking and posing" (Cowlishaw 2004), and hip-hop; between the construction of the NBA as a league of "overpaid, pampered, selfish thugs" ("Readers Express Little Sympathy for NBA Players," 2004) and its primarily black player demographic; between the "endless chest-bumping of the look-at-me showmanship, the gangsta image that [is] so much a part of youth culture, one that so many players identify with" (Reynolds 2004) and hip-hop/blackness are all transparent.

According to this logic, the NBA has been increasingly guided by a "middle finger mentality," which, according to Shaun Powell, was "merely an extension of the hip-hop culture they embrace, which promotes and encourages anger, violence, selfishness, bling-bling, excess, the exploitation of women, and showboating" (Powell 2004). In this vein, hip-hop has not only facilitated fan disillusionment, but also player contempt for the fans, the game, and civility in general, all of which boiled over on that frightful night (Powell 2004). Bryan Burwell, in "The NBA is Hip-Hopping its way out of the Mainstream," agrees with this interpretation as part of his effort to seek a "full truth" that challenges those who see Artest as "the only culprit." The Brawl was not the result of the choices and violent behavior of a single individual, Burwell argues, but a consequence of the NBA turning to hip-hop some years before.

> In its haste to keep a firm grip on its fading Dream Team popularity, Stern's marketing team decided to present professional basketball as an extension of the hip-hop culture. . . . But while selling their sports edginess they were playing with a loaded gun. They embraced hip-hop and hip-hop is now embarrassing them because they had no idea what they were messing with. They thought they were getting Will Smith and LL Cool J. But now they're discovering the dark side of hip-hop also infiltrated their game. (2004a)

Embracing a rhetoric that imagines black identity in general and, more specifically, that of hip-hop identity as encompassing both the "good" and the "bad," Burwell replicates a long-standing discourse of respectability—that of the "good Negro." The NBA's mistake was in not appreciating the complexity of black life, confusing gangsta rap with that of the wholesome, acceptable, Will Smith. According to Burwell, the dark side is evident in an "I-gotta-get paid" mentality, bling-bling, an "unregulated culture of possession," the "constant underlying threat of violence" and, most importantly, an inability to distinguish "between ballers who dress like thugs ('thugged up') and the athletes who behave like hoods" (2004a). Burwell's reference to "thugs" and "hoods" and, worse still, his assertion that the NBA's relationship with hip-hop is akin to "playing with a gun," serve to further solidify white supremacist notions regarding black criminality and danger. Ron Artest merely justified the furor already being directed toward a hip-hopped NBA, and confirmed the stereotypes held by many fans about today's NBA players, hip-hop, and blackness as a whole. Artest, like the NBA's presumed relationship with rap culture, "has helped perpetuate the notion of a thug league" (Wharton 2004). Of course, hegemonic notions of blackness guide those projects in imagining both the NBA and hip-hop culture as spectacles of pathology and criminality.

Michael Wilbon, in "Hip Hop Culture Contributes to NBA's Bad Rap," further elucidates not only the centrality of hip-hop to the debates and panics resulting from the Palace Brawl, but the entrenched dialectics of hip-hop, blackness, and criminality within the discourse.

> The point here is not that I think hip-hop is bad; some Eminem or Snoop Dogg CD is constantly playing in my car. The point is NBA folks probably didn't know what they were getting into, how much hip-hop's street code might appeal to the players, and how much the league's very mainstream ticket buyers and sponsors might be resentful of a subculture they don't understand or distrust, even if their white, suburban, well-to-do children inhabit the same subculture. And that doesn't even address the notion that basketball, a decidedly team sport, doesn't exactly work with the theme of "my, my, my." (2004a)

In other words, the selfishness exhibited by Artest, who put his ego and his preoccupation with machismo ahead of team, league, and fans not only resulted in the Brawl, but also substantiated the fan contempt for today's NBA. Likewise, the "themes of thug life that are admittedly the prerequisite values of hip-hop culture" (Wilbon 2004a) led Ron Artest and his peers into the stands. Moreover, the players' failure to respect the game, its history, or the values of society for the sake of "respect at any cost," including going into the stands and administering a beat down if somebody "disrespects you'" (Wilbon 2004a) explains why Ben Wallace was driven to push Artest because of a hard foul, why Artest responded to a cup thrown from the stands with such fury and violence, and why the incident spiraled into a near riot, and also the interconnectedness between this moment and hip-hop culture. The emphasis on respect, and the contempt for any sort of "dis," are seen as part and parcel with hip-hop culture. Accordingly, the recipe for the Artest Brawl, and the growing animosity exhibited by fans, starts and ends with the introduction and promotion of hip-hop culture within the NBA. The purported

obsession and pathological obsession with "respect" is represented as a cause
of Artest's storming into the stands and in the broader problems facing the
NBA (Lawrence 2004; Rhoden 2004a; Rhoden 2004b). "The NBA has
always had outcasts but today's head cases are disturbing because they follow
the same *beat*" (my emphasis), notes Shaun Powell. "They have a code: under
no circumstances will they be disrespected. Not by coaches, their own teammates, or fans. Anyone who challenges them will be dealt with and that's why
Artest climbed into the stands. He wasn't trying to defend himself. . . . He
was trying to get justice the only way he knows" (2004).

Given the discourse, it would seem that his association with hip-hop and
his ghetto upbringing explain why Ron Artest and his peers only know justice
through violence. Powell was not alone in linking Artest's behavior (and the
league's demise) to hip-hop's, and now the NBA's, preoccupation with the
"dis" and "respect." An editorial in the *Dallas Morning News*, entitled, "Artest
Outburst Typical of Street-Stupid Culture" lamented the impact of a mentality that says, "disrespect me, and I'll burn your house down" (2004). Likewise,
Geoffrey Norman argued that the fight resulted from Artest's investment in a
rap mind-set. "When he is 'dissed,' he fights. So when some fan threw a drink
on him, he charged" (Norman 2004). Tim Keown—like Rick Telander, whose
commentary about the Artest incident was entitled, "'Dis' Mentality: the
EVIL (my emphasis) behind the NBA Brawl" (2004)—similarly argues that
"this mess" wasn't the result of "loosening morals in schools or the war in
Iraq," but "the increasingly dangerous and misguided concept of disrespect"
(2004). Similarly, Rush Limbaugh told his audience that the Artest Brawl
represented a broader trend/issue plaguing the culture "that comes right out
of the hip-hop culture. . . . You know what the common theme that I'm hearing is? 'Well, I'm not going to be dissed. I'm simply not going to be disrespected. Somebody disrespects me, they're going to pay for it.' Meaning, 'A
fan disrespects me, that fan's going to pay for it,' not just another player"
("Limbaugh on NBA fight" 2004).

Notwithstanding the ubiquity of scapegoating of hip-hop, a few voices
worked to challenge this particular argument. According to Todd Boyd, "the
conversation is right back where you'd expect it: super-sized black men beat-
ing up on helpless white men. Black men gone wild. Let's blame hip-hop culture, the gangsta mentality, the rule of the street" (Boyd 2004b). Elsewhere,
Boyd questioned the media focus on hip-hop and, more generally, the tendency of commentators to extrapolate grandiose sociological commentaries
from the case of a very specific individual arguing, "Ron Artest is a special
case. It would be unwise to try and take this instance and link it to hip-hop. It
really has nothing to do with hip-hop" (Quoted in Wherry 2004). Focusing
both on Artest's own "violent, aggressive, anti-social behavior" (Quoted in

Wherry 2004) and broader cultural projects, Boyd points to the racial implications of those who have concluded that "hip-hop had come to represent all
that is wrong with the modern NBA. That the culture and the generation it
spawned were once again killing the game" (Quoted in Wherry 2004). The
scapegoating of hip-hop not only replicates long-standing cultural projects
that locate broader social and cultural problems within hip-hop and through
black bodies (Dyson 2007; Zirin and Chang 2007; Sewell 2006; Perry 2004;
Pough 2004b; Lewis 2003), but also simultaneously exonerates whiteness and
America as a whole. "When I was growing up, I use to go to Philadelphia
Flyers' games in the mid-1970s. I was at a game with a bench clearing Brawl
that made its way into the stands," recalled Larry Platt. "And no one said that
it was proof of a lack of character in 20–something Canadians. It wasn't a ref-
erendum on Canadian culture. And I think it's overly simplistic to point fin-
gers at the hip-hop subculture. I think any analysis that blames hip-hop is
trying to make a political point that doesn't really pertain to the specifics"
(Quoted in Wherry 2004).

Boyd also questions this logic, sarcastically asking what Artest's character or his actions reveal about the culture and politics of a post-9/11 America.
"If anything, you could talk about this violent, aggressive anti-social behavior
as being very similar to what's taking place at the highest levels of the U.S.
government right now. In an era of unilateral moves and preemptive strikes,
when people respond to threats, real or imagined, is that any different than a
guy getting hit with a plastic cub and deciding to go up into the stands and
go after the first person he sees?" (Quoted in Wherry 2004). Although arguing that George Bush or the Project for a New American Century are
responsible for the Palace Brawl "might seem a stretch" (Wherry 2004), so
should scapegoating an entire generation, cultural movement, artistic form,
and community, unless such claims are guided by the racial assumptions that
sit at the center of the ongoing cultural war directed at hip-hop and black
youth culture. The commonplace practice of demonizing and scapegoating
hip-hop may have reached its zenith in the aftermath of Don Imus's attack
on members of the Rutgers' Women's basketball team and Michael Vick's
criminal involvement with dog fighting.

The practice of demonizing hip-hop or, rather, employing hip-hop as a
one-size-fits-all scapegoat is not unique to the Artest situation or the NBA,
but instead reflects a commonly used trope within mainstream discourse.
Whether in regard to school violence, hyper-materialism, misogyny, racism,
sexism, or countless other social problems, hip-hop is frequently blamed and
invoked as key to understanding the basis of such problems. For example,
John Gibson, of Fox News, blamed hip-hop during his discussion of an incident where two teenagers gave marijuana to two toddlers.

Now to the "Big Debate," two teenagers were arrested this week in Dallas for allegedly giving two toddlers pot and then stupidly videotaping it. It is not hard to be smoking mad at them. But should we also direct our anger at a culture that glamorizes blunts, like the ones used in this video, and other drugs. I think the hip-hop industry has some of the blame coming to them for these tots being pushed to do pot. . . . Why shouldn't I blame hip-hop? I mean, I hear this talk about blunts, which are big fat marijuana cigarettes, in hip-hop records all the time. Why shouldn't I think those kids got that idea from listening to hip-hop? ("Hip-hop to blame for pot-smoking tots?" 2007)

On Monday, January 16, 2006, Bill O'Reilly, as part of his "Personal Story Segment," interviewed conservative commentator John McWhorter and Clarence Jones, a former speechwriter for Martin Luther King Jr. Using the King Holiday as a backdrop for discussing the problems facing black America and the failed efforts of prominent "black leaders" to address these problems O'Reilly stated, "The two big issues are out-of-wedlock births and gangsta' rap culture, which is decimating the children. The 70 percent out-of-wedlock birthrate among black Americans is the genesis of poverty, and I don't hear the leadership addressing that very much" (O'Reilly 2006b). Commenting on a *60 Minutes* piece concerning the "Stop Snitching" movement, Glenn Beck offered the following assessment of rap music and hip-hop culture:

You know, I saw a disturbing piece on "60 Minutes" last night with Anderson Cooper, who will be with me on the radio tomorrow to talk about it. I don't know if you saw it. It was an in-depth look at the hip-hop culture in America, and how rap stars refuse to report violent crimes to the police, because, as the saying goes—one that I've never heard before—"Snitches get stitches."

Here's the point tonight: the rap music industry is enslaving our children. And here's how I got there. There he said it: "They know what makes money." I don't know about you, but that should send a chill up your spine. It did mine. Now, it may be harsh, but when a few privileged people—white and black—are making money off the backs of others—white and black—by spreading the glorification of crime, sex and death throughout our community, that sounds like exploitation that borders on slavery to me. The chains of drugs, and violence and ignorance are just as real as the ones forged in steel. And we've got to stop it. (Beck 2007)

Oprah Winfrey has been similarly critical of hip-hop for its hypersexuality and misogyny, saying in one instance, "I respect other people's rights to do whatever they want to do in music and art and whatever. . . . I don't want to be marginalized by music or any form of art. . . . I feel rap is a form of expression, as is jazz. I'm not opposed to rap. I'm opposed to being marginalized as a woman" (Quoted in Clark-Florey 2006). Not to be outdone, Bill Cosby, who has in many ways blamed hip-hop for the problems facing the black community (Dyson 2005), described the hip-hop generation in the following way: "They think they're hip. They can't read; they can't write. They're laughing and giggling, and they're going nowhere" (Quoted in Hutchinson 2004).

Writing about the efforts to link hip-hop to Michael Vick's legal troubles and dog fighting in general, William Talley Jr., in his blog "Area 4:51," wrote the following: "This is little more of a continuation of the trend of making hip-hop the scapegoat for everything that's wrong with society. This is nothing new, ever since the attacks on NWA back in the early '90s. However, this trend seems to be re-energized more since the whole Don Imus scandal" (2007). Davey D concurs, arguing that, "Hip-hop is a convenient scapegoat because its communities don't have the political power or money to control the type of media images projected worldwide. This has resulted in unbalanced coverage and the maligning of a culture" (Davey D 2000).

Similarly, Jeff Chang and Dave Zirin offered the following assessment of the media and public discourse that resulted from Don Imus referring to members of the Rutgers' women's basketball team as "nappy-headed hoes":

> The idea that the black community in general and hip-hop in particular are to blame for Imus's rant is gaining currency across the political spectrum. From Oprah to Obama, the "teachable moment" on Imus has become a public meditation on racism and sexism not by whites in the media but by blacks. The anti-hip-hop furies fly far beyond the usual right-wing suspects. Even the great Bob Herbert of the *New York Times* compared Snoop Dogg with Imus and Michael Savage. And in the *Los Angeles Times*, civil rights attorney Constance Rice excused Imus as a "good-natured racist," guilty only of mimicking "the original gurus of black female denigration: black men with no class"—in other words, rappers. (2007)

Concluding that "the current national monologue about demeaning language and imagery is an exercise in scapegoating" that ultimately lays blame upon hip-hop (and its black constituency) for social and cultural ills rather than taking into account societal racism, sexism, and homophobia, or the interests/workings of those who profit from hip-hop's dissemination and commodification, Chang and Zirin illustrate the ways that the discourse about hip-hop serves to explain complicated problems that may implicate white America and the structures that govern American capitalism and democracy. "The only thing I'm saying is that the problem is bigger than rap music. Its cards need to be plucked, it's not only rappers who say things some people deem offensive, but also the white financial structure that manufactures and distribute records," argues Cheo Coker. "This same structure weaned an entire generation on sex and violence, so it's little wonder that rappers find such a huge audience hungry for themes involving sex and violence. Rap as a direct reflection of society, will change no sooner than the populace that influences it changes its attitudes" (1994). Despite the pervasiveness of patriarchy, misogyny, materialism, and other forms of violence within popular culture, public discourses continually scapegoat hip-hop. Gwendolyn Pough argues that "Rappers become grunt workers for the patriarchy; they sow the field of misogyny for the patriarchy and provide the labor necessary to keep it in operation, much as Black men and women provides the free and exploited labor that built the United States" (Pough 2004, p. 71). Mark Anthony Neal takes this a step further, focusing on the performative aspects of hip-hop—whether in the hypersexuality offered by male rappers and female dancers, or the pornographic displays visible on Howard Stern or in images of Spring Break—that mimic and capitalize on hegemonic notions of masculinity, femininity, and heterosexual sexuality. "Remember, some of the black men on the screen are 'performing,' performing their notions of how African American masculinity embodies power through force, violence and exploitation. Mr. 50 Cent isn't the only thug or pimp in the room; there are more than a few in the White House and at the Pentagon" (Neal 2005, p. 147). Stated in the most powerful terms, Ernest Hardy notes the absurdity, yet racial/cultural significance, of such arguments scapegoating hip-hop:

> Hip Hop is America. Its only real crime is being so much so. It boils "mainstream" standards and practices down to their essences, then turns up the flame. Violence, materialism, misogyny, homophobia, racialized agony, adolescent views of sex and sexuality. . . . These are the common, bankable, all-American obsessions. They're the underbelly items that have always defined this country's real, daily-life culture. What that means is the top-of-the-line hip-hop and its true artists (be they "mainstream" or "underground") soar on the same terms that America's real artists—and everyday folk—have always soared: by being un-America, by flying in the face of the fucked up values and ideals that are wired and corroded in this country's genetic code even as no-lip lip-service is given to notions of equality, justice, and fairness. (Hardy 2006, p. xiii)

It is true that the NBA of today is different from that of years past, but the claim that hip-hop is to blame for the NBA's current position within popular sporting culture is belied by a critical analysis of sport's location within

American life. Hip-hop is made a scapegoat for a culture that was created by product endorsements and consumerism; by overt pressure being put on talented, underrepresented youth; by coloring the money involved (no one questions the net worth of managers and owners, the vast majority of whom are white); and by an American public thirsty for a show.

CONCLUSION: ACCOUNTABILITY AND PUNISHMENT

> The perception problem was there, and therefore it was real. We were focusing on that issue even before the brawl, but it certainly was an exclamation point in terms of perception of NBA players. We've got to do a better job acknowledging it and working to correct it.
> —David Stern (Quoted in Dixon 2005)

The penalties issued today deal only with one aspect of this incident—that of player misconduct. The actions of the players involved wildly exceeded the professionalism and self-control that should fairly be expected from NBA players. We must affirm that the NBA will strive to exemplify the best that can be offered by professional sports, and not allow our sport to be debased by what seem to be declining expectations for behavior of fans and athletes alike.

There are other issues that the NBA must urgently focus on at this time. First, we must redefine the bounds of acceptable conduct for fans attending our games and resolve to permanently exclude those who overstep those bounds. Participants in and around the court must be assured complete protection from unacceptable fan behavior. Second, we must re-examine the adequacy of our current security procedures in Detroit and our other 28 arenas. The actions at Friday's game, though unprecedented, must now be factored into all efforts to guarantee the well-being of our fans. Third, we must develop and implement new NBA rules to assure that the unavoidable confrontations likely to occur in the heat of competition are not allowed to escalate to the level we witnessed on Friday even prior to the egregious behavior by individuals in the stands." (David Stern quoted in "NBA Commissioner David Stern's statement on suspensions")

In the wake of the Palace Brawl, media commentaries consistently called for both punishment and reform, all in the name of discipline and accountability. The initial calls for lengthy suspensions that dominated the discourse (Plaschke 2004; "Vile Conduct a Symptom 2004; Wilstein 2004b) quickly subsided with the celebration and applause for Stern suspending Artest for the rest of the season, Jackson for 30 games and O'Neal for 25 games (Canzano 2004; "In Our View" 2004; Moore 2004a; Page 2004; Rester 2004; Smith 2004a; Wilbon 2004b).[12] The demand for and approval of the severe punishments levied against the players was neither surprising nor striking. Given the ways in which "law and order" and "tough on crime" discourses govern a multitude of institutions (Mallory 2007; Davis 2003; Parenti 2000; Davis 1998a; Davis 1998b; Parenti 1997; Davis 1995), it makes sense that *The Daily Breeze*, like many other publications, would celebrate the suspensions without any questions, gushing "Kudos to the National Basketball Association for coming down hard on thuggery" ("NBA's Stern Punishment Merited after Brawl" 2004). Yet, what is revealing is the fact that these commentaries offer similar rhetorical devices, which clearly emanate from a discursive field of law and order. Calling for "Justice" (Canzano 2004; Wilbon 2004b), "the punishment [to] fit the crime" ("Flagrant Fouls" 2004), and for Stern to "decisively . . . lay down the law" (Rester 2004); referring to a suspension as being sent to the "League's slammer" (Moore 2004b); or calling for "the commissioner" to do "exactly what commissioners should do to knuckleheads: spank them" (Moore 2004a) all reflect the logics and commonplace rhetoric associated with the criminal justice system. In the same vein, Michael Wilbon describes the season-long suspension as "essentially a third strike punishment, or in Artest's case, a fifth strike" (Wilbon 2004b). Likewise, prior to the announced suspension, Michael Rosenberg pleaded for Ron Artest to "go away . . . go far way. . . . And now you need to disappear. . . . Not for a week, not for a month, and for any amount of time that can be defined in conventional terms. We're not measuring this in games missed. It goes beyond that" (2004). Ray McNulty suggested that Artest needed psychological help: "I hope he gets it," he said, "in prison" (2004). The same logics, ideologies, and discursive formulations that contribute to the systematic incarceration of black and brown youth (and their broader communities) also guided the commentaries that called for punishment, accountability, and "justice."

Yet, these same commentators also saw the problems facing the NBA as bigger than this one incident and, as such, worried that the punishment levied against the perpetrators wouldn't be sufficient to save the league, let alone society as a whole. "Applaud the strict stance commissioner David Stern took with Artest," notes John Canzano. However, "On Sunday we didn't get justice, we got a start. . . . Artest is gone. But if anything else warrants a season-ending suspension, it's the league's whining, unsportsmanlike, hyper-entitled attitude" (2004). Likewise, Phil Mushnick concludes that suspensions needed to be a starting point for cleaning up the league: "Suspensions? That's not a bigger question. Suspension serve to punish, not fix. Prevention? You can't prevent unless you identify how we got here, why we arrived at where we've been headed" (2004). Not surprisingly given the nature of the post-Brawl commentary, the "how" and "why" centered on hip-hop, criminality, and the behavior and values associated with its young black players, leading to calls for action and reform to deal with those problems. Larry Brown argued that "there are going to be a lot of ramifications to this" (Quoted in Stein 2004). Likewise, David Stern emphasized how the Brawl should lead the NBA to take a look in the mirror and reflect on its own failures. "Frankly we've got a lot of work to do in the next several days and coming weeks. . . . There may be other wrinkles" (Quoted in Litske 2004). Jim Litke, in "Stern will Drop Hammer Further," responded to Stern's assessment in the following way: "'Wrinkles' was an interesting choice of words for someone about to embark on one of the more ambitious sports overhauls in a while. Stern began by making his point about behavior to his own employees about as quickly and as forcefully as good judgment and his powers as commissioner allowed. He was smart enough to know the responsibility for the Brawl started there, but it didn't end there, either" (2004). Harvey Araton, almost predicting a serious change that would encompass "the wrinkles" that Stern spoke about, noted "Stern has never underestimated the racial conundrum, and he moved with a politician's élan to guarantee that he was on the case, and this his hip-hop N.B.A. would once again be rated PG" (Araton 2004a).

By the one-year anniversary of the Palace Brawl, the nature of the changes the league would experience, the specifics of those aforementioned "wrinkles," and the ways in which the "Motown Melee" had provided the league the needed leverage to properly discipline and punish its "out-of-control" black ballers, had become clear. "Both the league and the players got a quick and dramatic wake-up call about their perception in the public," argued Richard Lapchick. "When the NBA took corrective actions like the dress code, it showed how serious they took the threat to their business" (Quoted in Lage 2005). Mike Celizic took this rhetorical position a step further, not by linking the problems to a cultural shift within the league and calling to "rebuild the game," but by proposing the institution of programs and policies to teach (discipline) or punish the offenders. "It means taking the teenagers now coming into the league in hand . . . giving them a support system, hammering home the importance of fundamental values in their lives," he noted. "That begins with team play, the element that was so lacking in Athens. Respect your teammates and your fellow competitors and your fans and the people who write about you and make you famous, and you'll get it back" (Celizic 2004).

Similarly, David Ganis, president of Sports Corp Limited, a consulting firm in Chicago, described the Brawl as "a watershed moment" for the NBA,

With that fight, David Stern saw that something had to be done. He saw that the perception of the players had to be changed and that their attitudes toward the public had to change, too. There wasn't a monetary backlash against the NBA, but there was a cultural one. The fight became fodder for late-night comedians. People who had only a casual interest in the NBA looked at players as overpaid, thuggish athletes. To Stern's credit, he saw that this perception, even though it was wrong in most respects, had to be changed because it was becoming detrimental to the growth of the sport. So this was a real tipping point for the NBA, and you have to give him credit because he didn't wait. He didn't appoint a blue-ribbon committee. He started immediately. (Quoted in Lawrence 2005)

In other words, in the wake of the Palace Brawl, David Stern and others involved in the league, seized on the fear central to the media discourse and used/exploited it in order to implement a series of reforms—age restriction, dress code, and other new marketing strategies (NBA Cares)—designed to protect the NBA's economic solvency, a challenge complicated by the racial dimensions of the league. According to Billy Hunter, the executive director of the NBA's Player Association, the league was not simply responding to the Artest Brawl, but to the contempt and opposition that many fans have for the league and its players.

I understand David. David's got a $3 billion operation he's got to manage. He's got to send a message to those folks who support the game, to his sponsors and his fans that he's got everything under control. That's why he has to come down on Artest the way he does.

I understand his right to do it and his need to do it, because you have to reassure the fans and it goes back to this subliminal issue of image. The league is 85 percent black, and people have concerns about the cornrows and the tattoos. So he's got to reassure his fan base that things aren't going to implode.

So the question is, how much punishment do you have to impose to demonstrate to the public that you're taking control of things, that their safety is not at risk, the game is secure?

How much discipline do you have to impose to reassure them? How much is enough? (Quoted in Rhoden 2004b)

What the post-Brawl commentary revealed was that too many fans and commentators saw the NBA as "too Black" (Simmons quoted in Hammer 2009);

it was "Too black, too angry, too paid, too unapologetic" (Jackson 2010);[13] indeed the league had become "too edgy, too young and culturally black" (Araton 2004a); it was too "tattooed and bejeweled in the minds of many fans" (Wilstein 2004a), all of which necessitated intervention. The argument was clear from these commentators: the Brawl demonstrated that, whether their perceptions conformed to reality, fans viewed the league as too hip-hop, too black, and this had resulted in a fan disconnect that had itself been fueled by sensational media coverage of purportedly "thuggish" behavior by NBA players. "Athletes in the eyes of many fans are too spoiled, too loud, too 'hip-hop, too tattooed, too corn-rowed—all of which translates to players are 'too black'" (Zirin 2004).

More importantly, what becomes clear is that the loudness, the tattoos, the hair styles, the presumed thuggish/gangsta bravado, the trash-talking, and the ego are all seen as cultural markers, not only of hip-hop, but of blackness, aesthetics, and values that are constructed as destructive within both the NBA and broader society. This sort of logic is central to the discourse: in talking about the pathological and dysfunctional behavior of specific black athletes, the debate is purportedly colorblind, focusing on values, behavior, and culture, rather than race. According to this argument/discourse, the backlash was not against black people per se, and it certainly wasn't driven by racist ideology, because "a lot of black folks would agree" (Page 2004) with those denouncing hip-hop and its destructive influence on the once fantastic NBA. Instead, it was a revolt against a culture that was slowly ruining the NBA, along with the promising future of America's black youth. Its destructiveness and pathology was clear to many of these commentators on that fateful November night.

It wasn't simply the racial dimensions or the racial tensions that fueled both the backlash and the "corrective" actions that began with suspensions and moved forward with dress codes and age restrictions, but white suprema-cist logic, anti-black racism, that the league would not challenge. The threats to the league emanated from the players' refusal to adhere to their role as entertainers, as commodities, as "appropriate Sambos." Mark Anthony Neal makes this clear when he links the situation in the NBA to the history of minstrelsy.

> Whereas [Jack] Johnson was an singular object of disdain for many whites both for his professional skills as a boxer and for his extracurricular activities with white women, the heightened visibil-ity of highly paid black male athletes has helped create an industry of derision—sports talk radio being just one example—and indeed such derision, even hatred, is the price of the ticket for black male athletes who desire to be those highly visible, highly paid black bucks. Not simply the assets that help increase the coffers of the

owners of professional sports teams (and the attendant paraphernalia), highly paid black athletes—Sambos—are now targets for the legions of over-worked, under-paid, and disaffected white men. In the political economy of black male celebrity, highly paid black male athletes are the "shiny little ball" that diverts attention away from the reality of underemployment, lack of adequate healthcare, and aluminum foil ceilings (thinking about the assistant managerial class at your local fast food restaurant). In an effort to keep their fandoms happy and paying (this includes home subscription sports packages), owners of professional sports teams and sports commentators (the white gaze—though quite a few minstrels provide such commentary, Misters Steven A. Smith and Stuart Scott) often turn a blind eye to the rhetorical violence that black male athletes face and the threats of real violence that fester beneath the surface, not unlike that which exploded in Detroit last Friday night.

When the NBA's highly salaried overseer meted out punishment (David Stern's salary has been rumored to be as high as $20 million) to members of the Indiana Pacers and Detroit Pistons, his message was clear: Sambo you here to perform and part of that performance is to ignore those fans who pay good money to be entertained and who reserve the right to publicly despise you. As such the NBA, Disney, Viacom and the NFL offers little protection for their highly paid minstrels. Such is the case for the fame and fortune that now comes with "the real nigger show." As Slim Charles so eloquently reminded us during the current season of *The Wire*, "The game ain't changed, it just got more fierce." (Neal 2004)

Or, as one player told Dave Zirin, "I look at the seats and don't see anyone from my old hood or anybody that looks anything like me. It's like you're a monkey in a cage" (Quoted in Zirin 2004). Likewise, the resulting actions, and the post-Brawl commentaries, demonstrated the lack of commitment to challenging racism in both the league and the media. Just as Jim Crow and the legal support for it operated to placate white racist desires for the sake of profit and social control, those ubiquitous efforts that blamed the players, that insisted they change because of the views of the fans, accepted racism. Instead of protecting its primarily black players from the specter of violence, both rhetorical and real, the NBA and its media partners accepted and promoted the anger and racism of its fans, demanding change from the players, a fact not surprising given that the same sorts of ideologies that guide the criminal justice and educational systems also guides the sporting world.

The Palace Brawl is a strong indicator of the acceptance of a "new racism," one that suggests that, while people of color are capable of being "morally upright," they choose not to do so when/by committing violent acts. By choosing thus, Artest broke an unspoken social rule; players in the arena are there for a show and have no rights that exceed their value as entertainment. Despite Dave Kriger's call for "calm" and his argument that "this was a brawl, not a metaphor for the decline and fall of Western Civilization" (2004), the Ron Artest basketbrawl would guide the NBA's operations and the media/fan discourses because, at its core, it was imagined to be a challenge to western civilization, white supremacy, and American values. It was conceived, in some ways correctly, as a slave uprising quelled by the rhetorical violence offered by the media and fans, and by the NBA's disciplinary policy, which sought to recapture an acceptable black NBA player or, at least, a "40-million dollar slave" (Rhoden 2006).

3

A CRISIS INSIDE AND OUTSIDE AMERICA'S ARENA

Age Restrictions and the Real Color of Money[1]

INTRODUCTION

The 2007 FIBA Tournament of the Americas in Las Vegas not only saw the systematic annihilation of teams by the United States, but a surprisingly limited discussion about the age of the team members, which averaged 26.2 years old (compared to the previous year's world championship team, in which the average age was 24.5). Although the squad's youthfulness was still in play to the media, its usefulness as a marker for futility, dysfunctionality, and immaturity was negligible, despite the fact that 5 out of 12 team members (including three starters) did not attend college. Age is truly just a number, only significant within particular narratives. Although reflecting the success of this team and the immense talents of its members, the absence of a discourse about age signifies the conclusion of that part of the NBA's racialized culture war wherein its youth movement was curtailed by panics, demonization, and calls for discipline, resulting in an end to high school ballers jumping straight to the NBA, and in a discursive shift as well.

From 1986 to 1992, all but seven of the 35 top-5 NBA draft picks were college seniors. The three subsequent drafts saw 13 nonseniors out of 15 top-5 selections. At the 1995 draft, the first four picks were all sophomores, with the fifth pick, Kevin Garnett, entering the league as the first high school player to be selected since Daryl Dawkins and Bill Willoughby in 1975. The drafting of Garnett would signal a new trend: 13 prep stars were drafted between 1995 and 2001, nine who eventually secured places on teams. In fact, between 1995 and 2005, when David Stern and the NBA began requiring that all players declaring for the NBA be at least 19 (and be at least one year

59

removed from high school), 45 high school players jumped straight to the NBA, of whom 29 were drafted in the first round and 9 more in the second. Only seven of these players were not drafted (although two of them would ultimately make it into the NBA). In 2004 alone, eight high school players successfully bypassed college for the greener pastures of the NBA, with all eight having been selected by pick 19. As of the 2006 season, all but five remained in the league (one of those five was waived at the start of the 2006 season). In other words, since 1995, of the 38 straight-out-of-high-school players drafted in the NBA, an astounding 87 percent remained in the league. Of those drafted in 2004, approximately 33 percent were no longer in the NBA as of the 2006–2007 season; all eight high school players were still under contract.

High school players weren't the only youngsters flooding the league. According to Marty Blake, in 1996 there were 40 early entrants, an "incredible" shift given that in the history of the NBA, "Out of 271 underclassman who had declared 60 were not even drafted." Notwithstanding Blake's caution and skepticism, this trend continued throughout the 1990s and early 2000s. Yet, despite media reports, commonsense notions regarding those who skip high school, and the overall discourse concerning this group in the NBA, they have been immensely successful in terms of draft selection, remaining in the league, and excelling on and off the court—eight players have made all-star appearances and six appeared in the 2007 Olympic qualifying tournament. Not allowing facts to get in the way, the tide against the influx of prep-starts reached a boiling point in the wake of the Palace Brawl, which not only brought this issue back into focus—even though Ron Artest and Ben Wallace both attended college[2]—it also provided the league with the power and support to institute this new rule. The renewed visibility of the league's blackness necessitated intervention and greater control. While Stern and others had long desired an age restriction, the Palace Brawl provided the necessary leverage for mobilizing team, player, and fan support. In other words, in the wake of the fight involving Artest, the arrests of Kobe and A.I., and various examples of fan backlash (or at least media focus on fan backlash), the NBA enacted a rule appealing to the racial sensibilities of its fans, "the guys who can afford tickets and expensive merchandise, yet has trouble identifying with a culture, an athlete, and a lifestyle to which he can't relate" (Maese 2006).

The black baller and his authentic cultural identity/culture of pathology isn't simply "foreign," distant, and unknown to these fans, but demonized, feared, and otherwise constructed as a pollutant needing an institutional and structural remedy. As such, in an environment where the hip-hop baller posed a threat to the cultural value, profitability, and the overall success of NBA basketball, those straight out of high school, the most raw and authentic signifiers of hip-hop and the NBA's "new black aesthetic" (Boyd 2003), were scapegoated as the source of the league's problems and efforts to control, discipline, and rid the league of their influence emerged as a panacea of sorts. As in the broader society, black bodies, particularly those youthful (immature/undisciplined) forms taken to be authentic, functioned as spectacle, as a useful site for blame and societal redemption, as a means for changing not only the face of the NBA, but its soul. Moreover, neither the league's purported identity crisis, or its relationship to fans and sponsors provided the sole rationale for instituting an age restriction. Rather, both worked alongside a much more benevolent source of inspiration: the drive to help/save not only those future NBA stars, but the many (black) youth who had turned their back on education and discipline for the sake of an NBA career. "The NBA sold the public the rule based on the idea that these young athletes would be better served by at least one year of college season" (Maese 2006). While Maese's use of the term *seasoning* is instructive given its historic connection to the process of breaking down (seasoning) Africans into controlled and compliant slaves, it is also important to reflect the context of this rule and hegemonic ideologies regarding race and blackness. Not only did it exploit the widespread backlash resulting from the Palace Brawl, along with the widespread contempt directed toward the hip-hop baller, it also seized on long-standing constructions of black masculinity and the criminalization of black bodies.

Amid the widespread backlash against the NBA and the calls for reform, David Stern, who initially resisted the calls to stem the youth invasion by citing the successes of early entrants into the NBA, and noting the limited concern about teenage athletes in other sports, capitalized on this environment to successfully implement an age limit. Seeking to exploit the panics induced by the Brawl and the efforts to link the "demise of the league" to its youthfulness, Stern pushed hard to add an age clause to the 2005 collective bargaining agreement. During an online interview, Stern made his opinion on the matter clear, denying that the proposal had anything to do with the preparedness of players, financial incentives, or a desire to assist the college game.

> I have never said that the 18 year-olds can't play in the league. I just said that I don't think it's a good idea for us to have them in the league. And I never said that they shouldn't come into the league because they should go to college. Because I am not sure that college is necessarily for everyone. What I have said is that I don't think we should be setting an example for kids to be planning the rest of their lives around basketball, because it's not a very good thing to do. ("David Stern Media Conference")

Seeking to save youth of color by discouraging basketball and encouraging school, Stern's emphasis on role models and protecting children reflects the long-standing efforts of white saviors on behalf of the black community. Despite the inscription of "white man's burden," the proposed age limit cannot be understood outside of the widespread demonization of hip-hop and young black males, and the societal efforts to reform, discipline, and punish those other deviant bodies who persistently threaten the (NBA) status quo.

In the midst of widespread celebrations about the arrivals of Freddy Adu, Michelle Wie, Sidney Crosby, and Koby Clemons, as well as the praise afforded to European players who turned pro in their teens, the straight-out-of-high-school baller has now found a "do not disturb" sign hanging from the NBA's window. At one level, we find a clear contradiction in terms of the societal silence regarding youth participating in other professional sports, the entertainment industry, and even the military, but this is not the only contradiction here. According to Ian O'Connor, David Stern "wanted an age requirement to turn back the high school tide, and yet he found himself marketing high school players to his paying public. LeBron. T-Mac. Kobe. KG. In one breath, Stern celebrated their contributions to his game. In the next, he pledged his allegiance to the cause of stopping future LeBrons, T-Macs, Kobes, and KGs from showing up in his league before age 20" (O'Connor 2005a, p. 110). While we can note the paradox of a league that markets hip-hop and its youth movement to the hip-hop generation, all the while trying to exclude, demonize, and control these same bodies, these ruptures are less revealing than the points of continuity that exist between various discourses and practices.

This chapter, however, challenges readers to move beyond a focus on double standards—the NBA's selective embracing of hip-hop; the praise afforded to other young athletes, particularly whites engaged in individual sports; and the willingness that America shows in sending "its" youth of color onto the battlefield. It seeks to move past a focus on the long-standing racist practice of both demonizing and commodifying black bodies, instead arguing that the proposed rule and the nature of the debate reflect the hegemonic practice of policing young black males who defy dominant expectations with baggy shorts, trash-talking, bling-bling, and hypermasculinity. In society in general, and especially in spaces dominated by black youth, we expect control, reverence, and respect; as a society, we fear black youth and habitually demonize them as the source of America's problems.

In connecting the age debate to the increased levels of violence inflicted on youth of color, I attempt to not only center race and racism within this discourse, but to emphasize its connection to the increasing levels of state violence and the widespread efforts evident in American schools, the criminal justice system, and the sporting playgrounds to police, profile, punish, discipline, or otherwise render invisible deviant black bodies—to turn the victims of racism and white supremacist violence into the source of problems in need of control and correction. Here, I examine and reflect upon the justifications, rationalizations, and calls for an NBA age restriction, as a remedy not simply for the purported problems facing the league, but for the larger crisis facing black youth in America. In examining this discourse, and its broader context, this chapter underscores the centrality of racism and commonsense understandings of blackness as pathology, dysfunction, and problem in need of disciplinarity and punishment. This chapter builds on the broader themes of the work regarding a racialized culture war inside and outside America's arenas, demonstrating that the assumed paradox of a nation sending youth off to war, or black and brown youth into America's prisons, is not a contradiction but is guided by the same sets of racialized logic.

HISTORY OF AGE RESTRICTION

Stern's successful effort to institute an age limit reversed a 1971 Supreme Court ruling. In *Haywood v. the NBA*, the Court ruled against the NBA's requirement that entrants into the NBA draft wait until the graduation of their college class. Following the 1968 Olympics where he averaged 16.1 points/game shooting, an astounding .719 from the field, Spencer Haywood attempted to join the NBA. Having only played one year each at Trinidad College (Colorado) and the University of Detroit, Haywood wasn't eligible to turn professional. But, with a mother who struggled to live on the measly $2.50 a day she made as a cotton picker in Mississippi (Adande 2003), Haywood was determined. After signing with the ABA's Denver Rockets and dominating the league (averaging 20 points/game and 19.5 rebounds/game, he would be named ABA rookie of the year and MVP), he was drafted by the Seattle Super Sonics, which, despite the rules established by the NBA, signed Haywood prior to the graduation of his college class, prompting the NBA to threaten to disallow the contract and implement sanctions against the Sonics. Haywood, arguing that the NBA's rule regarding early entry violated the Sherman Antitrust Act, was initially successful in a U.S. District Court, which ruled that Haywood should be allowed to play in the NBA immediately and that the NBA could not levy sanctions against Seattle. The court concluded:

> If Haywood is unable to continue to play professional basketball for Seattle, he will suffer irreparable injury in that a substantial part of his playing career will have been dissipated, his physical condition, skills and coordination will deteriorate from lack of high-level competition, his public acceptance as a super star will diminish to the

detriment of his career, his self-esteem and his pride will have been
injured and a great injustice will be perpetrated on him.

However, during the 1970–1971 season, Haywood played in only 33 games as
a result of NBA legal action; throughout the season, the NBA filed injunc-
tions prohibiting him from playing, leading Haywood back to court where,
once again, the court ruled in his favor (Dye 2006). The backlash and obsta-
cles Haywood faced were not limited to the courtroom, but could also be seen
in the media and on the court. "Labeled a troublemaker" (Adande 1997) and
lacking support from his NBA peers, Haywood faced tremendous opposition.
He described his battle against the NBA in the following way:

> I took on the NCAA, ABA and the NBA. People were hitting me
> in my stomach, hitting me in my face, sucker punching me when I
> was going through this whole court case. Throwing bottles at me
> when I would walk on the floor during games. They would be like:
> "Ladies and gentlemen, we have an illegal player on the floor and
> he must be escorted off!" Because the NBA got an injunction. All
> kinds of things would happen. They put me out in the snow with
> just my uniform. ("Spoken Word: Spencer Haywood")

Additionally, when he took court for the Sonics, fans would boo and jeer,
screaming "Go home, Nigger! Go back to school and learn to read the rules.
Go back to Mississippi. Go back to Africa" (Haywood 1992, p. 150).
    In 1971, the Supreme Court also ruled in favor of Haywood, whose
attorneys had argued that the conduct of the NBA was tantamount to a
"group boycott" and thus in violation of the Sherman Antitrust Act. The
Court agreed, ruling that the NBA's draft policy was a "restraint on trade" and
therefore illegal under the Sherman Act (Brown 2000).
    Following the ruling, the NBA briefly required players to formally
request early entry status, basing its decision on the financial hardship of each
individual player. Although the hardship criteria were eventually eliminated,
the league had few early entrants. From 1976 through the 1994 draft, only
18.1 percent of the first round picks were early or foreign entrants, compared
to the almost 80 percent who were college juniors or seniors. Most of that 18
percent came after 1989 with the majority being foreign entries. The absence
of a salary cap (instituted in 1989), and the strict salary structures for draft
picks, which led them to negotiate directly with teams, lessened the incentive
to enter the draft early.
    In 1995, the owners and players negotiated a new Collective Bargaining
Agreement, which, among other things, addressed the concerns of veterans
and the league itself regarding rookies earning more than veterans. Although

prior to the youth invasion the NBA had seen an increasingly steady stream of underclassmen, Stern argued that a rookie salary scale that "locks players into a scaled salary structure for the first years of their careers" (Tellem 2001), thereby limiting their ability to secure fair market compensation, would dissuade teenagers from entering the league. Under the 1995 CBA, first round picks were given guaranteed three-year contracts, with salaries calculated using a predetermined scale linked to place draft, yet still allowing teams to exceed salary amounts by up to 20 percent. The terms of agreement also added provisions to address the status of second round draft choices, who were to be paid the league minimum without any guaranteed deals. This agreement ostensibly encouraged top rate high school and college freshmen/sophomores to enter the draft early so as to expedite achieving veteran status—three years of restriction resulting in free agency and market-driven salaries.

> They do not become true free agents until after their fifth season. Imagine an 18-year-old with the talent and desire to turn pro. Under the current system, he can seek an agreement that maximizes his earning potential at 22. At the expiration of his first post-rookie-scale contract, he will be young enough (28 or 29) to attract another significant deal. But if he were to attend four years of college, he would enter the N.B.A. at 22 and not be eligible for free agency until 26. At the end of that first major deal he would be 33—far less likely to command another major one. In Garnett's case, those four extra years of college could have cost him as much as $100 million. No wonder the N.B.A. wants to make teenagers wait! If Commissioner Stern really wanted high school players to attend college, he would reduce the number of years players are subject to the below-market salaries mandated by the rookie scale. (Tellem 2001)

To further illustrate this point, let's examine the salary history for Kobe Bryant. He was drafted in 1996, and as the 13th pick, he was paid approximately $999,600 in his first year and $1,074,500 in his second, signing an extension prior to his third season.[3] Bryant was able to sign this extension at a time when he had blossomed into one of the league's premier players. He signed a six-year, $71 million contract extension, which ended after his eighth season, by which time he had won three championships and become, in many people's opinion, the league's best offensive talent. He commanded a hefty salary on the open market, ultimately resigning with the Los Angeles Lakers in 2004, netting a seven-year, $136.4 million contract. Prior to the deal's expiration, Bryant signed a three-year extension worth nearly $90 million. It is impossible to know what might have happened to Kobe if he had gone to college given the experiences of Randy Livingston, Felipe Lopez, and Schea Cotton, all high school stars who would likely have been drafted straight out of high school, but who instead went to college only to have modest (or, in the case of Cotton, nonexistent) NBA careers due in some ways to injuries (or, with Lopez and Cotton, questions about talent). What is clear is that had he attended college it is fair to assume that Bryant would have lost out on millions of dollars, solely because of the salary structure of the league. One the one hand, the 1995 CBA successfully discouraged good players from entering the league soon, pushing them to go to college with hopes of making it into the first round after a couple years in school. On the other hand, it encouraged those potential superstars to enter the league as quickly as possible in order to maximize their financial possibilities (McCann 2002; Rosenbaum 2003).

This phenomenon would worsen with the signing of the 1999 CBA. In fact, the number of early entrants increased significantly following its signing from 47 percent of draft picks between 1995 and 1998 to 71.5 percent during the 1999–2004 seasons. The 1999 CBA lowered the pay scale for rookies, added a fourth-year team option, and implemented a set percentage salary increase for each player. The agreement provided incentives for teams to draft younger players because under the agreement they had to pay less for the next potential superstar. "The changes in the 1999 collective bargaining agreement gave teams even more incentive to draft early entrants," writes Peter Groothuis, James Hill, and Timothy Perry, in "Early Entry in the NBA Draft." "By lowering the rookie scale for contract salaries, and adding a fourth year option for teams at a predetermined percentage pay increase, the league and union added even more opportunities at the bargaining table for teams to recoup general on the job training cost" (2005, p. 8). To curtail the influx of young players the NBA could have reformed a Collective Bargaining Agreement that not only encourages early entrance for players seeking to secure market value as soon as possible, but for teams that have minimal cost, investment, and risk for players selected in the draft (McCann 2002; Rosenbaum 2003).

AN NBA CRISIS: THE DRAFT, AND CHILDREN PLAYING IN THE WRONG SAND BOX

For the NBA, the draft has long been important to its success. Held in New York City and broadcast on ESPN, the draft isn't simply about bringing the next wave of stars into the league or assisting struggling teams through an infusion of new talent, but as a marketing tool, a coming-out party where fans celebrate with players, teams, NBA executives, and corporate sponsors. Yet, to the many critics of the league who had long demanded an age restriction, the magic had been lost in recent years through the infusion of young unknown talent. In 1998, several years before David Stern would eventually institute an age restriction, Bob Ryan described the NBA draft as "one of the most depressing nights of the year" as an event where the "beast devours its young" (1998). To Ryan, the draft had historically given fans hope and inspired excitement about the prospects of their favorite college stars joining the professional ranks. Instead, the draft had, at best, become a day providing general managers and coaches with false hope, marking "the addition of more immature and almost certainly misguided players to the mix" (Ryan 1998). The uncertainty and luck factor associated with each draft hurt underperforming teams, which, because of the lack of certainty, would likely have a more difficult task in selecting players who could facilitate success (wins). "Now the draft pool is so diluted by unproven high-schoolers and unknown foreign teenagers that the NBA draft is nothing but an uneventful, yawn-inducing guessing game that seems more likely to kick more unrefined Kwame Browns that polished Tim Duncans" (Burwell 2004b). Or, as noted by Sally Jenkins in the *Washington Post*, "The NBA motive isn't altruistic" but rather, in forcing high school ballers to spend at least a year in college, "NBA teams" now have "a chance to judge their abilities. Drafting them will be less of a guessing game and lessen the chances of wasting a top pick on a spectacular failure." Failures during the draft don't simply lead to more and more losses, but to a decline in the streams of revenue collected from attendance, merchandising, playoff payouts, and television money (Jenkins 2007). "The draft historically is exciting, because of a chance to get immediate help," argued Jerry West, then general manager of the Los Angeles Lakers. "But that is not the case this year [1996]. There may be some good players, but their impact won't be immediate because they are young and unproven. Everyone is hoping to find someone who can help down the line, unless you are picking high" in the draft. Ironically, that year the Lakers would trade Vlade Divac for the Charlotte Hornets 13th selection, Kobe Bryant. According to this part of the discourse, the draft as a preview of the NBA's future stars was failing, just as it was failing to help those teams become competitive through the infusion of new talent because of the unpredictability and rawness (Neviuss 1999) of so much of that talent.

However, the calls for an age limit as a remedy for the "high school infiltration" (Parker 2005) and the ongoing crisis facing the NBA weren't simply about bringing greater certainty to the draft, or minimizing the costs associated with scouting so many players—from high schools and colleges to professional teams outside the United States—and those required for babysitting these "diaper dandies" (Sandoval and Steinberg 2004; Kiszla 2000), it was seen as a necessary step toward returning the NBA game to its rightful owners: the fans and corporate sponsors. According to Vicki Michaelis, the invasion of youngsters is "the latest in a plague of NBA ills. . . . How can the basketball public be expected to eagerly await the moment when the home-town NBA team will call the name they've rarely, if ever, read about or seen play?" (1999). Moreover, given the ways in which colleges "season" players the intrusion of "unseasoned" black ballers threatened the profitability of the league and its corporate sponsors. At the same time, in part because of hege-monic fears of black youth, their entry alienated fans who wanted to feel good about themselves and society through watching presumably raceless athletes like Jordan or Magic, not a bunch of kids who had not been taught how to act like NBA stars (Andrews 2001c; Cole 2001; Andrews 2000).

Yet, the widespread calls for an age restriction within the NBA were not only about draft day or eliminating the guessing aspect of drafting for the future—"business considerations"—("NBA defends age limit policy in letter," 2009), but also about facilitating a dramatic alteration in the skills and men-tality of the NBA's future stars. In a letter to Representative Steve Cohen (D, Tennessee), NBA President Joel Litvin defended the age restriction as neces-sary because of their desire to have "incoming players" with "the requisite ability, experience, *maturity, and life skills* (my emphasis) to perform at a high level" ("NBA defends age limit policy in letter," 2009). Most importantly, it represented a systematic responds to the sense of crisis and doom facing an increasingly young, hip-hop-based, and noticeably black league.

DON'T BELIEVE THE HYPE:
CAUTIONARY TALES AND SAD STORIES

One of the most prominent arguments offered in support of the age restric-tion was the cautionary tale, the story of a once-promising career destroyed by bad decisions, bad advice, and, of course, immaturity (Beck 2005; Springer 2005; Broussard 2004; Sandoval and Steinberg 2004; Symonds 2004; Fatsis 2001; Heisler 2000b; Wise 2000; Nevius 1999; Nance 1996). According to David Stern, the league needed to highlight those cautionary tales in which young men don't use basketball to go from "rags-to-riches," but whose failure to secure their own dream results in a "rags-to-rags" narrative. "A troubling case to me is Lenny Cook. He had the ability to grow, and there were inter-ested hangers-on giving him bad information and flattering his ego," notes Stern. "It was designed to cause him to go a particular way to get him money in the short run, and it caused him to make decisions at a time when he didn't have good advice" (O'Connor 2005a, p. 113). In other words, the NBA has a moral, social, and economic obligation to protect these players, who could potentially live out their dreams and aid the NBA through development and disciplinarity, from themselves and those "greedy adults who see the chance to ride on a child's coattails into the bank" (Bortner quoted in O'Connor 2005a, p. 114). Like Stern, Debbie Bortner, Cooke's summer coach and the mother of one of his friends (Cooke at one point lived at the Bortner's house), describes Cooke's downfall as a tale of bad decisions and harmful influences ruining what could have been a story of greatness and the American Dream. Identifying the beginning of Cooke's problems as that period when he "started gravitating backward to what I call the ghetto rats in Brooklyn," Bortner makes clear the racial dimensions of not only trying to protect these young black males from bad decisions and a sad future, but of directing blame toward black "hangers-on": "But in the end, these young black kids don't need some rich old white lady. They need young black men in their lives doing good things in the community . . . and there's just not enough out there" (O'Connor 2005a, p. 114). In the absence of necessary advice, as a result of the failures of black men to sufficiently guide and discipline young black males, too many black players were falling short of their NBA dreams. As such, the league had a moral responsibility to not only prevent players from making bad decisions, but to publicize these NBA nightmares in order to scare players back to school: back to the classroom, and most importantly, back to a place where coaches and teachers garnered more respect than posses and the latest styles in hip-hop.

Commentaries and editorials consistently avoided facts regarding the history of financial and athletic success for those who have skipped college, instead claiming that an overwhelming number of cases have ended tragically. "For every Kobe Bryant, Kevin Garnett, and LeBron James, there are countless others, poor misguided kids who put their eggs in the NBA basket and have few options when it doesn't work out," wrote Pete Barth. "Thanks to the success of King James, naïve high school students around the country suddenly think they're NBA ready. In a large, large majority of cases there are not even close" (Barth 2005). Jeff Nix, a New York Knicks executive, agreed, stating: "Most of the high school kids are getting bad advice. Kids are worrying about who's the next LeBron, and some of them aren't even ready for our development league, the NBDL. It's really sad. The LeBrons, Kobes, McGradys, and Garnetts are so few and far between. LeBron was so far superior to other players; he was the varsity and everyone else the jayvee" (O'Connor 2005a, p. 113). Such hyperbolic (and racialized) language was commonplace within the debate, as have been the stories of three players— James Lang, Taj McDavid, and Korleone Young—all of whom are deployed as rationale for an age restriction. Each of these three entered the league hoping to turn their talents into NBA riches. In the estimation of the age restrictionists, each failed to meet his dream because he was not mentally or physically prepared for the grind of the NBA. The storyline of reasoning says that because of the allure of money, the bad guidance provided by "advisors," and a sport culture that overhypes young black athletes, the NBA has a moral and ethical obligation to teach "impressionable" youth the truth. Marty Blake, the NBA director of scouting service, notes, "The problem is these guys are being led to believe that there is this pot of gold at the end of the rainbow. They are told to come out; they play three years and then they don't get the big money. How are you going to get big money if you can't play? Or if you don't play. No one tells these kids that" (Quoted in May 1996). Likewise, an anonymous NBA team official is quoted in Josh Barr's "NBA Endures Underage Dunking: Despite Questions of Readiness More High Schoolers Making Jump" stating the following: "It is a false logic; the topic high school guys see their predecessors making it and they think they will make it. These are impressionable young people" (Quoted in Barr 2000). According to this official, many will not make it and they need to be informed about the potential failures and risks involved so they can make informed decisions.

The argument goes as follows: For every KG and Kobe there are dozens of unknown former high school legends who never made it, whose stories are not featured on *Sportscenter* or in *Sports Illustrated*, and about whose pathetic lives nothing is known by younger generations. For example, Steve Henson, in a profile on Tyson Chandler, states that "for every Garnett, there is a Leon Smith" (Henson 2001). Likewise, Roscoe Nance cautions players, fans, and the league not to believe the hype resulting from spots on MTV's *Cribs*, or the success of Kobe and LeBron: "But for every player who has come directly from high school, there an Ousame Cresse—another high school player who entered that 2001. He was selected by Denver in the second round but never played in the NBA" (2005). Over and over, the names of unknown black youth (Lenny Cooke, Tony Key, Deangelo Collins, Ellis Richardson, James Lang, and Korleone Young)[4] are juxtaposed against those of superstar black millionaires, not only to elucidate the consequences of bad decisions, but in order to make an argument that links early entry to their failed NBA careers and sad downward fall.[5]

Their conclusion is simple: With an education, with greater physical and mental preparation, many of these cautionary tales could have been stories of triumph, basketball excellence, and beautiful movie-of-the week stories about black youth going from rags-to-riches. For example, Stefan Fatsis argues that Korleone Young, "with maturity . . . might make a standout player and solid citizen in the NBA someday," wondering what might have been had this "pampered prep star who believed his notices" gone to college and not had to grow up so soon. After four years of bouncing around the league, and between the NBA and minor league teams, it was unclear whether Young would make it, whether he would have the opportunity to mature and grow into his proverbial basketball body. "Will he make it? Will any of the six high schoolers on the market next week? Who knows? Had Mr. Young had someone pushing him to attend college, he might be entering his senior year now. But he didn't and he isn't, and that was his choice. Systems have causalities, and Korleone Young may be one of them" (Fatasis 2001).

Additionally, much of this focus on the failures, these basketball nightmares, works to construct the success stories as aberrational, as the exceptions derived from the physical gifts, emotional maturity, and intellectual abilities of those players who made the early jump. Whether focusing on Kobe Bryant's suburban, middle-class upbringing (the need for him to go to college was certainly less because he knows multiple languages and realized that it is more important to buy a house than rims); Dwight Howard's Christian faith and police officer father; Kwame Brown's "maturity and athletic prowess" ("Athletic Drafts and Trades"); Jerome Mosio's knowledge of three languages and the fact that he was an "Old sophomore," not to mention French (May 2000); KG's soft-spoken and mature personality; or LeBron's "special blend of charisma and star power" (Adande 2003), the discourse assumes that the players who made the successful jump from high school to the NBA are the "special guys" (Ellie quoted in Murphy 2000) who didn't *need* to go to college in order to achieve personal growth and emotional maturation.[6]

One NBA scout made clear this process of racial/class differentiation in regard to Dwight Howard, noting how different he was from others in the league: "He can do everything and you can tell he's a good kid. No tattoos, clean-cut, his dad's a state trooper, his uncle's a district attorney" (O'Connor 2005a, p. 174). In other words, he is not a walking or free-soaring billboard of the hip-hop generation; he isn't a signifier of pathology and destruction, in part because his *father*, a police officer no less, instilled in him the discipline and cultural foundation necessary to excel in the NBA. While acknowledging that some of these guys took a few seasons to acclimate to the physical demands of the NBA, these commentators conclude that they had the skills and talents needed to succeed with the media, their teammates, and off the court. They had the willingness and capacity to continue learning and maturing as both players and men, even without college. Their "goodness" in turn crystallizes the failures of the hip-hop baller. Moreover, the shared blackness of both the "good" (the disciplined) and the "bad" (the undisciplined) contributes to the hegemonic denials of race within an NBA discourse.

Writing about the racial significance of Dennis Rodman, Melisse Lefrance, and Genevieve Rail offer the following assessment of the good/bad racial binary: "Rodman's 'badness,' especially when contraposed with Jordan's 'goodness,' facilitates mainstream media's dichotomized good/bad representations of black men." In other words, "black men are thus locked into a profoundly stereotypical representational politics that denies and even disavows the complexities of their cultural situation and the pluralistic nature of the subject position they currently inhabit" (2001, p. 41). Similarly Samantha King and CL Cole, within their discussion of *Hoop Dreams*, elucidate the power of the film as a source of American redemption in its celebration of two black youth (Arthur Agee and particularly William Gates) as something different from the authentic black youthful body. "While Gates figures the 'human,' a stated authorial intention, the sport/gang dyad remains stable, marking what and who are deviant both within the film and the national imagination." This process of bifurcation does not liberate or expose the fallacies of racial stereotypes, but solidifies them both within a hegemonic common sense and in practice. "In contemporary America, the compassion and connection felt toward Agee, Gates, and their families suggest that revenge directed at criminalized African-American youth through excessive punitive measures is legitimate, since what calls for punishment (typically identified in terms of inexplicable acts of violence) is obvious and justified, and it requires no interrogation" (2003, p. 240). Delia Douglas, in her discussion of Venus and Serena Williams, reflects on the ways in which binaries and particularly the trope of the good and bad black body, has been central to a white supremacist project: "Historically, white supremacist logic has long relied on the 'the use of a dichotomous code that creates a chain of correspondences both between the physical and the cultural, and between the intellectual and cognitive characteristic' (Hall, 1997, p. 290). In this context, blacks were understood as more body than mind" (Douglas 2005, p. 3). Writing about the support Kobe Bryant received from some fans Kobe Bryant was arrested on charges of rape, Kimmel and Katz highlight the hegemony of a good/bad dichotomy within the representational field of black athletes:

> Clearly race is a central fact, but not in the way some might assume. Kobe Bryant's trial offers a revealing glimpse into one of the historical characteristics of White American racism. Try a little experiment. Suppose that instead of Kobe Bryant standing accused of sexual assault, it was Allen Iverson or Latrell Sprewell. Would there be a comparable outcry in their defense, and a comparable unleashing of rage against their alleged victims. It seems unlikely, because Iverson and Sprewell are already seen by much of White America as caricatures: street thugs who happen to be talented basketball players. (In fact, both have been involved in assaults, and neither got anything close to public expressions of sympathy that Bryant has received). Now, try a different example. Imagine if were Reggie Miller or Allen Houston in the defendant's chair. Millions of fans—including millions of whites—would instantly rise to their defense. Why? Because in the eyes of many White fans, they're not

like those "other" Blacks. They're "our" blacks, "good" Blacks, the kind of Blacks that White fans love to cheer for. (Quoted in Ferber 2007, p. 21)

As noted by Ferber (2007), "the good guy space reinforces color-blind racism. By embracing the successful good guys, Whites can tell themselves they are not racist, and they can blame African Americans for their own failures (Leonard 2004)" (Ferber 2007, p. 212). The success stories represent the exceptional/the good—the exceptions, where as the bad, the criminal, and the otherwise unprepared are the rule, individuals who are not only slowly destroying the NBA, but their own lives as well.

> As always, there are exceptions—those who can conquer this monster and blossom. Kevin Garnett is clearly one, as is Kobe Bryant. But what should be made of this flood of kids now entering the NBA draft, the high school seniors and college freshmen and sophomores who cut short their education to take a crack at pro ball? They are transforming the NBA into a developmental league, and concurrently crippling the college game. (Myslenski 1999)

Worse yet, because of hopes of securing their own pots of gold and delusions of grandeur, they are ruining their own lives in the process, potentially even becoming parasites upon and dangers to the system.

Although the media coverage offers a spectrum of specifics associated with various cautionary tales—from that of Ellis Richardson, a top-100 California prepstar in the late 1990s who was "more interested in shooting the ball than playing defense" (Wharton 1998) to Ronnie Fields, who "did not take academics seriously" (Berkow 2001a) because he thought he could follow his teammate (Kevin Garnett) right into the NBA—media commentaries have repeatedly invoked the stories of Leon Smith, Taj McDavid, Korleone Young, and others to illustrate the necessity of an age restriction for the good of both the NBA and these tortured souls. According to an editorial in the *New York Times*, the NBA and urban America (i.e., the black ghettos) are facing an epidemic of sorts, with once great basketball players missing out on their dreams, only to return home to lives of poverty, despair, and perhaps even crime. "America's inner cities are full of playground legends who never made it through college and ended up on the street when a professional sports contract failed to materialize" ("Youth Movement in the NBA"). Similarly, the Policy Bridge, a black think tank based in Cleveland, Ohio, argued that, "No amount of money or strategy will close that gap as long as black children are raised in an environment that devalues education. Rap music, poverty, and pop culture celebrities to create an alluring 'cool-pose culture of self destructive behaviors'"

(Quoted in Rose 2008, p. 79). In other words, inequality and persistent levels of poverty was the result of disparities in educational funding, institutional racism, or the legacies of racial segregation, but the devaluing of education perpetuated by the decision of young African American males to forego college for the NBA.

Worse than the fact that these athletes did not make it, they didn't even get the college degrees that would have provided them with otherwise unavailable opportunities. "The prospects of a college degree for many fine young athletes grew even dimmer this week when the National Basketball Association held its annual, nationally televised draft. Four of the top 10 choices were teenagers who have decided to bypass college altogether. Astoundingly, only 4 of the 28 first-round selections had complete four years of college" ("Athletic Drafts and Trades . . ."). They, like Leon Smith and Taj McDavid, had turned their backs on that most valuable commodity, an education, leaving them with either basketball or nothing; the American Dream or the American Nightmare; a bright future, or one of despair, poverty, and crime, wherein the once celebrated black basketball star becomes just another statistic, a source of societal derision, and rightfully so, for he now stands on the street corner rather than the court, either selling dope or stealing. At least, this is the message that comes through in these "cautionary tales."

Leon Smith, "the more common antithesis of the happily-ever-after Kevin Garnett story" (Araton 1999), became a "poster child" for the problems facing the NBA. At the age of five, after being neglected by his mother and abandoned by his father, he became a ward of the state in Illinois.[7] Hoping to make his fortune, and leaving behind a life of poverty, pain, and despair, Smith decided to follow "The path of other prep superstars who skipped college and went right to the N.B.A" (Wise 2000). Although Smith wasn't a McDonald's All-American, and some argued that he wasn't even the best player on his high school team, NBA teams were impressed by his potential, his size, and his physical talents, although his perceived immaturity, limited life experience, and emotional/ psychological problems were a source of concern for these teams. After being drafted in 1999 by the San Antonio Spurs (29th overall) and quickly traded to the Dallas Mavericks, Smith's transition from teenage basketball star to NBA professional was anything but smooth. In his rookie season, he was arrested twice and spent a month in a Dallas psychiatric center following a suicide attempt with 250 aspirin. In a span of two months, he reportedly fired two agents. His difficulties were evident at their first practice where Smith got into a verbal exchange with assistant coach Donnie Nelson. With a player lagging behind during sprints, Nelson told the entire team to run again, to which Smith responded, "You go run the sprints" (Wise 2000). Shocked by the bravado of this 18-year-old kid, Nelson demanded that Smith repeat his comment. The altercation ultimately ended with Smith storming out of practice, something he would do again during his rookie season. As a result both of these events and questions about his readiness for the league, the Mavericks waived Smith in February 2000. He resurfaced two years later with the Atlanta Hawks, only to be traded to the Milwaukee Bucks, for whom he would never play a minute. His last taste of the NBA would come with the Seattle Supersonics, who signed him in April 2000, although he would only play one game in a Sonics' uniform. In the end, Smith played in 15 NBA games, averaging 2.2 points per game, yet given the tremendous amount of media coverage devoted to him, one would have thought he was an NBA star.

The offered narrative of Smith's NBA career not only systematically erased his limited basketball talent (he probably just wasn't good enough), it focused on both the failures of the NBA/Mavericks to successfully integrate, assimilate, and help this problem "child," and his own pathologies and problems. David Stern, who at the time questioned the media's use of Smith as a cautionary figure, later exploited his story for similar purposes: "It would be unfair to call Leon a poster child for anything but Leon. All of these young men are individuals. But I remain convinced that we need to disincentivize these players who have other options from coming into the NBA too young" (Quoted in Wise 2000). In other words, Smith, who had no other options and was so screwed up that the NBA ultimately could not help him succeed as either a player or a man, might not be a poster child, but his story should be widely disseminated in order to "disincentivize" those with other options.

The media certainly seized on the story, using it over and over as evidence for a crisis warranting an age restriction. By explaining away Kobe, LeBron, and KG as unusual exceptions, and focusing on the emotional and intellectual deficiencies of Smith. Mike Wise describes Smith's story as a sad tale that is being echoed by the experiences of far too many (black) youth:

> But if Kobe Bryant and Kevin Garnett are models of players who were mature enough athletically and emotionally to make that huge jump, Leon Smith's sad and tumultuous basketball odyssey is a cautionary tale—one that is forcing the N.B.A. to rethink how to decide which teenagers are capable of going right from high school to the pros and what to do with those who are not. (Wise 2000)

Likewise, Harvey Araton identifies Smith's career as that of a troubled young man whose upbringing and emotional problems created a situation in which the NBA's programs and efforts were not sufficient to protect or empower him. He was simply "the wrong player to walk it alone" (Araton 1999). He was mentally unstable and a criminal, at best the type of high school kid who shouldn't "jump" right into the NBA. "Bryant's sexual assault case, and Darius

Miles' antics in Portland aside, the bad apple remains Leon Smith, the Chicago pre phenom" (Hu 2005). Reflecting the tendency to overhype and overstate Smith's basketball ability and potential, thereby both exonerating the NBA and elucidating the trope of "what could have been," Hu also expresses the discursive tendency to link high schoolers to criminal misconduct within the league. Yet, as noted by Michael McCann, as of 2004, only three (Ellis Richardson, DeShawn Stevenson, and Kobe Bryant) of the 29 NBA players who skipped high school had faced criminal prosecution, and the charges against both Stevenson and Bryant were ultimately dropped (2004, p. 163). The tendency to obscure this reality and ignore the facts, and to play on the commonsense stereotypes that have athletes committing a disproportionate number of crimes (see Jeff Benedict 2005), aids the panics and the calls for NBA intervention regarding its youth movement (Lapchick 2003a; Lapchick 2003b).

Although Smith came to symbolize the discursive questions about the emotional and psychological (but not the physical/basketball) readiness of the straight-out-of-high school/straight-out-of-the projects/single-mother home/culture of poverty baller, Taj McDavid, James Lang, Lenny Cooke, and Korleone Young would come to represent a different threat to the NBA: the delusional, talent-challenged (mostly high school) player in search of easy riches through a quick jump to the NBA.

Taj McDavid, despite not having been recruited by any major college basketball program, entered the 1996 NBA draft. According to Ira Berkow, McDavid represented a classic example where the "wild imagination [is] outdistancing stark reality" (2001a), in that despite the lack of interest he received from major college teams, let alone from the NBA, McDavid skipped college in hopes of fulfilling his dreams. His parents believed in him, especially after he played in a pick-up game with Kevin Garnett, who allegedly complimented him on his game. Notwithstanding the endorsement of his parents and KG, McDavid wasn't drafted during the 1996 draft. Although he would ultimately and successfully petition the NCAA in hopes of playing at the college level, McDavid was never able to use basketball to make something better of his life. After the NCAA declared him ineligible for his freshman year, thereby granting him three years of eligibility in a landmark decision, he enrolled at Division II Anderson College. There, he struggled to stand out even in intramurals, and he didn't do much better with the school's collegiate team. The coaches described his abilities "As not up to the competition in their league" (Quoted in Berkow 2001a). Having failed to make it to the NBA, or even at the Division II level, McDavid dropped out of school, returning to South Carolina where he "hangs out at the mall" (Wharton 1998) and reportedly has his high school coach, Lawton Williams, "screen his phone calls to keep curious reporters at bay" (Drechs 2001). Many in the media used the story of McDavid's career, even though, realistically, he never had much hope of success, as the cautionary tale of a young man who, despite believing himself NBA ready, would never sign an NBA, CBA, IBL, or overseas basketball contract. "McDavid is that embodiment of the failed draft dream, the unfortunate footnote; the player who forgoes part of all of the college to pursue an NBA career in vain. Young players, like McDavid, are the other side of the fabled player like Garnett and Bryant who became professional stars after leaving school early" (Berkow 2001a). Worse, he—like Korleone Young, Ellis Richardson, James Lang, Leon Smith, and countless others—entered the NBA draft because of the presumed success of "the good ones." Accordingly, when the media, through cautionary tales, and the NBA, with an age restriction, began protecting these "impressionable" and "immature" youth from making bad decisions, the likes of McDavid and Smith would be the exceptions rather than the rule.

As already mentioned, these arguments lack substance in terms of the history of early entrants into the league. Michael McCann, in "Illegal Defense: The Irrational Economics of Banning High School Players from the NBA Draft," an article that appeared in *Sports Law Review* in 2004, illustrates the lack of supportive evidence for the argument of Stern, Barkley and others:

> [F]rom 1995 to 2003, over 80 percent of drafted high school play-
> ers became, or will become multi-millionaires by the age of 21, or
> how they have maximized their earning potential by gaining the
> ability to become unrestricted free agents—when as many as 30
> teams bid for their services—by the tender age of 22, when, coinci-
> dentally, some of their counterparts will graduate from college and
> become bound by the nearly non-negotiable rookie salary scale for
> three to five years.
>
> [M]ost players who skip college may earn as much as $100
> million more over the course of their careers than if they had done
> the "smart thing" and earned a college diploma . . . [H]igh school
> players who enter the NBA Draft are a small, self-selected group,
> comprised almost entirely of exceptionally talented players. Simply
> put, for every Korleone Young, there are two or three Kobe Bryants.
> (2004)

Out of 37 players who entered the draft straight out of high school, 30 were selected; as of this writing, 26 were still in the league. More revealingly, several of those who entered the draft early and were late second-round picks or undrafted did so because of low SAT scores (McCann 2004). If the NBA, NCAA, and others truly wanted to push high school players away from the

NBA toward college, they might push for an elimination of Proposition 48 (Lapchick 2002). For example, Ian O'Connor argues that Kevin Garnett would likely not have entered the 1995 NBA draft had he "achieved the necessary standardized test scores necessary to play college ball as a freshman" (O'Connor 2005a, p. 118). Of course, Garnett is probably not alone in this regard.

The focus on education, and the supposed importance of high school basketball stars spending time in college, is belied by the realities of the NBA and the nature of college athletics. For instance, in the 2001 NBA draft, only 4 out the 28 players selected were seniors, so the vast majority of NBA players did not graduate from college prior to entering the NBA. One need look no farther than the graduation rates of major college basketball programs to understand how disingenuous are the demands that all NBA players spend time in college because "education matters." In 2007, 30 out of the 65 teams who participated in March Madness graduated less than 50 percent of their players. The picture was much bleaker in terms of the graduation rates of African American basketball student-athletes, where all but 29 schools had a gap of more than 30 percent between the graduation rates of their white and black student-athletes (Tompkins 2007). Moreover, according to Michael Oriard (citing a NCAA study) approximately 20 percent of student-athletes were not able to major "in the field of their choice," with another 40 percent unable to desired classes (2009, p. 208).

None of this should be a surprise given national graduation rates, where only half of African American students graduate from high school (compared to 75 percent of white students) and a dismal 43 percent of black college students ever graduate from their respective college and universities (compared to 63 percent for white students) ("Black Student College Graduation Rates" 2007; "Hispanic And Black High School Graduation Rates Very Low" 2004). Yet, despite these dismal numbers, which in many regards reflect institutional inequalities and a lack of societal investment in affording equal educational opportunities, the discourse surrounding the NBA age restriction demonizes both black NBA players and the entire black community for their lack of educational values, sounding the alarm about the problems that result from their not attending college, a place where, as Michael McCann points out, practice and sport often take precedence over education (2004, pp. 160–161).

Shaun Powell, writing about graduation rates and the "academic divide" experienced by black student-athletes, questions "whether single moms, who head most black households, are equipped to provide the proper academic atmosphere at home" (2008, p. 73). The focus on the necessity for educational attainment amongst NBA stars not only rehashes commonplace efforts to scapegoat black youth for a spectrum of problems both inside and outside the NBA, it also furthers a white supremacist logic that says black youth—mired in a culture of pathology, poverty, single motherhood, and hip-hop—will succumb to self-destructive behavior without the guidance, paternalism, discipline, and values offered by a white school system. "The representational politics of pathology is purely psychological," writes Henry Giroux. "Devoid of any social context within which to situate behavior . . . further mobilizes mainstream contempt for victims while securing the indifference of government" (2003b, p. 124). Education and other disciplinary interventions have the potential to limit the impact of these psychological pathologies, but the failure to take advantage of them limits the liability and responsibility of the state and of racism, further arguments that blame black basketball players for the state of the game and the black community for the state of black America.

PHYSICALLY WEAK, MENTALLY AND INTELLECTUALLY WEAKER: BIG BODIES AND SMALL BRAINS/HEARTS

The widespread support for the age restriction as a remedy to waning fan interest and poor quality of play also identified it as a smart business move. This effort to thwart the flow of "diaper dandies" simply indicated the NBA's desire to "improve the [its] product, to develop a better product on and off the floor" (Zirin 2005). It was just good business given the struggles facing the league: the slumping quality of play and the off-the-court difficulties of players, both of which had led to increased divisions between player and fan.

Throughout the many commentaries supporting an age restriction, one of the most prominent arguments that emerged was that the rule would serve to improve the awful skills and on-the-court product that had led many fans to turn off their TV sets, and ultimately turn away from the once "fantastic" NBA. Anthony Cotton, in the *Denver Post*, concludes that the age restriction is needed given the precipitous decline in league-wide scoring averages, which had contributed to declining TV ratings, unappealing NBA finals match-ups, and an overall disinterest in the league. In giving the league a "mature rating for playing" (Denberg 1999), Stern would be able to alter the negative views of the league, while also improving the quality of its product both on and off the court. Eliminating teenagers from the league would challenge "the belief that the NBA isn't what it once was because players while athletically gifted, have little idea about fundamentals or what it takes to succeed in the league" (Cotton 2003). Harry Edwards concurred in noting the lack of success for the U.S. within international competitions. "Our kids can dunk and make the crowd go wild, but the other countries are playing team ball and at the end of the day, that's going to win" (Quoted in Araton 2005a,

p. 178). Describing the NBA as the "National Potential Association" (Temkin 1999), "a developmental league" (Myslenski 1999), "a place to refine skills, not develop them," (Adande 1996), and a league that could aptly be described as a place where the "quality of play [is] endangered" (Blinebury 1998), critics lamented the poor quality of play from a league that markets itself as having the world's greatest basketball players and athletes as a whole. Mike Kiszla, who called on the NBA to "ID players before letting them into the building," chastised the league for providing a substandard product at exorbitant prices: "fans being asked to shell out 50 bucks so they can sit and watch [LeBron] James, [Carmelo] Anthony, and [Darko] Milicic get schooled in the hard knocks of Hoops 101 are being set up to feel ripped off. If Kobe Bryant, Kevin Garnett and Tracy McGrady averaged a measly 8.3 points per game among themselves as rookies, how can James, Anthony, and Milicic possibly live to expectations?" (2003). Similarly, Tony Kornheiser saw an age restriction as a natural response from the league, given its "suffer[ing] at the gate and in TV ratings" (Kornheiser 2001), all of which reflected the unfulfilled desires from fans to see, witness, watch, and cheer for the best. "We are watching larvae; we want to watch butterflies," writes Kornheiser. "These kids who jump straight into the NBA from high school and the ones who bolt college after a year or two—they may have talent, but it's in the embryonic stage. If we wanted to watch things develop we'd by a ticket at a Petri dish" (2001). Evident here and elsewhere, criticism of the "baby ballers" (Kornheiser 2001) who dominate today's NBA didn't simply focus on their immaturity or the fact that their talents had yet to be developed, it emphasized their lack of fundamentals that, because they had decided to skip or simply pass through college, and because of the structure of youth basketball and the mentality of the hip-hop baller, would likely never develop and, therefore, would slowly destroy both the league and the dominance of American basketball on the international scene. Rob Babcock, an NBA scout, described his experiences at an under-19 international basketball tournament in bleak terms: "American basketball is declining. Last year I covered an International age-19-and-under tournament in Athens. The U.S. finished seventh and it was no fluke. Our kids are great at the kind of spectacular plays they seen on TV—slam dunks and the like. But if they're going to pass the ball, it had better be a spectacular pass. And body can set a pack to free a teammate for a job shot" (Quoted in Charland 1996). Michael Murphy, who lamented the "perceived erosion of the product on the floor," cited the age restriction as a necessary step toward forcing fundamentals back into the league. In his estimation, today's players, more than ever, needed to learn the fundamentals of how to play the game from the great college coaches. "Young players, who typically use little more than raw athletic ability to dominate the high school and AAU level to the point where they are attracting the interest of professional scouts do not have the fundamental basis to carry the kind of success in the NBA" (2000). "Teams must have the commitment to work with teens, allow them to develop. Such players often are lacking some basic skills such as shooting," writes David Dupree. "They might be great athletes who can run and jump and look good going between their legs with the ball. But they can't make a simple jump shot, run, or defend a pick-and-roll, screen a man off the glass or even make a simple bounce pass." Dupree goes on to argue that international teens are far more prepared for the NBA because ironically they turn professional at an early age (14 and 15), and because overseas there is a far greater emphasis on "fundamentals and basic skill development" than there is in the United States (2003). Charles Barkley agrees, arguing that "these kids today have no concept how to play. They just go out there and run and jump and they think they can play" (Adande 1996). With an emphasis on showboating and spectacular dunks, players need to be taught fundamentals and team concepts. "The problem with the NBA is that it's loaded with kids with great talent who never spent the time learning how to play basketball. Those players with limited knowledge about the fundamentals are likely to "find a place on the NBA benches for a few years while the qualified players can take care of the league" (Feigen 2001).

According to this argument, the absence of fundamentals and skills brought by these players, coupled with their immaturity and aesthetic performance, was systematically destroying the league. What becomes clear through the spectrum of media commentaries and the overall debate is that the absence of fundamentals should not really be surprising given the immaturity of these players; the cultural realities of hip-hop combined with ESPN and its perceived emphasis on flash, dunks, and showtime (Reynolds 2006; McGovern 2005; Temkin 1999); and the number of players who spent little or no time in college receiving the necessary "life seasoning" (Buhls 2001) and discipline provided by college sports. Then Denver Nuggets coach, Jeff Bzdelik, citing the number of young players entering the NBA, and the ubiquitous practice of high school players moving from one school to the next, wondered if there was any chance for reversing this trend, in which fundamentals are a rarity, an exception, unless the NBA and NCAA implemented some radical changes, such as an age restriction. "How can we expect players to know the fundamentals when they get to the league when they're [sic]really have never been somewhere long enough to be taught them and to work on them?" (Cotton 2003). Similarly, Sam Schuler, the president of basketball operations for the San Antonio Spurs, questioned the possibility of a healthy future for the NBA unless it stemmed this youth movement. "Look at the high schoolers; for the most part and there are always a few exceptions—but for the most part these high school kids are just not ready physically and emotionally for the NBA. It's not fair for them to be thrown into that situation; they need time to mature and grow into people. That's what the college does so well, and we're taking that away from them" (Quoted in Cotton 2003). At Sonny Vaccaro's Academic Betterment and Career Development Camp, a yearly summer event where the nation's best high school players come to learn about college and, most importantly, to compete on the basketball floor, George Karl "lectured" the predominantly black campers about "the right way to play," cautioning them that success in the league isn't only about talent and athleticism. "One thing you have to understand about the NBA is we worry about attitude as much as we do talent. I saw a lot of you guys work out yesterday, and I think you guys are acting a little too cool. Think about playing the game the right way" (Quoted in O'Connor 2005a, p. 36).

The emphasis on fundamentals speaks to the discursive focus on hip-hop ballers and, more specifically, blackness. Todd Boyd argues that, within the discursive field of basketball, race is crucial to the descriptors associated with different types of play. As such, he describes, "white basketball" as one "in which adherence to a specific set of rules determines one's ability to play successfully and 'correctly'" (1997, p. 115). Aaron Baker (2000) builds on this idea, arguing, "That since basketball functions as a metaphor for racial identities, the textbook style suggests a white ideology that accepts the rules of the game" (2000, p. 225). The allure of sports rests not only in its reification of white intelligence, but its valorization of white working-class identity. "Baseball and football were already predetermined to be extensions of the American blue-collar ethos, and at some point, the Cold War ethic," argues Todd Boyd. "Individuality was subsumed, contained, in the name of group productivity. This was the White American way of life writ large, and Blacks need only be concerned to the extent that were useful" (Boyd 2003, p. 26). Whereas commentators constantly praise white players for intelligence and fundamentals, African Americans are celebrated for their athleticism and creativity, yet critiqued for their lack fundamentals, team-orientation, strategy, and basketball intelligence (Boyd 2003; King and Springwood 2001; Platt 2000; Cole and Andrews 1996).

Reflecting on the Los Angeles Lakers' abandonment of the Triangle Offense during the 2004 season, a western conference scout concluded that their shift in strategy wasn't about the salary cap or shifts in the style of play within the league, but rather a manifestation of the type of player in today's NBA. "The Triangle is no longer a valid offense. To run it, you've got to have players who are able to make reads and make passes and today's players are not intelligent enough to do it. Their basketball IQ is not high enough" (Quoted in Brown 2004). William Jelani Cobb provocatively illustrates the power of this discourse, noting, "I am awaiting the day that music credits start praising Eminem for having 'sound fundamentals' when it comes to rapping. Both Em and [Jason] Williams are the beneficiaries of a type of cultural affirmative action for white men, which is to say that neither of them is unqualified, but both are object lessons in the benefits of diversity" (Cobb 2007, p. 25). Basketball, especially in regard to the influence of street basketball and hip-hop, threatened the usefulness of sports as not only a celebration of American identity, but of whiteness, and thus became the basis of a widespread culture war.

IT'S A MAN'S GAME

While still focusing on the limited skills and absence of fundamentals in the new generation of primarily hip-hopped ballers, fueled by a lack of training and preparation (i.e., basketball education), much of the discourse also focused on the mentality and immaturity of its "childish" players. The decline of the NBA isn't simply the result of the under (non) development of their athletic skills—or their inability to execute a bounce pass, a crab dribble, a 3 on 2 break, a box inbound play, or get into a defense stance ("the fundamentals)—it is also being affected by the intellectual and emotional immaturity of today's (black) players. Bill Plaschke, in the *Los Angeles Times*, describes the NBA underclassmen as "the most clueless players in the room" (2000). Similarly, John Thompson called on the NBA to end the influx of young people because their skills and limited respect for the game were systematically ruining the NBA:

> The N.B.A. needs this rule to preserve the game. As the aging veteran is replaced by the younger recruit, the sport's traditions will disappear. Respect for the game and institutional memory will be lost as older players are squeezed out by younger recruits, recruits who will have fewer fundamentals and less-developed skills. And if we won't draw the line at 20, where do we draw the line? Is 17 too young? Sixteen? If age is irrelevant, does that mean the N.B.A. will feature 15-year-olds? (2001)

Bryan Burwell concurs, arguing that high school kids, and those barely into college, are not only physically incapable of battling Shaq on the boards, or dealing with Karl Malone's physicality, but "grossly unprepared . . . to handle the overnight journey into millionaire adulthood" (2007). Although those skipping four years of college "won't have money problems . . . the sudden change in lifestyle can be startling if they don't know what's coming" (Dupree 1995). But to David Dupree there is more at stake than money; there is also a question of "maturity" and whether younger players can handle the pressures and demands of the NBA. Commenting on Greg Oden[8] and

Kevin Durant—who would likely have entered the NBA draft in 2006 right after high school, but instead attended one year of college each, only to jump to the league in 2007—Burwell is left with one simple conclusion: "The age rule is working because it is forcing kids like Oden and Durant to go to college to learn, to mature, and figure out what it takes mentally and emotionally to excel in the league" (2007). Although unspoken in this context, Roscoe Nance elucidates the nature of this argument as far back as 1996: "Generation X ball players are going to be the ruination of the NBA. That's the fear of many league veterans, who question how new age colleagues respect for the game, work ethic, and professionalism. . . . The skeptics say these youngsters lack the maturity to cope with the rigor and responsibilities of a being a pro athlete and that and the NBA would be better served by four years of college" (1996).

In 1999, following five straight years of high schoolers and underclassmen joining the NBA, Mark Heisler described these years as a "children's crusade" where "the children are still pouring over the wall" (1999). Other critics would similarly invoke the racialized rhetoric of invasions, panics, and crises to describe the straight-out-of-high school phenomenon. In 2001, a year that saw three high schoolers drafted in the first four picks, two more drafted later (8th and 47th), and a number of underclassman selected by teams, the opposition to this "youth" movement seemed to solidify within the media and throughout much of the league. Jeffrey Deneberg described the drafting of early entrants into the NBA as "an epidemic" (2001), while John Deshazier cautioned the league against this "alarming" trend (2001). Van Coleman, the publisher of *Future Stars* magazine and director of Future Stars scouting service, described it as "a dangerous trend" that presented "the possibility for more and more failures over time" (Quoted in Sappenfield 2001).

Beyond the rhetoric of invasion, panic, and crisis, what bound together a 10-year-old discourse (or the battle against the invading force of baby ballers) was the infantilization of these players, the suggestion that those straight-out-of-high-school ballers and underclassmen who were systematically destroying the league, and who were overwhelmingly African American, were nothing but children. Although a number of commentators simply referred to early entrants as "kids" or "children" (Stern quoted in Couch 2005; Hochman 2003; Kiszla 2003; Cotton 2001; Deshazier 2001; Sappenfield 2001; Wise 2001; Heisler 1997), others engaged in more detailed name-calling, describing the players as "immature overpaid brats" (Kiszla 1999), "impatient teenagers" (Feigen 2001), "precocious prepsters" (Charland 1996), "ill-prepared children" (Burwell 2004b), and "teenage millionaires" (Hindo 2004). Michael Murphy, writing about the 1996 NBA draft, described the overwhelming number of high schoolers and underclassmen "as well-dressed teenagers," who look as if they were heading off to "prom" (1996). Referring to the 1999 NBA draft as one that was "teen dominated," Mark Heisler deployed a powerful racial metaphor, describing the flood of (black) youth as a "jailbreak" (1999). Kirk Bohls went so far as to wonder if there would be a breaking point, giving voice to the oft-articulated slippery slope argument that goes as follows: "First 20 year-olds, then high school students, and then those in middle or elementary school. If David Stern has his way college, high school or over-achieving kindergartners must wait until they're 20 years old" (2004). Similarly, on the eve of the deadline to declare for the 1996 draft, when "there seem[ed] to be no stemming the tide of early candidates," Peter May lamented the number of kids entering the draft. "It will all end today, point guards from the Western Athletic conference, teenage centers from Lithuania, and third-graders from Los Angeles have until midnight to make a decision" (1996). The reference to third-graders in Los Angeles speaks to the dominant discourses regarding the overemphasis on basketball within the black community, claims about the physical superiority of black athletes—given that a third grader could potentially get drafted—and the overall threats facing the NBA. Additionally, the influx, or invasion, of immature, self-centered, and ego-driven youth was perceived as/considered to be excessively troublesome given that many would come from Los Angeles (read urban . . . black . . . ghetto . . . single mothers), from families and communities that don't value education or facilitate normal maturation, and that, despite their physical size and athletic gifts, these early entrants were not intellectually, emotionally, or practically ready for the rigors of the NBA, whether in terms of managing their time and money (Brady and Meyers 1997), or of simply being away from home (Hindo 2004). Roscoe Nance argued (and lamented) the fact that the NBA was putting young people in a "position" to "grow up much faster than they might have. They have no choice once they decided to venture into the adult world of the NBA" (1999). Donnie Walsh, then general manager of the Indiana Pacers, a team that drafted Al Harrington and Jonathan Bender straight out of high school and traded for Jermaine O'Neal, another early entrant from the high school ranks, questioned the preparedness of his young players. "They are not ready for the court. They will need a lot of support" (Quoted in Williams and Campbell 1996). Al Menendez, a scout for the Indiana Pacers, offered a similar assessment, noting, "They're not mature enough in their personalities and in their game" (Quoted in Spears 2000b). Worse, much of the discourse wonders if the star treatment afforded these youth; the influences of hip-hop, the sports media, agents, and other hangers-on; the absence of sufficient oversight; and most importantly, their lack of preparation and education, would prevent these players from ever growing up, permanently relegating them to a child-like state, though stuck inside the demanding "man's world" of the NBA. Focusing on those players who slip through the cracks and those "cautionary tales," Marc Spears gives voice to both the skepticism and disdain that define the almost decade long debate, arguing that because of the structure of the NBA, the culture that gives rise to and sustains the hip-hop baller, and the limited amount of education they will likely ever experience, these players will probably never grow up, leaving both the NBA and the society that idolizes them in serious trouble. He quotes Butch Carter, who had coached Tracy McGrady in Toronto. According to Carter, McGrady struggled with the adjustment to playing on Sundays, and without a parent around, he would continually stay up too late the night before, resulting in sluggish play the following day. "Young players need an incubator off the floor," noted Carter. "The guys draft high school players into the pros, but coaches don't want anything to do with players when practice is done. You leave a kid in a major metropolitan city by himself. You don't teach him how to occupy his time, go to the movie theater, go to library" (Quoted in Spears 2000a). Implied here is that, given who is entering the league early, this process of acculturation, maturation, and "seasoning" is that much more important, and that a failure to stem the tide or dramatically increase the instruments of education will inevitably lead to more occurrences like the Artest Brawl, declining fan support, and a waning civility in the game (Smith 2000).

The process of imagining the racialized other has long/always been a part of colonial/white supremacist projects. "Nor should we forget that Jim Crow took root and evolved in tandem with the growing obsession with blackface caricatures of African Americans as senseless children too simpleminded to participate in an allegedly democratic society" (Cobb 2007, p. 40). Evident in cartoons, minstrel shows, and other forms of popular culture, white supremacist discourse has historically represented blackness as not only immature, but perpetually child-like, resulting in a clear logic: if blackness equals child, then whiteness equals mature and rational adult with the necessary wisdom, values, culture, and knowledge to help (parent) the immature black child. "The logic of white supremacy has been premised on the inherent inferiority of blacks and the equally fallacious assumption of the superiority of whites by whites," writes Kimberle Williams Crenshaw. "Within traditional white supremacist paradigms, blacks were imagined to be lascivious, emotional, and childlike, while whites were regarded as industrious, pious, rational, and mature" (1997, p. 104). Franz Fanon argues that, within the white supremacist (colonial) imagination, "The Negro is just a child" (Fanon 1967, p. 27), incapable of self-government or personal responsibility. Reflective of both the media reaction to the Palace Brawl and the broader racial crisis/culture war facing the NBA, the efforts to institute an age restriction (and a dress code) reflect a broader discourse wherein "problems of race have been psychologized either as issues of character, individual pathology, or genetic inferiority" (Giroux 2003b, p. 123). The process of "individualizing disorder" (Allen Feldman quoted in Camp 2009, p. 715) and blaming the victims of racism and state violence provides legitimacy for paternalistic arguments and calls for self-help. This process is reinforced by "representations that portray black men as utterly infantile, lacking moral values, and in need of character development so that they can pick themselves up and allegedly take responsibility for their lives" (Giroux 2003b, p. 123). For the NBA to be saved, its black players need to take responsibility and grow up, because the backlash from fans and sponsors reflect the players' own failures, not broader issues of race. Given their flawed values, the NBA has an obligation to teach, to provide a foundation, so that self-help can ultimately work inside America's arenas, but also so that black youth can learn civility and proper values (Collins 2005; Gray 2005; Giroux 2003a; Giroux 2003b; Watkins 2003).

Many media reports recounted stories about early entrants designed to underscore the immaturity of these child-like young men couched inside super-heroic bodies, and describe the polluting cultural attributes they bring with them to the NBA inside their diamond encrusted Mark Echo designer bags. In a *USA Today* cover story, Roscoe Nance narrates a story told to him by Chicago Bulls Radio analyst and former player Bill Wennington. Late during the 2004 season, Eddy Curry,[9] whose potential continued to exceed his on-the-court contributions three years after graduating from high school, prepared for a game with the Detroit Pistons not by reviewing game film, checking out the scouting report, psyching himself up mentally or warming-up physically, but by answering his cell phone. He, like Tyson Chandler, had already been criticized by teammates and reprimanded by the organization because of his lack of professionalism and their perception that he did not take games seriously enough. "They were kids. Everything was a game. They didn't realize there were things you have to take care of" in order to excel or even have a career in the NBA (Wennington quoted in Nance 2005). Similarly, Nance cited Kwame Brown as another example of the almost hopeless immaturity of these players , evidenced by his daily consumption of fried chicken early in his rookie season because "he didn't know how to grocery shop" (2005). Worse yet, "Brown complained that he had nothing to wear despite having recently bought a closet full of new suits. It turned out that each time Brown wore a suit, he took it off and threw it in a pile. He didn't know he had to take the suits to a dry cleaner" (Nance 2005). In a profile on Marvin Williams, who entered the NBA draft after spending one year at the University of North Carolina, Chapel Hill, Ian O'Connor notes that Williams "Still watches cartoons in his spare time" and that "Sponge Bob Square Pants is amongst his favorites," although "anything on Nickelodeon will do" (O'Connor 2005b). While criticizing Stern's efforts to "lock the door" on future teen entrants, O'Connor, who would later question the age restriction policy, still emphasizes the child-like qualities of these entrants.

"Somewhere down the line, a talented kid will lose a shot at a new life because of this rule. He's probably watching Nickelodeon right now" (O'Connor 2005b). Similarly, in a *Washington Post* profile of Kevin Durant, an article that celebrates his forced college experience because of the league's rule change, Sally Jenkins describes Durant as "obviously childlike": "he still calls 'Mommy when he needs comforting' and 'eats gummy worms'" (2007). In other words, because he does not know how to take care of himself, he is a child. Jenkins concludes that "even a temporary stop in college" was "good for him," as it would be for countless others. She powerfully describes Durant as follows:

> His interests remain strictly undergraduate: he doesn't have a girl-friend, and when he's not in practice or study hall, he engages in marathon sessions of the video game "The Godfather" with fellow freshman, point guard D.J. Augustin. . . . He has only one other current passion: basketball in any form. He watches every brand played on campus, from women's games to intramurals, always visible in the bleachers. (2007)

To further emphasize the specifics of the discourse, and the widespread infantilization of black youth as justification for their exclusion, I would like to conclude this section with three separate quotes, each in different ways highlighting the dialectics between age, culture, race, and the physical, intellectual and emotional preparedness needed for the NBA. Writing about the 1997 draft, Anthony Cotton offered the following observation about the NBA's newcomers:

> The braces just came off of Adonal Foyle's teeth while Tim Thomas is only 1 year removed from picking out a tuxedo for his high school prom. He is still one up on Tracy McGrady, who a year ago was barely old enough to drive himself to his junior ball. (1997)

Likewise, in 2000, Mike Wise, in wondering if Darius Miles had the physical and mental makeup necessary to survive and succeed in the NBA, described Miles' presence at the 2005 draft in the following terms: "His baggy suit framed Miles' shoulders and he looked like the Josh Baskin character in 'Big,' the movie in which Tom Hanks morphs into a boy again and returns to the innocent life he know before he sprouted into a man" (2000). According to Wise, there was no turning back for Miles and the NBA: the harm to these "boys" and the league is irrevocable. Finally, Joan Ryan pines nostalgically for the older NBA as opposed to today's league dominated by "young men—too young to rent cars on the road or drink beer in the locker room, kids barely old enough to order the Arch Deluxe at McDonalds" (1996). She further argues that "they will be paid like kings, enabling them to transform their own and their families' lives but also inviting temptations that a young mind and body might find difficult to resist" (1996). Although she doesn't doubt the attractiveness of the NBA, which can provide one with the wherewithal to fulfill the American Dream, she wonders about both the short- and long-term costs, calling on the NBA to protect these vulnerable and naive children, and arguing that the NBA, the media, and fans alike share a responsibility to save these boys. In other words, since they can't, or won't, protect either themselves or the league, we must protect them, because, if we don't, it is not just the players who will suffer, but also the league, the culture, and the game we all used to love.

What becomes clear through the media coverage is that black youth—because of their immaturity, because of cultural and communal dysfunctions, because of the absence of fathers, and because of the pampered lives of basketball kings—are particularly at risk when entering the NBA early. Those who are most likely to be pulled into the league early lack the skills (life and basketball) needed to excel and lead the league into the new millennium. Worse, those pulled (pushed) into the NBA without these skills will likely never grow up because they lack the incentive, the foundation, and the necessary guidance/accountability to ever become productive members of society. Following in the tradition of Richard Herrnstein, Dinesh D'Souza, and David Horowitz—and more recently the rhetorical offerings of Bill Cosby, Juan Williams, and Jason Whitlock—the discourse surrounding the state of the NBA "rework[s] the language of racism and social responsibility in ways that eliminate those larger systemic and structural inequalities that give racism such persistence" (Giroux 2003b, pp. 122–123). For example, Shaun Powell, in his recent book on the state of black athletics, illustrates the profound linkages between the hegemonic discourses surrounding the NBA and those concerned with the behavior of black urban youth. "It was fairly evident that NBA had a growing problem as the new millennium approached. A fair number of teenaged players, almost all of them black, were coming into the league carrying attitudes and maturity issues." He further notes that, "as teenagers from the street, they behaved like teenagers from the street" (2007, p. 104). The debates surrounding the problems facing, and the needed remedies for, the NBA place blame on a failing black family and culture that have left black men in a perpetual state of pathological childhood. Yet, this process of infantilization furthers the demonization of black youth. "Black youth seemingly have been in the eye of a public storm against crime, drugs, and the alleged erosion of traditional values," writes S. Craig Watkins. "As a result, new punitive technologies and legislation have been initiated in order to exercise greater control over black youth," whether in the form of racial profiling, dress codes, or incarceration (Watkins 1998, p. 1). Writing about *Baby Boy*, Henry Giroux describes this film as one that "echoes the conservative call for black males to stop complaining and pick themselves and the larger society up by exercising some self criticism aimed at the infinite and irresponsible lives they lead" (Giroux 2003b, p. 130). Excoriating the discursive "concern" with black masculinity, bell hooks describes the discursive and ideological foundations that provide legitimacy for the media's denunciation of black ballers, and its calls for widespread regulation both on and off the court, in the following ways:

> The portraits of black masculinity that emerges in this work perpetually construct black men as "failures," who are psychologically "fucked up," dangerous, violent sex maniacs whose insanity is informed by their inability to fulfill their phallocentric masculine destiny in a racist context. . . . It does not interrogate the conventional construction of patriarchal masculinity or question the extent to which black men have historically internalized the norm. It never assumes the existence of black men whose creative agency has enabled them to subvert norms and develop ways of thinking about masculinity that challenge patriarchy. (1992, p. 89)

The justification and support for NBA restrictions take this a step further, concluding that black ballers—and those who hang on their every move, hoping to win the NBA lottery—are incapable of pulling themselves up by their bootstraps, grounded as they are by delusions and privileges, necessitating that the NBA force discipline through a series of wake-up calls.

MATURATION AND EDUCATION

Although those who demanded and/or defended the NBA's age restriction invoked cautionary tales and cited the declining quality of play and the immaturity of today's NBA players as rationale for curtailing the flood of teenagers entering the league, the discourse also celebrated its eventual implementation as a step toward protecting unknowing black youth by requiring them to go to college. Taking the decision out of their hands served to protect players from making "bad choices" (Weir 1999), from the "peddlers and hanger[s]-on who," David Stern says, "conspire to get these kids to turn their backs on school" (Quoted in Kornheiser 2001), from agents who encourage them with promises of a first round selection to leave school early (Spears 2001), and from those who "indoctrinate" these kids with misinformation (Wise 2000). Moreover, the rule would protect the hip-hop generation from "the get-it now attitude" (Cotton 2003), and from the false allure and glam-our of a league where, shortly after Darius Miles arrived in the NBA, his jersey was being "worn by hip-hop artists and rappers in videos" (Cotton 2003). Serving as something akin to a "protective father" (Burwell 2004b), the NBA's requirement that players be at least 19 shielded these kids from "peer pressure" (Feigen 2001; Moran 2001) and from the idea that anyone who went to college was a second-rate baller.

At the core of this effort to "protect" in the way that any "responsible" (Heisler 2000a) grown-up would do was an emphasis on the importance of NBA players going to college to learn how to play and how to deal with the pressures of the league, to mature, to have something to fall back on, and ulti-mately to serve as role models for the (black) youth of future generations ("Going for It" 1996; Burwell 2007). Bryan Burwell, two years after the last high schooler entered the NBA draft, wondered what was wrong with "putting a 17 or 18-year old kid in a college environment . . . letting him grow up at a natural pace" (2007). He also explained that he was "having a hard time under-standing how it is such a bad deal to allow a kid to be immersed in a social and academic setting that encourages him to discover himself" (Burwell 2007). Seven years earlier, Bill Plaschke had called for the NBA to force kids to go to college. Referring to "the NBA's underage attractions," he offered the follow-ing analysis about early entrants' intellectual and emotional maturity, arguing that a college experience would likely improve this situation:

> They are as deep as a whirlpool. They are sophisticated as ball rack. With rare exceptions—such as Kobe Bryant—talking to underage NBA players is like talking to one of their very expensive, and very empty briefcases. In a college environment, they would not be clue-less. They would be kids. Their perceptions would be shared. Their observations would be validated." (2000)

Likewise, Sally Jenkins celebrated the age restriction as an effort by the NBA to get "out of the child-rearing business, to see that prodigies aren't ruined psychologically" by sending them to college and seeking to draft "more skilled and mature players" who have already benefited from the college experience (2000). College would provide these players with the discipline needed to succeed in the NBA and the maturity to stay out of trouble.

Describing them as "long-legged freaks" (Camunas 2005), and "unpre-pared emotionally" (Kerr 2005), the discourse consistently demanded that the NBA's future stars be forced to attend college so they could be helped by Roy Williams, Coach K., and others to "grow, to remove the pimples from their faces, to become men on the court and *gentlemen* (my emphasis) off the court (Camunas 2005; see also Adande 2005b; Barth 2005; Gibron 2005; Kerr

2005). Steve Kerr, in defense of raising the age limit, penned the following statement: "Perhaps Kobe Bryant would have dealt with adversity in a more positive manner had he spent a season or two playing for Mike Kryzwezski at Duke" (2005). A few years with Mike Kryzwezski, Bob Knight, or any number of other white NCAA coaches was seen as the answer to the influx of the hip-hop generation player. "The coach is similar to the White male father figure, whereas Black male athletes are like children, under the father's control and subject to his rule," writes Abby Ferber. "It is only when they accept and lay this role that they are fully embraced and accepted and seen as non-threatening. Their bodies can be admired as long as they are perceived as controlled by White males. These athletes are then defined as the 'good blacks'" (2007, p. 20).

David Stern consistently argued that the reason for an age limit was not that "young players can't play," but rather that "it's better for them to stay in school" (Quoted in Shields 2004). In addition, "My continuing observation is that because we're a sport that's very popular and easily accessible, there's going to be tens of thousands and hundreds of thousands of 10-year-olds thinking they are the next Sebastian Telfair or LeBron James. And I just don't feel great about being associated with that" (Stern, quoted in O'Connor 2005a, p. 110). As with so much of the discourse, such commentaries erase a broader context and history, reducing the problems facing the black youth of America's schools to personal failures, bad role modeling, and, of course, cultural priorities. In imagining that the choices of Kobe Bryant or LeBron James have been responsible for dropout rates, educational gaps, or poor graduation rates, the arguments behind an age restriction deny the effects of racism and structural inequalities. Gone are discussions of inequality in school funding, which might reveal that those states with the "highest poverty school districts" and those with "highest-minority school districts get less funding than the lowest-minority districts" (Carey 2003, p. 3).

To focus exclusively on role models, pathological values, and an undervaluing of education within the black community is to rehash long-standing racist ideologies evidenced in culture of poverty theories and other blame-the-victim discourses. Stern and many commentators seem to attribute educational shortcomings to the examples set by those skipping college for the greener pastures of the NBA, but one has to wonder how funding inequities contribute to black and brown children being left behind. Likewise, how are black and brown youth impacted by their criminalization within American schools, whether in the form of racial profiling, dress codes, various forms of mistreatment, or an overall jail-like environment. Kenneth Saltman, in his introduction to *Education as Enforcement*, cautions about the blowback effects of transforming American public schools—those places of education where youth of color are confined by their color—from places of education to instruments of discipline and control that resemble prisons and military insti-tutions: "Military generals running schools, students in uniforms, metal detectors, police presence, high-tech ID card dog tags, real time Internet-based surveillance cameras, mobile hidden surveillance cameras, security con-sultants, chainlink fences, surprise searches—as U.S. public schools invest in record level of school security apparatus they increasingly resemble the mili-tary and prisons" (2004, p. 1). The impact of the widespread age restriction debate is therefore extensive because it, like so many of today's conversations regarding black and brown youth, denies the importance of race or racism and instead invokes personal, cultural, and communal failures. The argument is clear: black youth are unable to secure the American Dream because they are spending too much time trying to be like Kobe or KG, from whom they have learned that bouncing a basketball is more likely to secure a bright future than reading or studying. Worse, parents, community members, and the culture of hip-hop offer no correctives measures, resulting not only in the sad stories of Lenny Cooke, Leon Smith, and Taj McDavid, but countless other black youth who fall through the cracks. In a given year in Chicago, class sizes decline by half between 9th and 12th grade. Chicago schools graduate 15,633 students, with 17,404 dropping out yearly. New York City may be even worse, with graduation rates hovering at 35 percent for black students and 31 per-cent for Latinos (Daniels 2007, pp. 156–157). Commentators and the NBA spread panic regarding the sad tales of Smith and McDavid, but are silent about the many children left behind by failed policies and persistent inequal-ity who have ultimately been pushed through the cracks into America's expanding prison system. Societal discourse, as evidenced by the arguments offered in support of an age restriction, identifies cultural and individual fail-ures as the impetus behind these numbers, thereby silencing any potential conversation about state violence, structural inequalities, or persistent racism.

PUT DOWN THAT BALL:
SAVING AMERICA'S (BLACK) YOUTH

The rationale for implementing an age limit were rather simplistic in that its proponents sought to only save those players who have already attempted to jump straight from high school into the league and failed, but future genera-tions as well. Michael Wilbon, expressing an opinion shared by many others, stated on *Pardon the Interruption* that the policy was a good idea because it would send a different message to hundreds of young black men who are operating under the disastrous misapprehension that they too are headed for the NBA and therefore don't need to concentrate on school. Asked why he was so adamant about a 20-year-old age limit, given the on and off court successes of LeBron James and Carmelo Anthony long before their 20th birth-days, Stern contended that the rule had nothing to do with the NBA: "I have never said that the 18 year-olds can't play in the league." With "Carmelo and LeBron," and "the long list of Jermaine O'Neal, Kevin Garnett, Kobe Bryant, and Tracy McGrady" there is "a veritable All-Star team" ("David Stern Media Conference" 2004). Similarly, one year before he would finally implement the age restriction, at a moment when he didn't foresee his efforts being success-ful (before the Palace Brawl), he argued that a rule prohibiting anyone under the age of 20[10] from entering the league "would be a good thing to send a message to 10- and 11-year-olds that they should really plan to do something with their life other than play basketball between the ages of 18 and 20" (Quoted in Dupree 2003). Claiming that he had "no hidden agenda" and that his crusade against teenage ballers wasn't about "marketing," he argued that this effort was about "standing for the right" and sending a message to the "now-thousands of would-be LeBrons" that they should pursue success through education, rather than basketball (Quoted in Dupree 2003). Some two years later, after the age restriction had been implemented, and despite the various problems facing the NBA, Stern maintained this rationale: "Because we're a sport that's very popular and easily accessible, there's going to be tens of thousands and hundreds of thousands of 10-year-olds thinking they are the next Sebastian Telfair or LeBron James. And I just don't feel great about being associated with that" (Quoted in Couch 2005). Since King James, Kobe, and KG are "rare," it was important for the NBA to counteract the image and message sent by an "influx of teenagers," which "set a bad example for high school players who are focused solely on a pro career instead of going to college." Stern stated that one of the reasons he ultimately saw an age restriction as necessary was because of the NBA's effects on children, and the complaints he was hearing from parents: "Huge numbers of kids whose parents are already approaching me, saying 'My son is 11 years old, he can bounce a ball well and he ain't going to college,' because he think he's going to the NBA. Everyone assembled here knows the chances of that young man become a rocket scientist are better than making the NBA" (Quoted in Beseda 2004). William Reed concurs, arguing that an age restriction pushes education back into focus, making unnecessary those scare tactics that point out that less than 1 percent of 250,000 high school athletes will receive a col-lege scholarship, and even fewer will make the NBA. It forces them to focus on getting into college, with or without a basketball (Reed 2003).

Three of the more instructive comments supporting an age limit because it would send a message to black youth came from John Thompson, Michael Wilbon, and an anonymous school teacher. Thompson, who vociferously praised Stern and the NBA for implementing this rule, defended this move by pointing out that any society "has to improve itself by encouraging education" and that "not drawing the line goes far beyond the 58 players selected in the N.B.A. draft. . . . As a society, we are creating a new disenfranchised segment of the population because we are baiting young men into following role models who have avoided college in pursuit of wealth" (2001). Thompson celebrated the dawn of a new era (or at least a return to an older one), where (black) youth would find role models who had attended college, reminding them of the importance of education. Similarly, a teacher whose thoughts appeared on freedarko.com, before being reposted on "The Starting Five,"[11] while questioning the substantive impact of the NBA move, celebrated its cultural importance:

> The implementation of the age limit will not close the achievement gap. It won't force books into the hands of inner city youth and supplies into their classrooms. But it will enable teachers and parents to tell their budding 7th grade superstar of the future that the road to the NBA runs through college. How can a 7th grader who knows he needs to go to college not be better off than a 7th grader who thinks college is for failures? ("Widening the Waters" 2006).

Although crucified for his "ghetto paternalism" on "The Starting Five," this teacher was certainly not alone. Michael Wilbon expressed his support for an age restriction, not in order to protect LeBron, Kobe, or even Leon Smith and Korleone Young, nor to improve the NBA product, but to save the children "left behind" by false dreams, false hopes, and false promises. In his estimation, limiting the NBA to adults (those over 20) sent a message to (black) youth who have foolishly attempted to follow in their heroes' footsteps, stepping in "potholes" that inure self and community.

> My concern is for the hundreds of boys in Southeast Washington, the Bronx and West Philly and the South Side of Chicago and in Detroit and East St. Louis and South Central Los Angeles who look at Telfair and immediately think, "Me, too." . . . My concern is a giant chunk of a fairly large culture is drunk with a risky obsession of one pursuit. See, the ripple effect is a killer when the rock skips through the wrong pond. (Wilbon 2004d)

Wilbon argues that the age restriction is a reminder to us all, particularly (black) youth confined to America's ghettos, that "education is not an impediment to success," and that given the fact that "these same neighborhoods that produce the basketball phenoms are decimated with gun violence and drug trafficking and teenage pregnancy and illiteracy," change is sorely needed (Wilbon 2004d). According to Wilbon, education and its emphasis, rather than multimillion dollar contracts, will ultimately lead to transformation and growth within these communities. To further emphasize his point that being a first-round pick or appearing on SportsCenter won't fix today's ghettos or the problems that define them, Wilbon implies that false dreams and an overemphasis on basketball are actually part of the problem: "Basketball has made a lot of careers [but it has] left exponentially more 45-year-olds sitting in the same playgrounds where we left them nearly 30 years ago, drinking a 40-ounce while wondering where the next meal is coming from" (2004d). The problems facing the black community, whether in terms of poverty, the achievement gap, illiteracy, teenage pregnancy, incarceration rates, or inequality are thus attributable to the choices and culture of the black community, a culture in which youth "would rather grow up to be Paul Piece who makes 13 million a year than Paul Allen who owns a team and is worth billions" (Irving[12] quoted in Wilbon 2004d). As such, limiting access to the NBA and forcing black youth to go to college would address these problems.

Tony Kornheiser, in his brilliantly titled commentary "Commissioner is Tossing Pennies in Wishing Well," questions the connection between the NBA and efforts to "save black youth," explaining that he is "leery of people who talk about 'the culture of basketball' and how teenagers jumping to the NBA create 'a ripple effect in urban America'" (2001). To Kornheiser, this is not an "epidemic," but a blip on the cultural screen. Yet, he offers no explanation as to why "this cultural blip" has been constructed as an epidemic not only in terms of the "NBA crisis," but also as source and remedy for the broader black community. Kornheiser doesn't seem to want to bring race into the discussion, arguing, "that race, of course, will add to the volatility" (2001). Others are not so tepid in their analysis.

Len Elmore, who played in the NBA for eight seasons, and went on to work as a sportscaster and NBA agent, describes this type of thinking in the NBA as "we know what's best for you poor, undereducated people" (Quoted in Araton 2005a, p. 177). Harvey Araton, who didn't deny the profit and marketing implications/basis of an age restriction, also wonders about the discursive and ideological links between a ban on teenagers and long-standing belief systems about race inside and outside the NBA arena. He, like others, recognizes the all-too-familiar strategy in the almighty pursuit of profit, but also speculated that it was driven by a "perhaps a paternalistic manipulation of minorities. . . . [Len Elmore had a more strident name for those who practice such subterfuge: puppet masters]" (Araton 2005a, p. 177). Richard Jefferson, then of the New Jersey Nets, although describing the restriction as only "bordering on racism," clearly identified the policy and its stated effort to send an educational message to black youth as racial and racialized: "As young black males, we always seem to be in a position of people telling us what's best for us, as if we can't figure this stuff out for ourselves. . . . Why is it you never hear anyone telling athletes in baseball and hockey and that they should go to college?" (Quoted in Araton 2005a, p. 176). Mark Anthony Neal—like Elmore, Jefferson, and Araton—sees the demands for NBA stars to go to college before entering the league as being part of a larger societal practice of white supremacy wherein the white power structure both concludes what is best for people of color and sees school, with its emphasis on discipline and control, as crucial to the advancement of communities of color. These guys are screaming that LeBron should go to college for a year or two because would make him a "better person," argues Neal. "Why does the young African American basketball player have to go to college to become a better person and the white tennis player doesn't?" (Quoted in Araton 2005a, p. 108). The answers to this question not only illustrates the racial double standards in operation, along with the systematic ways in which blacks are treated as children in need of education and advice, but also the long-standing ideology regarding control and disciplinarity that operates in this context. Although not limited to the criminal justice system, "the methods of controlling crime develop an informal and formal policy of disciplining black males" (Watkins 1998, p. 216). According to Robin D. G. Kelley, "The Right blames personal behavior, weak morals, and a pathological culture for the current state of black urban life" (Kelley 1997, p. 11). Even more than for white youth, black and brown youth need education as a means for repairing the pernicious effects of single mothers, a culture of poverty, and hip-hop. Ngugi Wa Thiong'o links colonial education to processes of control and cultural genocide, all in the name of power. It "annihilate(s) a people's belief in their names, in their languages, in their environment, in their heritage of struggle, in their unity, in their capacities and ultimately in themselves. It makes them see their past as one wasteland of non-achievement and it makes them want to distance themselves from that wasteland. It makes them want to identify with that which is furthest removed from themselves" (1986, p. 3). The discursive emphasis on helping and educating black youth replicates a long-standing history that both places the burden of help in whiteness and the burden of failure within those black bodies.

POLICING HIP-HOP

The desire to establish an age limit cannot be understood outside the backlash against the hip-hop baller in the wake of Kobe Bryant's nontrial, the Palace Brawl, and a host of other events, each of which would supposedly marked the demise of the league if it didn't wrestle control back from the tattooed, braided, bling-bling-displaying, posse rollin, street ballin straight-outta-high-school ghetto baller. Although the calls to stem the "tide," the

"flood" (Kiszla 2003), and "the unprecedented number of talented" high
school ballers (Sandoval and Steinberg 2004) have been longstanding—sur-
facing with the arrival of Kevin Garnett in 1995, and increasing during the
late 1990s and early 2000s—the clamor reached its pinnacle shortly after the
Palace Brawl. League and media demands for a blockade to the "flood" of
black youth into the NBA increased as concerns about tensions between fans
and players publicly materialized, while the opposition to the influences of
hip-hop on the NBA fueled the debate. According to Ian O'Connor, who in
The Jump documents the decision-making process of Sebastian Telfair, who
ultimately entered the NBA right after graduating high school, the calls for
and implementation of an age restriction "revolved around the idea that Stern
sees a disconnect between players and fans, which wasn't helped by the brawl
in Auburn Hills" (Quoted in Sullivan 2005). The rule thus was not simply
about "stemming the invasion" of teenagers into a man's league, but also
addressing media and corporate sponsor concerns, all while placating fan's
fears and contempt about the young black baller. "The age limit is an outrage,
a transparent public relations move by Stern," writes Jerry Sullivan in the *Buffalo News*. "He says an age limit will somehow 'protect' the game. From what?
From the notion that undisciplined thugs (black youth—my insertion) are
spilling directly from high schools on the NBA floor" (Sullivan 2004). The
policy, in ridding the league (although more symbolically than actually) of
black youth and the many signifiers attached to their bodies, sent a clear message to fans, the media, and the NBA's corporate sponsors: the NBA is "a
safer, more mature game" (Sullivan 2004). Dave Zirin concurs, questioning
whether the league's motivation is purely racial. "There is no economic
reason; no reason with regard to the stunting of talent, which justifies Stern's
move. That leaves race. Stern is simply expressing a policy, the long-held concerns by NBA executives that a league whose base of talent are America's
bogeyman, the YBT (young black teenager) is unsustainable" (Zirin 2004).
Ira Berkow, who challenges the arguments of benevolence and protection,
instead describing the age restriction as part of the NBA's assault on the
influences of hip-hop, writes the following: "Stern's promoting of college life
for the youth of America is self-serving and cynical. It is a fear of image with
incoming hip-hoppers (remember when the N.B.A. official magazine airbrushed out Allen Iverson's tattoos for its cover photo)" (Berkow 2001b).
Rick Maese likewise identifies the age restriction as an appeal to the (white)
fans, "the guy who can afford tickets and expensive merchandise, yet trouble
identifying with a culture, an athlete, and a lifestyle to which he can't relate"
(2006). In fact, in numerous interviews regarding the issue, David Stern did
not even deny these contentions, only challenging those who emphasized the
racial and cultural implications of the debate and instead focused on business,

fans, and age. He told Armen Keteyian, during an interview for HBO's *Costas Now*, that he sensed a level of condemnation from the fans, "that we are too young, that we were in effect robbing the cradle, and that we're grabbing kids at a young age." Although Michael McCann and Billy Hunter agreed with Stern regarding the dialectical workings of an age limit and league fears about a fan backlash, both men told Keteyian that the proposal reflected an effort to scapegoat straight-out-of-high school ballers for the league's image problems. "I really think it is a way to indirectly address the image issue. I think he and owners feel that they have to give the fans something," noted Hunter, the National Basketball Association union president. "The idea is what can you give the fans to convince them that you are in control of the game and that it hasn't gotten out-of-hand. And that [the Brawl] is just part of it. . . . Some individuals have problems have difficult that so many players have tattoos or corn-rows or they're saying that there a bunch of spoiled millionaires, etc. The problem may not be with the 18-year olds, but if we can make that the result, so be it" (Quoted in Keteyian 2005).

While the soaring signifiers of the hip-hop baller and the influence of hip-hop were most evident in the discourse surrounding, and the broader historical moment of, the production of an age restriction, it remained a coded presence throughout much of the media debate. Not only was the NBA getting younger and younger, and blacker and blacker, within the dominant imagination, but the intrusion of a hip-hopped baller resulted in an even younger, blacker, more selfish, immature, and undesirable player, who was ruining the league in terms of both quality of play and character. Given that these players had not been "seasoned" or "domesticated," they would bring not only their "raw" athletic talents, but also their hip-hop aesthetics and attitudes. To illustrate the coded ways in which hip-hop was connected both to the presumed immaturity of today's (black) players and the danger they posed to the NBA's future, I offer a few examples, followed by a short discussion of them as a whole.

Mark Kiszla rhetorically asked the following about today's players, making the link between hip-hop and a problematic NBA clear: "How does a coach get a teenager who could afford the Hope Diamond to listen to the truth rather than the hype" (2003). Four years earlier, Kiszla had interviewed then–Colorado State basketball coach Ritchie McKay about the NCAA possibly reinstituting a rule that limited freshman participation, thereby curtailing the influx of "immature overpaid frats, unprepared on and off the court." McKay responded: "In this age of instant gratification, I'm not sure it would work. In our society, today, we want instant growth, instant, maturity, instant wealth. You're taking a kid who has played all his life and telling him he can't do it for a year" (Quoted in Kiszla 1999). Likewise, Joan Ryan described the decision to enter the NBA "early" as one "about youth and money, class and family, the lure of fame, and the brevity of athletic careers, the craving for instantaneous gratification" (1996). Three of the more transparent, yet still coded, efforts to link hip-hop and the youth movement to the demise of the NBA can be found in the following arguments. In 1999, Phil Jackson, in what seems a ringing endorsement for sending future NBA players to college in order to break down their bad habits and curb the effects of negative cultural influences, offered the following assessment of hip-hop culture and its effects on the NBA product: "I don't mean to say [that] as a snide remark toward a certain population in our society, but they have a limitation of their attention span, a lot of it probably due to too much rap music going in their ears and coming out their being" (Quoted in S. Jackson 2005b). Moreover, in focusing on the aftermath or end result of a hip-hop youth invasion, Bernie Linicone argued that today's (black) athletes were not learning the values associated with basketball, instead presumably learning from hip-hop and the broader culture of "me": "What was once an extension and reflection of the college experience—athletics—is as far from the point of higher education as the power plant is from the light bulb. The lessons athletics are supposedly to reveal—teamwork, loyalty, selflessness, honor, integrity—are found in an ethics class, not that any athletes will be found there" (1999). John Thompson identified a clear link with the following:

> Those who argue against the N.B.A. 20-year-old rule may cloak themselves in words like freedom and opportunity, but let's look at their case. Aren't those, who say there should be no minimum age for someone to play professional basketball, saying: "Forget college. Cut to the chase and jump to the N.B.A. So what if you're unprepared for the level of competition because you lack fundamentals. Just shout, 'Show me the money!' Who cares if you have no idea how to handle your finances, the attention or the life style? 'Show me the money!' Who says the deterioration of basic skills or the loss of fan identification in the sport is your problem? 'Show me the money!' What does it matter if you don't actually last long enough to have a career in the N.B.A.? 'Show me the money!' Why worry about what's best for you? You'll be surrounded by a bunch of agents, lawyers, family and associates who will also shout, 'Show me the money!'"
>
> While I would be the last person to deny the importance of money, we need to keep the bigger picture in mind. Teaching young people that education is unimportant and may be skipped in the pursuit of money hurts everybody. Because of basketball's popularity, failing to adopt some rule that stems the tide will flood the

nation with this lesson in a way that baseball, hockey, golf and tennis never could. We need to motivate young people to pursue education, not avoid it. (2001)

The constant links to instant gratification, materialism, and financial rewards, as opposed to stability, education, and maturation, are telling given the ways in which these descriptions are used to define the aesthetics and meaning of hip-hop culture. Within popular culture, evidence can be found in representations of the hip-hop-influenced black athlete in films like *White Men Can't Jump*, *Any Given Sunday*, and *Jerry McGwire*, each of which not only presents the black athlete as driven by ego, love of money over game, and showmanship, but links these practices to hip-hop culture. Then White House Press Secretary Tony Snow described the cultural values of hip-hop in the following terms: "Take a look at the idiotic culture of hip-hop and whad-dya have? You have people glorifying failure. You have a bunch of gold-toothed hot dogs become millionaires by running around telling everyone else that they oughtta be miserable failures and if they're really lucky maybe they can be gunned down in a diner sometime, like Eminem's old running mate" (Quoted in Cobb 2006, p. 88). Similarly, John McWhorter, in "Hip-Hop Holds Back Blacks," argues that hip-hop, because of its values and its promotion of thuggish, pathological behavior, "retards black success."

> The attitude and style expressed in the hip-hop "identity" keeps blacks down. Almost all hip-hop, gangsta or not, is delivered with a cocky, confrontational cadence that is fast becoming—as attested to by the rowdies at KFC—a common speech style among young black males. Similarly, the arm-slinging, hand-hurling gestures of rap performers have made their way into many young blacks' casual gesticulations, becoming integral to their self-expression. The problem with such speech and mannerisms is that they make potential employers wary of young black men and can impede a young black's ability to interact comfortably with co-workers and customers. The black community has gone through too much to sacrifice upward mobility to the passing kick of an adversarial hip-hop "identity." (McWhorter 2003)

Whether talking about African American basketball stars or black youth, the discourse ubiquitously focuses on the ways in which hip-hop's ingrained cultural values and aesthetics not only limit the opportunities afforded to the black community while perpetuating stereotypes, but demonstrate a refusal to accept the cultural values embraced by white America. "What angers and alarms so many is the fact that of these players have no interest whatsoever in imitating the ways of mainstream white society," writes Todd Boyd. "This is evident in the style choices favored by so many contemporary players. Corn-rows have replaced the bald head. Long baggy shorts are de rigueur. Tattoos are the order of the day" (Boyd 2003, p. 181).

William Rhoden describes the history of sports in the years following integration as "an intense struggle to control the extent to which African American 'style' was expressed through sports," which he characterizes as a process wherein dominant sporting institutions want "black muscle but not the attendant zeal and style . . . , baggage that a history of living in a white supremacist country had helped to pack" (Rhoden 2006, p. 167). The efforts to rid the league of the influence of hip-hop, while continuing to profit off it as a desired commodity, reflects a broader discourse that sees hip-hop (black-ness) as a dysfunctional cultural movement that encourages misogyny, materi-alism, selfishness, and contempt for the accepted, civilized, and established (white) values of both basketball culture and society as a whole. The NBA age limit functions as a gatekeeper, a means for preventing the infiltration of the "dark side of hip-hop" (literally) while still appeasing critics and placating fans. It also represents an effort to put black male bodies and styles under sur-veillance and control. The effort to exclude under-20 ballers from the NBA, while also motivated by owners not wanting to pay first-round dollars to players who might take years to develop and college programs wanting to profit from the unpaid labor of America's top ballers, reflects a desire to push America's best players into attending college so they can join the league having been already "seasoned" and "domesticated."

A RACELESS ISSUE?

Asked about the racial implications of the proposed age limit that the NBA was then planning to add to the 2005 Collective Bargaining Agreement, Jer-maine O'Neal stated: "As a black guy, you kind of think (race is) the reason why it's coming up," O'Neal told the *Indianapolis Star*. "You don't hear about it in baseball or hockey. To say you have to be 20, 21 to get in the league, it's unconstitutional. If I can go to the U.S. Army and fight the war at 18, why can't you play basketball for 48 minutes and then go home?" (Quoted in Adande 2005b). He went on to say that, "In the last two or three years, the Rookie of the Year has been a high school player. There were seven high school players in the All-Star game, so why we even talking (about) an age limit?" ("Stern wants NBA age limit raised to 20" 2005).

Before he finished his last sentence, the vultures began to circle, attack-ing O'Neal for his statements. Questioning his intelligence, education, and his past behavior, he was quickly dismissed (Leonard 2005). More importantly, columnists and others used this opportunity to further make their case against high school ballers. Evidence by O'Neal's decision to "play the race card" and fight fans during the Palace Brawl or the ubiquity of braids, tattoos, and large diamond earrings, the downfall of the NBA rests on the backs of those players who have entered the league without a stint in college.

Specifically, both defenders of the proposed age limit and its "colorblind" opponents saw race as a nonissue. A number of commentators dismissed O'Neal's invoking of race because the rule would affect all players. For example, Nick Prevenas scoffed at the mere implication of racism: "The proposed NBA age limit has its share of problems, but it's not a racist initiative. The age limit is an equal opportunity discriminator. The 20-and-under barrier wouldn't only affect American high school kids—it would have a massive impact on overseas prospects" (2005). Bill Gibron, like so many others (see Whitlock 2005b), denounced O'Neal for introducing race into the conversation: "Worse yet, the 'r' word—race—has crawled into the conversation, making its potent presence known. While a Caucasian cabal out to keep the young black man out of the NBA may not exactly be the message of Indiana Pacer's Jermaine O'Neal's now famous comments, it surely is what he's suggesting. The sad thing is, had he not decided to go down the path of least logical resistance (as bringing ethnicity into an issue will often do), his anti-age limit sentiment might have sounded astute" (Gibron 2005). A majority of the commentaries not only dismissed race as a valid point for discussion, but also used O'Neal's discussion of race as evidence for why all players need to go to college. "Jermaine O'Neal has no idea what racism is. . . . He's every bit of twentysomething" (Moore 2005b). Jason Whitlock concurred, denouncing O'Neal in a series of demonizing comments about him and his generation of players: "O'Neal is the stereotypical NBA Million Dollar Baby. His youth, lack of formal education and bank account all stand in the way of his grasping the big picture" (Whitlock 2005b).

Often noting how the NBA was one of the few places where racism no longer mattered, the outright dismissal of O'Neal's comments as those of an ignorant black male willing to play the race card, reflects the power of colorblindness within post–civil rights America. "Denial in this case is not merely about the failure of public memory or the refused to know, but an active attempt on the part of many conservatives, liberals and politicians to rewrite the discourse of race as to deny its valence as a force for discrimination and exclusion either by translating it as a treat to American culture or by relegating to the language of the public sphere" (Giroux 2003c, p. 194). The popularity and visibility of the NBA, the prominence of blackness, the presumed dominance of the black community, and the rhetorical focus on basketball as an anti-political force propels the denials about race and racism within an NBA discourse. The denials not only repel injections of racial awareness into

NBA discussions, but also provide legitimacy to cultural arguments in that if it's not about race or racism it must be about the personal and collective (cultural) failures of the black community. "Within the colorblind perspective it is not race per se which determines upward mobility," writes Charles Gallagher, "but how much an individual chooses to pay attention to race that determines one's fate. Within this perspective race is only as important as you allow it be" (Quoted in Giroux 2003c, p. 198). In other words, in a moment of racial transcendence or post-racialness, "race becomes a matter of taste, lifestyle, or heritage but has nothing to do with politics, legal rights, educational access, or economic opportunities" (Giroux 2003c, p. 199).

Commentators also sought to delegitimize O'Neal's comments by saying that the rule was not motivated by race, but money and a desire to enhance the quality of the NBA product. Although certainly part of the motivation behind the rule, money doesn't invalidate racism as an explanatory factor—wasn't slavery driven by both financial greed and white supremacy? In fact, the systemic process of exploiting the bodies of black athletes is in keeping with the long history of racism in America.

A third argument stems from the idea that an age limit finds support among people of color, whether players (Shane Battier, Reggie Miller), commentators (Charles Barkley, Michael Wilbon), or fans. Again, this does not undermine the legitimacy of O'Neal's comments, but rather demonstrates the complexity of race, and the power of racist ideologies. Lastly, the argument that the rule cannot be racist because it ultimately seeks to help black youth is both absurd (imperialism, colonization, and institutions of enslavement have always invoked paternalism and helping as basis of endeavors) and baseless.

RACE MATTERS

With the vast majority of media pundits and online chatters scoffing at O'Neal's reference to race, only a few detractors emphasized the importance of race here. J.A. Adande (2005b), like Harvey Araton (2005c), Michael McCann (Quoted in Smith 2004) and Scoop Jackson (2005b) supported O'Neal's effort to add "a teaspoon of race" into the mix on this turbulent topic (Adande 2005b). Rick Maese linked the age restriction to the racially motivated cultural and policy shifts within the NBA. For him, it reflected the "NBA's ever increasing need for control—rules dripping with racial undertones—and indicative of an ever shrinking autonomy afforded to today's professional basketball player" (2006). Likewise, Michael McCann wondered, "If there's a race issue. This goes to an underlying stereotype that they need to be in school" (Quoted in Maese 2006). Others did not doubt the racial basis and implications of the rule. "Tennis players, golfers, they leave school early all the time. Baseball players, many go straight from high schools. Have those sports suffered? Have those players ended broke, with broken lives?" asked an anonymous NBA official. "No. But you have black kids whose families have no money, who have a chance to earn millions doing what they are going to be doing, two or threat years from now, anyway . . ." (Quoted in Williams and Campbell 1996). Todd Boyd asked similar questions, focusing on the racial meaning evident in this double standard:

> Interestingly, no one had lodged similar complaints about sports like tennis or gymnastics, where participants often start competing nationally and internationally at an even earlier age than they do in basketball. Tennis, for example, tends to be more white and middle- to upper-middle class in its orientation. . . . Yet there is a sense that it is wrong or poses some threat when a young Black man from the 'hood attempts to do the same on the basketball court." (Boyd 2003, pp. 177–178)

Noting the effects that such a rule would have on African Americans, and how similar debates have not taken place about hockey, baseball, tennis, or acting, these commentators concluded that the age restriction was indeed racial, and that it demonstrated a double standard for black athletes and whites—yet another hypocritical move by the NBA brass (Knapp 2005; Stein 2005a; Rhoden 1999), especially because it concerned issues of education. J.R. Smith, then a rookie with New Orleans after entering the league straight out of high school, questioned the double standard: "Something like an age requirement should not be considered for basketball. It doesn't happen for tennis, golf, or soccer, so it just doesn't make sense to me" (Quoted in Reid 2005). Likewise, Greg Anthony described the age restriction as not simply hypocritical, but a direct attack on black players (although he waffles) in the NBA: "I think that it's what's popular in society. In my mind, I don't want to say it's a racist position but you have young people in other sports like golf, tennis, and gymnastics that are not predominantly Black athletes and they go out and play effectively and there is no outcry" (Quoted in Stein 2005b). Anthony, like Smith, Zirin, and Adande, functioned as a minority voice within this dissenting discourse. More importantly, the double standard wasn't limited to differences between sports, but evident within basketball itself, where little has been made about international players who turn professional around the age of 14. In fact, these players are often celebrated for their maturity and fundamentals, qualities surely developed while playing professionally.

Yet others (O'Connor 2005b; Shields 2004; Shaw 2001; Stein 2005a; Stein 2005b; Williams and Campbell 1996) seem to construct the NBA's decision as simple hypocrisy, noting the ways in which white, black, and Latino athletes in other sports are embraced and even celebrated at a young age. Citing Chris Evert, Pete Sampras, Andre Agassi, Venus and Serena Williams, Eric Lindros, Derek Jeter, Manny Ramirez, and Wayne Gretzky, Arn Tellem, a prominent sport agent, questioned the NBA's decision in a *New York Times* op-ed, citing the legal and cultural standards established within the United States: "The N.B.A and its hallelujah choir talk often about 'making choices' and 'drawing lines' in support of their age-limit agenda. Well, our nation's court and legislatures have already set 18 as the age at which a young man can get married, vote and fight in foreign wars. Surely that same teenager can handle the pressure of playing in the N.B.A." (Tellem 2001). Bud Shaw (as well as Ira Berkow 2001b and Stein 2005a) also wondered how the NBA could reconcile its rules with the broader cultural standards and practices outside of sports, especially in a post-9/11 context when young men and women in the military are risking their lives:

> Declaring for an NBA draft shouldn't carry a stricter age restriction than signing up for a job that might put you in Bosnia or the Persian Gulf. They're both choices, thanks goodness. And except for those occasions when Juwan Howard is bearing down on you while you're airborne, the NBA is safer than war. Teenagers can keep our shores safe. They can even protect business interests overseas when U.S. shoe manufacturers build plants and hire cheap labor. But anyone under 20 shouldn't be allowed to wear those sneakers in an NBA game? (2001)

Despite their efforts to unsettle the hegemony of colorblind rhetoric, none of these commentators offered any insight into the ways in which racism and white supremacy function within and through this debate.

In discussing the racially determined debate concerning Kobe Bryant and Drew Henson turning professional straight out of high school, in which racial difference was "the difference that makes a difference," King and Springwood illustrate the racialized discourse that guides public debate regarding (black) athletes, age, and turning professional. In their estimation, Henson's decision to take $2 million to play minor [league] baseball went unremarked in the national media. There were no arguments about his maturity and no mention of the value of a college degree in his case. The same cannot be said for the coverage of Bryant's decision to skip college. In his case, numerous feature stories/commentaries emphasized what Bryant was lacking in terms of preparation, as well as how his decision broke the established rules of the NBA. Furthermore, these commentators suggest that the African American athlete needs training, regulation, and discipline that his

Euro-American counterpart does not. He needs the refinement and upward mobility secured by college in spite of his background that Henson does not. In college sports, the linkage between race and deviance imposes discipline, control, and improvement on the black body (King and Springwood 2005, pp. 198–199).

The double standard (racial specificity) evident in this debate is also clear when considered within the broader historical context. As noted by Russell Curtis Jr., little was made of Mickey Mantle or Ted Williams's decision to bypass college and enter major league baseball at the age of 18 (1998, p. 886). In fact, these two men are frequently invoked as (nostalgic) signifiers of the greatness of baseball's yesteryears. The absence of black bodies within much of sport during 1940–1960 not only explains the absence of concern for their decision, but also serves as a fulcrum for such nostalgia. Similar examples are evident in the careers of Jimmy Connors, Tracy Austin, Kerri Strug, Ty Tryon, Maria Sharapova, and countless others. In 2005, in the wake of the widespread debate regarding the appropriateness and effectiveness of allowing players to the enter the NBA straight out high school, little was made about the ages of either Sidney Crosby, the first pick in the NHL, or Koby Clemons, an 18-year-old who originally signed a letter of intent with the University of Texas, only to sign with the Houston Astros after being their eighth-round pick (Araton 2005c).

The debate concerning the NBA also erases the European baller, who is rarely mentioned, and if included at all, it is merely as an afterthought used to silence those who see race within the discourse. Through history, across sports, and within different spaces, the age debate has served as a discourse of control, disciplinarity, and punishment for intruding, transgressing, and rule-breaking black bodies.

It is crucial to see the racial dimensions of the discourse—its double standards, its guiding racialized ideologies and inherent "racial paternalism," and that it takes place within the context of long-standing white hegemonic efforts to discipline and control the Other—but it is also crucial to situate the debate within the realities of a post–civil rights discourse. Just as with Ted Williams and Jimmy Connors, there has been little public debate concerning the efforts of major league baseball to sign 16-year-olds (or younger) from Latin America to professional (cheap) contracts. To note the absence of outrage and panic for this practice—not to mention the worldwide exploitation of child labor within the shoe, diamond, garment, and agricultural industries—is not to say that race is unimportant here. Nor do the varied reactions to Freddy Adu and Michele Wie, both of whom are youth of color who have been celebrated for their childhood successes, demonstrate that such debates are colorblind. The fact that many commentators have simultaneously called for age restrictions within the NBA and celebrated Freddy Adu and Michelle

Wie does not legitimize claims of colorblindness ("they are both black"). Rather, it demonstrates the complex ways in which race, gender, and nationality construct and saturate post–civil rights (sporting) discourses.

YOUNG ATHLETES OF COLOR: MODEL MINORITY DISCOURSE AS ANOTHER EXCEPTION

Michelle Wie and Freddy Adu appeared on the American sports radar in 2004 as America's youngest golf and soccer sensations, respectively. While having played previously in a few LPGA events, Wie, for her part, generated a great deal of excitement with her entry into the PGA's (aka the men's tour) Sony Open. Wie had long made the golf world marvel with her sheer strength and her mastery over some of America's most difficult courses. At the age of 12, she qualified for an LPGA event; at 13, she became the youngest winner of the U.S. Women's Amateur Public Links Championship. Yet, her performance at the 2004 Sony Open elicited the biggest stir, earning praise from fans and her male peers on the tour.

After shooting a 68 and missing the cut by just one shot, Davis Love III had nothing but compliments for Wie: "There was an argument whether she should be playing or not. But once she's here—I mean, it's the talk in the locker room when I walked in there. The guys that got outhit and the guys that got beat. It's an incredible story. Just a year ago we were wondering if an L.P.G.A. or lady player could play out here" (Quoted in Brown 2004). Although debates raged about whether this girl without a tour card (she was provided an exemption given the interest her participation would generate for a tournament in her home state) should play in a PGA tournament, no one seemed to care that she was 14. Not a single announcer, commentator, or male golfer questioned her maturity or the appropriateness of her playing professional golf. Rather, they gawked at her talent and potential, describing her as a protégé, the future of golf, and the next Tiger Woods. In 2005, Jerry Sullivan pointed out the different nature of the discourses surrounding the LPGA and the NBA, despite the equal number of "precocious kids" within each sport. "Sunday was one of the most compelling days in women's golf history. Heading into the final round of the U.S. Open, three American teenagers were within striking distance of the lead," wrote Sullivan. "It did not occur to me that Michelle Wie (15), Morgan Pressel (17) and Paula Creamer (18) were a threat to golf. I don't recall anyone urging the USGA to restrict high school girls from playing in the Open" (2005). Arguing that opposing discourses and diametrically opposed rules (although the USGA does limit golfers under the age of 18 to six events, unless granted a waiver) reflect the differences in which each sport is read by the public, Sullivan argues that an age restriction "protects" fans "from the notion that undisciplined thugs are spilling directly from high schools onto the NBA floors" (2005). Whereas Wie and Pressel were seen as safe young girls who enhanced the image and marketability of the LPGA, the straight-out-of-high-school baller was imagined as the complete opposite: a pollutant, immature and dangerous to the game and the entire culture. Whereas those who play golf, tennis, and even soccer are imagined as young and mature, NBA players are represented as young and hyperimmature. Accordingly, for some athletes age is simply a number, but when age meets blackness, being under age represents a source of panic, fear, and demonization. In this regard, the implementation of an age restriction was not simply about minimizing and controlling the invasion of unambiguous black bodies.

Only hours after Wie teed off, Freddy Adu sat in anticipation of fulfilling his dream of a professional soccer career. Adu became the youngest professional athlete in the past 100 years after D.C. United drafted him first in the 2004 amateur draft. Like Wie, Adu has amazed the American sports public with his talent and maturity. Deemed a "strong kick for American soccer" (Starr 2002) by sports writers, celebrated as a "preteen phenom" (Starr 2003) by the popular press, his talents in the classroom have been emphasized as much as his juggling skills and rocket off the left foot.

The praise for these two athletes, however, cannot be understood outside the constant critique of those young black males seeking entry into the NBA—race, class, gender, nationality, and sport all play into fan/commentator reception and perception. In this context, David Aldridge lamented the connections between the NBA and the youth movements in other sports, illustrating the ways in which race, sport and identity affect media and societal reception. "In Major League soccer, 14-year-old Freddy Adu signs a contract . . . and is treated to fawning press coverage. . . . Even though no one expects him to be a superstar next season . . . no one begrudges him the opportunity to play. . . . In the NBA, 18 year olds routinely sign contracts . . . are not treated to fawning press coverage. Even though one experts them to be superstars . . . they are routinely blamed for destroying the league" (Aldridge 2003). While Adu and Wie have also been subjected to scrutiny and condemnation, making it clear that phenoms of color better be successful if they want good press, each benefited from the broader racial discourses that imagine Asian-American and certain immigrant groups as model minorities who have pulled themselves up by their bootstraps through hard work and education.

This double standard does not merely reflect America's love/hate relationship with professional basketball, but the hegemonic adherence to policing young black males, who defy dominant expectations with baggy shorts, trash-talking, bling-bling, and hypermasculinity. In society in general, and especially in spaces dominated by black youth, we expect control, reverence, and respect; as a society, we fear and scapegoat black youth.

As a soccer player and golfer, Adu and Wie are low on the American sports radar, although certainly not off the map given the hoopla each experienced. Surely, the lack of interest in these sports, and their often-mentioned immigrant identities, played into the absence of discussion surrounding the rise of these 14-year-old athletes. Moreover, the realities of race in the United States, its meaning within the sports world, and the racialized discourse surrounding the NBA also explains the varied reactions. Ultimately, neither Wie nor Adu were seen as reflective of the country's troubled (black) youth, allowing them to enter the world of professional sports freely, without critique or surveillance.

Each case shows the necessity for intersectional analysis that reflects on race, class, gender, nationality, and discourse. Both illustrate that the specificity of reactions to high school ballers is part of a larger project to discipline black male bodies and the corresponding panic generated by a deviant and rule-breaking (through hip-hop) black male body and aesthetic. "Perhaps such public concerns and panics are best understood as a form of racial paternalism in which white America struggles to come to terms with its (exploitative) enjoyment of the African athlete by advancing a linkage between the ostensibly moral and disciplinary space of the university and big time sports" (King and Springwood 2005, p. 199). Perhaps the lack of pleasure derived from foreign (African and Asian) bodies that play tennis, soccer, and golf, drives varied reactions. Perhaps the lack of danger imagined in the bodies of Adu and Wie, also guides the discussion. Race and racism operate on different planes, through different contexts, and Adu and Wie neither threaten the social order nor appear to be breaking the rules—they have not inspired any cautionary tales or catalyzed any media-induced panics. Whereas young black ballers represent a threat (to the white fan; to the profitability of the league; to the rules of the game; to its aesthetics) that needs to be contained and disciplined, whether through restricting the length of shorts, controlling the influences of hip-hop, curtailing showboating, or requiring that ballers be seasoned at America's college plantations, Adu and Wie pose no such threat.

A NOTE ON THE DEFENDERS:
THE AMERICAN DREAM AND MERITOCRACY

One of the most striking elements of this dissenting discourse is its celebration of both the American Dream and meritocracy. That is, those who oppose the NBA's decision to institute an age restriction do so not so much because they object to the racist logic by which the rule is informed, but because it counters the dominant ideology of the American Dream and meritocracy. A core American value has long been the belief that those who work hard and are deserving of financial awards, accolades, and advancement will receive them, a belief that can lead even those individuals born into dire circumstances to rise above their pain and despair and achieve greatness. "It is quite impossible to live in the United States and not be bombarded by images of materialism and economic achievement. . . . The dream has inspired heroic individual success stories, but it also has expressed itself in nightmares and human misery" (Cernkovich et al., 2000, pp. 131–132). Sports, especially basketball given its association with black youth and America's ghettos, "affirms that those on the bottom can ascend this society even as it is critical of the manner in which they rise" (hooks 1995, p. 22[13]). Likewise, King and Springwood identify sports as a powerful space of mythmaking regarding the occurrence and nature of the American Dream:

> In particular, the commonsense notions of the self-made man, and the American dream work against personal and collective engagement with the materiality of racial difference. Individuals, effort, and ability to obscure the conditions and effects of racial hierarchy. . . . These life histories map out opposite itineraries, success, superstardom, and the American Dream juxtaposed with failure, obscurity, and a societal nightmare. They individual, they assert, makes his or her fortune based on his or her effort and ability. The system is open, fostering upward mobility for individuals with talent, character, and *discipline* (my emphasis). (King and Springwood 2001, pp. 31–32, p. 34)

To many, the NBA, which had long been a means for "making it," for securing financial security and living the American Dream, especially if you were a young black male left behind in a post–civil rights America, had turned its back on this tradition. Stern's age restriction was a betrayal to not only the rags-to-riches American Dream experiences that had been provided by the NBA, but to a core American value. Reflecting on the possibilities of Sebastian Telfair entering the NBA straight from high school, or getting drafted in the middle to late part of the first round, Ian O'Connor describes his family's mind-set as one that not only connected the NBA to the American Dream, but saw it as a means for transcending the entrapment and confinement that define so much of modern black life: "That meant the first real chance to escape the crime and poverty that were as much a part of everyday life as Surfside Gardens as seagulls hovering over the boardwalk across the street" (O'Connor 2005a, p. 11). Greg Anthony also questions the fairness of the rule because it denies high school players the opportunity to enter the league, to be judged on the merit of their basketball talents. "The bottom line is that America is about opportunity and if you have the ability you should be afford the opportunity to perform. I always say if you have a problem with it, don't draft them. Just because a player declare for the draft doesn't mean they have to get drafted. If the league doesn't want them in the NBA, don't draft them" (Quoted in Stein 2005b). Similarly, Myles Brand, then NCAA president, wonders whether it would even be possible to dissuade kids from entering the NBA early, given the prospects it offers for living their dreams while also providing financially for their families. "The opportunity some athletes to earn 3 million a year after they have come out of an underprivileged background, which gives them a chance to help their parents is tough to compete with" (Quoted in Neviuus 1999).

The denial of the immediate opportunity to enter the NBA is a denial of the meritocratic-induced American Dream, resulting in "a dream deferred." More importantly, this exclusion does not simply deny opportunities to deserving black youth otherwise alienated from mainstream society, it also signals an ideological rupture where the ideological usefulness of sports is lost. Discussing the social, cultural, political, and economic usefulness of the icon otherwise known as Michael Jordan, Mary McDonald reflects on the importance of the "American Dream" within sporting discourses:

> In an era famous for attacks on affirmative action, lukewarm enforcement of civil rights laws, and the dismantling of the welfare state—of which disproportionately affect people of color—icons of success such as Michael Jordan and the NBA's best players serve as an ideological role: they suggest that the achievement of the American Dream is a matter of personal perseverance rather than the province of those born into [white, male] privilege. (McDonald 2001, p. 157; also see McDonald 1996)

The rule doesn't simply exclude 18-year-olds or establish a hip-hop blockade; it denies entry to the "Africanized Horatio Alger" (Patton quoted in McDonald, 2001, p. 157), the "army of athletes who possess the (new) right stuff with modest beginnings, skill, and personal determination" (McDonald 2001, p. 157). According to this hegemonic logic, the rule denies young black males the opportunity to provide for their families (another core value of the United States, one that celebrates and legitimizes patriarchy) and leaves them with bleak futures—confined to violent ghettos and impoverished situations where, in the best of circumstances, their parents are forced to live paycheck to paycheck (O'Connor 2006; Hollis 2001; "When Hoop Dreams Come True" 1998; Ryan 1996). Moreover, it forces these youth to secure an education,[14] which might not be needed, desired, or even feasible, denying them the constitutional and culturally sanctioned right to cash in on their physical gifts to the betterment of self, community and family (Berkow 2001b; May 1996). For Joan Ryan, getting drafted is "like winning the lottery" (1996), meaning that the rule does nothing less than deny a group of impoverished, yet talented, young men the right to buy a ticket. "The physicality of certain sports (like basketball); the eroticizing and racializing of the bodies participating in these spectacles; and the tendency to invest those bodies with the hopes, dreams, and aspirations of a mythic, heroic working class keep most popular commercialized team sports at a safe distance from the world of high culture" (Kelley 1997, p. 65). The hip-hop baller, situated amid a societal-wide racialized culture war, fails in this regard, representing the nightmares, disdain, and fears of a post–civil rights movement in America, in that sports, rather than being imagined as a source of redemption, pleasure, and fulfillment of the American Dream, denote the persistent dangers signified by black male bodies.

A CRISIS INSIDE AND OUTSIDE AMERICA'S ARENA

Within a context of increasingly vocal denunciations of black youth culture, efforts to funnel money away from social services to institutions of social control, and arguments linking criminality to blackness, black youth have suffered significantly. The shifting emphasis on building and populating prisons has resulted in a massive increase in America's prison population, the brunt of which has been felt by black and Latino males. Between 1970 (200,000) and 2000 (2,000,000), America's prison population increased by 500 percent, compared to a mere 45 percent increase in its overall population. As of the late 1990s, there were more than 50 million criminal records on file in the U.S., with at least 4 to 5 million "new" adults acquiring such a record annually. As of 2000, the total number of men and women behind bars, on parole, and on probation, had reached 6.3 million, more than 3 percent of the adult population. In the 1990s alone, nearly 2 million people were imprisoned (Davis 2003; Miller 1997; Parenti 1999; Davis 1998a). At the current pace, by 2020, 4.5 million African American men will be locked up, with an additional 2.5 million Latino men. "Prisons thus perform a feat of magic. Or rather the people who continually vote in new prison bonds and tacitly assent to a proliferating network of prisons and jails have been tricked into believing in the magic of imprisonment," argues Angela Davis. "But prisons do not disappear problems, they disappear human beings. And the practice of disappearing vast numbers of people from poor, immigrant, and racially marginalized communities has literally become big business" (Davis 1998a).

At present, people of color account for more than 70 percent of America's prison population, with Latinos representing nearly 20 percent and blacks accounting for more than 50 percent. As of 2004, there were more than 1 million black people confined to prison. That represents 1 out of every 35 men; if you split that in half, it constitutes 1 out of every 17. Now, if you remove the very old and very young, this number drops to 1 in 10, and if you include those on parole or probation, the number is 1 in 4; for those in their 20s, it is just 1 in 3. In America, the "land of the free," black males have a more than 30 percent chance of doing time at some point in their lives. When compared to Latinos, who hover around 16 percent (1 in 6), and whites at about 4 percent (1 in 24), it becomes clear that the effects of the prison industrial complex are especially egregious to/disproportionately felt by the black community. Although formal Jim Crow ended with the efforts of activists and organizers throughout the 1960s, the existence of the prison industrial complex (PIC) represents a twenty-first-century manifestation of Jim Crow (Alexander 2010) that entails disenfranchisement, family dislocation, virtual enslavement, and forced confinement (Mauer 2001; Miller 1997).

The web that defines the prison industrial complex connects the political and economic interests of America's elite: laws; zealous prosecutors; the legislative, judicial, and executive branches at the local, state, and federal levels; the media; transnational corporations; schools; churches; the police; and virtually every other American institution, as well as the ideologies/rhetorics of racism, fear, crime and punishment. All of these components work together to maintain the world's largest prison system.

> The prison industrial complex has thus created a vicious cycle of punishment which only further impoverishes those whose impoverishment is supposedly "solved" by imprisonment. Therefore, as the emphasis of government policy shifts from social welfare to crime control [and because "criminality and deviance are racialized"], racism sinks more deeply into the economic and ideological structures of U.S. society . . . The emergence of a U.S. prison industrial complex within a context of cascading conservatism marks a new historical moment, whose dangers are unprecedented. (Davis 1998a)

Moreover, "its uncontrollable growth ought to rattle a national consciousness now complacent at the thought of a permanent prison class" (Davis 1995, p. 260). These institutions and ideologies not only hold a dialectical relationship with one another in the growth and maintenance of the prison industrial complex, they possess various interests in sustaining a system of mass incarceration, despite the fact that a majority of people suffer under these conditions. From Ronald Reagan's Willie Horton ad to the media's exploitation of black female bodies in its depiction of the welfare problem, from *Cops* to discourses of hip-hop, it is crucial to understand the interconnectedness of crime, fear, race, and the media (Andrews 2001c; Davis 2003).

It is equally important to understand how fearmongering, processes of criminalization, and the rise of the prison state affect youth of color who, despite their supposed immaturity, innocence, and redemptive qualities, have borne the brunt of the "tough on crime movement." Vijay Prashad, in *Keeping up with the Dow Joneses*, notes that 56 percent of juveniles detained in correction facilities are black; an additional 21 percent are Latino. In total, half of the 700,000 youth in juvenile prison were confined following a first offense, usually a drug or property crime. Barry Feld describes this space as "one of violence, predator behavior, and punitive incarceration" (Quoted in Prashad 2003, p. 90). Prashad concurs, although arguing that the violence, dehumanization, and inequalities that define life for a juvenile on lockdown mirror the experiences of those confined to America's ghettos and barrios. "For the kids who are not in jail, the working class neighborhoods that they live in have become a vast prison," notes Prashad. "We've already encountered the ordinances against gangs, but we should also bear in mind the curfews in place" and the other forms of surveillance and violence that youth of color are subjected to on a daily basis (Prashad 2003, p. 90). Explaining why he is a prison abolitionist, Brooks Berndt notes that both standards of justice and the societal perception of criminals (those who may not be redeemable or need severe state intervention—state-sanctioned discipline—in order to be rehabilitated) are clearly racialized.

> Black youth, for example, were 15% of the youth population in Illinois in 1999. However, in Illinois that year, black youth were 50% of the youth arrested, 55.2% of the youth in detention, and 85.5% of the youth sent directly to adult court.
>
> For drug crimes in Illinois, black youth were 59% of the youth arrested and 88% of the youth sentenced to prison. This contrasts sharply with national statistics suggesting that white youth in Illinois would likely use and sell drugs at the same or a higher rate than black youth. (Berndt 2003)

According to a report authored by Xochitl Bervera, of Families and Friends of Louisiana's Incarcerated Children, similar inequalities have defined the experiences of youth of color there. Although only a third of the state's population, young black men account for 78 percent of those youth confined to Louisiana's correction facilities. "For Black youth, this is not the time of

rising expectation—these are the days of mass incarceration, ugly demonization, and full-out criminalization" ("Katrina, Jena, and the Whole Damn
System" 2007). The increased power of the state has resulted in the daily
harassment of youth of color, manifest not just in incarceration rates, but in
police brutality, profiling by officers, prosecutorial abuse and societal condemnation (Parenti 2001; Mauer 2001; "Katrina, Jena, and the Whole Damn
System" 2007).

In 1994, President Bill Clinton signed the Gun-Free Schools Act, which
mandated a one-year expulsion for bringing weapons to school. This legislation, which has resulted in the suspension and expulsion of children across
the nation for such "crimes" as bringing a toy gun, plastic knife, or nail file to
school, has contributed to the widespread policing of youth of color (Verdugo
2002). In 1998, when black students accounted for 17.1 percent of U.S. student populations, they represented 32.1 percent of students suspended for
disciplinary infractions (Johnson 2001, p. 15). Throughout the nation, youth
of color have been increasingly subjected to suspensions and expulsions, while
at the same time their schools have come to seem more and more like prisons
(Verdugo 2002). "A national survey of high school students found that the
number of students reporting the presence of security guards and/or police
officers in schools increased from 54 percent in 1999 to 70 percent in 2003"
(Sullivan 2007, p. 7). According to a study by the Applied Research Center
(Oakland, California), black students have disproportionately endured the
impact of zero-tolerance policies. The study "reported higher than expected
rates of suspension and expulsion for black students in all 15 major American
cities studied" (Skiba 2000, p. 12). With metal detectors, security guards, and
fences being used almost exclusively in schools with more than 50 percent
students of color, the late 1990s saw many of America's schools coming to
resemble its prisons in terms of their efforts to discipline and punish, as well
as the number of youth of color in attendance (Johnson 2001, p. 17).

To understand the racialization of crime (disobedience) and the acceptance of a culture of law and order (disciplinarity, accountability) is to understand both Willie Horton and Ron Artest, zero-tolerance policies in
schools[15] and the NBA's age limit in that all of these things reflect a desire to
control, discipline, and ultimately disarm black bodies. The increasing level of
intolerance for the NBA's youth movement and the calls to institute restrictions is not particular to sports, but rather part of a larger movement evident
in growing prison populations; shrinking social welfare budgets; overzealous
police, prosecutors, and judges ready to throw children into jail; and teachers,
principals, and school administrators increasingly expelling students (of color)
for even the smallest infractions. The mere fact that many states are investing
in prisons and the police rather than schools and education—"in California
the average prison guard now earns $10,000 more than the average school
teacher, and increasingly more than many professors working in the state uni-

versity system"—demonstrates a greater political, economic, and cultural emphasis on disciplinarity and control rather than on education and empowerment (Giroux 2003a, p. 559). The increased focus on law and order and discipline has been disproportionately directed toward youth of color, as is evident in the passage of curfew, loitering, and truancy laws, "designed not only to keep youth off the streets, but to make it easier to criminalize their behavior" (Giroux 2003a, p. 559). Henry Giroux further notes:

> The National Criminal Justice Commission report claims that while "get tough" policies are likely to be more severe when dealing with children, they are particularly repressive when applied to youth of color, especially as a result of the war on drugs and the more recent eruption of school shootings. Numerous studies have documented that unlike middle-class white youth, minority youth are "more likely to be arrested, referred to court, and placed outside the home when awaiting disposition of these cases. . . . [Moreover all things equal, minority youths face criminal charges more often than white youths for the same offenses. Also, African American youths are charged more often than whites with a felony when the offense could be considered a misdemeanor. . . . Minority youth are also more likely to be waived to adult court, where they will face longer sentences and fewer opportunities for rehabilitative programs" (Donziger, 1996, p. 123). Fed by widespread stereotypical images of black youth as superpredators and black culture as the culture of criminality, minority youth face not only a criminal justice system that increasingly harasses and humiliates them but also a larger society that increasingly undercuts their changes for a living wage, quality jobs, essential services, and decent schools. Within such a context, the possibilities of treating young people of color with respect, dignity, and support vanishes. (Giroux 2003, p. 560)

Of course, the denial of opportunity to play in the NBA straight out of high school, the demonization and humiliation endured by NBA ballers, and the widespread demands for reform and discipline mirror these broader social processes. The logic governing such processes, including the white supremacist orientation, have not surprisingly governed the efforts and demands for an age restriction in the NBA.

HYPOCRISY OR THE CONSISTENCY?

Jermaine O'Neal's denunciation of the proposed age limit focused on the hypocrisy of instituting such a restriction given the societal acceptance of

18-year-olds fighting in Afghanistan and Iraq. Recognizing that many of those fighting to "preserve freedom at home" and spread democracy else-where are youth of color from low socioeconomic communities, O'Neal found Stern's plan troublingly inconsistent. In fact, No Child Left Behind requires public schools to assist the U.S. military in its recruitment efforts by targeting all students above the age of 14, further revealing that age only matters in certain places. "The armed forces believe that children as young 14 should consider a career traveling to far away places, guarding oil pipe lines, and killing people," writes Dave Zirin. "But the NBA commissioner David Stern contends that 18 and 19 year olds may be able to vote, work shifts at Abu Ghraib and watch Sin City, but they have no place in his league" (Zirin 2005).

The call for and successful implementation of an age restriction in the NBA cannot be understood outside the context of the (increasing) hegemonic practice of trying youth of color accused of crime as adults. Like the NBA age limit, in terms of its ideological orientation and obvious effects, the efforts to try teenagers as adults have disproportionately affected communities of color. Beginning in the 1980s, calls for law and order and truth-in-sentencing resulted in an increased effort to not only incarcerate youth, but to try them as adults. By the mid- to late 1990s, 43 states had enacted laws facilitating the transfer of children into the adult criminal justice system, laws that have led to the gradual erosion of the 100-year-old juvenile justice system. Founded on the belief that children, because of their vulnerability and immaturity, are entitled to a range of special protections, the juvenile court was intended to shield youth from the deleterious effects of the adult justice system. However, the 1990s saw a paradigm shift in which age came to represent nothing but a number to prosecutors, the police, and the larger criminal justice system. Currently, all 50 states have laws on the books allowing juveniles to be tried as adults. According to a 2008 report from the Equal Justice Initiative, roughly "2,225 children under the age of 18 are serving life sentences in US. Prisons; almost two-thirds are children of color" (Jung 2008).

Rather than prompting outrage and demands that the system protect youth (a United Nations resolution that called for the abolition of life sentences for children resulted in a 185–1 vote, with the U.S. being the sole country who voted against the resolution), laws allowing juveniles to be tried as adults have received overwhelming support. For example, in California, 62 percent of voters supported Proposition 21, the Juvenile Crime Initiative, in 2000. Proposition 21 provided prosecutors, rather than juvenile court judges, the power to transfer cases to the adult court and, additionally, mandated adult trials for all juveniles older than 14 accused of murder or specified sex offenses. Pete Wilson, then governor and principle sponsor of the initiative, noted that "Proposition 21 will help win the war on youth crime, concentrating the Juvenile System's resources at rehabilitating nonviolent offenders but at the same time sending the clear message that there will be serious consequences for violent criminal acts" ("Proposition 21 Approved by California Voters" 2000).

In reality, Proposition 21, as with much of the "reform" in the criminal justice system, was not part of a universal "war on youth crime," but one against youth of color. Proposition 21 exacerbated the existing inequity in the treatment of youth of color within the criminal justice system. One study of the juvenile justice system in California from 1996 to 1999 found that minority youth, particularly African Americans and Latinos, consistently received more severe sentences than white youth and that they were more likely than white youth convicted of the same offenses to be committed to state institutions. Relative to their populations and levels of arrest for every offense category, minority youth offenders are much more likely than their white counterparts to be sentenced to incarceration in California Youth Authority facilities. Although studies reveal proportionality in terms of youth committing violent offenses in California, Latino youth are 2.3 times as likely, African American youth 6.7 times as likely, and Asian/other youth 1.3 times as likely as their white peers to be arrested for a violent offense ("Proposition 21 Approved by California Voters" 2000).

Across the nation, similar trends are evident. A 2000 Justice Department report found that "black youth are forty-eight percent more likely than whites to be sentenced to juvenile prison for drug offenses" (Quoted in Giroux 2003a, p. 138). A civil rights report from the Youth Law Center and the National Council on Crime and Delinquency, a criminal justice think tank, noted that black youth are six times more likely to be locked up than their white peers, even when both are without prior records and charged with similar crimes. Citing racial bias in every step of the juvenile justice process, the study concluded that efforts to charge youth as adults have a disproportionate effect on youth of color who are more likely than white youth who commit comparable crimes to be arrested, prosecuted, tried as adults, convicted, sentenced, and sent to adult prison. Of youth with no prior records arrested for violent crimes—including murder, rape, and robbery—137 out of every 100,000 blacks were incarcerated, compared with 15 out of every 100,000 whites (Mauer 2001).

Neither the increasingly prevalent practice of incarcerating youth of color, nor the support garnered for legislation to try youth as adults, can be understood outside of contemporary racial politics. The efforts to try youth within the adult criminal justice system have been tantamount to waging a war against youth of color, replicating long-standing efforts to police youth of color via surveillance, the control of their movements, and other forms of discipline and punishment.

At first glance, the support for and successful implementation of an age limit in the NBA, coupled with a simultaneous effort to try certain youth offenders (of color) as adults, appears to reflect a societal contradiction. Is the desire to protect and deny early entry into the NBA draft for those under the age of 20, in a society that increasingly treats age as irrelevant within its criminal justice system, an example of hypocrisy? Although a superficial examination might lead to such a conclusion, the NBA's age restriction and the efforts by the criminal justice system to increasingly try youth (of color) as adults share in common the fact that both seek to discipline deviant bodies, control those who transgress societal boundaries, and ultimately, punish young bodies of color. This is clear throughout the media discourse, given the rhetorical devices used [Heisler even refers to basketball court as "juvenile court" (Heisler 2005)] and the ubiquitous calls made for enforced disciplinarity of those corrupting and dangerous bodies in the NBA.

King and Springwood rightly connect these practices in their discussion of the spectacles of college sports: "Disciplinary mechanisms such as these limits on celebration and nineteenth-century prohibitions of Native American dance are informed by a fear that these racial others have impulses that demand a civilizing force in order to rein them in" (King and Springwood 2005, p. 201). Furthermore, Michel Foucault describes the dialectic between state institutionalized power and calls/demands for discipline in the following way: "Discipline produces subjected and practiced, 'docile' bodies. Discipline increases the force of the body (in economic terms of utility) and diminished these same forces of the body (in political terms of obedience)" (Quoted in Parenti 2001, p 136). The widespread efforts to discipline bodies rendered deviant and pathological by society are not simply rhetorical exercises, nor are they limited to societal debates. They facilitate, rationalize, and inspire the increased policing and profiling of black youth evident in both the policies of the NBA and the rise of the prison industrial complex. Reflective of and facilitated by the logic driving the discourse concerning the NBA, one that denies the paradoxes and slippages that define contemporary American life, the United States has moved:

> From punishing the body directly to controlling subjectivity, the soul, or the human interior, thus making bodies docile, and useful. Foucault focuses on the spectacular public torture rituals of the ancient regime, in which the sovereign re-established power by taking revenge upon the body of the criminal. Foucault then traces the ruptures that lead to modern "disciplinary" forms of control; forms of power that act upon human consciousness and subjectivity, and thus enlist us in the useful, productive regulation of ourselves and our bodies. Thus he writes, "[t]he soul is the effect and instru-

ment of a political anatomy: the soul is the prison of the body . . ."
Here deviance is no longer seen as individual sickness, as it was
during rehabilitation's heyday. Rather the surplus classes are simply
bad people made so by a corrosive "culture of poverty" or, in the
Charles Murray school of thought, by crypto-racist, "genetic" deficiencies. Thus the "super-predators"—as neoconservative criminol-
ogist Di Julio calls the impoverished pre-teens of America—and
"lost generations" of the ghetto cannot be saved, or used efficiently.
And so we see state power once again manifest in an increasingly
violent, ritualized politics of terror. As "actuarial" crime control
becomes the name of the criminological, whole communities
became the target of social control. (Parenti 1999, pp. 136–137)

Foucault, like Parenti, King, and Springwood would have understood the proposed age restriction within the NBA to be part of a larger body of "disciplinary power" and league sanctions that allow "the hegemonic forces within a
society to manipulate the bodies of its citizens and to exact from them greater
degrees of social control, so that imperial discipline might supersede punishment" (King and Springwood 2005, p. 201; Foucault 1979). Whether considering the criminal justice system or the NBA, we must understand laws and
rules as efforts to impose discipline prior to punishment.

Moreover, with efforts to both try youth (of color) as adults and push
youth (of color) to college instead of the NBA, the white paternal body (the
NBA commissioner and the state) seeks to enact policies that discipline and
punish, not only thwarting deviant behavior, but also working toward the
protection of white interests (accommodating/ placating their needs and
fears). Additionally, each racialized project works through dominant discourses that construct cultural deficiencies (dysfunctional values; culture of
poverty; single parents) as the basis for deviant behavior, whether through a
lack of emphasis on education that leads black youth to select the immediate
gratification of NBA riches over a college experience, or a culture of poverty
that fosters criminality and poor decision-making (Quoted in McCann 2004,
p. 147).

Writing about the ways in which American racial discourses imagine the
relationship between sport and the black family, C.L. Cole furthers our
understanding of both the proposed age debate and the criminalization of
youth of color.

In the absence of the modern family unit, sport is positioned as "the
most powerful, and by far the most economical system for keeping
human brings human." Sport is narrated as indispensable to community production and well-being as the figure of the coach is

made to represent the sanctioned nurturing father-child relationship depicted as unavailable in the African American community.
The "breakdown of the black family" and its pathologization
through the figures of the matriarch and the absent inseminating
black male are historical mechanism for displacing the social, economic, and political forces that shape the lives of the urban poor.
(Cole 2001a, p. 69)

The fact that a majority of NBA players, particularly those who were early
entrants, supposedly emanate from single-mother homes in America's poorest
communities is a point emphasized by much of the public commentary to
explain both the necessity for early entry and the problems experienced by
early entrants. Whether because of financial need, poor parenting, or a culture
of immediate gratification, efforts to join the league are pathologized and
linked to a culture of poverty, mandating intervention by the noble white
parent who ultimately knows what is good for young black males: discipline
and punishment. The realization that the NBA was indeed black in wake of
the Palace Brawl led to increased calls for disciplinarity in the form of zero-
tolerance policies and other forms of control. The restriction on entry and the
efforts to oversee who could enter the league and under what conditions
became increasing necessary once it became clear that racial transcendence
was an illusion and thus the league was indeed inhabited by (undisciplined)
black kids.

CONCLUSION

In this racism, the Other's identity warrants its very annihilation
because it is seen as impure, evil, and inferior. Moreover, whiteness
represents itself as a universal marker for being civilized and in
doing so posits the other within the language of pathology, fear,
madness, and degeneration. (Giroux 1994, p. 75)

In an interview in *Sports Illustrated*, Phil Jackson denounced the NBA for its
increased emphasis on young talent, offering insight into long-standing discursive articulations about the necessity and burden of whiteness controlling
savage, child-like blackness. "It doesn't matter whether they can play or not.
We've ended up becoming a service for growth. Now it's, 'We'll hire a chef,
we'll hire laundry, we'll hire Mom, we'll hire somebody to come and live
with them so that they can perform at this level'" (Quoted in Thompson
2004, p. 84).

David Stern's successful institutionalization of an age limit for those under 19 did provide an answer to Phil Jackson and others calling for a blockade to the NBA's youth movement. That wasn't it's true motive. It did, however, seek to appease fans by projecting its purported image problem onto the backs, bodies, and cornrows of young straight-out-of-high-school ballers. While the sports world celebrates the youth movement in golf, soccer, and tennis, with media pundits describing Freddy Adu and Michelle Wie, among others, as "prodigies" and geniuses (Kroft 2005), the opposite seems to be the case in the world of basketball.

Today's NBA and its surrounding media discourse often construct an authentic blackness (through youth) as menacing and threatening, a pollutant that requires surveillance and control, whether through increased rules or more prisons. More specifically, although dominant popular culture continues to imagine young black inner-city youth as authentic embodiments of blackness, the proposed rule change and corresponding backlash against the infusion of hip-hop into the league reflect desires to police "authentic blackness." The efforts to push out those young black men who have jumped straight into the league reflect desires not only to regulate bodies in the league (and send symbolic message to fans), but to push future players into conditions and spaces that will ultimately produce a controllable, yet still commodifiable, version of today's hip-hop baller.

Imani Perry argues that the backlash against hip-hop is nothing new or unique, but rather reflects the white supremacist practice (and logic) that renders black bodies and cultural styles as menacing and dangerous. "The isolation of black bodies as the culprits for widespread multiracial social ills is not unique to rap. It has occurred in critiques of the welfare state, in the demonization of early release programs from prison, in the image of drug trafficking, and in the symbols of sexist aggression" (Perry 2005, p. 27). Likewise, the ways of mediating and controlling these dangerous bodies find similar logic within both the world of sports and the criminal justice system. The age restriction is the NBA's version of various juvenile crime initiatives, working to constrain and control those who have secured a piece of the American Dream through basketball; more importantly, it utilizes the same racist logic that identifies black bodies as threats to white hegemony and pleasure, conceiving of rules, state power, and surveillance as proper and necessary methods to save both the game and community. To protect the streets, thus, necessitates more police and prisons, while protecting the NBA mandates increased rules and regulations of bodies, whether by minimizing trash talking; establishing regulations regarding shoe and sock color, headwear, and lengths of shorts; airbrushing away player tattoos; or, in the end, restricting who can and cannot enter the league.

The racial implications here are as undeniable as is the policy's intent to control black male bodies and aesthetics. Scoffing at those who denounced Jermaine O'Neal for his comments about race and the proposed age limit, Scoop Jackson wrote, "Let's define stupid. Stupid is Barry Bonds still working out with Greg Anderson. Stupid is Mike Tyson still fighting for a title shot. Stupid is the Lakers not getting at least one All-Star in return for Shaq. An NBA superstar finding something racially motivated when the principals involved are specifically of one race? That's not stupid. That's conscious" (Jackson 2005). Can you imagine a media commentator or citizen of the 1960s denouncing a civil rights worker or even a black laborer for questioning the racial implications of Jim Crow? Just as then, the motivations of profit and appeasing white customers define the age debate; yet, at its core is an agenda to control black male bodies while maintaining profits derived from the exploitation of those same bodies. More than in fears and repressed dreams, the black body exists in the courtroom and on the court as "a site of spectacle, its blackness" existing as "a potential measure of evil, and menace," necessitating containment and control (Denzin, 2001, p. 7), although the problems facing the NBA, have little to do with high-school ballers entering the league. Stern's ultimate denial of entry into the professional ranks follows long-standing white supremacist logic that "focuses, organizes, and translates blackness into commodifiable representations and desires that [can] be packaged and marketed across the landscape of American popular culture" or otherwise confines it outside the dominant racial order (Gray 1995, pp. 68 and 165). In other words, black bodies will continue to be called into the NBA in the name of global capitalism, while those same bodies will also continue being subjected to the rules and logic that emanate from white supremacy. Likewise, their brothers and sisters, again in the name of global capitalism, will be subjected to the surveillance and walls that define the criminal justice system, which also finds its legitimacy and ideological basis in the rules and logic that emanate from white supremacy.

The panics, the discourse of crisis, the calls for policing and disciplinarity, and ultimately, the age restriction represent a paradox in that the exploitation and control of black male bodies is both aided and undermined by the same policy. In 2003, Rasheed Wallace offered the following assessment of the NBA and its quest to get younger and younger: "In my opinion, they just want to draft niggers who are dumb and dumber—straight out of high school. That's what they're drafting all these high school cats, because they come into the league and they don't know better. . . . It's as if we're going to shut up, sign for the money, and do what they tell us" (Quoted in O'Connor 2005, p. 117). Reflecting a common response to inserting race into the discussion, especially from black players David Stern called him "a very confused and enraged young man who doesn't understand what he's saying" (Quoted in

O'Connor 2005, p. 117). Similarly, Jason McIntyre, who questioned whether "Wallace thinks at all," wrote about the absurdity of his argument: "Professional sports and exploitation is a misnomer. How can it exist when 75 percent or more of the NBA is making over a million dollars a year? And those who aren't in the upper crust salary-wise aren't appearing in any league promotions anytime soon. How are they being exploited?" (McIntyre 2003). What is lost here is not only the exploitation of college athletes, which Ian O'Connor describes as a "system . . . set up so that the only way a high school or college player could profit from his or her skill was to take gifts from people who weren't allowed to give them" (O'Connor 2005, p. 171), but the ways in which the NBA seeks to control physically, mentally, spiritually, and culturally the bodies, minds, and spirits of black athletes, attempts that are often presented as being part of a benevolent effort to civilize these athletes, both for their own good and that of the community. Noting the racial implications, Representative Steve Cohen described the age restriction as "a vestige of slavery" (Beck 2009). Likewise Mark Anthony Neal illustrates this connection, describing college sports as a plantation of sorts:

> The connection I make is to the plantation: How do you keep these kids on it? When they come, people ask, do they have the right to be here? When they go, it becomes, why aren't they grateful? When you set up a system in that context and then come up on the other side with multimillion dollar contracts, that adds to the sense of these kids being undeserving, ungrateful, unwilling to be educated. That creates an ongoing judgment on the performance of blackness." (Quoted in Araton 2005, p. 96)

Thinking about the rhetorical connections between plantations/slavery and sports does not end with an analysis of the ways in which black athletes become unpaid commodities within the college sporting industry, but it is illustrative given the emphasis of college as a place for "seasoning," a place where black men are broken down, disciplined, and re-created as productive, rule-abiding cogs in the professional sports machine. "The ultimate effect of the conveyor belt is not much to deliver young black athletes to the pros, but to deliver them with the correct mentality," writes William Rhoden. "They learn not to rock the boat, to get along, they learn by inference about the benevolent superiority of the white man and enter into a tacit agreement to let the system operate without comment. By the time they reach the NBA, the NFL, or the MLB, black athletes have put themselves on an intellectual self-check: you don't even have to guard them, they'll miss the shot" (2006, p. 194). The demands for an age restriction thus function along multiple lines, not only pointing to the economic needs of college and professional sports,

4

"No Bling Allowed"[1]

The NBA's Dress Code and the Politics of New Racism

The NBA does have an image problem. It's made too many head-lines in recent years for violence, drug abuse and sexual misconduct. TV ratings for its championship finals, which once topped the World Series, now trail both the NFL and baseball. How the play-ers behave is more important than what they wear. But there's no harm in asking them to be more presentable for the impressionable youngsters who mimic their style, and for the affluent audience the league and its sponsors covet. One of the NBA's youngest players, LeBron James of Cleveland, had it right: "This is a job, and we want to have fun, but it's a job and we should look like we're going to work. ("Drugs, Bling and Tears")

For too long the NBA has courted the hip-hop street culture. That side of town's idea of "business casual" is ridiculously expensive sneakers, game jerseys and baggy shorts down to the knees. It is a culture that the NBA has been selling ever since the smooth era of Michael Jordan and Magic Johnson. Now all of a sudden it's time to change course. Why? Because Stern fears things have gone too far. That they have become too street for the average NBA cus-tomer. (Borges 2005)

The Palace of Auburn Hills eventually was the site of last Novem-ber's epic brawl that has come to symbolize the gulf between play-ers and fans and, in Stern's case, made a conservative reformer out of a New York liberal. (Araton 2005)

127

INTRODUCTION

Not only unsuccessful on the court, the 2004 Olympic basketball team caused a significant amount of embarrassment for the NBA in the wake of its efforts to conceal blackness from the league. Once a source of national pride, given the long-standing dominance of American basketball over the world, the 2004 installment was more of a nightmare than a dream team. In anticipation of the Olympics, members of the basketball team attended a dinner in their honor at a fancy Belgrade restaurant. While other guests, including members of the Serbian National Team, wore matching sport coats and dressed "appropriately," Allen Iverson, Carmelo Anthony, LeBron James, and other members of the American team showed up in sweat suits, oversized jeans and shirts, large platinum chains, and, of course, diamond earrings. Larry Brown, the team's coach and the often-celebrated benevolent white father figure of the NBA, was appalled, coming close to sending several players back to the hotel. Mike Wise, in the *Washington Post*, described the incident as transformative for the NBA's league officials.

> Word of the fashion faux pas eventually made its way to the office of NBA Commissioner David Stern in New York, where concern was already on the rise about how some players were dressing and, more broadly, how the game's appeal was slipping. The NBA had tried mightily to fuse its product with hip-hop culture, viewing its young players and their street fashion sense as a way to connect with a new generation of fans in the post-Michael Jordan era. But that wasn't happening. Indeed, Stern and some of his closest advisers concluded, they might be driving fans away from the sport. (2005)

Shortly after the debacle in Athens, and less than two months after the Brawl at Auburn Hills, the NBA sent a clear message about the future of hip-hop and those bodies who embraced/reflected/signified this "ghettocentric imagination" (Watkins 1998). Shortly after he was traded to the Sacramento Kings, the NBA formally admonished Cutino Mobely for conducting interviews wearing a skullcap. Despite the fact that he donned headgear baring the insignia of the NBA, and that he was considered "a good guy," Mobely's fashion choice impelled league officials to remind its players about professionalism and the league's new unofficial policy concerning hip-hop. In this instance, with the NBA's simultaneous commodification and demonization of hip-hop and its black male signifiers now visible, the efforts to police the league's new black aesthetic illustrated the complex and contradictory roles played by aesthetics, cultural values, and bodies that are constructed as both fashionable (desirable and cool) and suspect (dangerous).

In the aftermath of the Palace Brawl, the failures of the 2004 Olympic basketball squad, the sexual assault allegations against Kobe Bryant, the arrest of Allen Iverson, and the overall perception that the NBA was being overrun by "criminals," gangstas, and those otherwise prone to "bad behavior" (Philips 2005), David Stern announced plans for a league-wide dress code in October 2005. Concluding that ad hoc policies and team-directed rules[2] were incompatible with their efforts to "rehabilitate the image of a sport beset with bad behavior," the league instituted a dress code policy that governed players all while sending a message to fans and corporate partners. While denying that the dress code was part of the NBA's master plan to appease white corporate interests and those of Red State, Middle America—or even that it was directed toward the NBA's black, hip-hop baller—Stern repeatedly acknowledged the connection between the dress code and the Palace Brawl. "It was a low point in the perception of our league. . . . Our players are really good guys who deserve more respect than that" ("Code Makes Debut to Mixed Reactions Across League"). In other words, the dress code represented an effort to counteract the negative publicity that had plagued the NBA during recent years by restricting assumed signifiers of blackness.

The 2003–2005 seasons were a low point for the NBA in a number of ways. The NBA experienced a sharp decline in fan support. Television ratings for the 2005 finals that pitted the Detroit Pistons against the San Antonio Spurs were down 30 percent from the previous year; its ratings for that year were last among the big three American sports (baseball and football). During this time, the NBA office and its teams saw an increased number of complaints from corporate (Lorenz and Murray 2005). Public opinion polls ranked basketball players as the least liked professional athletes among all the major American sports leagues. In response to falling ratings, dissipating corporate support, a deluge of publication relation's nightmares, and unrelenting criticism from much of the media, the NBA hired Matthew Dowd, a Texas strategist who had previously worked with George W. Bush on his reelection campaign. Having successfully helped Bush find immense support within Middle America, Dowd was brought in "to help" Stern "figure out how to bring the good 'ol white folks back to the stands" (Abramson 2005). As a result, the league office directed players to be more accessible to fans in terms of signing autographs, while also participating in "season-ticket-holder events." It also initiated the NBA Cares project, a global public service outreach initiative, which was intended to facilitate the donation of $100 million to charity, provide 1 million hours of community service donated by the players themselves, and build 100 youth centers by 2010. Both these initiatives represented the NBA's effort "to look a little less gangsta and more genteel" (Eligon 2005). It was part of a public relations strategy that emphasized the quality and good nature of NBA players.

Yet, the dress code would come to embody the NBA's most systematic effort to alter its image in order to bring back its red state fans and corporate sponsors. According to an NBA official, the dress code was designed to appease corporate anxieties about the league's hip-hop image and protect the NBA's economic (television contracts) future. "If you speak to 100 people on the street and most of them think our players are the worst of the lot in pro sports, there's a problem" (Quoted in Wise 2005). Notwithstanding these anonymous explanations, or the media's praise for the proposed dress code as a necessary challenge to the hip-hop/gangsta invasion of the NBA, David Stern and others consistently downplayed these motivations, instead focusing on the dress code as a means for combating the unfair demonization of its players. It was the NBA's attempt to help its (black) players be seen in a proper light. In a letter outlining the dress code, which was sent to players, coaches, and owners,[3] the NBA provided the following rationale for the policy:

> We know that you share our desire that NBA players be appreciated not only for their extraordinary talent and hard work, but also for their accessibility to fans, their community service, and their professionalism—both on and off the court. To that end, we will be instituting, effective with the start of the regular season, a league-wide "minimum" dress code. Many teams have previously issued their own dress codes, designed to demonstrate the seriousness with which their players take the representation of their teams, their cities, and our league; our new dress code is not intended to affect any of those that are more formal than what is set forth below in the new NBA dress code. ("NBA Dress Code: Dress Code Policy" 2005)

The policy required that players "wear business casual attire" whenever participating in league events or team functions, or when conducting "team or league business," defined as any "activity conducted on behalf of the team or the league during which the player is seen by or interacts with fans, business partners, members of the public, the media, or other third parties." The policy restricted the clothing choices of players engaged in a number of tasks: participating in league events, promotional appearances, or media interviews; sitting on the bench when not in uniform; leaving or arriving at the stadium, and, potentially, riding on team buses or planes. In addition to regulating dress in particular (public and private) spaces, the policy also stipulated what constituted "business attire," noting that to be in compliance players must wear dress shirts and/or sweaters, dress slacks, dress jeans or khakis, socks, and either dress shoes "or presentable shoes." Beyond the above description of business attire, it required that those players sitting on the bench out of uniform wear jackets along with the other mandated clothing options.[4] It additionally offered a series of prohibitions, thereby clarifying its intent, against the following: sleeveless shirts, shorts, jerseys, T-shirts, sports apparel (unless event appropriate), chains, pendants, medallions, sunglasses (indoors), and headphones (unless on team plane, bus or in the locker room). The breadth and specificity of the regulation is clear: "Headgear of any kind while sitting on the bench or in the stands at a game, during media interviews, or during a team or league event or appearance (unless appropriate for the event or appearance, team-identified, and approved by the team) is to be excluded" ("NBA Dress Code: Dress Code Policy" 2005). Although Stern and others inside the NBA spoke of the policy in universal terms, as an effort to highlight the professionalism and "goodness" of all its players, numerous players saw the policy as something else: a racist assault on hip-hop and yet another instance of the NBA attacking its young black male stars.

WHAT'S RACISM GOT TO DO WITH IT: PLAYER OPPOSITION AND A CULTURE OF DENIAL

Shortly after the NBA announced its plans to implement a dress code policy, players began to voice their concerns through the media. Although not uniform in their opposition, with some players (LeBron James, Antonio Davis, and Shaquille O'Neal) even expressing support for Stern's decision, many denounced the impending dress code. Unconcerned with how the media would position their comments as further evidence of the "problems" in today's NBA, numerous players voiced their concerns about and opposition to this measure. Before discussing the specific reactions of several players, it is important to understand the heterogeneity of player response, especially in light of those efforts to paint the players as sharing a single opinion about the policy; as being immature and irrational children, race-card playing punks so blinded by their allegiance to hip-hop and a culture of bling that they were unable to see the dress code as an effort to rehabilitate the NBA's image and protect *their* business (Elder 2005; Lynch 2005; McNulty 2005; Page 2005; Pitts 2005; Rorrer 2005).

Although players' opinions ranged from support to complete opposition, what becomes clear through analysis of those expressed opinions is that players generally supported some restrictions, especially those establishing rules against "do-rags," hats, and jeans. However, players were generally uncomfortable with the league mandating suits and ties, even on transcontinental, late-night flights. The players did not uniformly oppose any dress code policy, but they sought a more commonsense approach that considered their concerns. For example, Tim Duncan told the *San Antonio Express News*, "I think it's a load of crap. I don't understand why they would take it to this level. I think it's basically retarded. . . . I don't like the direction they're going, but who am I" ("One Size Fits All" 2005). Raja Bell also questioned the focus on player-corporate relations, arguing, "I understand they're making it out to make us look better to corporate and big business. But we don't really sell to big business. We sell to kids and people who are into the NBA hip-hop world. They may be marketing to the wrong people with this" (Quoted in "NBA Adopts 'Business Casual' Dress Code" 2005). Vince Carter told the *New Jersey Bergen Record*, "I just think people should be able to express themselves. I know they took out the 'do-rag' stuff; I understand that. As far as guys wearing what they want to wear, I am all for that. Who really cares about what they wear from the bus to the locker room" (Quoted in "One Size Fits All" 2005).

Stephen Jackson, who noted his support for a dress code ("I think we should dress up. A lot of guys have gotten sloppy") challenged the racial motivations of the policy: "But as far as chains, I definitely feel that's a racial statement. Almost 100 percent of the guys who are young and black wear big chains so I definitely agree with that at all" (Quoted in "One Size Fits All" 2005). While Tim Duncan called the policy "retarded" and "a load of crap,"[5] Paul Pierce voiced his opposition to the policy because of its targeting of black players and for its efforts to curtail the creativity and individuality that define hip-hop culture. "When I saw the part about chains, hip hop and throwback jerseys, I think that's part of our culture. The NBA is young black males" (Quoted in Brunt 2005). Both Jermaine O'Neal and Allen Iverson also questioned the racial dimensions of the proposal. O'Neal sarcastically asked "What's next, we can't wear our hair in cornrows? You wonder where this is all going. . . . Do we have to change everything about ourselves? The message to us is that we're too urban" (Quoted in Roberts 2005). Likewise, Allen Iverson offered an insightful critique of the policy, a powerful commentary on racism and the widespread criminalization of young black males, noting that "you can put a murderer in a suit and he's still a murderer" (Quoted in "Allen Iverson & The NBA Dress Code"). In countering Stern's claim that a dress code would send a positive message to American youth by reestablishing the NBA as a haven for role models, Iverson noted: "It sends a bad message to kids. If you don't have a suit when you go to schools, is your teacher going to think you're a bad kid because you don't have a suit on" (Quoted in Weiss 2005).

Like Iverson, Marcus Camby, who was referred to as yet another "disgruntled millionaire crybaby," made his opposition clear, describing the dress code as sending a bad message "to our youth." Additionally, he objected to the league's implementation of an unfunded mandate, making clear that he felt it shouldn't happen "unless every NBA player is given an NBA stipend to buy clothes" (Quoted in Elder 2005). To Iverson, Jackson, and O'Neal, the policy was clearly directed at black players as part of an effort to improve the NBA's image by ridding it of the aesthetics of hip-hop and disciplining those who jeopardized its future. These players expressed outrage at the policy because of its demonization of black youth culture. In their estimation, the dress code revealed that unprofessional, sloppy, undesirable, and unacceptable clothing were considered the purview of the aesthetics and styles of black youth culture.

It is not a coincidence that these players, all of whom are often associated with hip-hop, were constructed as the representative voices of player opinion.[6] In fact, throughout the discourse, these four men not only served as representative voices, but also evidence for the irrationality, anger, and lack of common sense by which the me-first hip-hop baller is defined. For example, on hearing these concerns and criticism expressed by several black players, David Stern offered the following assessment of player reaction: "You get a guy half-naked in a locker room and put a microphone in front of him and he'll say anything" (Quoted in "Dress Code Reactions Amuse Stern" 2005). Stern sarcastically proposed a scholarship for those who make less than $8 million per year. Others were equally dismissive, questioning the intelligence and values of those complaining players. Michael Wilbon, in the *Washington Post*, described Camby's "stipend speech" as "the dumbest and most offensive thing uttered in the last five years, surpassing the 'I've got to feed my family speech'"[7] (Wilbon 2005). In the *Northwest Herald*, Joe Stevenson described Camby's comments as offensive, illustrative of the immense problems facing the league and the need for the changes ushered in by David Stern. Responding to Camby, Iverson, Jackson, and others, Stevenson noted, "And players wonder why they are not more beloved by their fans. Maybe if they even pretended to live in our same world, we might care" (Stevenson 2005). Stern, Stevenson, and Wilbon, among others, made clear that NBA players needed to shut up and play because their racial rhetoric and complaints about injustice were growing tiresome.

What is striking about the discourse surrounding the player responses, beyond the erasure of their heterogeneity, is the way in which the media used players' references to race and racism as justification for a dress code. The players' lack of respect for the game, for the fans, and for decency, as evident by their chains, diamonds, do-rags, and saggin' jeans, as well as their incessant "whining" and playing of the race card, all demonstrated the importance of disciplining the NBA player. The dress code was seen as having the potential to assist in a maturation process, changing the league's dismal image. Several sports columnists came to David Stern's aid, refuting accusations of racism. Larry Elder accused the players of "crying racism" without any evidence. Terrence Moore agreed, noting, "Commissioner David Stern didn't become

the league's Bull Connor with his latest edict involving the dress code"
(2005). Although less diplomatic, Jason Whitlock similarly argued that players and their enablers needed to be looking in the mirror, rather than accusing
Stern and the league of racism. In his estimation, such a charge was not only
unfounded but absurd given that the intention of the rule was to help players
by protecting their wallets and rehabilitating their poor image. In a column
that appeared in the *San Diego Union-Tribune*, entitled "Black NBA players
Need to Realize Stern is on Their Side," Whitlock penned a letter to the
NBA's black ballers that celebrated the dress code as a way to take a stance
against hip-hop's presumed grip on the NBA, the black community, and
those black youth enamored with this "prison culture."

> The owners and the commissioner have decided one of the main
> things standing in the way of growth is the negative, thug image
> NBA players have here at home and abroad. Now, if you like, you
> can blame the "racist" American media for this negative image.
> Besides being a cop-out, it won't change the negative image.
>
> Too many young, black professional athletes have too closely
> aligned themselves with the hip-hop culture, which in reality is
> nothing more than prison culture.
>
> Shut up! You know it's the truth. Gun-toting, drug-dealing,
> full-body-tattooed, gang-repping rappers have overrun hip-hop
> music and hip-hop culture and have poisoned just about the whole
> scene.
>
> It's comical to listen to you all call Stern's dress code racist
> when black-owned nightclubs have been enforcing similar dress
> codes (and using metal detectors) for years just to keep the hip-hop
> thugs out. (Whitlock 2005)

The fact that the modes of dress being criminalized are coded as black
further demonstrates the racialized orientation of the dress code. Calling hip-
hop-inspired dress a form of prison culture not only demonizes an entire
industry, but also inscribes it as a visual marker of Otherness and danger, the
sole purpose of which is to disrupt the supposedly balanced, colorblind multiculturalism on which the NBA's decision makers rely.

Noting that "racism and the NBA mix like Mondays and Me," Dave
Golokhov rhetorically denied the racial implications of the dress code, chastising those "radicals," from players to commentators like Scoop Jackson and
Chris Broussard, who seemed intent on "stir[ing] the pot—quite obviously
not the melting pot" (2005). In an attempt at humor and sarcasm, he offered
the following assessment of the dress code: "You see, dress codes have nothing
to do with company representation or company image. It has everything to do

with taking away from black people." To make clear his opposition to such "logic," he went on to question the presumptive argument that the dress code was an attack on black culture, since oversized clothing and diamond necklaces are certainly not culture. Likewise, he concluded that, "David Stern is not saying forget your culture, forget your roots and follow my ways. He's not asking you to convert your religion. He is saying when you come to work or when you are affiliated with the NBA follow the dress code. When you're done for the day, drape yourself in as much velvet as you like" (2005). In other words, the dress code was not based on race, nor was it racist, because it merely asked all players to accept and follow a universally accepted definition of professionalism.

To those players and commentators who wanted to talk about race, who wanted to use the dress code as an excuse to interrogate the racial dynamics of the NBA, much of the media was dismissive, arguing that the code was about professionalism, marketing, and the undesirability of hip-hop/gangsta culture, not race. Operating under a very narrow definition of racism, which denies its existence if a rule or policy does not explicitly single out a particular community, much of the media declared that references to racism were absurd. Joe Bell, in the "NBA's Dress Code is Reasonable," argued that that the mere mention of race "diverts discussion from the real issue," and thus has no place in the public discourse. "It is neither unfair, nor as some have suggested, racist. Every player regardless of color is expected to abide by both the same dress code and both black and white players have objected" (2005). Likewise, Josh Smith described the NBA's dress code as "an acceptable idea," scoffing at claims of racism, while celebrating it as a smart decision that would enhance the image of the league and its players: "Finally, some people argue that it just is a racist attack on the NBA's 'hip-hop culture.' But these rules don't apply just to African American players. They apply to everyone. No group of people has a monopoly on bad taste. Shirts, t-shirts, and sandals are viewed as unprofessional and damaging to the NBA's image" (2005).

Interestingly, Smith failed to mention that the new dress code prohibited chains, headphones, jerseys, and headgear, all things associated with hip-hop and a new black aesthetic. Instead, he and others focused on the ban of shirts and sandals, presumably racially universal clothing styles. Additionally, they concluded that because Steve Nash, Dirk Nowitski, and even Jason Williams[8] had to comply with the code, race had nothing to do with the discussion (Collins 2004; Gray 2005; Leonard 2006). Despite commentators' arguments to the contrary, the intent of the policy, although never explicit, and its context make it clear that the proposed dress code was about regulating the behavior and style of the black baller.

Numerous commentators also denied the racial implications of the rule by noting that many members of the African American community not only

supported the dress code, but held negative views about hip-hop and its influence on the NBA. Dr. Jessica Johnson argued that the dress code was not
about race but dollars and cents, that the league's "thuggish image" and marriage to hip-hop had "alienated older white and black fans and caused concern among corporate sponsors" (2005). Accordingly, black people supported
the implementation of the dress code, so race and racism were irrelevant. As
many of the people who criticized hip-hop were African American, such
opposition was obviously colorblind. Dave Golokhov, with "Does the NBA
Dress Code Attack Black Players," followed suit, stating, "Plenty of Black
people (particularly parents) scoff at this type of style as much as I do." Mir-
roring denials of racism that claim "some of my best friends are black,"
Golokhov and others (Smith 2005; see Cervantes 2005; Rutland 2005)
argued that because African Americans, including Charles Barkley, Magic
Johnson, Michael Wilbon, and numerous unnamed parents and fans, supported the dress code, their support had nothing to do with race. In fact,
within a number of commentaries offered by white sports writers, the opinions and analysis of Charles Barkley, John Thompson, LeBron James, and
other African Americans were cited as evidence of their own colorblindness
and that of the dress code, David Stern, and the NBA.

Bonilla-Silva, noting some common rhetorical phrases, describes the
process of racial denial in the following way: "Phrases such as 'I am not a
racist' or 'some of my best friends are black' have become standard fare of
post–Civil Rights racial discourse. They act as discursive buffers before or
after someone states something that is or could be interpreted as racist"
(2003, p. 57). Similarly, Allan Johnson reflects on the ways in which dominant discourses and practices seek to "deny and minimize" the importance of
racism, and by so doing, legitimizes the status quo and the privileges derived
through hegemony (Johnson 2006, pp. 108–109). "When women and people
of color are accused of 'whining,' for example, they're essentially being told
that whatever they have to deal with isn't that bad and they should 'just get
on with it.'" He writes further that, "when you deny the reality of oppression,
you can also deny the reality of privilege that underlies it, which is just what it
takes to get off the hook" (Johnson 2006, p. 109). Throughout the media discourse, commentators minimized, dismissed, and ridiculed critics (particularly
players) for inserting race where it did not belong. In citing African American
support for the dress code, the universal nature of the dress code, and the fact
that the code was designed to "help" black players, the discourse invoked
dominant rhetorical devices to deny the significance of race.

Another mode of denial came with a focus on the broader racial context
of the NBA, contending that accusations of racism reflected a lack of knowledge and understanding of the equity and diversity of the NBA, especially in
comparison to other sports leagues and broader society. "When I hear players

say that a dress code is racist and anti-hip-hop, I take it with more than a grain of salt. For more than 15 years the NBA has had sports' best record in terms of hiring practices in front offices, from team presidents to general managers to head coaches to senior administrators and regular professionals," wrote Richard Lapchick in "NBA Players Should Dress Up." Citing findings by the University of Central Florida's Institute for Diversity and Ethics in Sport, an institute that he himself directs and which had given the NBA an "A" for racial-hiring practices, Lapchick denied the significance of either race or racism, arrogantly lecturing the players about their ignorance in relation to the dress code: "This decision was not about race or culture. It was about professionalism in the workplace. It just so happens that the NBA's workplaces are basketball arenas" (2005). In reducing racism to an individual action (because David Stern has pushed for racial equity in hiring, how could this policy be race-based?), a zero-sum binary, and defining it as an issue of access and diversity, Lapchick reflects a hegemonic understanding of racism. Using this logic, because the cabinets of the Bill Clinton and George W. Bush administrations were more "diverse" than those of their predecessors, policy-based discussions of racism (in terms of welfare, prisons, education, etc.) are unnecessary. Just as when the Virginia's House of Delegates passed a bill, which "target[ed] those who wear baggy, sagging pants or low riding pants that reveal underwear in a 'lewd or indecent manner,'" race mattered in that commonsense ideas about blackness guided the discussion about the legislation and the positive and negative reaction to its proposal (Bellantoni 2005; Chery 2005).

Beyond the deployment of hegemonic understandings of race, the denials of racism reflect long-standing practices of white supremacy. Much of the discourse painted those who invoked racism as stupid, irrational, and, of course, angry. William Rhoden, in *Forty Million Dollar Slaves*, describes this discursive practice in the following way: "This is a problem with black athletes, the notion that they should be grateful that they've earned, that they should come hat in hand in gratitude for the money and power that they themselves generate" (2006, p. 189). In other words, the virulent reaction to the few players who publicly spoke out against the dress code—and the overarching argument that athletes should accept the dress code because, without the NBA, none of them would have fame, fortune, and privilege—rearticulated hegemonic ideas of black masculinity that imply that, without basketball, these whining ballers would likely be in jail or unemployed. More to the point, many reacted to those protests against the dress code with a simple reminder: players, particularly those who want to talk about race, should shut up and play; they should do what they're told and, if they don't like the dress code or don't want to follow it, they can find a different job, although they'd be hard pressed to find another that would pay them millions of dollars for

playing a "kid's game." For example, Jerry Sloan, in response to their complaints, reminded players of their options: "If you don't like this business you
can always go work somewhere else" (Buckley 2005). Likewise, Josh Smith
instructed players that they should be grateful and not complain, offering the
following assessment of the dress code: "Let him quit his cushy lifestyle and
get a job at McDonald's flipping hamburgers. Then I might listen to him
when he complains about his uniform" (2005). Not to be out-done, Terrence
Moore used his column to give "some advice" to those players unwilling to
"shed the thug look" in spite of both Stern's policy and the needs of the game,
fans, and those who put money in the players' pockets: "Just dress up and shut
up. Either that, or find another job that will pay you millions with your desire
to do your best Flavor Flav routine" (2005). What is revealing both here and
throughout the discourse is the argument that black NBA stars should not
only shut up and play, but be grateful for anything and everything "given" to
them; that without the NBA, its owners, David Stern, and most importantly,
the fans, they would be working some minimum wage job. The deployment
of racialized stereotypes that form this discursive shadow works in concert
not only with the media praise for the dress code, but the ubiquitous calls for
black athletes to just shut up, be grateful, and entertain. The widespread trope
of black athletes as ungrateful, out-of-touch, whining, spoiled, and otherwise
unemployable thugs (criminals) does not merely operate within media and
fan discourse, but infects player identity formation as well. "America loves
their Black entertainers when they behave properly and stay in their place,"
writes Todd Boyd. "When the players realize their value, their significance to
the game, and try to capitalize on this, they are held in the highest contempt"
(Boyd 2000, p. 65). Rhoden notes further: "This is a crucial problem with
black athletes, the notion that they should be grateful for the things .that
they've rightfully earned, that they should come hat-in-hand in gratitude for
the money and power that they themselves generate. It's this sense of gratitude and subservience . . ." (2006, p. 189).

In 1995, the owners locked out NBA players in the hopes of securing a
collective bargaining agreement that better served their financial desires.
Kenneth Shropshire describes this NBA lockout and "the dominant public
reaction" in distinctly racialized terms. He argues that the public opposition
to the players emphasized that they "should be grateful for what you have"
(Shropshire 2000, p. 83). Ultimately, the success of the owners in curtailing, if
not eliminating, the power of the union and negotiating a deal that solidified
their own control and bolstered the financial interests of both themselves and
(white) agents, reflected the racial politics of the NBA and its broader history.
"The NBA is a very black league, so we must be careful of the message we
send" (John Salley quoted in Keteyian, et al. 1997, p. 80). To Salley, the ves-
tiges of "1970s racial perceptions," of a drug-infested, thug league, were diffi-

cult to erase, particularly for its white corporate supporters and white fan-base. The media coverage and fan reactions during the lockout merely extended and perpetuated this racial animosity. Receiving salaries averaging more than $600,000 (Keteyian et al. 1997, p. 68), and being led by black lawyers, players were easily cast as "ungrateful, greedy" punks. Armen Keteyian, Harvey Araton, and Martin Dardris describe the racial context and animus that defined the 1995 lockout:

> Sadly he [Salley] may have been right, judging by the media's response to the summer of labor strife. After at least acknowledging baseball and hockey players had the right to fight for their best deal, many sports journalists more or less rolled their eyes and advised the basketball players to be happy with whatever they got. Stern was held up as the sport's shining knight. Jordan, as if he needed the money, was cast as a greedy infidel. One national sports commentator referred on television to Jordan's involvement as the "equivalent of a drive-by shooting." (1997, pp. 80–81)

Not only did the lockout reveal the racial double standards within American sports culture, and the powerful role race plays within its dominant discourse, it also provides an important historic backdrop for understanding the recent racialized culture wars within the NBA. It reveals the historic presence of a "shut up and play" and "shut up and be grateful" mentality, because "without US—the NBA, its white fans and white corporations—you would be dead or in jail" sentiment. This commonplace attitude is not simply a populist reaction to the exorbitant amounts of money paid to contemporary athletes, but reflects a racial (racist) ideology that expects African Americans to serve and entertain whites (Lott 1995; Lhamon 1997). It additionally elucidates the belief that black males are incapable (intellectually; morally) of doing anything other than playing sports and rapping and, therefore, should be grateful to the NBA for affording them the opportunity to make millions of dollars, despite their own personal, cultural, and communal flaws. In return, these players needed to be compliant.

Connecting the demonization of black athletes as ungrateful to the absence of sustained protest from today's black athletes, William Rhoden argues that high school and college sports nurture black athletes who arrive in the professional ranks: "with the correct mentality: They learn not to rock the boat, to get along, they learn by inference about the benevolent superiority of the white man and enter into a tacit agreement to let the system operate without comment. By the time they reach the NBA, the NFL, or the MLB, black athletes have put themselves on an intellectual self-check: you don't even have to guard them, they'll miss the shot" (Rhoden 2006, p. 194). So, the limited public opposition from NBA players, the absence of a collective response, is neither surprising nor indicative of support for the dress code, but rather reflective of the power of this trope and the overall efforts of the NBA conglomerate (including its media partners) to facilitate disciplinarity in its black players. It is evidence for Rhoden's point regarding the power of a "conveyor belt," which "dulls racial consciousness," (Rhoden 2006, p. 177), "breeds complacency, not militancy," (Rhoden 2006, p. 183) "fosters complacency" (Rhoden 2006, p. 177), and "introduces them to a world of few African Americans" (Rhoden 2006, p. 193). It is reflected not only in the silence about the dress code maintained by some and the public support voiced by others, but in the extensive backlash experienced by those who challenged and/or refused to be grateful for a dress code. The demonization of Allen Iverson, Stephen Jackson, and Marcus Camby as ungrateful, out-of-control hip-hop ballers (as angry and black and therefore unable to function as the desired racially transcendent players)— and the construction of David Stern as their benevolent white father working tirelessly to protect their interests— demonstrate the dialectics between the dress code and race.

THE DRESS CODE: SMART BUSINESS OR INSUFFICIENT CHANGE?

Amid denials of racism and the demonization of those who inserted race into the discussion, two prominent arguments emerged: (1) One theme focused on the dress code being a smart decision, a corrective measure intended to counteract the negative publicity associated with the league and its players, thereby reinvigorating its relationship with corporate/middle (white) America. Given the Palace Brawl, the Kobe nontrial, the arrests of a number of players, the public "feud between Shaq and Kobe," the NBA's lockout, and a host of other incidents that highlighted the blackness of the league within the white imagination, the NBA needed to "reassure the Gated Community Crowd" (Perace 2005). Reebok Chairman Paul Fireman elucidates the context for the dress code in clear terms: "There's a perception by some that NBA players have a diminished quality of characters just because they look different: tattoos, cornrows, do-rags. What the commissioner is trying to do is find an answer for that" (Quoted in "NBA Attempts to Dress Up its Image" 2005). As such, Matt Bonner, then the player representative for the Toronto Raptors, concluded that the dress code simply represented a smart business decision prompted by the negativity surrounding the NBA: "We have the worst image rating out there of all the sports, and I think anything we can do to improve that is good. The dress code's a start" (Quoted in Feschuk 2005). Thus, it had nothing to do with race or racism and everything to do with the NBA being a smart business (Kerridge 2005; Lapchick 2005; McWhorter 2005; Schlussel 2005; Weiss 2005). (2) A second prominent argument that emerged was that, although the dress code was a good start, it would ultimately be insufficient for reversing the downward course of the NBA. Simply changing the NBA baller's attire would not dramatically improve the quality or character of the NBA "product," nor would it transform fan opinions about the league and its thug players. In other words, the problems facing the league, those resulting from the presence of corrupting and dangerous black bodies, could not be solved with a mere makeover. A clothing makeover would not be enough to reverse the blackness of the league.

SMART BUSINESS

Upon learning about the NBA's proposed dress code, Phil Jackson, then head coach of the Los Angeles Lakers, voiced his support for the policy because it would curb the influence of hip-hop, a cultural intrusion that, in his estimation, alienates fans. "To the majority of these young men, the rap stars, hip-hop guys, are really like heroes or colleagues," he noted. "And it's not the same audience. Our audience is corporate businessmen and businesswomen and kids. So it's a different audience that you're dealing with and these players should be aware of it" (Quoted in Murray and Lorenz 2005). Jackson, however, saw the dress code as not simply an accommodation to those market forces, but an outgrowth of the players' failures to respect the traditions and values of the NBA's fans and its corporate partners: "I think we've noticed a number of situations in the playoffs, when the full attention is on the NBA, when it reaches its pinnacle and you have a player step to the podium wearing a do-rag and sunglasses . . . and it sends out a message . . . of prison garb and thuggery" (Quoted in Lorenz and Murray 2005). Jackson was not alone in linking the NBA's hip-hop style to prison culture, with others describing the rule as a war against the invasion of the cultural values and aesthetics of the ghetto, gangstas, punks, the street, children, inmates, and criminals (Hans; 2005; Hutchinson 2005; Jayne 2005; Johnson 2005; Robinson 2005; Taylor 2005; Will 2005; Wise 2005; Whitlock 2005). An editorial in the *Michigan Daily*, playing on long-standing racial fictions that imagine blacks as lazy, concluded that the dress code was about regulating those "multi million dollar athletes too damm lazy to put forth a respectable image" (Kerridge 2005).

Beyond the connection of hip-hop (blackness) to thuggery and criminality, the discourse identified the dress code as a move toward delivering fans nonthreatening and appealing (desirable, consumable) black bodies. Although Jackson and others would deny its racial context and implications, the rationale for winning back (white) fans and corporate sponsorship by controlling the signifiers of hip-hop (blackness) has clear racial meaning. "So Stern has elected to enhance his league's image. He has elected to prevent Allen Iverson from wearing a sideways baseball hat during press conferences," notes Greg Jayne, the sports editor from the *Columbian*. "He has elected to stop Rasheed Wallace from wearing headphones during interviews. He has elected to require proper work attire when players are on the job, just as any self-respecting employer would" (2005). The racial implications are evident in the purported brilliance of the dress code because it: (1) allows the NBA to better control the league's black baller (as signified by Wallace and Iverson); (2) enables the league to rid itself of the polluting influences of hip-hop; and (3) sends a message to the players; and (4) represents an invitation from the NBA to white fans and its corporate sponsors to give the league, with its new look, another chance. Phil Mushnick, a sports commentator for the *New York Post*, surmised that the dress code was a response to players "looking like recruitment officers for the Bloods and Crips, a fact that surely wouldn't prompt fans to shell out hundreds of dollars for tickets and jerseys" (Quoted in Deford 2005). Tony Snow, then host at Fox News, took this opportunity to not only celebrate Stern's efforts, but also demonize and pathologize hip-hop as well. "You see the bling, what is it? It's a reference to a hip-hop culture that glorifies violence and glorifies sexism. And I don't care if it has to do with somebody's roots, but if you're making $15–$20 million a year, perhaps you need to be a role model rather than someone filled with nostalgia of back in the old days then guys were popping each other back in the neighborhood" (Quoted in Zirin 2007d, p. 116). George Will also celebrated the NBA's dress code for not only being a smart business that would bring virtue and civility back into the NBA, but for its effort to decry the influence of a criminal culture that had rendered black NBA ballers indistinguishable from gang members and other criminals:

> The well-named David Stern, commissioner of the NBA, recently decreed a dress code for players. It is politeness to the league's customers who, weary of seeing players dressed in "edgy" hip-hop "street" or "gangsta" styles, want to be able to distinguish the Bucks and Knicks from the Bloods and Crips. Stern also understands that players who wear "in your face" clothes of a kind, and in a manner, that evoke Sing Sing more than Brooks Brothers might be more inclined to fight on the floor and to allow fights to migrate to the stands. (Will 2005)

Citing image consultants, media commentators consistently celebrated the dress code as an economically savvy response to fan outrage and resentment. "Dress creates a first impression," notes Marion Hatley, the CEO of Powerful

Presence, an image-consulting firm in California, in *USA Today*. “For the league, it needs to be controlled. One bad apple can ruin things for the whole league” (Quoted in Dixon 2005). Sandy Moore, an image consultant at Image Talk in Portland, Oregon, agreed, emphasizing that hip-hop and family-friendly entertainment had proven to be incompatible, as evidenced by the declining popularity of the league within American families. “The fact that the NBA is family entertainment makes it incumbent on players to address that audience” (Quoted in Dixon 2005). Amid a racialized culture war, which purportedly led to declining interest in the league and, thus, dissipating revenues, players needed to present themselves in an appealing (commodifiable) way to their white fan base; they needed to be less threatening, less noticeably black. They needed to dress in clothes that were seen as race-neutral (white), thus deracializing their bodies and that of the NBA.

The following comments best represent not just the widespread celebration of the NBA's dress code as a policy “that's wiped out the so-called hip-hop element” (“The Answer Grows Up” 2005), but the media's depiction of the code as a necessary method for controlling the NBA's black bodies, thereby returning the league to a time when white fans loved black players. Tim Dahlberg, in “What's Next, Traveling Calls in the NBA,” which appeared on Sportsnews.com, offers the following assessment of the dress code:

> OK, so NBA players can't wear baseball caps or sunglasses while on the team's dime anymore. The baggy jeans are gone, and so are the sneakers that bring the big money for the bling-bling. Wait, cover up the bling-bling, too? Just what is David Stern up to anyway? Why not bring back the two-handed set shot and short shorts while you're at it? Better yet, start calling players for traveling. Soon this may really be your father's NBA. . . . Stern finally declared to the hip-hop culture that helped sell the league that its time has passed: He instituted a dress code. (2005)

To Dahlberg, the dress code was a publicity move, reminding fans and corporate sponsors that the NBA was still their product.

It does send a message. It sends it to a corporate America apprehensive of being involved with a league whose players brawl on one kind of court and are often dragged into another. It sends it to parents who might be a put off by Carmelo Anthony appearing in a video where a man warns that people who snitch to police about drug deals “get a hole in their head.”

Similarly, Hugh Adami praises Stern for trying to minimize the financial backlash by reigning in players “with their hooded sweatshirts, heavy neck metal, lingo and arrogance,” while also reaching out to “the conservative corner of the NBA market" (2005). Scoffing at the insertion of race into the discussion, he celebrates the dress code as a necessary response to player deficiencies and the intrusion of hip-hop. "Quite simply, many NBA fans, and even those on the periphery, have been turned off by too many tatted, mean talking toughs whose musical tastes include tunes that promote murder and misogyny" (Adami 2005). Although the dress code did not represent a panacea, it did make clear to the NBA's (white) fans and its corporate partners that, in the war between hip-hop and mainstream America, between gangsta values and those of red state America, between the new NBA and those who wanted a return to its "glory days" and, ultimately, between the NBA baller and white America, the league and David Stern would no longer be allied with the dysfunctional hip-hop culture that was destroying the NBA.

Michael Wilbon, in his aptly titled column "There's No Dressing up Bad Attitudes," voices his support for the dress code. While hoping the league would clean up its image, Wilbon praised the dress code for making a statement about the unacceptability of a league dominated by "jail culture" and players who "now look like bums on the street" (2005). According to Wilbon,

> The NBA, as it turns out, knows now that people don't want to pay $200 a night to see jail culture. If they can't see Magic and Michael, they want to see people who make the attempt to look something like Magic and Michael. This is why the league went from one extreme to the other, from hip-hop to forging a relationship with Matthew Dowd, chief campaign strategist for Bush-Cheney 2004. It'll be interesting to see whether Commissioner David Stern, who has been carrying a big stick the last 18 months on issues of comportment and image, will back down now that so many players have complained. (2005)

Likewise, Ray McNulty concludes that the dress code was not truly of Stern's doing, but that of fans and corporate interests who had made clear their disgust and outrage about the gangsterization and hip-hopization of the NBA, not simply through public pronouncements and media commentary, but through their watching and buying habits.

> Clearly, somebody told Stern the NBA's urban, hip-hop image was losing its appeal, especially in Middle America, particularly with the white, middle-aged, middle-to-upper-income fans who buy the bulk of the tickets. Somebody—probably a lot of somebodies, from Madison Avenue to Main Street—told him to do something before

these fans turn their backs and the TV ratings dwindle and the corporate dollars disappear. (2005)

A number of commentators went beyond theory and abstraction, arguing that the dress code would facilitate a return to the glory years of Michael Jordan, a man who not only dominated on the court, but whose appearance, professionalism, and demeanor made him one of "the good ones." Moreover, the constant references to Jordan, or the style of Alonzo Mourning, Magic Johnson and others, reaffirmed the hegemonic claim that demanding players wear professional clothing has nothing to do with race. Not only did the above arguments mention players who adhere to a socially defined standard of respectability, but made clear that donning a suit and tie in no way compromised cultural markers of blackness. The necessity for a dress code and the absurdity of accusations of racism were evident in the NBA's own history, given that, throughout the 1980s and 1990s, the black players who were celebrated, praised, and idolized all presented themselves with professionalism and civility.

Christopher John Farley notes that Jordan "understood what the public wanted" and "never left the locker room before slipping into a tasteful suit" (2005). Frank Deford, likewise, laments the transformation from the "impeccable and classy Michael Jordan" to a bunch of gangsters (2005). Michael Wilbon equates the success of the league during the 1980s and 1990s with the players' professional demeanor and clothing choices when he writes that Magic and Jordan "looked so stylish and sophisticated every night that CEOs wanted to buy what they were selling" (2005) and Terrence Moore chastises today's players for "keeping it real, as in keeping it real stupid." Rather than travel the path pioneered by Michael Jordan ("his airness" and "his Armani")—who "took dressing beyond presentable all the way to legendary" and "dress[ed] for success" because he was in to "keeping it classy" (2005)—today's players have chosen a less reputable and respectful path. "The bigger question," asks Wilbon "is whether the rebels outnumber the players who look back at the previous generation of NBA stars, even some holdovers like Shaq and Mourning, and realize the upside, both short term and long, and see how stupid it is to equate dressing up with selling out" (2005).

Yet, even those who expressed nostalgia for the Jordan-era and saw the dress code as a method for re-creating a better time in the NBA questioned its potential effectiveness, given the fundamental cultural pathologies and problems of today's players. Tim Kawakami agrees that the dress code was not simply a response to falling ratings or the Palace Brawl, but part of a larger plan to bring about a return of the Jordan era and thereby attract fans and sponsors back to the game. In his estimation, resurrecting either Michael Jordan or the greatness of the league during the 1980s and 1990s was impossible, yet it was plausible that the demeanor, attitude, and identity of yesteryear could be re-created. Kawakami, however, wonders about the effectiveness of the policy in this regard, noting, "It's silly to believe you can replicate Jordan just by asking his players to dress like him" (2005). Similarly, Mark Starr, while sympathetic to Stern's desire to turn the clock back to the era of "Michael, Magic, and Larry," questions whether a wardrobe change for Allen Iverson or Ron Artest would matter to fans—the quality of the basketball product, and most importantly, the character of the players would remain the same. "Still nobody believes that if you dress Allen Iverson in a suit he'll be mistaken for Michael Jordan. The dress code is simply a modest symbolic gesture to mainstream America. And it's only a small part of a series of more substantive initiatives . . . aimed at getting NBA players to grow up" (2005). To ask this generation of players to grow up is one thing; to ask them to embody a racially transcendent, self-made man is quite another. To re-create Jordan out of gangstas, punks, and hip-hop criminals was, in their minds, an impossible task. Still, it was one worth attempting given the ideological, political, and racial importance of Michael Jordan to the NBA and contemporary racial politics.

The constant references to Jordan elucidate the racial text and context of the dress code. The celebration of a Jordan era is a celebration of the league when he entered into the dominant white imagination as "a black version of a white cultural model, who by his very simulated existence, ensures the submergence and subversion of racial Otherness" (Johnson and Roediger 1997, p. 231). As evident in the debates concerning the dress code, Jordan represents a better moment for the league not simply because of his greatness, his turnaround jump shot, or his gravity defying dunks, but because he offered the public a more marketable and palatable inscriptions of blackness. In the white imagination, he was not a thug, a criminal, or someone to fear, but an "All-American image. . . . Not Norman Rockwell values, but a modern American image. Norman Rockwell values, but a contemporary fair" (David Falk quoted in Andrews 2000, p. 174).

Yet, what was clear to Stern, these commentators, and presumably, the vast majority of fans was that Michael Jordan and the hip-hop baller are incompatible. In order for the NBA to return to its "fantastic era," it would need to purge itself of these pollutants, these cultural cancers, and of its blackness, by which the greatness of MJ and others was being diluted. More significantly, what becomes quite clear through this nostalgia, through the constant references to Jordan and his clothing/identity choices, is that the greatness of Michael Jordan was not simply composed of his accomplishments on the court, but also his constructed identity.

What also becomes clear is that, if the players were either incapable or unwilling to perform these desired identities, to traverse the paths and conform to the standards established by Jordan, it was incumbent on the league to save itself from these ungrateful, prison-loving, gangsta-ballers. Given that the problems rested within a pathological and self-destructive non-Jordan (hip-hop) culture, change would only come about by policing, disciplining, and curtailing the infiltration of criminal attire (Hans; 2005; Hutchinson 2005; Jayne 2005; Johnson 2005; Robinson 2005; Taylor 2005; Will 2005; Wise 2005; Whitlock 2005) into the NBA.

YOU SAY GOOD BUSINESS, I SAY RACISM

Amid the denials of racism and the significance of race, much of the media commentary focused on the dress code as a corrective course for the NBA's identity crisis. It was seen as an attempt to mediate the conflicts and tensions between the league's white fans/corporate partners and its black players. Equally important, these commentaries consistently argued that the dress code represented the NBA's attempt to rid itself of the influence of hip-hop and that it was about professionalism and marketing, not race. However, as we unpack the discursive and rhetorical meanings of "identity crisis" and "professionalism" and focus on the tensions within the league, it should become evident that the dress code was only one part of a broader effort to unblacken the NBA. It was an attempt to discipline and punish those players who attempted to assert their blackness in the faces "of those good ole' fans" who demanded a "cleaner" and "less-ghetto" product (Abramson 2005). "Underlying this dramatic tension is another white anxiety—also implied in the Stern quote—about the lack of civility that Black men (freshly out of the ghetto) are tempted to exhibit when they suddenly become rich and famous" wrote Glen Hughes on the NASSS listserve. "(This is the joke driving the Barkley Right Guard 'uncivilized' ad from awhile back.) Teaching Black men how to behave—how to dress, speak respectfully, and generally assume a humble affect—is a paternalistic task for management, for the league, for white people who know better. It's the basic plot of *Any Given Sunday* and, in some ways, *Jerry McGuire*" (2005).

In chronicling the history of race and commodification, the dialectics of race, gender, imperialism, and modernity, Anne McClintock offers an insightful discussion of discourses about civilization and hygiene, and the "uncertain boundaries of class, gender, and race identity" (1995, p. 211). She claims that access to and concern with cleanliness and hygiene, amplified through commodity culture, represented a clear break between the civilized and the uncivilized, the desired and the undesirable, the citizen and the Oth-ered subject. "Soap offered the promise of spiritual salvation and regeneration through commodity consumption, a regime of domestic hygiene that could

restore the threatened potency of the imperial body politic and the race"
(1995, p. 211). The dress code functions in similar ways, serving as a civilizing
mechanism, a tool for regeneration, by which, once and for all, "they" would
either be cleaned up or excluded from the NBA all together. Stacey Lorenz
and Rod Murray aptly describe the intent of the rule, and the basis for its
widespread support, as fundamentally racist. "By getting rid of bandanas,
sideways ball caps, and gold chains, the NBA hopes to rehabilitate its image
among its mainly white fans and advertisers who feel uncomfortable with the
league's embrace of street fashion and urban black style," write Lorenz and
Murray. "Rather than defiant black males in unsettling gangster gear, the
NBA wants to display more deferential players who conform to the cultural
standards of corporate and Middle America. Historically, this is the type of
black athlete that has been viewed most favorably by whites" (2005). The
dress code is clearly directed at black players, specifically those black players
who embrace the signifiers of blackness that scare and alienate white fans and
corporate supporters. An editorial in the *Windsor Star* similarly argues that
the racial implications and basis for the dress code are quite clear given that
the policy targets hip-hop, a style and aesthetic associated with the league's
black players. More significantly, the editorial suggests that, despite arguments that the dress code will enhance the image of the league's often-dispar-
aged black players, it will actually have the opposite effect:

> A dress code specifically designed to clean up young black players
> so they're not mistaken for punks only reinforces the prejudice that
> black men sporting baggy pants and throwback jerseys are just sec-
> onds away from a mugging or other crime. A punk is still a punk is
> a suit. And a decent, law-abiding youth doesn't his abandon [sic]
> values when he dons a do-rag. Just like nobody should judge a book
> by its cover, nobody should judge a basketballer by his bling. ("NBA
> Dress Code 2005," p. A8)

Reflecting these racial ideologies, the discourse repeatedly questioned
whether merely altering clothing would bring fans back to the game, since "a
gangsta in a 3 piece suit is still a gangsta" (Murray and Lorenz 2005). To
these folks, the dress code was a surfaced and incomplete attempt to rid the
league of polluting styles, cultures, and bodies.

NOT ENOUGH: ONCE A GANGSTA, ALWAYS A GANGSTA

Amid the widespread celebration of the dress code as a colorblind demand for
professionalism, a benevolent attempt to win back (red state) fans by ridding

the league of hip-hop, and a necessary effort to discipline the NBA baller, much of the media commentary also questioned whether the dress code would have lasting effects. Although it was needed and motivated by the best intentions, the problems facing the league would ultimately render the dress code impotent. For example, Ron Borges, in "Dress Code Won't Solve the NBA's Woes," argues that Stern is attempting to conceal rather than address the core character and identity problems plaguing the NBA.

> But what he fails to realize that it's not the attire that is the problem. It's the headlines.
>
> Not once can I recall a headline that said: "NBA star arrested for baggy jeans."
>
> Not once can I recall a headline that said: "NBA star sued by girlfriend for wearing hooded sweatshirt."
>
> Not once can I recall a headline that said: "NBA stars leap into stands to attack fashion police."
>
> Not once can I recall a headline that said: "NBA star accused of carrying a concealed cardigan."
>
> The problem has nothing to do with what the players wear, but everything to do with how they think and act. Do you think the fans would have felt any different about Ron Artest if he'd been wearing a three-piece suit when he entered that stands in Detroit last year?
>
> The NBA's stuffed shirts need to understand you can't simply dress up the problems the league is facing. After all, who dressed better than Martha Stewart?
>
> And what happens next if corporate sponsorships don't pick up or season ticket sales fall? Unbraid your braids? Cover your tattoos?
>
> The NBA should worry more about the contents of a man's character and less about the contents of his closet. It's a problem for a sociologist and a psychologist to solve, not a tailor (2005).

According to Borges, the proposed dress code did not address the criminal influences of the league, nor did it deal with the pathological and dysfunctional cultural intrusions into the NBA locker room. Instead, it attempted a makeover, not simply in terms of image, but in an effort to erase from the white public's imagination the destructive cultural influences that are harming the league—it erases the symptoms rather than treating the disease. Borges is not alone in this opinion, with numerous other commentators also questioning the efficacy of a dress code that will not rid the league of its thugs, gangstas, and criminals, but merely seeks to hide them behind a new look.

According to Greg Jayne, the motivations of the league are "goal worthy," but their choosing to polish the league's image has led them to "ignore the shortcomings of the product he [Stern] is selling." To Jayne, the NBA's problem is with its game and its players, the "pushing" and "grabbing" all too commonplace in today's NBA, not with its sideline attire. More to the point, he decries both the league's inability to enforce basic rules of basketball (traveling) and the players' "lack of fundamentals" as significant problems facing the NBA, evident in the persistent failure of American NBA blacks to dominate on a world stage. "Yes, the NBA has an image problem, but it was reflected more in an Olympic loss to Puerto Rico than in anything around Iverson's neck" (Jayne 2005). Dressing like a "thug" and a criminal are "bad enough," but failing to fulfill the most essential obligation of American athletes—dominating the world's competition—necessitates action, requiring changes beyond a dress code. Jayne makes this clear, wondering how the dress code will impact this problem, while acknowledging the dialectic between aesthetics and the bigger deficiencies of the NBA.

Phil Taylor, like Jayne, questions the efficacy of the dress code not because of its racism, but because it won't necessarily meet the goal of bringing back "more conservatives" who aren't likely to spend their time and money on players dressed like people they might cross the street to avoid under different circumstances. To respond to this problem requires more than a wardrobe change; it necessitates disciplining, regulating, and potentially ridding the NBA of those (toxic) black bodies incapable of assimilation as racially transcendent commodities. Phil Taylor writes:

> But if league officials are so concerned with image, they would be better off focusing on behavior instead of appearance. This is the same league that downplayed the significance of its players fathering children out of wedlock at alarming rates, for example. It is a league whose public perception has been soured by the small segment of its players who get involved in drug scrapes, sexual misconduct or dustups outside strip clubs. If the league office wants to avoid alienating fans, there are several problems that need attention more than what Iverson is wearing when he walks through hotel lobbies.
>
> Sure, the league has a right to be concerned with the image its players present to the public, but a man's clothes are not necessarily a reflection of his character. Maybe the NBA ought to trust its fans to realize that. (Taylor 2005)

Daved Benefield, in the *Province*, although sympathizing with Stern's efforts to use the "Queer Eye Guys to teach straight guys how to dress" professionally and respectfully while "still keeping it real," wonders if a dress code would have any impact given the difficulties "black athletes" experience "with the English language" during "interviews" (2005). Mark Starr, while supporting the dress code because "any hint of increased professionalism should bolster the league's image somewhat," questions whether a public relations move would be enough to save the league from the immense problems plaguing its future:

> But it doesn't address a growing conviction among longtime fans that have watched NBA all-star aggregates get their butts kicked at the Olympics and world championships, the NBA no longer has game. Or at least the same game that America once loved. Instead of teaching its players to don a sports jacket, the league might be better served by schooling them in once-upon-a time fundamentals like a bounce pass or how to hit a 10–foot jump shot. (Starr 2005)

Playing on the long-standing racial discourse where black ballers are imagined as selfish, street, and lacking fundamentals, Starr imagines a time in which the NBA's greatness stemmed from the prominence of textbook, team-oriented, and, presumably, Jim-Crowed basketball. The NBA's current configuration has betrayed that history by emphasizing flash and individual play.

To Starr, Borges, and others, whether he is donning hip-hop gear or a Brooks Brother Suit, a thug is still a thug. The celebration of the NBA's dress code and those questions as to whether it would make a difference given the league's blackness reflect the hegemonic ideologies that suggest "these innately physical males (black athletes) would be misbehaving" without sports—without the interventions and disciplinary oversight of white coaches, fans, and owners (Andrews 2000, p. 182). For many, the dress code represents a desired intervention, a moment of oversight and disciplinarity, that might save the game and, in so doing, save black athletes from themselves. For others, however, the pathological and destructive realities of blackness meant that either the dress code had no chance of reforming the unredeemable and unreformable, or it was merely a first step in the laborious task of taking out the NBA's trash. Described as a band-aid public relations stunt that would be ineffective in addressing the problems of "character, ethics, and integrity," much of the discourse concluded that a dress code would not impact the fundamental problems facing the NBA; you could take the NBA player out of the ghetto clothing, but you could not take the ghetto out of the NBA player. Interestingly, the other problems purportedly plaguing the NBA—excessive physical play, selfishness, the absence of team ball, criminal behavior, and the thug mentality of its players—are also associated with blackness and, particularly, with the NBA's black ballers.

RACISM: TAKE 2

Franz Fanon argues that, in the history of American racial discourse and praxis, "criminal" and "deviant" have been conceived as equivalent to "black" within the white imagination (Fanon 1992, p. 166). Although there are a handful of counter examples—Sidney Poitier, O.J. Simpson in the 1970s and 80s, Michael Jordan, Kobe Bryant in the 1990s, Tiger Woods before December 2009—those desired black athletes are imagined in relationship to a stereotypical image of "black masculinity as threatening, irresponsible, and hypersexual" (McDonald 2001, pp. 154–155). The signs of deviance, cultural pathology, and danger are all inscribed onto bodies, mandating control and surveillance, whether through castration, lynching, incarceration, or the regulation of bodily movement and appearance. "The inscribed body serves as its own discursive action set that can be read—if the body remains agent or subject—or written on—if the body becomes Otherized or object," notes Ronald Jackson in *Scripting the Black Masculine Body.* "The racially encoded inscription of the Black body, especially during lynching, represents a referred boundary between Blacks and Whites, a prohibition that annuls any possibility of the Black body becoming subject" (Jackson 2006, p. 18).

Writing specifically about the 1980s, as well as the broader issues of media and the criminalization of black men, Herman Gray argues that the black body continues to mobilize consent for law and order discourses and demands for regulation, surveillance, and control. "Television represented and thereby constructed the public sphere as the site of an increasing but necessary regulation and surveillance that depended on race, even though it was overtly expressed as moral panic and political disputes over immigration, welfare, and crime" (Gray 2005, p. 23). He further argues that:

> In the media discourse of regulation (where fear and menace are the key touchstones of a society seen as out of control), the black male body operates symbolically to signify the erosion of morality and threats to manhood. . . . In television news, national political ad campaigns, and Hollywood cinema, while the physical body of black women has often been present, her subjectivity has not (especially as the primary subject of narrative cinema). In the discourse of regulation, the black body has more often than not functioned symbolically to signal the erosion of family, the deleterious consequence of single-parent households, and the purported threat to a patriarchal moral order. (Gray 2005, pp. 23–24)

The skepticism about and celebration of the dress code underscore the historic ambivalence and contradiction surrounding black bodies within the

United States. Although integral to the success and economic viability of the U.S. politic, blackness has long been imagined as incongruent with the U.S. democratic project. David Theo Goldberg makes the link between race and state formation, as it relates to cultural projects of citizenship, quite clear:

> The drive to exclude is not antithetical to modernity but constitutive of it. Domination and exploitation assume new forms in modernity and postmodernity, not in contrast to an increasingly expressed commitment to "liberty, equality, and fraternity" as well as to cultural preservation but as basic to the realization of such ideas for those espousing the commitment. Moreover, the self-conception of "modern man" [professional man—my addition] as free, productive, acquisitive, and literate is not delimiting of racisms' expressions but a framework for them. It forms the measure by which racialized groups are modern and deserving of incorporation, or premodern and to be excluded from the body politic. (Goldberg 1993, pp. 108–109; quoted in Rodriguez 2006, p. 67)

Similarly, Dylan Rodriguez, whose work on prisons underscores the ways in which racialized bodies are included and excluded from the polity at the physical, cultural, and social levels, notes that "regimes of 'rational' discipline, moral correction, and 'progressive' (rehabilitative) incarceration are, in this sense, invited, institutionalized, and reproduced through the abstracted figure of the (potentially) wayward white (male) subject, the categorical 'human,' whose body and soul require incorporation into the eminent domain of the modernist historical telos" (Rodriguez 2006, p. 67). Sports scholars have argued that within the media a disproportionate attention is paid to the alleged discretions of black athletes (Ferber 2007; King and Springwood 2001). According to Katz, "media coverage seems to increase when black males are alleged perpetrators" (2006, p. 139). Sporting discourses, even among the hypercommodification and celebrity afforded to contemporary black athletes, thus, becomes the space in which dominant discourses about pathological and abhorrent black bodies are circulated, legitimized, and articulated. The dress code not only normalizes whiteness while simultaneously demonizing and criminalizing the abject black body, it also reveals who is desirable, who has the potential to be included in both the NBA and the national polity.

Moreover, its supporters fail to see the ways in which race overdetermines the position and signified meaning of today's NBA players. Daved Benefield interestingly (and ironically, given his other points) elucidates the proposal's explicit racism and, consequently, its limited usefulness given the varied meanings of whiteness and blackness used/employed in and around contemporary NBA culture:

Does the so-called hip-hop street wear that many athletes "chill in" after games scare fans when you see these millionaire players emerging from the secured player parking lot in their Range Rovers, and Bentleys?

Why is it Justin Timberlake can wear the gear and be considered the hip" boy next door?

But Allen Iverson wearing the same clothes may carjack you?

What kind of suit would make Ben Wallace seem as non-threatening as Al Roker?

David Stern has never got on an elevator in a suit and tie and watched a lady shift her pursue from one side to the other

Did she hear the hip hop playing in my Ipod? Sometimes I want to scream, "I don't want what's in your ratty knock-off Prada purse!" . . .

Look, David, I know you want the fans to love your players and the league.

But the fans have to be able to judge a book by something more than its cover. Unfortunately we are still in full court press by something that goes deeper than baggy clothes and hats turned backward. (2005)

In other words, the NBA dress code, David Stern, and the policy's many supporters erased, ignored, or simply failed to see the broader realities surrounding the players, the fans, the league, the teams, and sports culture in general. These are realities to which Malcolm X once rhetorically referred when he asked a black liberal arts professor, "Do you know what white racists call black Ph.D's? 'Nigger!'" (Malcolm X and Haley 1987, p. 290) and by which jokes such as "What do you call a black man in a coat and tie? Defendant" have become widely uttered and accepted. Because of the intransigence and centrality of white supremacy, the wardrobe change would not alter the meaning or position of black bodies either inside or outside America's arenas. It is the blackness and the meaning of blackness within the white imagination that overdetermines the image and reception of the NBA player so that altering clothing, especially in a post-Artest, would have little success in changing racial signifiers.

THE POLITICS OF RESPECTABILITY AND SELF-HELP

Alongside the sports media's calls for disciplining the black baller, and in so doing, returning the NBA to red state America, black leaders, including Al Sharpton and Jesse Jackson, former and current NBA players, including

Charles Barkley, Magic Johnson and LeBron James, and a number of black sports columnists all endorsed the NBA ban on bling. While offering a spectrum of reasons for their support, many of those black voices focused on the connection between the dress code and black respectability.

Terrence Moore celebrates the dress code because it sends a message not only to those in the NBA, whom he sees as almost hopeless, but to the millions of youth who emulate and idolize NBA stars. Noting that few high school players will make a career out of basketball, he celebrates the dress code as a lesson to black youth about professionalism and respectability. Such an education, he argues, is both necessary and infrequent, given the types of models available and the problems that exist within the black community. Ignoring the realities of racism, Moore instead focuses on the cultural and aesthetic lessons taught by today's NBA ballers who, like single mothers, have contributed to the dysfunctionality and criminality of the black community. Their choice "is the reason why a slew of them don't find real jobs after they fill out applications while wearing their versions of a jumbo cap turned sideways over a do-rag, a throwback jersey and enough bling bling to make the sun look for shades" (2005). Jessica Johnson concurs, noting that NBA players should adhere to and respect the dress code because the "majority of young black males . . . will have regular nine-to-fives," and "you can't wear a do-rag and heavy jewelry in the workplace" (2005). In other words, the dress code isn't simply about protecting NBA players, or better appealing to the white masses, but preparing black youth for successful futures in the workplace.

Although deploying similarly racialized language as their white counterparts, echoing the emphasis on discipline, professionalism, cultivating desirable role models, and purging the NBA of its negative influences (i.e., hip-hop), the discursive context and meaning of black media commentators, players, and leaders is entirely different. To fully understand the public support for Sharpton and Magic Johnson, John Thompson, and Michael Wilbon, Jesse Jackson and J.A. Adande, along with numerous others, is to examine the dress code within a larger history of "black respectability."

Mark Anthony Neal describes the importance of calls for black respectability within a broader history of the black freedom struggle during his discussion of the immense silence among African Americans in Durham, North Carolina, in the wake of the Duke Lacrosse case. Neal writes the following:

> But such demonization takes on another dynamic within the world of "black respectability." It was clear from the outset, that for some black communities in Durham, NC, the young woman was not a "respectable" victim. The concept of "black respectability" can be traced back to the struggles of African-Americans in the early days

following "emancipation," where so many of the former enslaved sought to find common ground—a shared humanity—with the white citizenry. The strategy behind "black respectability"—exemplified in the late 19th and early 20th century by the Black Women's Club Movement and the New Negro Movement and much later by the NAACP *Image* Awards—was to put the "best face" of the race forward. Accordingly, it also meant that less savory black bodies and antics had to be reduced to so-called "dirty laundry"—never to see the light of day. It was a logical strategy, given the pervasiveness of white supremacy in the century after emancipation and the desire of many black leaders to fight racism, disenfranchisement and racist violence on moral grounds. But it also created the context where those black bodies and practices that were not thought to be respectable enough were jettisoned to the margins of black life and culture. (Neal 2006)

Writing about *Coach Carter* and *Friday Night Lights*, Jared Sexton highlights the powerful ways in which a "politics of respectability" functions within the broader history of white supremacy:

We have long struggled with the variously nourished mythological insistence, noted above, that the salvation of black communities lies with black men's arrival within (and not their struggle against) dominant formations of gender and sexuality and their concomitant ascension to (and not their struggle against) the middle and upper classes. *Coach Carter* participates in this cinematic "politics of respectability" with a vengeance (White 2001). Not only for the ways it systematically writes off the mass of black youth—its target audience (?) and its putative filmic antagonist—as the statistical casualties of everyday urban life, or even its unconcealed recasting of (even the most recent) progressive political movements as viciously personal aggrandizement. Not only for its single-minded meditation on the welfare of men and boys, its clear relegation of female gender to the margins of narrative movement, sequestered to spectacle and sideshow, the forced choice of support/obstruction for male fortunes. But also, a point that might be made more often in related discussions, because it sells a lie even to those young black men whose identifications it solicits in such evident bad faith. For the uniformed black male—here in the sports arena, other times among the troops (*Antwone Fisher*) or behind the "thin blue line" (*Training Day*)—the game is rigged and not least (nor most) for himself. (Sexton 2006, p. 115)

The extensive support for the dress code expressed by civil rights leaders, black sports columnists, and both former and current players does not indicate a raceless debate but, in fact, demonstrates the centrality and salience of race to the discussion. Beyond disciplining the current slew of black players and teaching them to display a modicum of professionalism, this support continues a historically based hyperfocus on respectability, especially among youth and the underclass, as a means for challenging and overcoming the racism of American society. Daniel Howard, a 19-year-old from Brooklyn, who co-directed *Bullets in the Hood: A Bed-Stuy Story*, a documentary that explores gun violence in this New York City community, challenges the ways in which the politics of respectability contributes to a stereotypical vision of black urban youth: "So not only do we have white people stereotyping us but sometimes we have our own Black folks stereotyping us as well. . . . It is like there is a class system, a border between Black professionals and Poor Black people that needs to be broken" (Quoted in Daniels 2007, p. 89). Similarly, Mary Pattilo-McCoy, author of *Black Picket Fences: Privilege and Peril Among the Black Middle Class*, argues that the politics of respectability practiced by the black middle-class reflects their desire to change, reform, and civilize the black poor. "They surely want to change the behavior of the poor, Black people who live there" (Quoted in Daniels 2007, p. 89). Likewise, Cora Daniels concludes that because a politics of respectability builds upon hegemonic notions of the black poor race is salient: "The 'they' in this case are Black professionals moving back to the, well, ghetto. Unfortunately, when the two worlds collide, there ends up being a lot of tsk-tsking going on" (Daniels 2007, p. 89).

Kobena Mercer describes this process within popular culture as a "social engineering project," wherein black artists and image producers profess a responsibility to challenge stereotypical representations of blackness through positive imagemaking. Cornel West, like Mercer, questions both the desirability and plausibility of a social engineering project, arguing, "The social engineering argument claims that since any form of representation is constructed—i.e., selective in light of broader aims—Black representation (especially given the difficulty of Blacks gaining access to positions of power to produce any Black imagery) should offer positive images, thereby countering racist stereotypes. The hidden assumption of both arguments is that we have unmediated access to what the 'real Black community' is and what 'positive images' are" (West 1999, p. 130). West and Mercer rightly perceive these representational movements as futile challenges to racism, which put the burden on African Americans to perform and embody a respectable and desirable image of blackness to be consumed by the public. Writing about the controversy that surrounded the release of Spike Lee's *School Daze* in the 1980s, S. Craig Watkins describes it as a generational battle wherein "an

older generation of" African Americans "committed to the notion of promoting respectable—or in other words, bourgeois—images of blackness"
(Watkins 1998, p. 118) denounce, demonize, and police any and all representations that aren't "respectable," that don't elevate the community by challenging stereotypes. To further illustrate the presence of a politics of
respectability, it is important to reflect on a few examples and their broader
context of meaning.

Jason Whitlock describes the dress code as yet another example of how
David Stern "is quite possibly the best friend the black American-profes-
sional athlete has ever had in the commissioner's seat of a sports league"
(2005). As the archetypal benevolent white father figure, "a classic, New
York-liberal do-gooder," David Stern is not only protecting the league's
financial future, but that of his players—his children. He, unlike the players,
who Whitlock argues are unable to see the big picture because of their lack
of education and because they have been coddled for too long, recognizes
the implications of a society in which black males are stereotyped as
gangstas. He understands the potential consequences of perpetuating these
racialized representations. With a dress code, and other policy proscrip-
tions, Stern is simply trying to protect the league, a "place where elite, black
American athletes can thrive and earn a nice living" (2005). In his own estimation, and in that of many visible and publicized black voices, Stern's
actions were that of an anti-racist who sought to put the players in a more
positive light. Take Earl Ofari Hutchinson, who argues that Stern's the
dress code are systematically protecting players from the prejudices of fans,
from those who would prejudge them because of their style and clothing.
Clothing profiling is not reserved for inner-city youth harassed by cops, as
any "Rhodes scholar, National Science Medal winner or junior achievement
awardee, could find himself tagged as a gangster simply because of their
dress." He notes further:

> The players that complained they're targets of NBA officials trying
> to spiff them up to please the league's corporate boosters don't have
> a free pass from the negative typecasting that they've generously
> contributed to either. When the final buzzer sounds, and they step
> out into the streets, they can also get the dress profiling treatment.
> There are more than a few cases where pro athletes have been
> spread eagled by police beside their expensive Mercedes, BMW,
> SUV, or Hummer. If the cop stops an NBA player and is not a bas-
> ketball buff all their protests about their name, money and fame
> won't mean much. They're still just another black suspect. . . . It was
> a bum rap, of course, the majority of NBA players are not violent,

criminals, and many quietly and selflessly donate to charities, participate in education programs, perform community service and endow programs at their alma maters. . . . Clothes may not make the man, but they sure make the stereotypes. NBA officials recognized that even if some players don't. (2005)

Yet, Leonard Pitts, in "Is the NBA Dress Code Racist? Who Cares?" not only celebrates the dress code as a challenge to the stereotyping of black youth, but identifies the policy as nonracial:

As for race: Let's grant that for some individuals, all young black men, indeed, all black men, period, are scary looking, regardless of dress. Still, to believe the dress code is racist, you must ignore the fact that the gangsta look is not particularly popular among middle-aged black folk, but is often embraced by young white ones. Point being, this is less racial than generational.

Meaning a generation of young black people choosing a style of dress that connotes criminality and street corner values. And it's childish to say, as Camby did, that, "You shouldn't judge a person from what they wear." Unlike skin tone, unlike nationality, unlike sexual orientation, clothing reflects a conscious choice. (Pitts 2005)

Similarly, John McWhorter links Stern's edict to a broader civil rights struggle that will ultimately hold black people accountable for their own failures and shortcomings. "We did not fight for our freedom to be rebels. We fought for our freedom to be normal," writes McWhorter. "The idea that poverty, violence, and rebellion are the heart of being black is not normal nor is it deep. It is outdated, counterproductive and self-indulgent. The NBA players might even find that wearing jackets on camera enlarges their 'culture' which will add to their repertoire of dress styles. Call it a new kind of multiculturalism—or maybe we can just call it civility" (2005).

The logic here is quite clear: embracing the dress code, and the resulting respectability with which it is associated, isn't merely a response to declining attendance numbers or shrinking corporate sponsorship, it is a means for taking a stance against racist stereotypes and the profiling experienced by black youth. Charles Barkley notes that "If a well dressed white kid and black kid wearing a do-rag and throwback jersey came to me in a job interview, I'd hire the white" kid (Quoted in Stewart 2005).

Not surprisingly, neither Hutchinson nor Barkley, and certainly not Stern, reflect on the ways in which blackness overdetermines the experiences and opportunities of black youth. For example, in 2003, Marianne Bertrand

and Sendhil Mullainathan found that applicants with "white sounding names" were 50 percent more likely to receive a callback after submitting a resume than were those with "black sounding names." In fact, according to their study, whiteness was as much an asset as eight years of work experience, demonstrating that race has a significant impact on one's job future. In their study, "Are Emily and Greg More Employable than Lakisha and Jamal? A Field Experiment on Labor Market Discrimination," the authors conclude, "While one may have expected that improved credentials may alleviate employers' fear that African-American applicants are deficient in some unobservable skills, this is not the case in our data. Discrimination therefore appears to bite twice, making it harder not only for African-Americans to find a job but also to improve their employability" ("Employers' Replies to Racial Names" 2003). Similarly, researchers at the Discrimination Research Center, in their study "Names Make a Difference," identify racial discrimination as a significant obstacle within the contemporary labor force. They sent out 6,200 resumes to temporary employment agencies throughout California, all of which described applicants with similar qualifications, concluding that those with names associated with the Latino and white communities received callbacks more frequently than those presumed to be African American or South Asian/Arab American (called back the least frequently) (Miller 2004).

Another study found that white applicants who had spent time in prison were more likely to receive callbacks than were African Americans without any prison records (Von Zielbauer 2005). Devah Prager and Bruce Western concluded that "black job applicants are only two-thirds as successful as equally qualified Latinos, and little more than half as successful as equally qualified whites" (Quoted in Rose, 2008, p. 80). In fact, according to the work of Praeger, in *Marked: Race, Crime, and Finding Work in an Era of Mass Incarceration* (2009), African Americans who lack any sort of criminal record still are less likely to secure a job than a white man recently release from prison. By focusing on choices and role models, the emphasis on the clothing of NBA stars elides any discussion of the racial realities inside and outside the NBA. Moreover, none of these commentators bother to think about white privilege in this context, about how an NBA baller can wear either a suit or a throwback and, regardless, never be thought of as anything like a middle-class professional, but always and certainly a threatening gangsta. Equally important, the erasure of race here not only speaks to the ways in which the NBA sought to deracialized the league after Artest, but the widespread efforts to explain and justify the experiences of African Americans, whether in the form of white fan resentment/anger or a potential employer choosing a white applicant.

DRESSING FOR THE PART: ROLE MODELS

At the heart of the public debate about the dress code and the future of the NBA was the subject of role models. Regardless of past statements from Charles Barkley ("I am not a role model"; "I am not paid to be a role model"), which illustrate his refusal (just like that of Iverson, Paul Pierce, Jermaine O'Neal) to "accept the race man ideology" and adhere to a politics of respectability (Boyd 1997, p. 33), or the complaints by players about the unfair burden of being labeled a role model (Hill 2005; Murray and Lorenz 2005; Sharp 2005; Thomas 2005; Wise 2005), many inside the discourse concluded that, as role models, NBA stars have a responsibility and obligation to act respectably both on and off the court. Some focused on the universality of this responsibility, but many black commentators focused on the particular responsibility of black NBA players given the dire future facing America's black youth. As a result of countless problems facing the black community and because of the failures of single mothers, the pernicious influence of rap music, and the absence of black fathers, black NBA stars needed to become a frontline defense against the crisis facing black male youth specifically (Williams 2006). Commenting on the demeanor and attitudes of many of today's NBA players, Marques Johnson illustrated the links between the world of the NBA and broader discussions of identity, blackness, and family. "Some of these . . . African-American players today come from single-parent homes," said Johnson, "where there's no strong father figure in the home" (Quoted in Elder 2002).

To understand the impetus behind and desire for an NBA dress code requires an examination of the long-standing discourse concerning the "endangered black male" and the "failed black family." During the 1990s and, to a lesser degree, through the first part of the twenty-first century, "the plight of the black man [has] continued to be an evening news staple, splashed across newspaper headlines, the topic of roundtable debates, films about the hood and talk-radio discussions, and of course shouted in rap lyrics" (Hopkinson and Moore 2006, pp. 24–25). The NBA's dress code is imagined as an intervention against the conditions that have led to more black men being in jail than in college, to the problems facing the NBA and to an "endangered black male future." Such problems are imagined to be the result of individual and communal failures rather than racism, inequality, privilege, or state violence. Consequently, a cultural and aesthetic makeover is seen as a proper intervention. Writing about "racial realists," Michael Brown et al., argue that today's hegemonic racial discourse describes racial inequality and the gaps in achievement and success as manifestations of cultural and communal failures. "As they see it, the problem is the lethargic, incorrigible, and often pathological behavior of people who fail to take responsibility for their own lives" (2003, p. 6). More significantly, "persistent and deep black poverty is attributable to the moral and cultural failure of African Americans, not to discrimination" (Brown et al. 2003, p. 6). Similarly, Robin D.G. Kelly, in *Yo Mama's Disfunctional*, describes the dominant racial discourse in the following way: "The clamor for 'color-blind' social policy not only delegitimizes race-based explanations for inequality but it camouflages the racist underpinnings of much contemporary political discourse. Welfare mothers, criminals, and the underclass are the most recent code words for black people." Kelley continues, "Each of these terms," like hip-hop, or even NBA baller, "reflects a growing 'common sense' that black behavior—whether we call it nihilism, a culture of poverty," hip-hop, "or plain irresponsibility—is the source of urban poverty and violence and a drain on our national resources" (Kelley 1997, p. 91). "The solution to poverty, therefore, doesn't lie in a collective movement. It lies in the will and discipline of the individual people who dedicate themselves to living moral lives, striving to improve their circumstances, and providing greater opportunities for children (Mark Goldblatt quoted in Rose 2008, p. 61). In this context, the styles, aesthetics, and values embraced by today's players are not only contributing to the league's decline, but facilitating pathological behavior from those who look up to NBA stars, contributing to criminality, poverty, and joblessness. In these terms, the NBA dress code is reimagined as a policy intervention, as a critical response to an endangered black male.

Orlando Patterson, in an effort to insert "cultural attributes" into the discussion of "the tragic disconnection of millions of black youths from the American mainstream," recycles the long-standing "culture of poverty" thesis in his *New York Times* op-ed, "A Poverty of the Mind." Patterson focuses on the cultural values that have contributed to educational deficiencies and joblessness. "I call this the Dionysian trap for young black men. The important thing to note about the subculture that ensnares them is that it is not disconnected from the mainstream culture," writes Patterson. "To the contrary, it has powerful support from some of America's largest corporations. Hip-hop, professional basketball and homeboy fashions are as American as cherry pie. Young white Americans are very much into these things, but selectively; they know when it is time to turn off Fifty Cent and get out the SAT prep book" (Patterson 2006). Although not discounting the potential importance of history, or even the context produced by America's political economy, Patterson sees cultural attributes as key to understanding the crisis facing Black America. Arguing that a "cool pose culture" contributes to the exceedingly high drop-out rates among black students, Patterson describes this culture in the following ways: "For these young men, it was almost like a drug, hanging out on the street after school, shopping and dressing sharply, sexual conquests, party drugs, hip-hop music and culture, the fact that almost all the superstar athletes and a great many of the nation's best entertainers were black" (Patterson 2006). Patterson isn't alone in mixing culture of poverty theories with the scapegoating of hip-hop for the problems of the black community. "The arm-slinging, hand-hurling gestures of rap performers have made their way into many young blacks' casual gesticulations, becoming integral to their self-expression," argues John McWhorter. "The problem with such speech and mannerism is that they make potential employers wary of young black men and can impede a young black's ability to interact comfortably with co-workers and customers." He challenges the supporters of hip-hop to highlight how and "just where, exactly, the civil rights–era blacks might have gone wrong in lacking a hip-hop revolution. They created the world of equality, striving, and success I live and thrive in. Hip-hop creates nothing" (Quoted in Rose 2008, p. 83). In other words, the culture of hip-hop and the interrelated corporate trends in basketball have led black males to see schooling, disciplinarity, and development of the skills and values necessary for success as antithetical to blackness. In the end it leads to and produces nothing.

Reflecting on the "flurry of studies" and commentaries about "the plight of black men," Cora Daniels concludes that Orlando Patterson "decided to veer" the conversation in a different direction, away from policy, history, or even racism, arguing that despite his "sloppy grouping of hip-hop, basketball, and homebody" and his "leaning on a crutch that hip-hop equals evil," that the cultural acceptance and promotion of a ghetto mentality, culture, and style were systematically leaving behind a generation of black youth. "On a gut level we understand what Patterson is trying to say. . . . I felt Patterson was on to something even if he couldn't pinpoint exactly what it was" (Daniels 2007, pp. 166–167). Such arguments are not new; they are recycled from earlier works on "soul" and the "cool pose." Robin D.G. Kelley describes a cool pose thesis as an effort to explain "the essence of young black male expressive culture," arguing, "Like earlier constructions of soul, they too believe that the 'cool pose' is an adaptive strategy to cope with the particular forms of racism and oppression black males face in America" (Kelley 1997, p. 31). The debate concerning and support for the NBA dress code demonstrate the persistent power of these debates in terms of race, representation, and policy.

THE DRESS CODE AND QUESTIONS OF AUTHENTICITY

Although the opposition to hip-hop's intrusion into the NBA and the support for the dress code emanating from black sports commentators, the civil rights establishment, and former (African American) NBA stars were often cited as evidence of the insignificance of race and the importance of generational or class divisions within the black community, race—even in those comments coming from African Americans—remains of central importance here. The demands that black NBA players alter their looks and, potentially, change their identities to accommodate white fans/corporate interests illustrate its racial orientation on one level. Yet, on another level, the call for black men to change their clothes operates through the idea that bourgeoisie values/white aesthetics are inherently more respectable, proper, and professional. Although it is certainly true that the hip-hop aesthetic is not an authentic signifier of blackness, just as the suit and tie are not an essential marker of whiteness, each are imagined as such. In other words, the demonization and regulation of a hip-hop aesthetic and a blackened body within the NBA are inextricably linked to the contempt and fear of blackness. Its undesirability, and even its desirability, stem from its connection to a discourse of authenticity, which ubiquitously reduces blackness to a criminal and cultural pollutant. Greg Tate encapsulates the complexity here:

> Perhaps the supreme irony of black American existence is how broadly black people debate the question of cultural identity among themselves while getting branded as a cultural monolith by those who would deny us the complexity and complexion of a community, let alone a nation. If Afro-Americans have never settled for the racist reductions imposed upon them—from chattel slaves to cinematic stereotype to sociological myth—it's because the black collective conscious not only knew better but also knew more than enough ethnic diversity to subsume these fictions." (Quoted in Kelley 2005, p. 119)

In "On the Question of Nigga[9] Authenticity," R.A.T. Judy describes "authenticity" as nothing more than "hype," a constructed idea that is crucial to the commodification of blackness. "Designating the contradiction (other/appropriate) that is constitutive of popular culture, nigga defines authenticity as adaptation to the force of commodification. Rap becomes an authentic African American cultural form against its appropriation as transnational popular culture" (2004, p. 114). In other words, hip-hop as manifested within the world of the NBA represents the power and possibility of a commodified blackness, yet its authenticity and presumed danger are inherently counterproductive to the NBA's global mission. John L. Jackson argues further that the discourses surrounding authenticity function as scripts, which "provide guides for proper and improper behavior" (2005, p. 13). He identifies racial authenticity as a "restrictive script" that "limit[s]" an "individual's social options" (2005, p. 13). The power of the discourse surrounding the NBA dress code is that it simultaneously authenticates blackness as criminal, underclass, pathological, and urban hip-hop, thereby denying the possibility of these identities existing as proper, desired, or authentic NBA identities. Because a ghetto or criminalized identity is presumed to be an authentic and hyper-real black identity, blackness, in its most natural and true form, is seen as an inherent threat to the NBA and the culture at large.

Likewise, the desirability of a more professional aesthetic for the NBA's black baller stems from the presumed respectability and goodness of styles imagined as white. Allen Iverson, in his statements about the dress code, makes clear his belief that the NBA's ban on bling to be racist because it reduces hip-hop to blackness, and hip-hop/blackness to criminality, danger, and undesirability. On the other hand, professionalism functions as a stand-in for whiteness, signifying goodness, respectability, and desirability. Iverson elucidates the dialectic between goodness and aesthetics (clothing) and, thus, the link between race and productive/desired bodies.

> Just because you put a guy in a tuxedo, it doesn't mean he's a good guy. It sends a bad message to kids. If you don't have a suit on when you go to school, is the teacher going to think you're a bad kid? I never wore a suit going in any park I ever went to when I was coming up. I just came from Japan, where I saw thousands of kids; all of them dressed like me, from the biggest guy to the smallest. It's just not right. It's something I'll fight for. I promised I wouldn't get up here and try to destroy anybody trying to make that [rule], but it's not right. (Quoted in Chiles 2005)

Noting that the dress code does indeed send a message to kids, Iverson questions how policing the clothing choices of black youth challenges racism given the power and centrality of race in American life. Jason Richardson concurs, noting how black youth are being judged because of societal prejudices. As argued by Dave Zirin, it reflects, "the politics of racial profiling, the argument that dress determines who you are—and jeans, chains, and sneakers somehow constitute predictors of anti-social behavior" (Labidou and Zirin 2005). Although the discourse focuses on issues of style and the appearances of black youth, the demonization reflects the signified meaning of blackness within the white imagination. Responding to Phil Jackson's comments about the dress code and hip-hop, all the identifying his hypocrisy given the profits generated by hip-hop within the mainstream, Scoop Jackson disentangles hip-hop from blackness, and blackness/hip-hop from criminality, dysfunctionality, and pathology:

> Would you rather us be like Karl Rove or Tom DeLay or Lewis Libby, Phil? Would you rather your Lakers players and the rest of

the ballers in the NBA present themselves more like Enron's Kenneth Lay or Jeff Skilling? Arthur Andersen's Joe Berardino? Tyco's
Dennis Kozlowski? WorldCom's Bernie Ebbers?

Maybe you'd rather them dress like Catholic priests.

Define prison garb, yo.

Or maybe in your next comment about "us" will you single out
Lil' Kim, use her as an example of the jail mentality that comes
with hip-hop's influence, but conveniently fail to mention Martha
Stewart?

Or maybe you'll remember to mention that most of the "thuggery" clothes we buy (especially those worn by NBA players) come
from Neiman's, Macy's and Saks, where entire floors are devoted to
our fashion and designers. Does that irritate you, Phil? Make you
wish that these upscale department chains wouldn't carry such
urban outfits? If so, why not scream them out too?

Clothing not cool for your players to rock, but OK for Fortune
500 stores to sell? (2005)

In this sense, the dress code simultaneously erases and invokes the logic of
racism: the authentic meaning in various black bodies is overdetermined by
the meaning of blackness, so that hip-hop as blackness represents a marker of
decay and unprofessionalism necessitating intervention, disciplinarity, policing, and correction. Yet, as noted by Iverson, Richardson, Scoop Jackson,
Marc Lamont Hill, and others, this imagined blackness, whether clothed in
baggy jeans, a Starter jersey, or a black Armani suit, is presumed to be criminal and undesirable, be it inside NBA arenas, on a street corner, or inside
America's schools.

The logic is clear in this regard: blackness equals hip-hop and hip-hop
equals blackness; because hip-hop is dysfunctional, dangerous, criminal, and
corrupting, blackness embodies these same pathological elements. Blackness,
confined to a hip-hop (urban/gangsta/Nigga) aesthetic, is thus marked as
essentially disruptive, uncontrollable, as a source of "cultural degeneracy."
Blackness exists as "a problematic sign and ontological position" (Williams
1998, p. 140). Given that the NBA does not want to rid itself of its black
players, the dress code seeks to lighten, if not whiten, these players in the
national (white) imagination. It sought to re-create the illusion of racial transcendence among its African Americans players. It works to sever the ties
among LeBron, Dwyane, and Kobe and hip-hop, blackness and the criminalized black body, at least within the white imagination. Jason Richardson again
makes this clear: "They want to sway away from the hip-hop generation. You
think of hip-hop right now and think of things that happen like gangs having

shootouts in front of radio stations" ("Pacers' Jackson: dress code is 'racist'").
Rod Murray and Stacey Lorenz describe the dress code as follows:

> Like earlier attempts to alleviate worries about "mannish" women,
> the NBA's new fashion rules are intended to mollify concerns about
> "thuggish" black men.
>
> At the same time, we must not forget that the mandatory
> business casual dress code is still code for respectable, white,
> middle-class masculinity. The messages being sent to black players
> and fans, many of them from lower-class backgrounds, may not be
> overtly racist, but these not-so-subtle subtexts about race and class
> cannot be casually dismissed.
>
> Unfortunately, some of the opinions we've heard expressed
> around the water cooler and on radio talk shows also have an indi-
> rect, but unmistakable, racial edge. It is difficult to escape the sense
> that many (white) people seem pleased that a group of young,
> black, millionaire basketball players are finally being put in their
> place. (2005)

Bomani Jones concurs, helping us see the connections between the NBA
dress code and similar initiatives in America's urban schools, where youth of
color are subjected to disciplinarity, punishment, and regulation of their
bodies, minds, and styles.

> Much like a high school principal might do, Stern recently rolled
> out a dress code, one that requires players to be outfitted in business
> casual attire for team functions such as arena arrivals and depar-
> tures, team flights and public appearances. The commissioner hopes
> to add some "professionalism" to the league, one sport coat at a
> time. But what does it mean for players to look professional? After
> all, we're talking basketball players, not diplomats. A fancy jacket
> can't make a player look any more or less professional, especially if
> cornrows dangle above his collar and pinball-sized diamonds gleam
> from his earlobes. Armani hasn't come up with a suit that snazzy
> yet. No matter the attire, nothing says "professional" in basketball
> like being 6 foot 9. Or are braids and earrings the next to go? (B.
> Jones 2005)

Reflecting on how the dress code merely perpetuates a long-standing tradition of whites treating blacks as children in need of parenting—whether in
schools, the social welfare system, or sports—Christopher John Farley

describes the code as "Silly. It makes the players in the league look like they are children who can be ordered around by their parents. That's not going to help the league look cool" (2005). Likewise, whiteness, whether embodied (or worn) by Kenneth Lay dressed in a three-piece suit or the Trench Coat Mafia dressed in trench coats, is seen as innocent, desirable, and ultimately, the benchmark of all that is good. In response to Renford Reese's editorial in support of the dress code, sports sociologist Samantha King criticizes the ways in which the discourse has linked white bodies to goodness, civility, professionalism, and desired citizenship, while blackness, in body and clothes, is linked to that which is threatening, undesirable, criminal, and destructive. To King, the dress code:

> Seems to suggest that a smattering of good old-fashioned discrimination might be okay so long as it encourages a handful of black players to learn the bourgeois etiquette that is "equate[d] with character and social responsibility." Ken Lay and Jeffrey Skilling wore nice suits too but that didn't stop them robbing millions of dollars from their employees and shareholders. These corporate criminals were also lavish spenders, but conspicuous displays of wealth (which are often not understood *as* conspicuous) by white men (in the form of renting private boxes at NBA games, for example) don't make white America feel uncomfortable in the ways that large pieces of gold jewelry worn by black men apparently do. This suggests to me that the policy is also reflective of a sense of anxiety about black wealth and a belief that riches are the proper domain of the already middle or upper class white. (2005)

The dress code and its celebrators are better understood in relationship to new racism, wherein culture becomes a stand-in for race. "Racial realists categorically reject biological explanations for racial inequality while subscribing to the notion that any possibility for reducing racial inequality is undermined by black behavior and values" (Brown et al. 2003, p. 8). The authors of *White-Washing Race* further note that:

> White racism, in their view has very little to do with black income and wages or persistently high poverty rates. It clearly makes much more sense, these people think, to look at the counterproductive and antisocial choices of poor blacks—choices that lead young women to have babies out of wedlock, young men to commit crimes, and young men and women to drop out of school. (2003, p. 10)

Likewise, Kimberle Williams Crenshaw argues that the hegemonic racial discourse consistently teaches, "that the absence of certain attributes accounts for the continued subordination of blacks" (2000, p. 554). To her, the only difference between contemporary arguments that focus on cultural deficiencies and those of the past, which tended to center on biological explanations, is that the "former explains subordination through reference to an unspoken social norm. That norm—although no longer explicitly white supremacist—nevertheless remains a white norm" (2000, p. 554).

That is, the slipping ratings and cultural capital of the NBA—like the declining graduation rates and increased rates of unemployment, incarceration, or health disparities—have nothing to do with race or racism, but, rather, reflect the failures of African Americans to uphold and represent the basic standards and values necessary for excelling in and out of America's arenas. It reflects their inability to subscribe to the norms—white norms—established by mainstream (white) society in terms of clothing choices, the right way to respect the game, and so on.

BEYOND THE DRESS CODE: THE NBA AND THE CRIMINALIZATION OF BLACK BODIES

The significance of the dress code transcends the debate surrounding the dress code, or even the ongoing racialized culture war in the NBA, reflecting and perpetuating commonsense ideologies that imagine black culture as pathological and blackness as criminal. "The prevailing public profile of the violent black offenders is manufactured by collapsing the image of a distinctly small minority of black violent offenders with the presumption that runs deep in racist culture of a naturally violent and oversexed black people" (Goldberg 1997, p. 161). Writing about Charles Stuart and Susan Smith,[10] Vijay Prashad reflects on the power of a racial discourse that naturalizes and reduces black men to a perpetual class of criminals. "In both cases, the public initially accepted as normal that a black man would randomly kill whites or else rob them with excessive violence. Black men are dangerous, was the message particularly when they are young" (Prashad 2003, p. 73). In other words, "the international Muslim terrorist and the domestic black criminal stand as alibis for revanchism" (Prashad 2003, p. 75). The long-standing practice of imagining an authentic black identity and culture—blackness—through a prism of the underclass contributes to a discourse wherein "the social conditions of the undeserving poor can be blamed upon their own character" (Goldberg 2000, p. 155). The "production of social knowledge about the racial Other, then, establishes a library or archive of information" (Goldberg

2000, p. 155). The hegemonic representations of the underclass, hip-hop, black youth, and the black NBA "[describe] a state of mind and a way of life." reflect "as much a cultural as an economic condition" (2000, p. 166). To be a member of the underclass and a hip-hop baller is to be "reduced to individual pathologies and the poverty of culture that generates the social disease of deviance" (2000, p. 166); it is to live with an "absence of the moral virtues disabling individuals from 'deferring gratification, planning ahead and making sacrifices for future benefit'" (2000, p. 166).

The discourse surrounding the dress code solidifies those sincere fictions that construct blackness as hip-hop and hip-hop as blackness, and that see/describe both as destructive and pathological (and resulting from a culture of poverty). Such logic manifests itself within everything from the Palace Brawl and claims about selfish play, to arguments about disinterested students and criminal behavior. Not only solidifying notions of an authentic (and destructive) black culture in hip-hop, the focus on hip-hop as the basis for the NBA's problems reinforces those who blame black youth and their adherence to a hip-hop identity for dropout, incarceration, and poverty rates (Cosby 2004; Williams 2006). Debates about inequality or racial injustice elide reflection on structures of inequality or even racism, instead focusing pathological and self-defeating culture that is harmful to future generations, black youth who see ballers as role model.

Sean Gonsalves, in "The Hypocritical NBA Dress Code," writes, "Maybe life does imitate art. The new NBA dress code will make the league look more 'professional' but it also validates the fictional black thug caricature so frighteningly real in the popular imagination" (2005). While Harvey Araton encourages his readers to take off their "hats and do-rags" to Commissioner Stern for "a much-needed dialogue on the N.B.A. identity crisis," he also expresses concern about the blowback effects of such a policy (2005). He questions the usefulness and appropriateness of placing the focus and, thus, the blame for the problems facing the NBA on its black players, "surrendering to the almightily American stereotype" of black men being criminals, threats, and culturally uncivilized. "Blaming the N.B.A. slide on how players present themselves is like attributing the president's plummeting poll numbers to images of him clearing brush in a work shirt and jeans" (2005). Dave Zirin may have put it best, and most succinctly, when he wrote the following in *Welcome to the Terrordome*:

> But the dress code doesn't just make bad business sense, it is morally repellent. Trying to control what NBA players wear off the court, as if that's the root of the league's problem, gives weight to people's worst stereotypes about the young, Black, and gifted among us. It sends a message that players are "out of control" and

need some kind of external discipline or the league will go to hell. It also gives credence to the deeply reactionary idea that you can profile antisocial behavior through clothes. If someone wears baggy jeans and a chain, they must be on drugs, packing a gat, or on their way to see one of their twenty babies. This is a slap in the face to every baller who lives clean and, as a grown man chooses to wear what he damn well pleases – not to mention the young urban audience that the NBA depends on. (2007d, p. 116)

Given the constant description of the league as filled with gangsters and criminals in need of a makeover, it is clear that the dress code merely reinscribes these fictions. In 1990, the University of Chicago's National Opinion Research Center found that 62 percent of nonblacks polled believed that blacks were lazier than other racial groups in the United States. It additionally found that 56 percent of respondents viewed blacks as more prone to violence, while 53 percent believed that blacks were less intelligent than other racialized groups (Brown et al. 2003, p. 40). A study in the *Journal of Alcohol and Drug Education* where 95 percent of respondents pictured a black drug user when prompted to imagine a drug user or another study that found "60 percent of viewers who saw a story with no image falsely recalled seeing one/70 percent of those viewers believed the perpetrator to be black" (Alexander 2010, p. 103) illustrates the power of anti-black racial framing. Similar studies about persistent implicit bias (see Alexander 2010), and the persistence of stereotypes (see Feagin 2010) demonstrate how "young + black + male is equated with reasonable suspicion, justifying arrest, interrogation, search and detention" (Alexander 2010, p. 194). These many studies and poll, as well as countless others exploring the criminalization of African Americans, should not be surprising given the representations and discourses disseminated by academics, politicians, popular culture, and sports.

Between the flowering of the civil rights movement and the Reagan years, the image of black youth in particular underwent an extraordinary transformation: The brave little girl walking up the schoolhouse door in the face of jeering white crowds was replaced by fearsome young black men coming down the street ready to take your wallet or your life. The cultural transformation of black youth from victims of injustice to remorseless predators was mirrored in public policies that quietly reduced funding for programs that had historically served minority youth. (Brown et al. 2003, p. 132)

Moreover, these shifting mediated representations of blackness rationalize and justify policies of surveillance, incarceration, and disciplinarity, whether in zero-tolerance initiatives in schools, the war on drugs, mass incarceration efforts, or dress code policies from the NBA and various school districts. Arguing that the contemporary era is defined by a "secluded, camouflaged kind of racism" that ultimately "naturalizes black people as criminals," (1997, pp. 270–271), Angela Y. Davis laments the significance of mediated representations in the advancement of the prison industrial complex.

> When the structural character of racism is ignored in discussions about crime and the rising population of incarcerated people, the racial imbalance in jails and prisons is treated as a contingency, at best as a product of the "culture of poverty," and at worst as proof of an assumed black monopoly of criminality. The high proportion of black people in the criminal justice system is thus normalized and neither the state nor the general public is required to talk about and act on the meaning of that racial imbalance. (1997, p. 265)

The dress code not only substantiates these practices, but does so in a way that provides legitimacy to the argument that if black youth wear baggy jeans and do-rags, they should be treated as criminals deserving of police surveillance and undeserving of jobs. For example, Phil Jackson who, despite being long known (and celebrated) as an example of the NBA's countercultural, rebellious spirit, voiced his support for the dress code as a necessary curtailment of "prison garb" in the NBA:

> I think we've noticed a number of situations in the playoffs, when the full attention is on the NBA, when it reaches its pinnacle. And you'll have a player step to the podium wearing a do-rag and sunglasses and holding a child on his lap and it sends out an image, I don't know, of prison garb or thuggery or smells of defiance in a way. (Quoted in Lorenz and Murray 2005)

To Jackson, the influence of hip-hop on this generation of NBA players has had a deleterious effect, not simply in terms of their clothing choices, but their on-the-court behavior and their demeanor, values, and attitudes. Following the announcement of the proposed dress code, he elucidated the links between hip-hop and the problems facing the NBA and its black players with the following: "I think it's important that the players take their end of it, get out of the prison garb and the thuggery aspect of basketball that has come along with hip-hop music in the last seven or eight years" (Quoted in S. Jackson 2005).

Likewise, the fact that support for the dress code was, at times, coupled with reservations about its potential for success reveals the power of the criminalized black body within the white imagination. You can take the black NBA player out of his baggy jeans and put him in a three-piece suit, but ultimately, a trip to Men's Warehouse or Armani cannot eradicate his criminal tendencies or pathological cultural subscriptions. No rule has the power to completely deracialize (or whiten) the purportedly genetically and culturally polluted black body. Lamont Jones seems to argue this point, questioning whether a dress code will have any impact given both the constructed deviance of the players' bodies and the anti-black racism, which will continue to flourish regardless of their clothes. "Band-Aid dress codes—and that's what the NBA's is—seldom work. The jobs of these pro ballers are inconsistent with business attire. They don't make their living in office parks and board rooms. It's ridiculous to assume, as the NBA does, that grown men with amazing talent, super-sized egos, a love of style and money to burn will behave how bosses want them to behave if they look the way bosses want them to look" (L. Jones 2005). Jarold Wells likewise severs the links between professionalism and whiteness, between normalized definitions of "proper" and civility, both of which are wrapped up in traditionally racist visions of white and Othered masculinity. "One of the most important factors in professionalism is taking pride in your appearance. A person should take care to ensure that he is well groomed and neat, that his clothing reflects money and time spent to ensure quality. Whether the manifestation is a $345 jersey or a $400 suit, both meet the standards recently mentioned. . . . . He [Allen Iverson] is no less a professional because his style is more 'urban'" (Wells 2005). Additionally, Bomani Jones, in "A Dress Code is Dangerous," makes clear the incongruity of professionalism and blackness within the white imagination, given the hegemonic racial contexts of the NBA and the broader American culture.

> A fancy jacket can't make a player look any more or less professional, especially if cornrows dangle above his collar and pinball-sized diamonds gleam from his earlobes. . . . The problem, of course, is that not everyone likes what is seen. Much is made about what's wrong with today's athlete, and the NBA gets the most league-specific criticism. The rap goes that *all* athletes are spoiled and unappreciative and are too concerned with "respect," but *NBA players* keep going to jail, keep contributing illegitimately to global overpopulation, and keep getting pulled over with forbidden firearms and horticulture in the consoles of their tricked-out Lexuses. And all of it is stereotypically associated with the gaudy jewelry, oversized T-shirts and roomy jeans so many players in the league wear (along with that music they listen to). (B. Jones 2005)

Illustrating the incongruity between blackness and professionalism within a dominant imagination—how unnatural it would seem to see a black man, particularly a young black athlete, donning professional attire—Scott Ostler describes the prospects of putting Allen Iverson in a sport coat as the "most incongruous look on TV since Milton Berle dressed in drag" (2005). Despite claims to the contrary, the dress code merely played on, utilized and reinforced dominant inscriptions of black male bodies in which those bodies are criminal, dangerous, and threatening. "In trying to appeal to the corporate crowd upon whose spending power the NBA has decided to rely (even as it also depends heavily on selling merchandise to young kids who find urban hip-hop style appealing), the league is helping to reinforce an already entrenched fear of blackness in U.S. culture that has, among other things, contributed to the criminalization and mass incarceration of several generations of young black men" (King 2005). So argues Samantha King, who despite the praise of others, concludes that, "this is for me the most troubling implication of the policy and why, unlike [Renford] Reese, I find it irredeemable" (2005). The governing discourse mandates a marriage between blackness and criminality, and between whiteness and professionalism, innocence, and goodness. "A dress code will do nothing to change the perception of players. They will remain a group that is young, predominantly black and thoroughly washed in the blood of a counterculture that is incorrectly—though somewhat understandably—associated with handcuffs instead of cuff links. (That culture is pretty indifferent toward the latter)" (B. Jones 2005). Kevin Powell, who describes the dress code policy as the NBA's effort to appease a white fan base "unhappy with these black boys gone wild," offered a more historic analysis and presented the code's usefulness as evidence for the power of white supremacy in dictating and controlling black cultural production. He goes on to say:

> Many white American males in power positions have a history, dating back to slavery, of wanting black labor, black entertainment, black bodies while simultaneously not respecting or appreciating our language, attitude, fashion or ways of viewing the world. Which means also that Mr. Stern, uncomfortable with the bling, throwback jerseys, and vernacular of these hip-hop heads, who also happen to be star basketball players, would rather try to restrict them than have an honest dialogue about race, class and culture in America. (Quoted in Hayes 2005)

These commentators did not simply challenge the racist assumptions of the dress code or the links it presumed between hip-hop, blackness, and criminality, they questioned the usefulness of the policy given the standing and meaning of blackness within contemporary America. As blackness signifies danger, criminality, and hypersexuality within the dominant imagination, this gimmicky marketing strategy was seen as perpetuating centuries-old ideologies of white supremacy. Unlike the many mainstream commentators who questioned the impact of the dress code because "they" (the gangstas, ghetto punks, and criminals who dominate the league) can't be helped and because their influence on the game transcends the styles they wear, these critical voices predicted that the dress code would ultimately fail because it was insufficient in transforming the American racial landscape; it wouldn't/couldn't alter the racial meaning of blackness or its long-standing function as signifier and symbol of decay and danger. "Dressing up black stars like Allen Iverson in sport coats and sensible shoes won't radically change the culture or image of the NBA," notes Murray and Lorenz (2005). The meaning of blackness within contemporary America transcends the aesthetic markers of clothing, class status, and other signifiers of membership to America's professional elite. This is evident in the instances of racial profiling experienced by middle-class African Americans (even those wearing suits), the difficultly that a group of black secret service agents (yes, they were wearing suits) faced in trying to get served at a Baltimore Denny's, or when executives at Texaco referred to African Americans as "black jelly beans" (Brown et al. 2003, pp. 36–37; Feagin and Sikes 1995). Whether reflecting on the violence experienced by black college students (who often wore suits) during the 1960s sit-in campaigns, or the well-documented incidents involving professionally dressed African Americans unable to get some dinner, receive a loan, or make a purchase, it is clear that race and racism inscribe meaning onto black bodies regardless of clothing choices (Cose 1995; Feagin and Sikes 1995).

What might be most striking about the league and media response to the dress code is that so many voiced outright denials regarding the significance of race and racism. Given both the policy's regulation of a hip-hop aesthetic and its celebration as a necessary response to the hostility between fans and corporate investors (the majority of whom are white) and NBA players (almost 80 percent black), and with columnist after columnist demonstrating the necessity for a dress code by making reference to gangstas, criminals, and the ghetto destroying the quality and appeal of the league, it is rather ludicrous to deny the racial context and implications of the code. Lamont Jones makes this clear, chastising those who deny the racial/racist orientation of the dress code, given the assumptive and essentialized links between hip-hop, blackness, and criminality.

> The new policy is about the Benjamins. The NBA has decided that a dress code is necessary to help address declining viewership, skittish corporate investors and mostly white ticket holders who admire the slam dunks and fancy footwork but can't identify with the highly paid, mostly young black athletes they cheer and jeer.

The code's racial overtones can't be denied when one considers that the soon-to-be taboo fashions and accessories are part of the black-created hip-hop culture and are basically worn by black players.

So, what's next? A ban on braids, cornrows and dreadlocks? A provision against gold and diamond dental ornamentation?

The need to control or eradicate what you dislike, fear, or don't understand is strong, but it makes for bad policy when it leads to reactionary decisions based upon cultural stereotypes. (L. Jones 2005)

Although clearly operating through a racial discourse—given the effort to use the dress code to discipline and, if necessary, punish those violating (black) bodies who choose hip-hop (blackness) over professional and respectable (white) clothes—the policy not only criminalized the performance of a particular aesthetic inscription of blackness, but focused on the problems of a *culture* rather than a racial group. The fact that culture was being used as a stand-in for race, hip-hop as a code for blackness, in some way explains the denials of racism here.

Yet, what is powerful within this discourse is that racism is seen as irrelevant because of the truisms emanating from the dress code discourse. John McWhorter makes this clear in his *Wall Street Journal* commentary, wherein he too celebrates the dress code as an antiracist demonstration that thuggery and gangster poses are not a "black thing." Responding to players' insertion of race into the discussion, McWhorter penned the following: "Stephen Jackson of the Pacers grouses that the NBA is afraid of being seen as 'too hip-hop'— well, given the public doings of rappers who provide the soundtrack to the dress style, is the NBA completely out of its mind?" (2005). As such, it is not racist to link hip-hop (blackness) to criminality, pathology, danger, and corruption, since all these links are based in a purported reality. Similarly, Tamar Jacoby is reported to have the following note above her desk, illustrating the power of a discourse of truism: "If you can't call a black thug a thug, you're a racist. It is an idea I stand by" (Quoted in Brown et al. 2003, p. 7). In other words, the defenders of the NBA dress code, like other "racial realists," don't fall for the traps of "liberal racism," but are willing "to acknowledge the failures of black people," a practice that doesn't legitimize accusations of racism because it arguments purportedly rely truthfulness and honesty (Brown et al. 2003, p. 7).

Race sits at both the center and periphery of the policy, determining its widespread support, the rhetoric used to sell its necessity, and its overall significance as part of the NBA's plan to change its image (whiten) and discipline its "problem-causing" black players. However, we have to wonder what might be next: a ban on cornrows, dreadlocks, Afros, braids, or even a high-top fade? A rule requiring the surgical removal of tattoos and the removal of earrings? The elimination of headbands, throwback jerseys, black shoes or socks, and "shorts that extend more than 14 inches below the navel" (Broussard 2005a). Broussard sarcastically predicts the changes that will be implemented next:

> There will be no rap music—including hip-hop-inspired R&B—played in NBA arenas, and rap artists must sit in the nosebleed section, dress in preppy clothing and enthusiastically wave Thunderstix while attending games. . . .
>
> The Slam-Dunk Contest is replaced by a free-throw shooting competition, and Funkmaster Flex and Kid Capri will be replaced at All-Star Saturday by someone related to Casey Kasem.
>
> Players must wear a perpetual smile at all team functions, especially games. High fives are no longer allowed, but teammates may congratulate one another with a pat on the back or a firm handshake in which they look each other squarely in the eye. The popular soul brotha' shake that's followed by a one-armed hug and finger snap will not be tolerated.
>
> The iPods of every player in the league will be erased and refilled with country western and soft rock hits. (2005a)

The path that the NBA is traveling is one where, ultimately, it may fully accommodate white demands for a league without hip-hop or even a perceived blackness. In this new NBA, the banning of tattoos, headbands, and cornrows could actually happen. While certainly adopting a comedic and farcical tone, Broussard—like Bomani Jones, Lamont Jones, Dave Zirin, Scoop Jackson, and several others, including a number of players—not only illustrates the racial basis of the dress code, but elucidates the new racist reality of an NBA that simultaneously tries to commodify and demonize, profit off of and police, accept and deny, the aesthetics and signifiers of hip-hop and blackness. "NBA execs courted hip-hop and ghetto-fabulous to boost interest and profits, but they didn't expect some of the baggage that came with it," writes Lamont Jones. "A dress code that addresses a symptom rather than a cause might make some people feel better, but it won't unbake the cake that the NBA wants to have and eat, too" (2005).

CONCLUSION

The NBA's crusade against creativity, individuality, hip-hop, and blackness, especially in regard to control and ownership over bodies, did not end with the establishment of a dress code. Shortly after the start of the 2005–2006 season, the Players' Union filed a grievance over the league's fining of several players ($10,000 dollars) for violating the league's prohibition against shorts extending 0.1 inch above the knee. Although the celebration of the dress code invoked Michael Jordan, the adoration of the Jordan rules obviously did not carry over into the battle over the length of shorts. While Michigan's Fab 5 is mostly responsible for the popularization of long shorts (and black shoes and socks), Michael Jordan apparently asked Champion to makes his shorts extra long, so that when he was tired he could hang on his shorts (Whitaker 2005). As with the dress code, long shorts weren't just a matter of personal choice or player comfort in that long, sagging, shorts are visible markers of the influence of hip-hop/the penetration of a black aesthetic in the league and, therefore, required league intervention.

Similarly, during the following season, David Stern and others around the league made clear their opposition to the trend of players wearing full length tights, announcing that, starting in the 2006–2007 season, players would no longer be allowed to wear tights while playing, unless dictated by a medical necessity. Through the 2006 season, star players from Kobe Bryant and Dwyane Wade to LeBron James, Vince Carter, Michael Redd, and Jerry Stackhouse began wearing tights. Some said they did so for comfort and others noted that tights prevented injuries, but the league saw it as a challenge to the uniformity of their product, and, consequently, outlawed tights. What is striking here, beyond the regulation and control of these predominantly black bodies, is the indication of a continuing fear that hip-hop (in this case tights) was becoming too prominent in the league, making the presence of tights, the visibility of personal marketing, and the potential trends of white suburban kids wearing tights troubling to league officials. Moreover, given the obvious and ongoing fears about white fans rooting for overtly masculine black men, it is somewhat ironic that the wearing of tights prompted such a backlash. In fact, whereas hip-hop gear, brawls, or trash-talking crossed the line in terms of acceptable and profitable inscriptions of black masculinity, the use of tights seem to cross the opposite line, signifying the undesirability of a presumably feminine black aesthetic. For example, Brad Rock, in the *Desert News*, celebrated an end to the era of tights not because the league was now rid of a hip-hop or gangsta aesthetic, but because the banning of tights thwarted the infiltration of a feminine identity: "Ballet is ballet. But even I am a bit nonplussed when it comes to the trend of NBA players wearing tights under their shorts. It's strange. I've never even seen anyone in the WNBA wearing them. So men are wearing tights but women aren't. What is this, the Renaissance?" (2006). He then went on to ask whether Andrew Bogut would still wear tights if they came in "pink?" (2006). Similarly, Marcus Camby made clear that the protective sleeve he wore on his leg was different from spandex tights, noting, "I don't wear pantyhose" (Quoted in Jenkins 2006). When LSU's Glen Davis donned tights during a game at Alabama, fans subjected him to chants of "ballerina" (Quoted in Jenkins 2006). While a spectrum of issues seem to be at work here, including the fact that a number of athletes wearing the tights were under contract with NIKE, which began selling the tights, what is striking here is that the regulation of the performed identities of black athletes was designed to protect NBA profits; it was about black bodies functioning as commodities and the regulation of those bodies in accordance with profits, all of which was deployed through long-standing hegemonic stereotypes of blackness.

"Dirty Nigger! Or Simply, Look a Negro" (Fanon 2000, p. 257). So writes Frantz Fanon, in "The Fact of Blackness," arguing that within the white imagination, dirty or not, professionally dressed or not, law-abiding or not, employed or not, an African American is always a "dirty nigger." To be black is to remain black within the white imagination; it is to remain dirty, dangerous, destructive, and dysfunctional, all while maintaining a relationship to the "ontology of whiteness," which is assumed to embody "rationality and universality" (Bhabha 2000, p. 355). Homi Bhabha further clarifies the significance and meaning of blackness within a white supremacist context, what it means to be essentially "a Nigger, . . . a member of the marginalized, the displaced, and the Diasporic." He writes: "To be amongst those whose very presence is both 'overlooked'—in the double sense of surveillance and psychic disavowal—and at the same time over-determined—physically projected made stereotypical and symptomatic" (Bhabha 2000, p. 355). The discourse surrounding the NBA dress code in the aftermath of Artest and the code itself brings to light Bhabha's poignant and provocative commentary, in that black NBA players, and their brothers and sisters living outside America's arenas and in America's "new Jim Crow" (Alexander 2010), are simultaneously subjected to state-mandated acts of violence—"surveillance and physical disavowal"—and the logics of racism that reduce black bodies, aesthetics, styles, and cultural performances to little more than those of a "dirty Nigger." As evidenced by both the demonization of the black baller (the references to him being a child in need of David Stern's guidance; his stupidity, etc.) and the hypercelebration of the presumably race-neutral Michael Jordan, we see the hegemony of white racial framing:

> The black is both savage (cannibal) and yet the most obedient and signified of servants (the bearer of food); he is the embodiment of rampant sexuality and yet innocent as a child; he is mystical, primitive, simple-minded and yet the most worldly and accomplished liar, and manipulator of social forces. In each case, what is being dramatized is a separation—between race, cultures, histories,

within histories—a separation between before and after that
repeats obsessively and mythical moment of disjunction. (Bhabha
quoted in Young 2005, p. 282)

The dress code reveals the racial logic that governs the NBA after Artest not
only in terms of the demonization of black bodies and the ubiquitous pathologizing of the black underclass—along with the widespread support for the
surveillance, disciplinarity, and control of (those deviant, which includes all)
black bodies—but in the normalization of whiteness and the denial of the
significance of race and, more importantly, racism. As black bodies who
refuse to play by "their" (the NBA/society) rules are scapegoated for the problems facing the league, the black community, today's youth and society as a
whole, the state, whiteness and racism are in turn let off the hook. Although
police and prison guards, both of whom wear suits, are "the deadliest (people)
of all" (Kevin Cooper quoted in Zirin 2007a), those donning chains and sagging their pants are systematically perceived as threats to the NBA, its corporate sponsors and, most importantly, white Americans. We have been told
over and over that the future of the NBA is in jeopardy and can only be saved
by David Stern and his institutionalization of policies. Only by holding those
deviant criminals accountable, by fostering a return of players like Michael
Jordan, and ultimately, by civilizing, domesticating and concealing its black-
ness/black bodies will the NBA return to its promised land.

5

THE PALACE BRAWL AND THE COLORBLIND FANTASY

INTRODUCTION

I have argued throughout this book that, on a certain level, the Palace Brawl represented a moment of rupture for the NBA. It provided the ideological and cultural leverage for ushering in substantive policy shifts within the league; in highlighting the blackness of the league, the fight necessitated systemic intervention. Likewise, it represented an ideological break from the NBA's and the larger society's fantasy of colorblindness. Whereas the era of Jordan was marked by purported racial progress and colorblindness, along with the widespread articulation of a commodifiable type of blackness, a post-Artest moment has been marked by the rearticulation or reinscription of racism. In other words, Artest, with all of the signifiers he embodied, was the ultimate reminder of the blackness of the NBA, and his actions catalyzed a series of policy shifts and a systematic cultural backlash. Just as the arrest of O.J. Simpson's concretized his blackness (Crenshaw 1997) and rape allegations against Kobe Bryant serve as a reminder of his blackness (Mipuri 2011; Markovitz 2006; Leonard 2004), and even as the entry of Jeremiah Wright into the 2008 presidential campaign underscored Barack Obama's blackness, the Palace Brawl elucidated the blackness (and therefore the dysfunction, danger, and pathology) of the NBA.

In "Color-blind Dreams and Racial Nightmares" Kimberle Williams Crenshaw offers the following description of the racial logic that guided the dominant narrative concerning O.J. Simpson prior to his arrest: "Simpson was not thought of (by whites) as an African, but as simply a 'race-neutral' celebrity." She notes further, "such 'assurances' unwittingly revealed an underlying racial logic in which blackness remained as a suspect category that Simpson had been fortunate to escape" (1997, p. 100). Writing about Simpson's "symbolic 'return' to his essential blackness" the blackening of Simpson on the cover of *Time* magazine, Williams argues that the cover "simply offered a graphic depiction of the narrative that its competitors were hawking elsewhere" (p. 113).

The Jordan era was also defined as a time when Jordan (constructed/ painted/cast as the model and desirable representative of the league) and the NBA as a whole were imagined to have successfully transcended the suspect category of blackness. According to Michael Hoechsmann, Jordan was "the point guard for what was Reagan and Gingrich's version of America, a black stripped of racial connotations who 'proves' that hard work and determination are the keys to the American Dream" (2001, p. 273). His career was defined by "his desire to live beyond race, to be 'neither black nor white'" (Patton 1986, p. 52), to be "viewed as a person" (Vancil 1992, p. 57), a process that not incidentally elevated the status of the league (Dyson 2001, p. 265). Not only because of his on-the-court play, but because of his public and commodified persona, Jordan did "not just transcend race in the United States, he trans-form[ed] race for white viewers, providing a desired alignment for white folks with a black personality who does not appear to pose a threat" (Hoechsmann 2001, p. 273). More importantly, Jordan transformed the relationship that white America had with basketball because of his racial markers or, rather, his perceived lack thereof. "Basketball, a game associated with inner city—read "black"—America has been subject to an astute marketing effort which has raised it to All-American status with baseball and football" (Hoechsmann 2001, p. 273). The Artest Brawl was sort of death knell for this fantasy of col-orblindness (which had long been on its last legs), demonstrating without a doubt that the NBA was not race-neutral; that it was a black league and, therefore, a suspect, dangerous, and problematic space in need of policing and surveillance.

The 10 to 15 years prior to the Palace Brawl had been defined by the fantasy of a post-racial United States characterized by the colorblindness evi-dent in the popularity of a racially transcendent Michael Jordan. Jordan, the symbol of the NBA, was imagined as outside the set of the accepted markers of blackness, including those associated with hip-hop. He had transcended race and provided not only hope for a colorblind NBA future, but a paradigm for erasing race. However, race, which had been "suspended in the buffer zone, remain[ed] ready to reappear as an interpretative frame to justify racial disparities in American life and to legitimize, when necessary, the marginal-ization and the circumvention of African Americans" (Crenshaw 1997, p. 103). After Artest, race resurfaced and all of the corresponding, ideologies, frames, narratives, and requirements of disciplinarity and punishment there-fore became both necessary and justifiable.

Artest reminded the league, its media and corporate partners and the culture at large of the blackness (and consequent undesirability) of the NBA.

The fight, and the ensuing media/fan backlash, burst the bubble of Jordan, post-racialness and colorblindness. It demonstrated that the NBA/culture had not reached a post-racial moment, and that Jordan's popularity was not evidence for such a moment because he was not perceived or imagined in relationship to hegemonic notions of blackness. With his exit, the fantasy ended, finally bursting at the Palace Brawl, leaving behind a vacuum that was filled by dominant white racial frames: the colorblind racial frame was thus replaced by the white racial frame.

Artest is where the pendulum swung. Artest, the Palace Brawl, and all of the intrusions of an imagined blackness that had proceeded this moment, demonstrated to the public at large the problematic nature of the NBA after Jordan. His post-racialness had been replaced by hip-hop, gangsta ballers, guns in the locker room, tattoos, hypersexuality, and violence both on and off the court. Jordan's acceptability had been replaced by a "real" (and ultimately bad) blackness as imagined in the dominant white racial frame. *After Artest* reflects on a game change in which the NBA, its surrounding media culture, and dominant white culture were awoken from the fantasy of post-racialness, resulting in multiple demands for disciplinarity and punishment in/for the very black NBA.

Artest was the final piece of evidence for the blackness of the NBA and thus the failed colorblindness/racial transcendence marked by Jordan. It was the ultimate counternarrative to the fantasy that Jordan had fostered a progression of the NBA (and the nation as a whole) into a post-racial territory. As such, it led to an open war on blackness and its perceived cultural markers within the league. Before reflecting in greater detail on the ways in which *After Artest* has highlighted the dialectics between race/racism and the NBA's culture war, I want to provide one additional example of how, in the aftermath of Artest, the reinscription of white racial framing and the penetration of blackness into the dominant media framing of the NBA played out, in this case in a second brawl that occurred at Madison Square Garden.

THE PALACE BRAWL 2.0:
MADISON SQUARE GARDEN MELEE

All was business as usual at Madison Square Garden December 16, 2006: the Knicks were headed for another humiliating double-digit loss. However, what happened with 1:15 minutes remaining on the clock was not extraordinary,[1] yet still it sparked debate and hyperventilation regarding the state of the NBA. Sam Mitchell, among others, questioned whether the Madison Square Garden Melee was even a fight, but much of the media and basketball's media pundits lamented the Knicks-Nuggets as something much worse than a fight. Described as a "horrendous brawl" (Beck 2006), a "fracas" ("NBA Shows its Immaturity" 2006; "Summit to Address Fracas" 2006; Ventre 2006), a "riot" (Martin and Berman 2006; P. Vecsey 2006), a "black eye for the NBA" (Mahoney 2006), a "wild brawl" (Mahoney 2006), "ugly" (Burns 2006; Celizic 2006; Deveney 2006; B. Lee 2006), a "boorish brawl" (B. Lee 2006), and a night of "mayhem" (M. Lee 2006; Olson 2006; "Suspensions Total 47 Games from Knicks-Nuggets Fight 2006), the post-Artest Brawl media coverage constructed this fight as chaotic, dangerous, and violent, yet not out of the ordinary. Peter Vecsey described this NBA fight night as one of "repulsiveness"—"a reenactment of the Melee at the Mecca" and the "league's latest outbreak of senselessness" (2006). Michael Ventre labeled the brawl "worse than the 'Malice at the Palace'" (2006). As did much of the discourse, these commentaries tried to contextualize and link this incident to the broader cultural problems plaguing the NBA. Described as being perpetrated by "basketballbrawlers" (Povak 2006)—a term used after the Pacers-Pistons-fan fight, as "yet another hit to the NBA image" (Luhm 2007), as "a stain on the game that isn't going to wash away quickly" (Celznic 2006), and as "another moment where the NBA has a big fight against perception" (Sorensen 2006), the on-the-court "fight" was imagined as symptomatic of a broader set of problems destroying the NBA from the inside out. Childs Walker, in the *Baltimore Sun*, predicted that this brawl would likely elicit a discussion about "the sociology of the NBA" (Walker 2007). Not surprisingly, more than 62 percent of respondents on ESPN's Sports Nation poll viewed this brawl as bad as the Pistons-Pacers fight, with 65 percent believing that the fight would lead to policy changes within the NBA.

Given the ongoing racialized culture war evident within the NBA discourse, it is not surprising that this fight elicited widespread condemnation, panic, and outrage. Facts aside, the signifiers of blackness, basketball, and fighting—in and of themselves sufficient to trigger such a response—were all present. Eschewing a narrative that focused on the ubiquity of violence in other sports and in society as a whole, or one that constructed the fight as either unusual or unfortunate, numerous commentaries used this instance to once again excoriate the league, its players, and the purported cultural and criminal influence of hip-hop on the league.

Replicating much of the media discourse concerning the NBA and its culture wars, the commentaries elicited by the Knicks-Nuggets "fight" infantilized the blacks involved in the "fracas," suggesting that the fight and the problem facing the league reflected the immaturity of its players. Throughout, they were referred to as "whippersnappers" (Red Eye 2006) and "crybaby millionaires" ("NBA Shows its Immaturity"); accused of "acting naughty" ("Brawling Bad Boys") and fighting as if the court was "the playground" (Lupica 2006); and described as "pro athletes with the emotional make-up of

3–year olds" who don't need to be suspended but sent "to detention and sand-box duty" (Sloane 2006). The *Las Vegas Sun* condemned the coaches for their involvement in the brawl, complaining that they were supposed to be "the adults of the sport" and asserting that, "It is beyond time for the league's coaches and players to start growing up" ("NBA Shows its Immaturity"). Others simply called on the league to discipline and punish the players in order to help them "grow up" ("Brawling Bad Boys"). Once again, the dis-course reduced the (black) NBA, along with George Karl, the white coach of the Nuggets, to immature kids in need of parenting, guidance, and discipline from both the league (the benevolent white parent) and the media (the grandfather determined to provide some tough love).

The predominant argument also included a contention that the fight between several Knicks and Nuggets players was not merely a result of the players' immaturity and lack of self-control, but also of the persistent influ-ence of hip-hop on the NBA and its immature players. In a sense, hip-hop was imagined as a promoter or purveyor of the immaturity and criminality evident in the league. Brian Mahoney answered his own question about what caused "the meltdown" with a simple conclusion: "the Knicks felt dissed" (2006). An editorial in the *Las Vegas Sun* also attributed the brawl to the Knicks feeling "dissed." Ignoring long-standing questions, all of which pre-date hip-hop, about sportsmanship, running up the score, and the supposed unwritten rules about how players and teams with a big lead are supposed to behave, along with the history of fighting within American sports, these commentators insisted that the brawl stemmed from the importation of a hip-hop ethos concerning respect and disrespect. Mitch Albom, on ESPN's "The Sports Reporters" (December 17, 2006), bemoaned the fact that "play-ers seem to want to settle issues of respect with their fists." This isn't surpris-ing given that Albom had discussed the Palace Brawl in similar terms, although here he indicted the fans alongside the players in his implication of a warped vision of respect as the reason for the fight. "Fact is, respect is what started this in the first place. Oh, not real respect. Real respect has traces of kindness. Real respect is deferential, like a young apprentice and his patient mentor. Real respect knows, at its core, humility," wrote Albom. "I'm talking about the bastardized "respect" in today's sports world—where the word means nobody does anything to you that you don't like, want, accept or appreciate" (2004). Likewise, Jerry Brewer called on players to "stop scowling, stop barking, stop littering the court with macho garbage" (2006).

Although arguments about the maturity of the NBA player and the pur-ported polluting influences of hip-hop shaped the discourse in more subtle ways, the efforts to construct the brawl as yet another sign of the criminality of today's (black) NBA were overt. Ryan Norris asked if Carmelo Anthony was the "new NBA Thug?" (2006). Michael Ventre, who described the brawl as worse than the "Palace Melee," called on David Stern, a trained attorney, to use his "gavel" and "black robe" with care. He summed the situation up this way: "Two years after the Malice at the Palace caused the terms 'NBA' and 'thuggery' to become inextricably linked in the minds of basketball fans the world over, the Knicks and Nuggets disregarded the greater good and flailed away at each other like rival bikers at a road house. In fighting for individual honor they brought dishonor upon the game. Stern also wisely opened up a jumbo-size can of legal whup-ass" (2006).[2] Ventre, like Peter Vecsey, who encouraged Stern to "lock up Nate Robinson and throw away the key" (2006), framed the Knicks-Nuggets fight in legal and criminal justice terms, playing on hegemonic frames of reference that systematically imagine the black body as a criminal threat that is justly contained, controlled, policed, and punished by a colorblind system that maintains societal law and order. Steve Dimatteo, in "Basketball Brawls: The 'Thug' Mentality of the NBA," highlights this element of the discourse, writing:

> Thanks to the media influences, the players' close ties to the rap industry, and the overall thug mentality of the league, the NBA is now known as nothing more than a bunch of vastly overpaid gangster wannabes.
>
> By no means is this a racial issue because all one needs to do is look at the facts to see that the NBA is out of control. How often is there an NBA player in trouble for something? Granted, all sports have their legal issues but none translate quite so prominently onto the playing field as professional basketball does in the U.S. There is nothing the league can do about it because the players are going to act however they want. The outside influences and temptations are too strong for anyone to put an end to it and in the race to see who has the most tattoos or baggiest clothing, the league will continue to spiral downward into a moral pit of despair until the players themselves are gone and a new era can be ushered in. (2006)

Similarly, Lisa Olson describes the brawl as "criminal behavior" that "once again gave the impression that it was a league perpetuated by thugs" (Olson 2006). Responding to Nate Robinson's claim that he was simply "trying to protect family," a rhetorical argument commonly used after sports fights to highlight the team as family unit, Olson further elucidates the dialectic between race, crime, and culture (hip-hop) evident in the media coverage: "Good Lord. What a way to pile shame on top of the disgrace. Had some masked man just broken through the window and stolen Robinson's bling? Had his fancy ride been carjacked?" (2006).

The Internet was littered with rhetoric pronouncements and narratives—echoing the sentiments of Olson, Dimatteo, and Ventre—that imagined the brawl as the simple consequence of allowing a criminal contingency to infiltrate the NBA. On FreeRepublic.com, in response to polling on ESPN.com concerning the fight, posts in the comment section consistently referred to the players as "thugs" and demonstrated a lack of surprise about the fisticuffs given that "Carmelo 'Stop Snitching' Anthony'" is "the thuggiest thug who ever thugged." On AOL Sports, Fanhouse posters frequently labeled the players "thugs" as well. "D" offered the following assessment of the situation: "I guess the NBA stands for N*ggas Brawling Again. Guess you can take the man out of the hood, but you can't take the hood out of the man" ("Carmelo Anthony Drops Mardy Collins" 2006). Mike Oritiz seemed to agree, concluding that the brawl should surprise no one given the culture of the league and the nature of its players:

> Hello . . . what do you think will happen when you take nothing but common street thugs, pay them a ton of money to boost their ego's [sic] even more, and throw them on the basketball court with rival gangs. That's all the NBA is anymore. Over-paid, overdressed, under-educated, street gang members. Instead of fighting on the streets, they bring it here. They are no better than Mr. Drumline, "earlier post," that can't even speak proper English. They are uneducated, ignorant, thugs. I say it's a ONE shot deal. Start a fight, say goodbye to the NBA. These ignorant, mindless apes are suppose [sic] to be role models for our children? No thank you. I remember a time when all athletes were roll [sic] models. Respected, admired and looked up to. Never going to happen in this lifetime again. ("Carmelo Anthony Drops Mardy Collins" 2006)

Likewise, Mike Celizic described the Brawl as reaffirming "the perception that it's [the NBA's] a haven for thugs which it isn't—at least not any more than any other sport" (2006). Avoiding complexity for the sake of racialized tropes, this post-Brawl commentary illustrated the centrality of race to the NBA's culture war and its entrenched nature.

Such racial language is an important illustration of the racial and racializing language that followed Artest, but these commentaries were also contested. Demonstrating the ways in which the NBA functioned after the Palace Brawl as a space of narratives and counternarratives about race, the pretense or charade of colorblind discourse had been pushed aside for powerful racial talk. According to several commentators, the post–Madison Square Garden Brawl discourse was littered with racial tropes, stereotypes, and the usual scapegoating, which not only revealed a racial double standard, but once again focused public attention on the failures—cultural, sporting, and personal—of the NBA baller specifically, and the contemporary black athlete in general (Bryant 2006; Hill 2006; Jones 2006; Zirin 2006a).

Noting how hockey, baseball, and football players—not to mention other members of society (e.g., college students)—engage in fights without triggering panic buttons, sweeping generalizations, and demonizing commentaries, much of the discourse debated why the brawl elicited so much media attention (Adande 2006a; Berger 2006; Brennan 2006; Bryant 2006; Jones 2006; Sharpe 2006; Sorensen 2006; Wilbon 2006). While Drew Sharpe specifically attributed the heightened scrutiny felt by the NBA to the popularity and celebrity of the league (2006), Christine Brennan focused on the different uniforms/gear of the different sports: "Look at hockey and football players. They are dressed for battle. NBA players look like they're reading for a photo shoot" (2006). David Stern, erasing race from the conversation, argued that the "visibility" of the NBA's players created extra "burdens" (Quoted in Berger 2006) for them. However, other commentators, as well as some players (Bryant 2006; Jones 2006), argued that the double standard resulted from the power of whiteness and anti-black racism. J.R. Smith, a member of the Denver Nuggets, surmised that the rampant hyperbole and denunciations embodied "A double standard: You see guys out there with tattoos and stuff like that, especially African American guys that makes people think ever worse about you than they already do. People are going to have their perceptions of you anyway" (Quoted in Bryant 2006). Steve Francis (New York Knicks) concurred, arguing, "In other sports there are incidents that are way worse than basketball. So many worse things happen every game or four or five times a year, but because there are more blacks in the NBA, it's under the microscope more than baseball and hockey" (Quoted in Martin and Berman 2006). Smith and Francis were not alone, with several other writers similarly attributing the double standard and the widespread demonization of the players to race and racism:

> But, for me, this thing has gone overboard. Everywhere I look another critic brands the players involved as "thugs." Everywhere I look, the fight is looked upon as a black eye for the league. I say hogwash and I call the critics hypocrites. The NBA is the only sport on earth where the players are deemed as practical criminals if a fight breaks out. (Jones 2006)

> They invoke clichés about thugs and punks and the two-year old Detroit Pistons-Indiana Pacers-Detroit fans brawl. Eventually, they

get around to cornrows and tattoos. They always get around to cornrows and tattoos. (Sorensen 2006)

The brawl I witnessed back in the early 1950s involved predominantly white players and I don't remember there being any outcry about white violence. (G. Vecsey 2006)

And every now and again after something like that, I'll hear some racist crack. Racists are always waiting for an opportunity to paint the NBA as a bunch of out-of-control players. It kills me to have these highlights all over the TV, knowing racist idiots in sports bars somewhere are seeing them feeling vindicated. (Henry Abbott quoted in "Garden Brawl" 2006)

Two things you could count on happening in the aftermath of the Knicks-Nuggets fight: (1) Over usage of the word "thug," which belongs right next to "race card" in the Phrases That Should Be Eliminated Hall of Fame; (2) Somehow this will all be blamed on hip-hop culture—the convenient scapegoat for everything wrong with the NBA. Forget blaming this on a petty feud between George Karl and Isaiah Thomas. Let's just point the finger at Ludacris.

Seriously folks, can we not make the same mistake with "Melee at Madison Square" that we did after the "Malice at the Palace"? Can we not smash the overreact button and realize Saturday's multiplayer brawl was just a regular ol' jock fight? (Hill 2006)

Meanwhile black basketball players apparently is such an issue that it even competed for weekend air time with other staple of saturation coverage—missing white people (on Oregon's Mount Hood). . . . Yes there will always be racial components when you're are dealing with a league in which more than 70 percent of the players are black. . . . Somehow NBA players have received status normally reserved for white people in America; the right to be judged individually, not collectively. After Timothy McVeigh blew up that building in Oklahoma City, security guards didn't cast a suspicious eye on every white man driving past a federal building. But ask any person of Middle Eastern descent how hard it was for them to board an airplane after Sept. 11. (Adande 2006a)

Folks in Atlanta from the other side of the track and from the country aimed their venom at the combatants. In the NBA land it's been vicious, racist and personal. (Evans 2006)

What is clear from those citing race as an explanation for much of the media discourse and fan reaction is not simply that a double standard exists in which NHL, MLB, and NFL players are celebrated for fighting while NBA players face a firing squad of sorts, but that rhetorical devices are used to criminalize the NBA's players/blackness, constructing the fight as an indication of the broader problems facing the league—hip-hop, the purported infusion of a "ghetto mentality," and the overall hegemony of blackness.

What is also striking about several of the commentaries that acknowledge the centrality and/or implications of race and racism is their simultaneous celebration of Stern for his application of swift justice in doling out several suspensions (Adande 2006a; Jones 2006; Smith; 2006; Vecey 2006). Richard Lapchick called Stern "realistic. He's trying to create a sense that the NBA is full of responsible citizens. That jumps into the face of the segment of our population that is racist. But by immediately reining in the players who fought he is saying, 'That's not us'" (Quoted in Brennan 2006). Similarly, focusing on appeasing white fans and protecting the financial future of the league in the wake of Artest (and the racial awareness/ anxiety about the league), Christine Brennan celebrated the suspension of the players. "He has heard the comments about the 'thugs' in his league, about all the tattoos," she wrote in "Fan Repulsion led to Stern Measures." "Stern effectively acknowledged that those words, fair or unfair, matter. If his league wants to play in Peoria and Topelo and Spokane, if the players want to sell merchandise and make money in cities big and small, there could be no slapping of wrists, not on Stern's watch" (2006). Celebrating the power of whiteness—that white players can get away with more without threatening the bottom line because their actions don't have negative implications on the league (i.e., they are individuals)—and the importance of accommodating and appeasing white fans, even those who are racist and/or operating on stereotypes, Brennan applauds Stern for his neoliberal approach to the NBA. Elizabeth Martinez and Anoldo Garcia argue that neoliberalism reflects a belief in "the rule of the market" and a systematic elimination of "the concept of the 'public' or 'community'" (2007). In this paradigm, justice, fairness, and equality are secondary; challenging racism isn't as important as the needs of the market. In his commentary on the fight, "A Hittin Image," Michael Wilbon describes the importance of economics to league decision making, how the needs of (white) patrons trump the rights of black players, justice, or equality:

> NBA players have endured more scrutiny, pertaining to image, than any other professional athletes in America. This was the case in the 1970s, when the league had to deal openly with the perception that the league was too black and too drug infested. And after a very

cozy period with patrons and Madison Avenue from, say, 1984 until about 2000, the league is back to dealing with the perception that too many of its players are thugs.

Whether that's racial code or not, the NBA is a business and Stern is its chief operating officer, and he's had to deal with the perception affecting the league's reality and bottom line. The recent adoption of an age limit, the dress code, and the crackdown on demonstrative complaining to the refs is all part of a larger effort to improve the league's image.

So was hiring a conservative operative to figure out how the league that had married itself to hip-hop could be better perceived by the people who buy the tickets and jerseys.

You can sugar-coat this any way you want but the bottom line is: A black league has to be palatable to white patrons. And black multimillionaires swinging at each other isn't part of the equation. If Stern doesn't send the message that the league has zero tolerance, it's incredibly bad business. . . .

This fighting issue and the way it attaches itself to the players is the NBA's burden to bear. "Those thugs" are going to have to be more red-state friendly in order to sell seats, much less jerseys and shoes. NBA players are the most identifiable of professional athletes. They make the most money. They've got the most intimate relationship with the patrons. They've got the longest shelf life (2006).

Wilbon, like many of Stern's cheerleaders, makes clear that racism necessitates intervention and harsh punishment by the league, unwittingly sanctioning the racial dimensions of the discourse. Such arguments are akin to arguing that the practice of racially profiling people of color driving in white neighborhoods that while unfair is understandable, or even politically smart, given the political power and social capital of white residents. The presence of people of color in white suburban neighborhoods elicits fear and anger and because white concerns matter, the police are justified in engaging in racial profiling, heightened surveillance, and even harassment.

Similarly, given that white fans and corporate sponsors have vocalized contempt for and fear of black bodies in the NBA, and given the potential threats to the league if those bodies violate their demands and expectations, it is argued that Stern has an economic and moral obligation to suspend any and all players involved in such a violation. The discourse, once again, celebrates Stern for challenging the players rather than racism, failing to recognize that the suspensions themselves provide legitimacy for the racist ideologies and prejudices that necessitate action. "This approach, in my mind, is rooted in generational and racial anxiety and efforts to assuage that anxiety among folks who can afford the pricey tickets at Madison Square Garden," writes Dave Zirin. "When Stern feeds the myth that players are out of control and uncivilized, it gives confidence to the apostles of fear" (2006). Recognizing Stern's accommodation to racial fear, Zirin argues that the logic and ideologies guiding the NBA are not unique: One could make a comparison between the NBA culture and suspension rates in American public schools, or even the NBA and the war on drugs. Fear and racism leads to policing and surveillance, which is then justified by a culture of racialized fear. Just as racial fear contributes to a Jim Crow-ed federal drug policy, where possession of 500 grams of cocaine historically resulted in the same sentence as having 5 grams of crack (the sentencing guideline/disparity was reduced to 18:1 in 2010), the media and league response to the "Mayhem at the Mecca" both played off the racial fear so prevalent within the discourse and, in so doing, justified that fear by further demonizing and criminalizing the league's black ballers. Responding to Henry Abbott's question, "Who cares what they [the bigots] think?," Paulsen wrote the following on the "Sports Media Watch" blog:

> David Stern does. And as long has [sic] he continues to, the NBA will suffer. David Stern has been catering to those bigots for going on two years now, and he will continue to in an effort to make attendance and television ratings increase.
>
> By playing to the ignorant majority, David Stern will destroy his league. The NBA will never be a favorite of the masses. How it ever was is a statement to just how amazing Michael Jordan, Magic Johnson and Larry Bird were. Any league with mostly black players is not going to have mainstream success, with the lone exception of the NFL. (2006)

Demonstrating the power of race and racism within the NBA media discourse, the post–Madison Square Garden Brawl debates revealed that the criminalized black body remained front and center, scapegoated as the reason for the fight and the problems facing the NBA. More importantly, the panics and fears, whether justified or not, of this criminalized black body necessitated action in the form of punishment and discipline implemented by David Stern. As with the judge who punishes/disciplines the black defendant or the principal who suspends/disciplines the black student, this moment in the culture war once again reinforced the idea that "helping" the NBA and its black players meant punishing and disciplining them.

THE CULTURE WARS

In 2004, Thomas Frank published a critically acclaimed and much talked about monograph on the divisions within America that resulted from "what he calls the 'great backlash'—the popular revolt against a supposedly liberal establishment" (2000 dust jacket). Wondering why so many Americans vote against their political and economic interests, Frank attempts to elucidate the reasons for this phenomenon. He concludes that the battles—both real and imagined (media constructed)—between liberals and conservatives, the secular and the religious, the unpatriotic and the patriotic, and those residing in blue and red states is nothing new. According to Frank:

> In the backlash America is always in a state of quasi-civil war: on one side the unpretentious millions of authentic Americans. On the other side, the bookish, all-powerful, liberals who run the country but are contemptuous of the tasks and beliefs of the people who inhabit it. When the chairman of the Republican National Committee in 1992 announced to a National TV audience "We are America" and "those other people are not," he was merely giving a more blunt expression to a decades-old formula. Newt Gingrich's famous description of Democrats as "the enemy of normal Americans" was just one more winning iteration of the well-worn theme. (2000, p. 13)

Likewise, in 1992, Patrick Buchanan argued that Americans were "at war for the nation's soul" (Quoted in Williams 1997, p. 1), bringing into focus his argument that the United States was not simply battling foreign enemies, but the cultural divisions within its own borders. Similar efforts to imagine America as a nation facing a culture war have been highlighted and used by the likes of William Bennett, James Dobson, and Bill O'Reilly. For example, in his book, *Culture Warrior*, Bill O'Reilly argues "there is a huge philosophical difference between secular-progressives and traditionalists, and that gulf will never narrow" (2006, p. 69). In fact, the past 20–plus years have seen ample arguments coming from media pundits and politicians alike concerning the divisions and battles for America's future.

> "We are witnessing a culture," we are told. The major political cleavage in American politics is no longer class, race, region, or any of the many social structural differences that divide the popular. Rather, a major realignment of sensibilities and controversial issues means that the body politic is now rent by a cultural conflict in

which values, moral codes, and life-styles are the primary objects of contention. (Williams 1997, p. 1)

The emphasis on this ongoing culture war and "the struggle to define America" has not been limited to the pulpit, podium, or sound bite, but has also manifested within the academy (Fiorina 2005; Gates 1992; Gitlin 1995; Hunter and Wolfe 2006; Jacoby 1994; Sine 1995; See Williams 1997, p. 1 for exhaustive list). Perhaps the most influential book within the academic discourse concerning America's culture wars has been James Davidson Hunter's *Culture Wars*. Focusing on religious/secular divisions, Hunter argues, "America is in the midst of a culture war that has had and will continue to have reverberations not only within public policy but within the lives of ordinary Americans everywhere" (1992, p. 34). More precisely Hunter concludes that the "cultural conflict" that plagues America "emerges over fundamentally different conceptions of moral authority, over different ideas and beliefs about truth, the good, obligation to one another, the nature of community, and so on. It is, therefore, cultural conflict at its deepest level" (1992, p. 49).

Similarly, while focusing on political struggles over needle exchange programs, gambling, prostitution and pornography, Elaine Sharp, in *Culture Wars and Local Politics*, offers her own description "of what James Davidson Hunter (1991; 1994) calls 'culture wars,' and Ken Meier (1994) calls 'morality politics'" (1999, p. 3). According to Sharp, the ongoing culture wars are: "grounded in moral concerns" (p. 3). In this sense, local and national deployment of the trope of "morality politics" reflects an effort to regulate and impose policy, "which involves efforts by some individuals to impose 'legal authority to modify or replace community values, moral practices, and norms of interpersonal conduct with new standards of behavior'" (Sharp 1999, p. 3; Tatalouich and Dayne 1998, p. 1). "Culture wars are often extraordinarily passionate and strident" (Sharp 1999, p. 3), Sharp argues. There is nothing moral or "business as usual" within the culture wars. The culture wars inspire significant debate and interest within the spectrum of constituencies and the public at large "because they touch on deeply held values and threats to those values" (Sharp 1999, p. 3). Finally, the discourse concerned with the culture war itself imagines the controversies through the prism of a binary, presenting the conflict in oppositional and simplistic terms: "morality issues can be presented in simple ways and can engage people that have no special expertise in the topical area" (Sharp 1999, p. 4). Rhys Williams, in the introduction to *Culture War in American Politics*, notes how, within this discourse, religion and religiosity represent the center, the basis, for the culture war. He further notes that, within the public and academic debates, culture is "defined as the beliefs, values, ideas and moral commitments that people share; these have become objects over which the two sides struggle. . . . Second, cultural is the means with which contemporary politics is pursued" (Williams 1997, pp. 6–7).

What is lost here is an understanding of how power defines and dissem-
inates culture and ascribes value and meaning to culture and cultural values.
Moreover, culture also functions as a commodity—an object, even a symbol—
that is bought, sold, and traded within the capitalist, political, and cultural
marketplaces. For example, the imagining of the culture war as a battle
between two communities (the religious/orthodox and the secular humanist)
of equal footing and standing, which constructs traditional (white, middle-
class Christian male) American values as being under assault, does not
account for racism, sexism, Christian hegemony, or the commonsense ideologies that guide American cultural and institutional practices. Michael Omi
and Howard Winant do not so much see a culture war as they do a response
by the right, formulated over several decades, to the great transformation ushered in by the social movements of the 1960s.

> The new right dream seemed within reach: to consolidate a "new
> majority" which could dismantle the welfare state, legislate a return
> to 'traditional morality,' and stem the tide of political and cultural
> dislocation which the 1960s and 1970s represented. The project
> linked the assault on liberalism and "secular humanism," the obses-
> sion with individual guilt and responsibility where social questions
> were concerned (crime, sex, education, poverty), with a fierce antis-
> tatism. The political strategy involved was populist. . . . Some ana-
> lysts see the new right as a status revolt by those who, according to
> Ben Wattenerg are "unyoung, unpoor, and unblack"—those whose
> identities and interests were articulated negatively by the social
> movements of the 1960s and the crises of the 1970s. They resent
> any mobility on the part of lower-status groups, and demand that
> the political process reorganize the traditional values to which they
> subscribe. Their anger is directed at those who are "not like them-
> selves"; this involves a racial dimension which is experienced as a
> cultural threat as much as an economic. one. (1994, p. 125)

In other words, Omi and Winant argue against much of the discourse that
imagines the culture war as cutting across racial, class, gender, and geographic
lines, illustrating the ways in which racism and hegemonic visions of blackness, whiteness, and the racial "other" guide both the rhetorical devices used
and the resulting political mobilization. They also elucidate the ways in which
the Right has used racial, gendered, and class-based ideologies to consolidate
power in the face of challenges from 1960s freedom movements. "The politics
of white identity is undergoing a profound political crisis. . . . White privilege
. . . has been called into question in the post-civil rights period" writes George
Lipsitz. "Far from being destroyed, however, the white 'politics of difference'
is now being trumpeted as an ideology of victimization. The situation would

be farcical if it weren't so dangerous, reflecting venerable white anxieties and fortifying the drift to the rich which, now as in the past, is highly conductive to race-baiting" (Lipsitz quoted in Watkins, p. 42). "Presently in America a war is being fought. Forget about guns, plans, and bombs, the weapons from now on will be the newspapers, magazines, TV shows, radio and film," notes Spike Lee. "It's war in the battleground of culture" (Quoted in Watkins 1998, p. 137). S. Craig Watkins, demonstrating the contradictory and contested nature of this culture war, concludes that it is not simply the result of the emergence of the New Right, but also the increased visibility of the black underclass within commodity culture.

> The ghetto has emerged as the dominant locus of social problems according to leading public opinion polls. For instance, public concern about crime, welfare, and decaying moral values invariably invokes the ghetto. On the other hand, the language, fashions, cultural productions, and allegedly nihilistic lifestyles associated with ghetto youth seem to give life to the production of new popular culture trends in the United States. (Watkins 1998, p. 175)

In this sense, blackness had become an organizing principal for America's culture war. Watkins, Stuart Hall, and Herman Gray each illustrate the significant ways that an imagined African American culture has been used to explain away problems, to place blame outside the realm of white American-ness, thereby substantiating claims of white victimization, white superiority, and the personal failures of the black community. Writing about Pat Buchanan's 1992 speech, Watkins argues:

> Buchanan's claim that the deployment of force was necessary to take back our cities and our country was, of course, premised on the widespread assumption that because black youth lacked discipline and respect for authority, they constitute a serious threat to the nation. The ominous tone of the speech dramatizes the manner in which black youth are implicated in some of the more prominent social and political episodes that define the culture wars at the century's end. . . . [The] rising tide of social conservatism [that] has developed tenacious racial characteristics. Black youth seemingly have been in the eye of a public storm against crime, drugs, and the alleged erosion of traditional values. As a result crime, drugs, and the alleged erosion of traditional values. As a result new punitive technologies and legislation have been initiated in order to exercise greater control over black youth. (1998, p. 1)

Focusing on the racial dimensions of the culture war—in terms of the demonization of racialized others, the consolidation of white power, and the hegemony of commonsense ideologies regarding blackness and whiteness—Stuart Hall, who notes that "blackness is never innocent or pure" (Gray 2005, p. 21), argues that cultural definitions of blackness as criminal, as threatening, guided politics in the 1980s:

> The themes of crime and social delinquency, articulated through the discourses of popular morality, touch the direct experience, the anxieties and uncertainties of ordinary people. This has led to a dovetailing of the "cry for discipline" from below into the call for an enforced restoration of social order and authority "from above." This articulation for the bridge, between the real material sources of popular discontent, and their representation, through specific ideological forces and campaigns, as the general need for a "disciplined society." It has as its principal effect, the awakening of popular support for a restoration of order through imposition: the basis of a populist "law-and-order" campaign. This in turn, has given a wide legitimacy to the title of balance within the operations of the state toward the "coercive" pole, whilst preserving its popular legitimacy. (Hall quoted in Watkins, p. 36)

Likewise, Herman Gray notes that the New Right successfully reduced "blackness as a marker of internal threats to social stability, cultural morality, and economic prosperity" (1995, p. 35). Considering the arguments of these authors suggests an answer to Thomas Frank's question about why so many Americans vote against their political and economic interests, one where race and racialized understandings of culture, community, and values are central. There may indeed be an ongoing culture war, a battle between competing ideologies and worldviews, but race and racism facilitate and guide this war. That is why, once the blackness of the NBA became so transparent (and thus troubling and dangerous) there arose a demand to control it. Protecting white hegemony is the fundamental motivation behind this simultaneously real and imagined war. For example, whereas much of the literature on the culture wars constructs welfare as a site of conflict guided by competing moral and political visions, Omi and Winant, Gray, Hall, Lipsitz, Watkins, Kelley, and countless others force us to think about the impact of race, racism, and racial ideology on this debate. The wars on welfare and drugs do not simply challenge certain values and behaviors, they define those values and behaviors in terms of their relationship to black bodies. "Constructions of deviant sexuality emerge as a primary location for the production of these race and class subjectivities," writes Micki Mcelya in *Our Monica Ourselves: The Clinton Affair and the National Interest*. "Policy debates and public perceptions on welfare and impoverished Americans have focused relentlessly on the black urban poor—blaming nonnormative family structures, sexual promiscuity, and aid-induced laziness as the root cause of poverty and mobilizing of welfare queens, teen mothers, and sexually predatory young men to sustain the dismantling of the welfare state" (2001, p. 159).

The basis of the culture war, the means/methods by which the war is waged, and its consequences, disproportionately impact the cultural positioning and opportunities afforded to communities of color, women, and homosexuals—it is about power and privilege. Writing about the demonization of the black underclass, Robin D.G. Kelley discusses "the cultural and ideological warfare that continues to rage over black people and the 'inner city' as social problems" (1997, p. 4). He goes on to note the importance of talking about the relationship between the culture wars and post–civil rights antiblack racism:

> If racism is essentially a thing of the past, as conservatives and many neoliberals now argue, then the failure of the black poor to lift themselves out of poverty has to be found in their behavior or their culture. . . . I deliberately used the popular phrase culture wars in the subtitle of this book because all of these essays, in one way or another, explore the ongoing battle over representations of the black urban condition, as well as the importance of the cultural terrain as a site of struggle. Some readers might find the term culture wars inappropriate since it is generally associated with curriculum debates, "political correctness" on college campuses, or the politics of the arts and humanities funding. However, there is more to the culture wars than whether or not Cleopatra was black, or if multicultural education constitutes a new form of academic tyranny. The culture wars continue to rage each day in the streets of urban America, in the realm of public policy, in the union halls, and at the workplace. This book is premised on the idea that culture and questions of identity have been at the heart of some of the most intense battles facing African Americans at the end of the century. And as the global economy grows, the terrain of culture becomes ever more crucial as a terrain of struggle. Not only has globalization continued to transform black culture, but it has also dramatically changed the nature of work, employment opportunities, class structure, public space, the cultural marketplace, the criminal justice system, political strategies, even intellectual work. The "ghetto" continues to be viewed as the Achilles heel in American society, the repository of

bad values and economic failure, or the source of a vibrant culture of resistance. Depending on who is doing the talking/writing ghetto residents are either a morally bankrupt underclass or a churchgoing, determined working class living in fear of young riffraff. Whatever the narrative and whoever the source, these cultural and ideological constructions of ghetto life have irrevocably shaped public policy, scholarship, and social movements (Kelley 1997, pp. 8–9)

George Lipsitz describes this process in the following way:

> Because they are ignorant of even the recent history of the possessive investment in whiteness . . . Americans produce largely cultural explanations for structural problems. The increased possessive investment in whiteness generated by disinvestment in America's cities, factories, and schools since the 1970s disguises the general problem posed to our society by de-industrialization, economic restructuring, and neoconservative attacks on the welfare state as racial problems. It fuels a discourse that demonizes people of color for being victimized by these changes, while hiding the privileges of whiteness by attributing them to family values, fatherhood, and foresight—rather than favoritism. (1995, p. 379)

Watkins, building on the work of Tricia Rose, pushes readers to think about culture not simply as a place of contested racial meaning, but as a site of policy making, racialization, and policing: "Tricia Rose contends that the policing of black popular culture has become synonymous with the increased surveillance of black youth in general. Politicians seeking election year votes, for example, make fighting black youth expressive culture tantamount to fighting crime" (Watkins 1998, p. 176). Taking the analysis of both Watkins and Kelley as a point of departure, I similarly argue throughout *After Artest* that the cultural and bodily influences of the ghetto, often imagined through narratives focused on hip-hop culture, are frequently seen as the main source of the league's pathology, dysfunctionality, and criminality. These narratives guided discourse about the NBA after Artest. Furthermore, the intrusion of the values and morals associated with ghetto life were believed to necessitate intervention in the form of discipline and punishment.

Joy James argues similarly, concluding that signifiers of black violence and markers of black sexuality enter into public discourses as sources of consumption and scorn, as "corrupting and pathological, whether on screen or through welfare debates" (1996, p. 135). "What is forbidden in American culture often seems to be projected outward onto the outsider or scapegoat," writes James. "Blackness has come to represent sex and violence in the national psyche. Although they gain notoriety as the most infamous perpetrators of unrestrained criminality, African Americans are given little resignation in media, crime reports or social crusades as being victims" (1996, p. 27). In the case of the NBA specifically, and sports and popular culture in general, conservatives and whites have positioned themselves as powerless, the victims of the war, assaulted by the sports world, with its selfish athletes, and by other cultural arenas pimping sex, drugs, violence and supposedly anti-Christian values. Whether manifesting in commentaries on the lack of emphasis on team ball, panics regarding the criminal activity of NBA players, debates about the stylistic choices of the NBA baller, or criticism over trash-talking, the culture war inside America's arenas and playing fields is historically and ideologically specific, and reflects long-standing fears about black and brown bodies. As Lauren Berlant laments in her discussion of cultural citizenship and the conservative focus on sex and intimacy, sexualized culture wars and conservatives' use of "divisive rhetoric" as the basis for seizing power post-Reagan have obscured the public debate about questions regarding justice, equality, and state violence within contemporary America.

> It is my view that critical engagement with what ought to constitute the social privileges and obligations of citizenship must be reorganized around these questions—of national capitalism, metropolitan and rural poverty, environmental disintegration, racist thinking, and ordinary concrete practices and other banalities of national evil. (1997, pp. 8–9)

Although the culture war represents a battle over values, between hip-hop culture and "middle America"—a term Watkins sees as neither "race-neutral" nor "ideologically neutral" (Watkins 1998, p. 43)—between an older and a younger generation (Boyd 2004b), the NBA's culture war is, at its core, both racial and racialized. Take Thomas Frank's *What's the Matter with Kansas*, which, despite giving voice to the ongoing culture wars in America, discounts the racial implications and consequences of these debates. "What we see here is something very different, and equally disturbing: the backlash in full cry without the familiar formula of racial conflict to serve as an interpretative guide" (180). While much of the literature tends to de-center race, focusing on class or generation as primary explanations given the popularity of hip-hop among white youth, *After Artest* works from what has increasingly become an unpopular argument that race sits at the center of the culture war. As such, this monograph builds on the work of Watkins, Berlant, James, and Gray, among others, illustrating the ways in which race is central to national panics and the resulting efforts to regulate and impose new policies. Examining the contemporary culture wars of the NBA and the surrounding media discourse illustrates the fallacy of the celebration of the NBA as a racially transcendent. Just as crime signifies blackness, and vice versa, after Artest blackness began once again to embody a pollutant within the NBA, necessitating surveillance and regulation.

THE NBA'S CULTURE WAR

Throughout the 1990s, the relationship between the NBA and hip-hop flourished, with players like Shaq and Allen Iverson producing their own rap albums, and the cultural aesthetics of hip-hop taking a greater hold on the NBA. Hip-hop became synonymous with the NBA to such an extent that Eric Barrow concludes, "hip-hop and the NBA are one" (2007). According to Kenny Smith, "basketball has always been connected to hip-hop and vice-versa. Old street ball at Rucker Park influenced hip-hop because the bravado of the player is what got the people out to the event" (Quoted in Broussard 2005, p. 45). Likewise, Lil' Wayne identified the relationship between hip-hop and basketball as natural given that they are ostensibly the same thing in different forms: "Hip-hop culture is about style, swagger and charisma, and so is basketball. Hip-hop is an up-temp thing and basketball is an up-tempo game. Also, there are a lot of young people involved in hip-hop and love hip-hop and basketball, of course, is a young people's game now. It goes like a hand in a glove" (Quoted in Hochman 2007). Ludacris attributes the symbiotic relationship between hip-hop and the NBA to the shared values of competition, confidence, and boldness associated with both rap music and basketball. Yet, others like Mark Cuban and Spike Lee see the prominence of hip-hop within the NBA as the result of markets and profit potential, (Broussard 2005, pp. 45–46). According to Mark Cuban, "if classical music were hot with 12– to 24 year olds, you'd be asking why the NBA is tied to Brahms" (Quoted in Reyes 2005). Still others focus less on marketing and the strategies of the NBA to court new fans and more on the ways in which the players, from the Fab-5 to AI, transformed the league in both its play and its style. "The league is more commercial and it's all based on image, but hip-hop is basically where a lot of the people in the NBA grew up," concluded Marcus Camby. "We grew up in the inner city, we grew up on hip-hop music" (Quoted in Thompson 2004, p. 1). Tattoos, braids/cornrows, and the "fuck it" attitude that define elements of hip-hop overtook the league as a new generation entered its ranks, while, at the same time, the NBA (and its media partners) attempted to use the cultural and economic power of hip-hop to sell the league. The influx of hip-hop has not been limited to the court, with Jay-Z and Nelly each owning portions of two different NBA franchises.

Yet, even as the league and its players have sold the game by exploiting its relationship with hip-hop, the NBA has tried to maintain a certain distance so as not to alienate its rich, white, corporate fans, or those living in America's red states. Although the emergence of the NBA baller (and hip-hop in the NBA) transformed the aesthetic and stylistic offerings of the league, ushering in a new era of popularity, its prominence refocused fan and societal attention on the blackness of the league. Hip-hop, in this sense, challenged the hegemony of Magic Johnson and Michael Jordan who, along with Stern, had transformed a league once associated with drugs and the ghetto (blackness) in the white imagination to one defined by racial transcendence. Hip-hop, in the eyes of many, unraveled this "progress" and created the need for action. At one point, the NBA put Allen Iverson on the cover of its official magazine, *Hoop*, with his tattoos airbrushed away so that he might look more "acceptable."

The Palace Brawl, on the other hand, demonstrated the impossibility of airbrushing away or sanitizing the blackness in the NBA. It not only raised questions as to whether hip-hop could continue to have such a prominent place in the NBA (given its connection to blackness), but also demonstrated a need to curtail the visibility and cultural power of the NBA's black bodies. Not surprisingly, the idea of a (racialized) culture war plaguing the NBA is ubiquitous to the discourse. Ethan Skolnick in, "It's an Athlete . . . Hide," describes the ongoing debate that followed the brawl at Auburn Hills as one of hyperbole, panics, and sensationalism.

> Raise the threat level to a fiery red, add provisions to the Patriot Act, bust out the duct tape. Call on elected officials to protect us from the true enemy within our borders, the real threat to our way of life, the imminent danger George W. Bush and John Kerry egregiously ignored on the stump.
>
> You know, the professional athlete. . . .
>
> Maybe you didn't hear Fox News' Greta Van Susteren ask, "Athletes out of control? What's behind the rage?" Or MSNBC's Mike Barnicle, subbing for Joe Scarborough, ask, "Has our society created monsters? Should they be role models?" Or radio host Laura Ingraham, while admitting she hadn't followed the NBA since college two decades ago, insinuating hip-hop culture caused Friday's melee.
>
> Maybe you didn't see the fear on the faces of parents invited to chat with Zahn on CNN.
>
> Almost as if they had seen the deficit.
>
> Or Desperate Housewives. Or Terrell Owens—gasp!— with the most desperate.

Maybe you've been too focused on footage from Fallujah to witness the horrifying guerrilla warfare of Auburn Hills. . . .

Now all should do the right thing: find a bunker, escape the evildoers, and still be sure not to miss Fox's season premiere of When Athletes Attack (2004).

Likewise, Jason Whitlock, while dismissing the importance of racism to the discussion, describes the ongoing battle as a "clash of cultures. A predominantly white fan base is rejecting a predominantly black style of play and sportsmanship" (2004). Whitlock is not alone in concluding that the NBA, prior to, during, and as a result of the Artest Brawl, faced a cultural struggle, increased tensions, and, ultimately, a clash between two distinct communities; that a series of shifts within and realizations about the NBA (culminating after the Artest brawl) made visible the league's blackness and revealed the illusion of the NBA as a space of racial transcendence, thereby prompting discomfort and, soon after, demands for regulation, control, and containment. "Maybe the NBA is too hip-hop for its audience," suggested Marcus Thompson two and half weeks prior to the Palace Brawl. "Maybe the urban culture, with its braggadocio and rebellion, is too much for the predominantly older, whiter ticket buyers and media." (2004, p. 1). Or, better said, maybe the league was too black for its white fan base and only after Artest was there a full recognition of its racial signifiers; with this recognition, there was no chance that hip-hop could exist in the context of white consumption and racial transcendence. As a result: suspensions, a dress code, excoriating commentaries, criminalization, rule changes, "no high school ballers allowed," and surveillance. While acknowledging that race matters, Thompson, Whitlock, Boyd, and others see the conflict as not simply being driven by racism, or broader discursive articulations, but also by cultural and/or generational divides. "It comes down to a generational difference," argues Boyd, as quoted in "Hip-Hop Culture Polarizing Older White Ticket Buyers." "The gate-keepers of the NBA are older and white. They want to make the league out to be something to fit them instead of taking the league for what it is. It's not just racial. There are many black people who don't like hip-hop either. It's a generational difference. People from older generations want to impose their beliefs on the younger generation" (Quoted in Thompson 2004). Repeating this same theme, three weeks later, Boyd argued that the Artest Brawl was indeed the result of a racialized culture war, although in his eyes, there was more to it than that:

So was it a race war?

Well, this is America, and race has something to do with practically everything.

But that's just the easy answer. What happened last Friday

certainly wasn't any kind of race war we're familiar with. There are too many other factors: wealth, the culture of the players, the assumptions of the fans.

The culture we live in today makes it more complicated than black versus white—just as the whole issue of race is more complicated than black versus white, and it's time we woke up to that. (Boyd 2004b)

Since 2004, the league has also gone to great lengths to sanitize and insulate itself from the influences of hip-hop. Whether by fining players for wearing excessively long shorts or engaging in too much trash talk, in recent years the NBA has been defined less by its style of play, or even its superstars, and more by its systematic effort to "fight a culture that pervades the league and will for a generation" (Barrow 2007) and its attempts "to make the sport more palatable to White America" (Barrow 2007). The visibility of blackness on the court and in the players' aesthetic offerings (style, swagger) had created an identity crisis for the league given that, within the national white imagination, blackness is represented as being "lascivious, emotional, and childlike" (Williams, 1997, p. 104). The NBA and its fans had been awoken from their racial fantasy, their claims of progress and racial transcendence, to not only see the league as black, but also to manifest discomfort, disdain, and animosity toward anything signifying blackness. "The NBA despises itself. It can barely stand to look in the mirror anymore. It hates what's staring back. . . . It's in Allen Iverson. It's in Carmelo Anthony. It's in Ron Artest. It's smack-talk and back-talk. It's brims to the side. It's do-rags. It's cornrows" (Barrow 2007).

While neither discounting generation, class, or gender, nor embracing a black/white binary, *After Artest* has argued that racialization, representations of blackness based in white supremacist ideologies, and blackened moral panics guided the racial contestations that followed the Palace Brawl; that the realization of the blackness of the league, and the post-racial bubble bursting, led to the reemergence of hegemonic white racial frames that, in turn, produced a war on the styles, aesthetics, and bodies associated with blackness.

FIVE YEARS LATER

On the fifth anniversary of the Palace Brawl, a series of television debates and online commentaries appeared to reflect on its impact and legacies. While many focused on how it transformed the lives of Ron Artest and John Green,[3] and how it impacted both the Pacers and Pistons, a good portion of these commentaries reflected on the broader significance of the event. In

"Five years on, Perceptions, Lessons of Infamous Palace Brawl Changing," Mark Montieth concludes that fans' focus on player behavior rather than the punishment directed at the players, or even the brawl itself, revealed the issues at work. "Many weary fans revised their opinions of the brawl, viewing it as further evidence of the players' poor character rather than unfair punishment. A parade of callers to local talk-radio programs labeled them 'thugs.'" As a result of fan anger and corporate concerns, "Stern reacted so swiftly and firmly—to send a message to fans and sponsors alike that his league didn't tolerate lawlessness" (2009). Similarly, Jemele Hill, with "The Brawl: Were Lessons Learned?" argues that the brawl foregrounded the racial tensions that had long been plaguing the league.

> As embarrassing as it was, the fight brought some fascinating issues to the surface, including the declining relationships between fans and players and, of course, the racial tensions created by a nearly all-black league being marketed, covered and consumed by a mostly white media and fan base. . . . (2009). But there is no doubt that, sadly, the Palace incident was a culmination of what most people had come to expect from NBA players. At the time, the league was bubbling with racial tension created by its alignment with hip-hop culture. You had young, black men making millions of dollars, unafraid to flaunt it with gaudy platinum chains and throwback jerseys—an image the NBA attempted to dissolve by instituting a dress code a year after the Palace brawl. (Hill 2009)

While not yet fully successful in transforming the league's image by controlling, regulating, and otherwise purging the presumed blackness of the league,[4] several lessons were learned from the Palace Brawl: (1) The league had not, despite claims to the contrary, created a cultural space of racial transcendence and colorblindness; race mattered, even if it lay beneath the surface; (2) in moments where race, or better said, blackness bubbled to the surface, action was needed in the form of discipline and punishment; (3) the association between blackness and hip-hop prevented the complete integration of hip-hop styles and aesthetics within the NBA. Because blackness always followed hip-hop, and because blackness signified pathology, savagery, and danger within the white imagination, hip-hop would ultimately threaten the profitability and cultural acceptance of the NBA; (4) most importantly, the Palace Brawl highlighted the blackness of the league—no amount of airbrushing or spinning could deny that reality. It was a spectacle, a confirmation of "the fact of blackness" in the NBA.

It was a moment akin to Fanon on the train, in which a young white girl uttered:

"Look, a Negro!". . . .
　　"Look, a Negro!" . . .
　　"Look, a Negro!"
　　"Mama, see the Negro!
　　I'm frightened!. . . .
　　"Look at the nigger! . . .
　　Mama, a Negro! . . .
　　The Negro is an animal,
　　The Negro is bad,
　　the Negro is mean,
　　the Negro is ugly;
　　look, a nigger. . . .
　　Negroes are savages, brutes, illiterates." (Fanon 2000, p. 257; p.
258; p. 261)

All of what followed—media commentaries, new policies, and the altered culture of the NBA—represented an attempt to curtail this fear and to otherwise control, discipline and annihilate "the negro"/ "the animal," "the ugly savage" "the nigga"/ "the thug"/ "the gangsta"/"the Nigger" from the cultural and physical landscape of the NBA. It has been an attempt to make her less frightened.

For five years efforts have been made to kill the "Negro," to rid the league of its blackness, to convince fans that they don't have to be scared, and to revive the dream of colorblindness and racial transcendence by erasing race and otherwise controlling the NBA's black bodies. Although the league has not been successful in putting the proverbial racial genie back in the bottle, of re-creating the illusion of racial transcendence/colorblindness—a fantasy that was dramatically undermined on that fateful night—the efforts to rid the league of straight-out-of-high-school players, hip-hop clothing, and other assumed signifiers of blackness has been central in an effort to recreate an NBA where blackness is another color. After Artest has not been the end of blackness within the NBA but it surely transformed the ways in which the NBA polices, manages, and controls the bodies associated with "the facts of blackness."

NOTES

CHAPTER 1. AFTER ARTEST

1. Artest described the confession as such: "The whole purpose of the testimony was to share problematic times in my life with the youth. There's a lot of kids out there right now that's going through the same things I was going through and they're able to relate" (Bresnahan 2009).
2. This section contains parts of a prior book written by the author entitled *Screens Fade to Black: Contemporary African American Cinema*, 2006. Said prior material is included herein with the permission of Praeger Publishers Inc., © 2004.
3. For purposes of clarity, discourse is thought of "as a set of ideas and practices that, when taken together, organize both a way a society defines certain truths about itself and the way it puts together social power" (Collins 2004, p. 350).
4. This is by no means an argument concerning the veracity or possibility of colorblindness, as colorblindness was never a reality in the NBA (or elsewhere), but rather one that emphasizes the importance and emphasis on colorblindness within the NBA brand.
5. This term was inspired by the work of Matthew Frye Jacobson whose book on the experiences of various white immigrant groups explores how their racialization led them to embody "whiteness of a different color."
6. Critical Discourse Analysis has advanced the theoretical arguments put forth by such luminaries as Antonio Gramsci, Louis Althusser, and Michel Foucault. While stressing the importance of ideology as an instrument of power, as a tool for "sustain[ing] and reinforc[ing] their social structures and relations" (Teo 2000, p. 11), each of these theorists pointed to the powerful role played by discourse. According to Omi and Winant, whose own theory of racial formation influences this research, "Gramsci's treatment of hegemony went even farther: he argued that in

order to consolidate their hegemony, ruling groups must elaborate and maintain a popular system of practices—through education, the media, religion, folk wisdom, etc.—which he called common sense" (p. 67).

7. Despite media emphasis on basketball as a ladder out of the ghetto, "the average baller doesn't come from the inner city" (Craggs 2008, p. 50).

CHAPTER 2. "I WENT TO A BASKETBALL GAME AND A VIBE AWARDS BROKE OUT" OR "NEGROES GONE WILD"

1. From free republic.com.
2. Page 2004.
3. Hip-hop only encompasses its five elements—Djing, MCing, graffiti writing, b-boying, and b-girling—but also represents an ethos, a worldview, a sense of community/belonging, and an imagined community. According to Jeff Chang, those connected by hip-hop "share a desire to continue to break down boundaries . . . to make urgent truth telling that reflects the lives, loves, histories, hopes and fears of their generation" (2007, p. xi). Chang and his contributors emphasize a myriad of aesthetic qualities that define hip-hop: competition/battles; sense of community; challenging binaries; "intellectual and social uplift" (Marc Joseph in Chang 2007, p. 13); "the urgencies of now" (Chang 2007, p. xi); "the democratic reclamation of public space" (Chang 2007, p. x); hybridity, spontaneity and creativity; and ultimately being a "voice of the people" (Doze in Chang 2007, p. 328). Yet at the same time, hip-hop is also a sign, a corporate strategy, a marketing ploy, and a mainstream commodity. In this vein, and because of a larger history of race and culture, hip-hop often functions as a stand-in to describe and discuss the black community irrespective of its multiracial/global history. The discourse surrounding it is used interchangeably with theories, such as culture of poverty, and hegemonic white racial framing that consistently stereotypes the black community as young, urban black males who listen to Jay-Z, who sag their pants, who wear starter jackets, and have cornrows, thereby erasing the diversity, complexity and heterogeneity of the black community.

   While recognizing the myriad of influences of hip-hop and understanding the heterogeneity of culture, identity, and community within the black community, *After Artest* explores the intersections/conflation of hip-hop and blackness. Despite arguments that the Palace Brawl and the connected culture wars merely elucidated fan discomfort about hip-hop, it will be argued here that at the core of the NBA's culture wars has been anxiety and animosity that emanates from anti-black ideologies. Hip-hop, while a code word for blackness (imagined as interchangeable), was not imagined as the central source of the NBA's problems, but rather the league's blackness. Accordingly, the influences of hip-hop were merely evidence of the league's blackness.

Hip-hop is a cultural movement, a form of popular culture and personal expression but also a trope to which the dominant media/political discourse rallies against (this is why I talk about hip-hop as a vehicle for the commodification of blackness). In *After Artest*, I explore how the demonization of hip-hop after the Palace Brawl not only emanates through critiques and rhetoric focused on hip-hop but did so in a way that saw little difference between hip-hop and blackness. It is important to make this clear so that readers don't misinterpret the argument to be saying something else. In no way is the argument offered here to suggest that hip-hop is synonymous with blackness. In fact, the opposite is the case in that the monograph is exploring the ways in which dominant media discourses use the trope/signifier of hip-hop as a way to talk about, ridicule, demonize, and control blackness.

More specifically, I explore the ways in which hip-hop is used as an acceptable stand-in for demonizing, criticizing, and blaming blackness for the purported problems of the NBA. Generally speaking, hip-hop is a vector to problematize and consume blackness within the contemporary NBA (and culture at large). The linkages between hip-hop and blackness emanate from the discourses connected to the NBA, and the commodification of particular bodies, styles and aesthetics.

4. There are a few instances where I am quoting white nationalists and white supremacists that have racist language. I include their words because it demonstrates the level of racism, the level of rhetorical violence, and the demonization directed at black NBA players/blackness.

5. I owe a debt of gratitude to Sanford Richmond concerning this argument. He has long argued to me that the Artest Brawl was the equivalent to 9/11 in that the NBA, like the Bush administration, converted the power and leverage resulting from crisis to institute change. Similarly, Frank Davis, a Pacers fan, described the Palace Brawl as "like 9/11" (quoted in Brady and Dodd 2004), "suggesting that the NBA might implement security measures similar in scope to changes at airport after the terrorist attacks" (Brady and Dodd 2004). While I take this argument a bit differently, arguing that Artest challenged claims of racial neutrality and transcendence within the league, necessitating changes in policy, media coverage, and the overall treatment of the NBA black players, his observations helped in the development of this argument.

6. Over this same period, 63 percent of whites polled, in 1993, expressed love/like for the NBA, with only 50 percent sharing this sentiment in

2003. For blacks, this number rose from 62 percent in 1993 to 92 percent in 2003.

7. This section contains parts of a prior essay written by the author entitled "The Next MJ or the next OJ? Kobe Bryant, Race and the Absurdity of Colorblind Rhetoric," which appeared in the *Journal of Sport and Social Issues*, 2004, Vol. 28, No. 3. Said prior material is included with the permission of Sage Publications Inc., © 2004, 2455 Teller Road, Thousand Oaks, CA 91320, http://www.sagepub.com. Thanks to C.L. Cole for her support. For additional discussion of crime and athletic discourse within the sport media, please see Leonard, "A World of Criminals or a Media Construction?: Race, Gender, Celebrity and the Athlete/Criminal Discourse," in Art Raney and James Bryant (Eds.), *Handbook of Sports and Media*, Taylor & Francis, 2006.

8. Richard Lapchick, in *Smashing Barriers* argues that the reporting about criminal misconduct from contemporary athletes "provides whites with the chance to talk about athletes in a way that reinforces these [black as more violent, prone to drug use, and inclined toward violence against women] stereotypes" (2002, p. 265). Noting the racial orientation here, he highlights the ways in which the media focuses not athletes committing crimes but those alleged transgressions by football and basketball (as opposed to hockey or baseball). The issue is not about crime and sports so much as it is about crime within sports dominated by African Americans. He (2003a; 2003b; 2002), as with a study from *San Diego Union-Tribune* (Schrotenboer 2007) found that, despite media sensationalism regarding criminal misconduct and NFL players, highlights the ways in which the media not only sensationalizes and overstates criminal misconduct from athletes, but how this coverage emanates from all the while confirming long-standing stereotypes about African Americans.

9. Of course, although Benedict does not provide specifics here, this image is one that was modeled after Jerry West, a white basketball player.

10. The media coverage surrounding rape allegations leveled at Kobe Bryant prompted a series of articles that contextualized the arrest of Bryant within a larger problem of crime-committing athletes. Chris Sheridan (2003), Bill Redeker (2003), and Rob Fernas (2003) not only reported the allegations against Bryant, but also used the moment to point to a larger problem facing the NBA. According to their reporting, the case against Bryant was reflective of a larger trend within the contemporary NBA. For example, in a section entitled "Here Comes Trouble," Redeker focuses on the out-of-control nature of the predominantly black NBA.

In recent years, the NBA and trouble seem to have become synonymous. In the past year alone, some of the biggest names in basketball—Jerry Stackhouse, Marcus Fizer, Darrell Armstrong, Allen Iverson, and Glenn Robinson—have all had runins with the law.

So many members of the Portland Trail Blazers have had problems with the law in recent years, sneering sports commentators have begun calling them the "Jail Blazers."

Some players have been charged with spousal abuse, others have been caught carrying guns, while still others have gotten into brawls with police. (2003)

11. This article was written prior to the Palace Brawl.
12. It should be noted that the celebrations were muted in some ways by disappointment that punishment was not even harsher and more severe.
13 Recognizing that these comments were not in the aftermath of the Palace Brawl, nor direct commentary on this event, I include above quotes from subsequent years because they capture the ongoing debate that preceded, yet increased after Artest, continuing into the present moment.

CHAPTER 3. A CRISIS INSIDE AND OUTSIDE AMERICA'S ARENA

1. This chapter contains parts of a prior essay written by the author entitled, "The Real Color of Money: Controlling Black Bodies in the NBA," which appeared in the *Journal of Sport and Social Issues*, 2006, Vol. 28, No. 2. Said prior material is included here with the permission of Sage Publications Inc., © 2006, 2455 Teller Road, Thousand Oaks, CA 91320, http://www.sagepub.com; the chapter also contains parts of a prior essay written by author entitled, "The Real Color of Money: Controlling Black Bodies in the NBA," which appeared on popmatters.com, May 10, 2005. The article is available at http://www.popmatters.com/sports/features/050510–nba-2.shtml; and finally, the chapter also contains parts of a prior essay written by author entitled, "Why Does a 14–year-Old Matter?," which appeared on popmatters.com, February 5, 2004. The article is available at http://www.popmatters.com/pm/feature/040205–freddyadu. Thanks to C.L. Cole, Cynthia Fuchs, and Tobias Peterson for their support.
2. Jermaine O'Neal and Stephen Jackson both did enter the draft straight out of high school, although Jackson was not initially drafted, leading to his attendance at a community college.
3. Please note that I have been unable to locate the exact salary structure for 1996 draft picks, and am thus using salary scale for 1999–1999

season; given history, the numbers of 1996–1997 season were presumably slightly lower.

4. Interestingly Robert Swift, a white center from the Seattle Super Sonics is not constructed as cautionary tale although he went straight from high school and despite being an early selection has been a flop. Similar, the many European teenagers—i.e., Darko Miličić—who despite being early draft picks have produced little on the court are rarely mentioned as cautionary tales, or even as flops.

5. Some of these players may not have ever made it with four years of college and who were drafted, so may not have been drafted after being exposed at the college level as just not that good.

6. Kwame Brown's place in the media coverage is quite interesting and instructive given that when he first entered the league he was celebrated as unique, as an exception, but in wake of his struggles on and off the court, including a 2006 investigation for sexual assault (he was cleared in July 2006), he quickly became an example of the problems of prepsters entering the league; he went from the exception to the rule. The short-lived success for Jerome Mosio and even the ample criticism directed at LeBron James following "The Decision," demonstrates how fluid this process can be and the selectivity and ephemeral nature of this narrative.

7. Interestingly, his life of poverty and despair was highlighted to ostensibly illustrate the desperation of Smith and the importance of the NBA as his only way out, his only way to provide for himself and his family, a possibility that was lost by his hasty entry into the league, and the failures of the NBA to protect these kids.

8. Oden, who because of injuries has been a "bust." To date, his usefulness to age restrictionists (unlike Durant) has been limited.

9. Curry, like Brown, has found limited/little success, which has been attributed to his lack of maturity and dedication

10. He would ultimately settle for a rule mandating that NBA entrants be at least 19 years old and have been out of high school for at least a year.

11. Both are blogs, with freedarko.com appearing to dabble in a spectrum of cultural happenings, whether sports or politics, whereas "The Starting Five" focuses on sports.

12. Larry Irving, who received his J.D. from Stanford University, spoke at a panel at Stanford University.

13. Here, hooks is writing about *Hoop Dreams*, concluding that the "film tells the world how the American Dream works" (1995, p. 22).

14. Red Auerbach, as part of his pitch to Ralph Sampson, a 7'4" center from University of Virginia, to enter the NBA draft early stated, "It's not like he's going to be a brain surgeon. He's going to be a professional basketball player (Quoted in May 1996).

15. According to Sullivan (2007) zero-tolerance policies have resulted in a disproportionate number of suspensions and expulsions directed at African American students. Although only 17 percent of the national student population, black students "account for 36 percent of the school suspensions and 31 percent of expulsions" (p. 6).

CHAPTER 4. "NO BLING ALLOWED"

1. Elder 2005.
2. For example, the New York Knicks had long required its players to wear jackets and ties for all team functions.
3. Interesting and more revealing, the coaches and owners would not be subjected to the dress code policy.
4. The policy also stipulates that players sitting on the bench have to wear dress shoes or boots, and socks, which is somehow different from the general policy, which states that all players must wear "appropriate shoes and socks, including dress shoes, dress boots, or other presentable shoes, but not include sneakers, sandals, flip-flops, or work boots." It also allows for players to leave the arena wearing either a "neat warm-up suit" as long as it was team-issued or proper business attire.
5. Little was made of his criticism of the policy or that of Wally Szerbiak, Steve Nash, or Greg Ostertag. The racial implications here are not lost on the author.
6. It should be noted that LeBron James, the "heir apparent" to "Air Jordan," who voiced support for the dress code was quoted prominently within the media discourse. As such, he was also positioned as the voice of reason and a positive force within the league.
7. In 2004, Sprewell is said to have been offered a three-year contract extension worth between $27 and $30 million dollars. Insulted, he noted, "I've got my family to feed."
8. Williams, known as "white chocolate" is depicted as the archetype example of a white player who represents the style and aesthetics of hip-hop/street basketball (the culture and game play associated with blackness).
9. Scholars like Fanon, Bhabha, and Judy invoke the racist language of white supremacy in an effort to capture this ideological component of white supremacy and the nature of racial violence (the ways in which it builds upon essentialist language that overdetermines meaning of black bodies). One of the core arguments of *After Artest* is that since the Palace Brawl the blackness of the league (imagined and represented in particular ways) became increasingly visible and seen as undesirable,

unmanageable, and threatening. This blackness—as defined primarily in cultural terms—countered the ways in which Michael Jordan embodied the league. Jordan was constructed as legally (and physically) black, yet as having transcended race (he was post-racial in a cultural sense). In a post-Artest context the blackness of another color embodied by Jordan became nonexistent within an NBA context resulting in cultural panics, demonization, and the regulation of black bodies. The language of Fanon, Bhabha, and others captures the ways in which blackness (and all of its associate meanings) overdetermines reception, representation, and positioning within the racial hierarchy. I see the value in including these quotes, but I do appreciate the history of this word and the complexity of my (as a white male scholar) using it even as a quote in this context.

10. Both Stuart and Smith accused black men of crimes that they ultimately were accused of committing.

CHAPTER 5. THE PALACE BRAWL
AND THE COLORBLIND FANTASY

1. The fight was initially ignited by a hard foul leveled against J.R. Smith (Nuggets) by the Knicks Mandy Collins as he attempted to complete a fastbreak bucket. Smith took exception to the foul, getting in the face of Collins. At this point the Knicks' Nate Robinson jumped into the fray, leading to him and Smith falling into the front row as they wrestled with one another. The altercation escalated after Carmelo Anthony (Nuggets) proceeded to throw a punch at Collins, leading the Knicks' Jared Jeffries to chase Anthony down the court. ESPN.com described the fight in the following way: "The brawl began when Collins prevented Smith from an easy basket by grabbing him around the neck and taking him to the floor. Smith got up and immediately started jawing with Collins, and Robinson jumped in to pull Smith away. Anthony shoved Robinson, and Robinson and Smith then tumbled into the front row while fighting. Just as things appeared to be calming down, Anthony threw a hard punch that floored Collins. Jeffries sprinted from the baseline toward half court in an effort to get at Anthony, but was tackled by a Denver player. By the time security finally contained Smith, the players were nearly at the opposite end of the court from where things started ("Suspensions Total 47 Games" 2006).

2. In the aftermath of the fight, the league suspended Anthony for 15 games, while J.R. Smith and Nate Robinson each received 10–game suspensions. Additionally suspended were Mardy Collins (6 games), Jared Jeffries (4 games), Jerome James (1 game), and Nene (1 game).

3. Green is said to have tossed the cup onto the court, leading Ron Artest into the stands.
4. Hill cites a 2008 *ESPN: The Magazine* poll, which found that nearly 50 percent of fans expressed "shame what's happening to the league."

WORKS CITED: POPULAR DISCOURSE

The vast majority of articles cited and analyzed for this book were retrieved through ProQuest database. Other articles were found via Google searches and other search engines.

Abramson, A., and Anastasis, L. (2005, October 20). Columnists argue whether NBA dress code is racial or professional. Retrieved August 7, 2006, from http://www.alligator.org/pt2/051020jumpball.php

Adami, H. (2005, October 23). So it's goodbye to the gangstas, bye-bye bling. *Ottawa Citizen*, D.4.

Adande, J.A. (2006, December 26a). A different scale is set for NBA players. *Los Angeles Times*, D.1.

Adande, J.A. (2005, October 20a). Dress code suits him. *Los Angeles Times*, D.1

Adande, J.A. (2005, April 14b). It remains an age-old question for the NBA. *Los Angeles Times*, D.1.

Adande, J.A. (2004, November 22). Making a play to the fans. *Los Angeles Times*, D.9.

Adande, J.A. (2003, September 25). Trailblazers for a cavalier; LeBron James is aware of contributions made by Earl Lloyd and Spencer Haywood. *Los Angeles Times*, D.1.

Adande, J.A. (1997, October 6). Haywood: A forgotten pioneer. *Los Angeles Times*, 8.

Adande, J.A. (1996, February 26). From the prom to the pros; Garnett goes from high school to NBA, the New York league. *Washington Post*, C.01.

Albom, M. (2004, November 21). Blame it on dumb view of respect. *Knight Ridder-Tribune News Service*, 1.

Aldridge, D. (2007, March 4). The Philadelphia Inquirer David Aldridge column. *Knight Ridder-Tribune Business News*, 1.

Aldridge, D. (2003, December 3). Why the west is best. Retrieved June 2, 2008, from http://sports.espn.go.com/nba/columns/story?columnist= aldridge_david&id=1678825

Alexie, S. (2007, March 22). Sherman Alexie on watching the NBA through a racial lens. Retrieved May 25, 2007, from http://myespn.go.com/ blogs/truehoop/0–24–98/Sherman-Alexie-on-Watching-the-NBA-Through-a-Racial-Lens.html

Ali, T. (2008, April 28). DeShawn Stevenson fined for making a threatening gesture. Retrieved May 12, 2008, from http://www.cavsnews. com/20080428–1135.php

Allen, P. (2005, November 1). Dress code getting more attention than it deserves. *Seattle Times*, F.1.

(Carmelo) Anthony may face stiffest penalty in wake of brawl (Knicks/ Nuggets fight)—A discussion (2006, December 17). Retrieved March 28, 2008, from http://www.freerepublic.com/focus/f-news/1754876/ posts

Araton, H. (2007, February 27). Stain of racism feeds N.B.A.'s renegade image. *New York Times*, D.1.

Araton, H. (2005, October 21b). The N.B.A.'s latest edict already looks threadbare. *New York Times*, D.1.

Araton, H. (2005, July 26c). College or pros? Answer seems driven by race. *New York Times*, D.1.

Araton, H. (2004, November 23a). Brawl evokes real story of N.B.A. and its fans. *New York Times*, D.1.

Araton, H. (2004, November 22b). Stern sends a forceful message. *New York Times*, D.1.

Araton, H. (1999 November 19). Breaking the bonds of innocence. *New York Times*, D.1.

Armour, N. (2004, December 25). Image is child's play: Younger player combined with bigger salaries can lead to social problems. *Columbian*, B.4.

Associated Press. (2005, November 2). Dress code makes debut to mixed reactions across league. *Daily Texan*. Retrieved May 22, 2007, from http://media.www.dailytexanonline.com/media/storage/paper410/new s/2005/11/03/Sports/Dress.Code.Makes.Debut.To.Mixed.Reac-tions.Across.League-1044207.shtml

Associated Press. (2005, November 2). Dress code reactions amuse stern. Retrieved November 3, 2005, from http://www.espn.com

Associated Press. (2005, October 20). Pacers' Jackson: dress code is "racist." Retrieved May 22, 2007, from http://www.msnbc.msn.com/ id/9730334/

Associated Press. (2004, December 9). Pacers, fan facing charges; 5 players charged for roles in brawl. *Telegraph-Herald* (Dubuque, Iowa), B.3.

Associated Press. (2004, November 22). Artest, 3 others, suspended indefinitely. Retrieved November 24, 2004, from http://nbcsports.msnbc.com/id/6534820/site/21683474/

Associated Press. (2004, November 21). NBA commissioner David Stern's statement on suspensions. Retrieved November 24, 2004, from http://www.usatoday.com/sports/basketball/nba/2004–11–21–stern-statement_x.htm

Associated Press. (2004, January 19). Excitement wanes without 14–year-old Wie. *Daily Express News*. Retrieved from http://www.dailyexpress.com.my/news.cfm?NewsID=24251

Barrow. E. (2007, January 7). NBA's culture of hate. *New York Daily News*, 64.

Barth, P. (2005, July 12). NBA age limit a good idea. *Sheboygan Press*. Retrieved July 5, 2005, from http://www.wisinfo.com/sheboygan-press/print/print_21401883.shtml

Basketball's thugs—Punish athletes who assault fans. (2004, November 24). *San Diego Union-Tribune*, B.8.

Beck, G. (2007, April 23). Al Sharpton speaks out against rap artist Cam'Ron. Retrieved from http://transcripts.cnn.com/TRANSCRIPTS/0704/23/gb.01.html

Beck, H. (2009, June 5). N.B.A. commissioner Stern wants to preserve age limit for players. *New York Times*. Retrieved February 19, 2010, from http://www.nytimes.com/2009/06/05/sports/basketball/05stern.html

Beck, H. (2006, December 19). Stirring the pot, but not getting burned. *New York Times*, D.2.

Beck, H. (2005, June 28). Draft will close book on high school stars. *New York Times*, D.1.

Bell, J. (2005, October 25). NBA dress code is reasonable. Opinion Editorials.com. Retrieved August 7, 2006, from http://www.opinioneditorials.com/guestcontributors/jbell_20051025.html

Bellantoni, C. (2005, February 9). "Droopy drawers" bill seeks end to overexposure of underwear. *Washington Times*. Retrieved May 17, 2007, from http://washtimes.com/metro/20050208–105116–2078r.htm

Benedict, J. (2003, August 5). Athletes and allegations. *New York Times*. Retrieved July 27, 2004, from http://www.ncava.org/articles/nytimeskobe.html

Benefield, D. (2005, October 19). Some casual observations on dress code. *Province*, A48.

Berger, K. (2006, December 19). Stern's actions are on the mark. *Newsday*, A.87.

Berkow, I. (2001, June 24a). They're still waiting for an N.B.A payday. *New York Times*, 8.1.

Berkow, I. (2001, May 17b). Ignore Stern: Teenagers should play. *New York Times*, D.1.

Beseda, Jim. (2004, January 26). The young and the NBA: How old should a player be? A 20–year-old minimum age limit would change many a roster—Including Portland's. *Oregonian*, E.06.

Blackistone, K. (2005, January 27). Kevin Blackistone says athletes in brawl deserve same treatment as other people involved. *Pittsburgh Post-Gazette*, C.2.

Blinebury, Fran. (1998, December 2). NBA defections hurt college game. *Houston Chronicle*, 1.

Blunt, C. (2005, October 19). Pacers' Jackson leads chorus of players against dress code. *USA Today*. Retrieved May 18, 2007, from http://www.usatoday.com/sports/basketball/nba/2005–10–19–sjackson_x.htm

Bohls, K. (2001, May 27). NBA, NCAA should grow up in age debate. *Austin American Statesman*, C.1.

Borges, R. (2005, October 20). Dress code won't solve NBA's woes. Retrieved June 2, 2008, from http://www.msnbc.msn.com/id/9679068/

Boyd, T. (2004, August 19a). They're playing bas-ket-ball. Retrieved July 8, 2006, fromhttp://sports.espn.go/com/espn/page3/story?page=boyd/040818

Boyd, T. (2004, November 26b). Did race play a role in basketbrawl? *Los Angeles Times*, B.15.

Boykin, K. (2005, October 20). Does the NBA dress code go too far? Retrieved October 22, 2005, from http://www.keithboykin.com/arch/2005/10/20/does_the_nba_dr

Brady, E., and Dodd, M. (2004, November 21). Police investigating after brawl in stands. *USA Today*. Retrieved November 24, 2004, fromhttp://www.usatoday.com/sports/basketball/nba/2004–11–21–brawl-cover_x.htm

Brady, E., and Meyers, B. (1997, June 25). Bryant: Put in hard work, then have fun. *USA Today*, 02.C

Brawling bad boys: Latest melee just blackens NBA eye. (2006, December 20). *Knight Ridder-Tribune News Service*, 1.

Brennan, C. (2006, December 21). Fan repulsion led to Stern measures. *USA Today*, C.2.

Bresnahan, M. (2009, December 4). Ron Artest is trying to be a role mode. Los Angeles Times. Retrieved July 2, 2011 from http://articles.latimes.com/2009/dec/04/sports/la-sp-lakers4-2009dec04

Brewer, J. (2006, December 23). Time to lose league's fake macho men: Some helpful tips for how the game should be played. *National Post*, S.2.

Broussard, C. (2005, October 17a). Dress code too tame? Retrieved September 25, 2006, from http://insider.espn.go.com/espn/blog/index? name=broussard_chris&month=10&year=2005

Broussard, C. (2005, February 28b). Walk this way. *ESPN: The Magazine,* 42–52.

Broussard, C. (2004, June 20). Draft becoming refuge for young and restless. *New York Times,* 8.5.

Brown. C. (2004, January 18). Golf: Els moves up at Sony, but still trails by one. *New York Times.* Retrieved September 24, 2008, from http://query.nytimes.com/gst/fullpage.html?res=9A0CE5DA1739F93 BA25752C0A9629C8B63

Brown, T. (2004, May 14). L.A. trades triangle for pick-and-roll. Retrieved May 21, 2007, from http://forums.yellowworld.org/showthread. php?t=16145

Brunt, C. (2005, October 20). Dress code targets blacks—Pacers guard. *Edmonton Journal,* D.2.

Brunt, S. (2005, October 21). NBA's dress code may be a disguise for another problem. *Globe and Mail,* S.3.

Bryant, M.F. (2007, January 21). When fighting becomes a racial double standard. *Gazette (Knight Ridder-Tribune News Service),* 1.

Bryant, M.F. (2006, November 6). No-tolerance plan expected to have effect. *Sunday Gazette-Mail,* 8.D.

Buckley, T. (2005, October 6). "Big O" no fan of NBA dress code. *Desert Morning News.* Retrieved May 21, 2007, from http:// findarticles.com/p/articles/mi_qn4188/is_20051006/ai_n15673736

Bulpett, S. (2004, November 21). The NBA: Riots about right: Ingredients always there. *Boston Herald,* B.16.

Burdekin, R.C.K., Hossfeld, R.T., and Smith, J.K. (2005). Are NBA fans becomingindifferent to race? Evidence from the 1990s. *Journal of Sports Economics,* 6(2), 144–159.

Burns, M. (2006, December 18). Anthony does irreparable damage to image in brawl. Retrieved March 28, 2008, from http://sportsillustrated. cnn.com/2006/writers/marty_burns/12/17/brawl.knicks.nuggets/

Burwell, B. (2007, February 28). Knight's take on NBA's age restriction rule is off the mark. *St. Louis Post-Dispatch,* D.1.

Burwell, B. (2004, November 22a). The NBA is hip-hopping its way out of the mainstream. *St. Louis Post-Dispatch,* D.1.

Burwell, B. (2004, May 28b). The kids are not all right, and Stern knows it. *St. Louis Post-Dispatch,* D.1.

Caltechgirl. (2005, October 200). "The NBA dress code": Not exactly rocket science. Retrieved May 18, 2007, from http://caltech girlsworld.mu.nu/archives/127655.php

Camunas, M. (2005, June 23). Not enough: NBA age limit too low. Retrieved July 5, 2005, from http://www.usforacle.com/vnews/display.v/ ART/2005/06/23/42bab2b24cdc0

Canzano, J. (2004, November 22). NBA deserves some blame for brawl. *Oregonian*, C.01.

Carbado, D. (2005, October 19). What's in a chain? Race and the NBA's new dress code. Retrieved July 8, 2006, from http://www.blackprof.com/ archives/2005/10/whats_in_a_chain_race_and_the.html

Carmelo Anthony drops Mardy Collins, runs like a girl (A discussion). (2006, December 17). Retrieved March 28, 2008, from http:// sports.aol.com/fanhouse/category/nba/2006/12/17/carmelo-anthony-drops-mardy-collins-runs-like-a-girl/6#comments

Celizic, M. (2006, December 18). Plenty of blame to go around for this brawl. Retrieved March 28, 2008, from http://nbcsports. msnbc.com/id/16245553/

Celizic, M. (2004, November 23). NBA's problems are cultural, not racial: League must help players improve image to middle America. Retrieved December 2, 2004, from http://msnbc.msn.com/ id/6561246/

Cervantes, A. (2005, November 20). Young blacks open up about problems. *Columbus Dispatch*, 08.B.

Chalifoux, M. (2005, October 26). Sports gospel: Ignorance or escalation? *Sports Fan Magazine*. Retrieved May 22, 2007, from http://www. sportsfanmagazine.com/sfm/articles.html?id=2095

Charland, W. (1996, June 25). Is drafting from high school a cool thing to do? *Christian Science Monitor*, 14.

Chery, C. (2005, February 10). Virginia passes bill, don't let those Polos and Girbauds hang low. Retrieved May 17, 2007, from http://www. sohh.com/article_print.php?content_ID=6714

Chiles, J. (2005, October 5). Allen Iverson & the NBA dress code. Retrieved August 8, 2006, from http://aofg.blogs.com/the_airing_of_griev-ances/2005/10/allen_iverson_t.html

Clark-Flory, T. (2006, June 22). Oprah vs. rappers: Rappers ask Oprah, "Where's the love?" Retrieved June 11, 2008, from http:// archive.salon.com/mwt/broadsheet/2006/06/22/oprah/print.html

Clay, G. (2005, November 2). The politics of the NBA's dress code. *Knight Ridder-Tribune News Service*, 1.

Clay, G. (2004, November 28). Sportsworld appears to be losing control. *Houston Chronicle*, 1.

Cobb, W.J. (2006, July 11). We still wear the mask (Gangsterism within hip-hop). Retrieved June 11, 2008, from http://www.thuglifearmy.com/ news/?id=2831

Comments: Stern warning (A discussion). (2004, November). Retrieved November 24, 2004, from http://www.fuckedsports.com/mt/mt-fsports.cgi?entry_id=2282

Cook, B. (2004, November 22). Kick out the sports. *Flax Magazine.* Retrieved June 2, 2008, from http://www.flakmag.com/sports/cook041122.html

Cotton, A. (1997, June 25). Senior citizen will be leader of the pack: Wake Forest's Duncan is likely No. 1, then youth will be served. *Washington Post*, C.01.

Cotton, A. (2003, June 29). The young and restless: Are teen players ready for prime time in NBA? *Denver Post*, A.01.

Couch, G. (2005, April 24). NBA guilty of flagrant foul on proposed age restriction. *Chicago Sun-Times*, 95.

Cowlishaw, T. (2004, November 20). NBA reaches a new low point with brawl. *Knight Ridder-Tribune News Service*, 1.

Craggs, T. (2008, February 25). Where they come from. *ESPN: The Magazine*, 50.

Dahlberg, T. (2005, October 18). What's next, traveling calls in the NBA? *Sporting News.* Retrieved August 7, 2006, from http://www.sportingnews.com/yourturn/viewtopic.php?t=27402&highlight=&sid=bdbac243fe5af765c7a1475c33a53b6d

David Stern media conference. (2004, April 12). Retrieved June 8, 2008, from http://www.insidehoops.com/stern-interview-041104.shtml

Davey D. (2000 July). A convenient scapegoat—Hip hop music blamed for inciting violence. Retrieved June 11, 2008, from http://findarticles.com/p/articles/mi_m1310/is_2000_July/ai_63845112/pg_1

Deford, F. (2005, October 26). Suiting up: NBA dress code draws criticism from many corners. *Sports Illustrated.* Retrieved August 7, 2006, from http://sportsillustrated.cnn.com/2005/writers/frank_deford/10/26/dress.code/

Denberg, J. (2001, May 13). Fat chance of stemming underage tide. *The Atlanta Journal-Constitution*, D.13.

Denberg, J. (1999, June 20). Inside the NBA; Stern wants to stop high school players from entering draft. *Atlanta Journal-Constitution*, E.12.

DeShazier. J. (2001, July 5). Stern message falls short: NBA commissioner can expect to see more youngsters in league. *Times-Picayune*, 01.

Deveney, S. (2006, December 16). Nuggets-Knicks game ends in brawl. *Sporting News.* Retrieved March 28, 2008, from http://www.sportingnews.com/yourturn/viewtopic.php?t=159805

Deveney, S. (2006, October 12). Players, not rules, will lift the NBA's image. *Sporting News.* Retrieved November 3, 2006, from http://www.sportingnews.com/yourturn/viewtopic.php?p=1241232

Deveney, S. (2004, November 22). Artest deserves most of the blame. *Sporting News*. Retrieved December 2, 2004, from http://msnbc. msn.com/id/6559232/print/1/displaymode/1098

Diamos, J. (2004, November 22). For Artest, today's troubles took root years ago. *New York Times*, D.3.

Dimatteo, S. (2006). The "thug mentality" of the NBA. Retrieved March 28, 2008, from http://www.helium.com/items/103948–basketball-knows-about-recent

Dixon, O. (2005, November 17a). One year later: NBA on the rebound; Stern tries to polish league's image tarnished by Pacers-Pistons Nov. 19 brawl. *USA Today*, C.3

Dixon, O. (2005, October 17b). New dress code unlikely to wear well. *USA Today*. Retrieved August 7, 2006, from http://www.usa today.com/sports/basketball/nba/2005–10–17–dress-code_x.htm

Douglas, R. (2009, December 5). NBA bad boy Ron Artest of L.A. Lakers admits he had a problem: Drinking during games! Retrieved December 8, 2009, fromhttp://www.hiphoprx.com/2009/12/05/nba-bad-boy-ron-artest-of-la-lakers-admits-he-had-a-problem-drinking-durin g-games/

Downey, M. Detroit taking an unfair hit in brawl game. *Chicago Tribune*. Retrieved June 8, 2011, from http://articles.chicagotribune.com/ 2004–11–23/sports/0411230270_1_pistons-fans-auburn-hills-palace-revolt

Drehs, W. (2001, June 18). Lure of stardom can glitter like fake gold. Retrieved June 1, 2007, from http://espn.go.com/nba/draft2001/ s/2001/0618/1215705.html

Drugs, bling and tears. (2005, October 20). *USA Today*. Retrieved August 7, 2006, from http://www.usatoday.com/news/opinion/editorials/ 2005–10–20–sports-edit_x.htm

DuPree, D. (2003, June 26). NBA experiencing teen crush: First round in tonight's draft could include 11 players under 20. *USA Today*, C.01.

DuPree, D. (2003, June 2). Stern "losing steam" on minimum-age rule to play in NBA. *USA Today*, C.08.

DuPree, D. (1995, June 28). NBA draft tonight/underclassmen expected to be leading choices. *USA Today*, 1C.

Dwyre, B. (2006, October 21). This NBA class has a rough beginning. *Los Angeles Times*, D.1.

Dwyre, B. (2004, November 23). Is it all just part of game? *Los Angeles Times*, D.1.

Dye, D. (2006, June 27). Haywood has "scars" from suit: NBA great opened doors by challenging draft eligibility rule, but he paid a steep price. *Detroit News*, D.3.

Editorials on NBA brawl. (2004, November 23). *Knight Ridder-Tribune News Service*, 1.

Elder, L. (2005, October 27)b. NBA: No bling allowed. *Jewish World Review*. Retrieved August 7, 2006, from http://www.jewishworld review.com/cols/elder102705.asp

Elder, L. (2002, August 22). The reparation desperation. *Jewish World Review*. Retrieved May 18, 2007, from http://www.jewishworl-dreview.com/cols/elder082202.asp

Eligon, J. (2005, October 19). N.B.A. dress code decrees: Clothes make the image. *New York Times*. Retrieved October 24, 2005, from www. nytimes.com/2005/10/19/sports/basketball/19stern.html?oref=login

Elmore, C. (2004, November 28). An image problem. *Palm Beach Post*, 1.B.

Evans, H. (2006, December 21–27). Don't dare call them thugs. *New York Amsterdam News*, 52.

Farley, C.J. (2005, October 21). The rap on NBA fashion. *Time*. Retrieved May 18, 2007, from http://aolsvc.timeforkids.kol.aol.com/time/arts/article/0,8599,1121820,00.html

Fastis, S. (2001, June 22). Kid stuff. *Wall Street Journal*, W.10.

Feigen, J. (2001, June 24). Youth not being well served. *Houston Chronicle*, 18.

Fernas, R. (2003, July 19). Athletes part of violent trend. *Los Angeles Times*. Retrieved July 23, 2003, from http://www.latimes.com/sports/la-sp-crime19jul19002426,1,5915255.story

Feschuk, D. (2005, October 19a). Stern mandate fashion mistake: For some reason, muzzles not mentioned. *Toronto Star*, E.03.

Feschuk, D. (2005, October 7b). Suit or straitjacket?; The NBA's new off-the-court dress code will do away with do-rags and jeans but some players of the hip-hop generation consider the league's plan a poor fit. *Toronto Star*, E.3.

Flagrant fouls. (2004, November 22). *USA Today*, A.14.

Flowers, S. (2005, October 30). Bravo to the NBA for setting example. Retrieved August 7, 2006, from http://www.roanoke.com/colum-nists/flowers/wb/wb/xp-38486

Freelove, M. (2004, November 21). Fallout from the Artest riot. Retrieved June 8, 2011 from http://blogcritics.org/culture/article/fallout-from-the-artest-riot/#ixzz1OkOTRpGo

Fuchs, C. (2004, December 2). Ballers, shot callers. Retrieved June 1, 2008, from http://www.popmatters.com/sports/features/041202–ronartest.shtml

Freelove, M. (2004, November 21). Fallout from Artest riot. Retrieved November 24, 2004, from http://blogcritics.org/archives/2004/11/21/203126.php

Garden Brawl (2006, December 16). Retrieved March 28, 2008, from http://sportsmediareview.typepad.com/sports_media_review/2006/12/garden_brawl.html

Gibron, B. (2005, May 10). Age before ability: Why college, not a contract, should be the next stop for the student athlete. Retrieved June 4, 2008 from http://www.popmatters.com/sports/features/050510–nba-1.shtml

Gilmore, J. (2005, November 1). NBA sets positive example. *Omaha World-Herald*, 01.E.

Going for it. (1996, May 13). *Christian Science Monitor*, 20.

Golokhov, D. (2005, October 24). Does the NBA dress code attack black players? *Sports Fan Magazine*. Retrieved August 7, 2006, from http://www.sportsfanmagazine.com/sfm/articles.html?id=2084

Gonsalves, S. (2005, November 3a). NBA dress code exposes prejudices. Retrieved November 8, 2005, from http://www.alternet.org/columnists/story/27770/

Gonsalves, S. (2005, October 26b). The hypocritical NBA dress code. Retrieved November 8, 2005, from http://www.alternet.org/columnists/story/27386/

Graves, E. (2005). The NBA dress code: Setting high standards. *Black Enterprise*. Retrieved May 22, 2007, from http://www.blackenterprise.com/ArchiveOpen.asp?Source=ArchiveTab/2005/12/1205–35.htm

Gurnett, K. (2005, November 1). NBA dress code a jump ball. *Times Union*, A.1

Hammer, T. (2009, October 30). Interview: Bill Simmons, ESPN's "The sports guy"/author of *The Book of Basketball*. Retrieved March 20, 2010, from http://bostonist.com/2009/10/30/interview_bill_simmons_espns_the_sp.php

Hans, D. (2005, November 12a). NBA gangs must fight dress code. Retrieved August 7, 2006, from http://www.hoopshype.com/columns/dress_hans.htm

Hans, D. (2005, October 16b). BackTalk; When Mr. Blackwell meets Mr. Shaqwell. *New York Times*, 8.9.

Hayes, M. (2005, October 22). New NBA dress code pressed on players. *Pittsburgh-Post Gazette*. Retrieved May 18, 2007, from http://www.post-gazette.com/pg/05295/593152.stm

Heisler, M. (2005, November 2a). League already needs to come in from code. *Los Angeles Times*, D.2.

Heisler, M. (2005, February 15b). Juvenile court: Drafting high schoolers such as Howard was once thought of as risky. Now it's how the NBA does business. *Los Angeles Times*, D.1.

Heisler, M. (2000, March 12a). Youth makes this draft irresistible. *Los Angeles Times*, 7.

Heisler, M. (2000, February 15b). The NBA: One-and-done plan what colleges or pros had in mind. *Los Angeles Times*, 10.

Heisler, M. (1999, July 4). Stern wants to tap the fountain of youth. *Los Angeles Times*, 11.

Henson, S. (2001, June 24). California lottery: At 7 feet, 228 pounds, Dominguez's Tyson Chandler is about to strike it rich. *Los Angeles Times*, D.1.

Hill, J. (2009, November 19). The brawl: Were lessons learned? Retrieved February 4, 2010, from http://sports.espn.go.com/espn/commentary/news/story?page=hill/091118

Hill, J. (2006, December 18). Just an Ol' jock fight. Retrieved May 13, 2008, from http://sports.espn.go.com/espn/page2/story?page=hill/061218

Hill, M.L. (2005, December 23). The barbershop notebooks: Thoughts on the NBA dress code. Retrieved May 18, 2007, from http://www.popmatters.com/columns/hill/051223.shtml

Hindo, B. (2004, July 5). Helping teens make a big leap. *Business Week*. Retrieved June 1, 2007, from http://www.businessweek.com/magazine/content/04_27/b3890125.htm

Hip-hop to blame for pot-smoking tots? (2007, March 8). Retrieved June 11, 2008, from http://www.foxnews.com/story/0,2933,257747,00.html

Hochman, B. (2007, February 16). Today's NBA mixes hip-hop energy and corporate America. *Newhouse News Service*, 1.

Hochman, B. (2003, June 22). Other high schoolers not stirring excitement. *Times-Picayune*, 01.

Hohler, B. (2006, November 10). Many players regard firearm as a necessity. *Boston Globe*. Retrieved November 13, 2006, from http://www.boston.com/sports/other_sports/articles/2006/11/10/many_players_regard_firearm_as_a_necessity/

Hollis, J. (2001, May 13). Under a spotlight: Brown agonized over his decision NBA draft: Youth takeover. *The Atlanta Journal-Constitution*, D.13.

Howard-Cooper, S. (2000, May 2). They're in a rush to leave: UCLA: Sophomores Moisio, Rush make themselves available for NBA draft. *Los Angeles Times*, 1.

Hughes, G. (2005, December 6). Post sent on NASSS Listserve.

Hutchinson, E.O. (2005, October 27). The NBA dress code: It's not the dress, it's the stereotypes. Retrieved August 7, 2006, from http://www.blacknews.com/pr/nba101.html

Hutchinson, E.O. (2004, July 22). The myths of Bill Cosby. Retrieved June 11, 2008, from http://www.blackcommentator.com/100/100_cosby.html

In our view: Rampaging thugs; NBA confronts a serious problem. (2004, November 23). *Columbian* (Vancouver, WA), C.6.

Jackson, S. (2010, January 29). The Gilbert Arenas comeback template. Retrieved March 20, 2010, from http://sports.espn.go.com/espn/commentary/news/story?page=jackson/100129

Jackson, S. (2005, November 1a). Sacred ignorance. Retrieved November 2, 2005, from http://proxy.espn.go.com/espn/page2/story?page=jackson/051101

Jackson, S. (2005, April 14b). Why can't O'Neal ask questions? Retrieved August 3, 2005, from http://sports.espn.go.com/espn/print?id=2036962&type=story

Jayne, G. (2005, October 23). NBA selling image, not product. *Columbian.* Retrieved October 24, 2005, from http://www.columbian.com/printArticle.cfm?story=11886

Jenkins, C. (2006, February 10). NBA players suddenly sporting tights. *USA Today.* Retrieved May 21, 2007, from http://www.usatoday.com/sports/basketball/nba/2006–02–10–men-in-tights_x.htm

Jenkins, S. (2007, March 15). For Durant, riches deferred; NBA's age minimum puts Texas freshman in college spotlight. *Washington Post,* A.1.

Jenkins, S. (2004, November 26). With Artest, a Human Quality. *Washington Post,* D.01.

Johnson, E. (2005, October 14). Hip-hop hooray for the dress code. Retrieved August 7, 2006, from http://www.hoopshype.com/columns/dress_johnson.htm

Johnson, J. (2005, October 30). NBA dress code is not about race: It's about business, not bling in the NBA. Retrieved August 7, 2006, from http://www.e-sports.com/authors/33/Dr.-Jessica-Johnson

Johnson, R. (2007, February 26). Time to look in our ghettoized mirror. Bar for what we think is acceptable is at its lowest. Retrieved May 13, 2008, from http://www.blackvoices.com/black_sports/columnists/roysjohnson/_a/time-to-look-in-our-ghettoized-mirror/20070226121009990001

Jones, B. (2005, October 11). A dress code is dangerous. Retrieved September 25, 2006, from http://sports.espn.go.com/espn/page2/story?page=jones/051011&num=0

Jones, L. (2005, October 30). With dress code, NBA does the wrong thing for the right reason. *Pittsburgh Post-Gazette.* Retrieved August 7, 2006, from http://www.post-gazette.com/pg/05303/596214.stm

Jones, T. (2006, December 27). Unfair labels: While sports are deplorable, NBA players singled out by critics. *New Journal* (Daytona Beach), 10.C

Justice, R. (2004, November 23). NBA has chance to reconnect. *Houston Chronicle,* 01.

Katrina, Jena, and the whole damn system. (2007, August 26). Retrieved September 8, 2008, from http://revcom.us/a/099/urgent-need-en.html

Kaufman, K. (2004, July 6). King Kaufman's sports daily. Retrieved November 7, 2007, from http://www.salon.com/news/sports/col/kaufman/2004/07/06/tuesday/index.html

Kawakami, T. (2005, November 1). Sorry Stern, clothes don't make the man. *National Post*, S6.

Keown, T. (2004, November 23). Why players and fans attack. Retrieved November 24, 2004, from http://sports.espn.go.com/espn/page2/story?page=keown/041123

Kerr, S. (2005, April 14). Quality control. Retrieved August 3, 2005, from http://sports.yahoo.com/nba/news?slug=sk-agelimit041305&prov=yhoo&type=lgns

Kerridge, W. (2005, October 21). In dissent: Dress to impress. *Michigan Daily*. Retrieved May 18, 2007, from http://media.www.michigandaily.com/media/storage/paper851/news/2005/10/21/Opinioneditorials/In.Dissent.Dress.To.Impress-1432269.shtml

Keteyian, A. NBA age debate. *Costas Now* (HBO), June 10, 2005, http://www.hbo.com/costasnow/episode/episode.02.html

Kindred, D. (2004, April 14). Punks and thugs are to blame here. *Sporting News*. Retrieved November 24, 2004, from http://msn.foxsports.com/story?contentID-3183918&print=true

King, S. (2005, December 5). Post sent on NASSS Listserve.

Kiszla, M. (2003, May 22). King James too young for NBA riches, royalty. *Denver Post*, D.01.

Kiszla, M. (1999, June 12). Basketball, this is your wake-up call. *Denver Post*, D.01.

Knapp, G. (2005, April 17). NCAA, pros are good at hypocrisy. *San Francisco Chronicle*, D.1.

Knott, T. (2007, February 28). NBA is guilty by association. *Washington Times*, C.01.

Kobe vs. Artest: Proof Artest will kill your team (2009). Retrieved December 8, 2009, from http://www.redsarmy.com/home/2009/05/kobe-vs-artest-proof-artest-will-kill-your-team.html

Kornheiser, T. (2004. November 23). A Stern test for the NBA. *Washington Post*, D.01.

Kornheiser, T. (2001, May 15). Commissioner is tossing pennies in wishing well. *Washington Post*, D.01.

Kriger, D. (2004, November 25). Rhetoric overshadows "the brawl." *National Post* (Toronto, Ontario), S.2.

Kroft, S. (2005, June 1). Prodigies: Bright lights in sports. *60 Minutes* and CBS News. Retrieved from http://www.cbsnews.com/stories/2005/07/01/60minutes/printable705753.shtml

Labidou, A., and Zirin, D. 10 questions for Zirin. Elevation Magazine.com. Retrieved May 20, 2007, from http://www.elevationmag.com/basketball/index.php?itemid=9

Lage, L. (2005, November 19). NBA trying to rebound from basketbrawl. *Edmonton Journal*, C.2.

Lawrence, M. (2005, November 13). Image up. A year after Pacers-Pistons brawl, NBA on right track. *New York Daily News*, 76.

LeBatard, D. (2004, November 21). Pull no punches because it's the fan's fault. *Knight Ridder-Tribune News Service*, 1.

Lee, B. (2006, December 28). NBA players who would rather fight shouldn't be in league. *Yakima Herald-Republic*, A.4.

Lee, M. (2006, December 19). Anthony suspended 15 games for brawl. *Washington Post*, E.01.

Lee, M. (2005, November 19a). NBA rights to regain image: One year later, brawl leaves a mark throughout league. *Washington Post*, E.01.

Lee, M. (2005, October 20b). New dress code draws a few threads of protest. *Washington Post*, E.03. Retrieved August 16, 2006, from http://www.washingtonpost.com/wp-dyn/content/article/2005/10/19/AR2005101902415.html

Leonard, D.J. (2005, February 5). Why does a 14–year old matter. Retrieved May 1, 2008, from http://www.popmatters.com/sports/features/040205–freddyadu.shtml

Leonard, D.J. (2003a, September 11). Racing sports: Kobe Bryant. Retrieved September 5, 2008, from http://www.popmatters.com/sports/features/030911–kobe.shtml

Leonard, D.J. (2003b, Summer). Yo: Yao! What does the "Ming Dynasty" tell us about race and transnational diplomacy in the NBA? *Colorlines*, 34–36. Retrieved September 5, 2008, from http://www.findarticles.com/cf_dls/m0KAY/2_6/103192536/p2/article.jhtml?term

Letters. (2004, November 28). *The Atlanta Journal-Constitution*, G.5.

Limbaugh, R. (2004, November 23). Limbaugh on NBA fight: "This is the hip-hop culture on parade." Retrieved December 1, 2004, from http://mediamatters.org/items/200411230007

Lincicome, B. (1999, May 9). Book on bolting underclassmen: They have a lot to learn. *Chicago Tribune*, 1.

Litke, J. (2004, November 22). Stern will drop hammer further. Retrieved November 22, 2004, from http://www.msnbc.msn.com/id/6551350/print/1displaymode/1098/

Lorenz, S., and Murray, R. (2005, December 6). NBA dress code smacks of racism. *Express News*. Retrieved December 6, 2005, from http://www.expressnews.ualberta.ca/article.cfm?id=7158

Luhm, Steve. (2007, January 7). NBA: Image takes another hit. *Salt Lake Tribune*, np.

Lupica, M. (2006, December 17). The garden of evil: Knicks are punching bags on and off the court. *New York Daily News*, 7.

Luster, P. (2005, November 23). Off-court dress. Fresh thoughts: A blog of the *Indianapolis Star*. Retrieved May 21, 2007, from http://blogs.indystar.com/freshthoughts/archives/001669.html

Lutz, B. (2004 November 23). NBA brawl overflowing with blame. *Star-Telegram*. Retrieved November 24, 2004, from http://www.dfw.com/mld/dfw/sports

Lynch, A. (2005, October 27–November 2). That's my word: NBA players need to grow up. *Call & Post*, 1C.

Maese, R. (2006, June 27). NBA draft doesn't get any better with age. *Sun* (Baltimore), 1.C.

Mahoney, B. (2006, December 21). MSG brawl. Another black eye for the NBA. *Tennessee Tribune*, C.1.

Mariotti, J. (2004, November 20a). No exaggeration to call the chaos a tragedy. *Chicago Sun-Times*, 101.

Mariotti, J. (2004, November 14b). Rap on Artest: A spoiled brat. *Chicago Sun-Times*, 102.

Mariotti, J. (2004, November 21c). Offenders deserve Stern punishment. *Chicago Sun-Times*, 126.

Mark. (2004, November 11). Pacers-Pistons all out brawl. Retrieved November 24, 2004, from http://www.conservativerevolution.com. Also Retrieved June 5, 2008, from http://coldspringshops.blogspot.com/2004_11_01_archive.html

Marrone, M. (2004, December 31). The brawl of them all. *New York Daily News*, 114.

Matthew Dowd, who helped Bush win. (2005, May 31). Retrieved June 5, 2008, from http://www.vianovo.com/english/news/vianovonews/2005_0531.htm

May, P. (2000, May 28). College exodus continues: Will they ever learn. *Boston Globe*, D.4.

May, P. (1996, May 12). School's out; draft is in—There seems to be no stemming the tide of early candidates. *Boston Globe*, 50.

McCann, M. (2005, October 6). Don't wear that! David Stern's paternalism strikes again with dress code. Retrieved August 7, 2006, from http://sports-law.blogspot.com/2005/10/dont-wear-that-david-sterns.html

McIntrye, J. (2003, December 15). Need a reality check, Rasheed? Retrieved October 6, 2008, from http://hoopshype.com/columns/wallace_mcintyre.htm

McGovern, B. (2005). Does the NBA need an age limit? Retrieved May 9, 2005, from http://probasketball.about. .com/od/nbadraft/i/nbaage-limit_p.htm

McNamara, J. (2005, April 12). Green only color that matters. *Daily Cardinal*. Retrieved April 13, 2005, http://www.dailycardinal.com/media/paper439/news/2005/04/13/Sports/Green.Only.Color.That.Matters-922170.shtml

McNulty, R. (2005, October 25). New code not racist, just good business. *Seattle Post-Intelligencer*, D.2.

McWhorter, J. (2005, November 8). Stern rules. *Wall Street Journal*. Retrieved December 19, 2005, from http://www.opinionjournal.com/la/?id= 110007518

McWhorter, J. (2003, Summer). How hip-hop holds blacks back. Retrieved September 8, 2008, from http://www.city-journal.org/html/13_3_how_hip_hop.html

Michaelis, V. (1999, June 29). NBA school by bad draft incentive plan to play to save game. *Denver Post*, D.01.

Modesti, K. (2006, October 29). Stern hand strikes the NBA. *Daily News*, S.1.

Montieth, M. (2009, November 19). Five years on, perceptions, lessons of infamous palace brawl changing. Retrieved February 4, 2010, from http://sportsillustrated.cnn.com/2009/writers/mark_montieth/11/19/brawl/1.html#ixzz0eb4TrLjZ

Moore, G. (2005, December 22a). Maybe the hip hipsters of sports will understand the importance of dress from a man who knows how to be a successful black businessman. Retrieved August 7, 2006, from http://www.blackathlete.net/artman/publish/article_01374.shtml

Moore, G. (2005, April 14b). NBA needs age limit to protect the quality of play. Retrieved April 13, 2005, from http://www.blackathlete.net/artman/publish/article_0608.shtml

Moore, T. (2005, October 19). NBA dress code restores sanity to ludicrous image. *Atlanta Journal-Constitution*. Retrieved August 8, 2006, from http://www.ajc.com/blogs/content/shared-blogs/ajc/sportscolumns/entries/2005/10/19/nba_dress_code.html

Moore, T. (2004, November 22a). Sterner penalties deserved. *Atlanta Journal-Constitution*, B.1.

Moore, T. (2004, November 21b). When players join thugs, they become star culprits. *Atlanta Journal-Constitution*, G.1.

Moran, M. (2001, May 17). NBA draft pool the youngest ever league, colleges fret as players go pro early – multimillion-dollar deals, peer pressure lure youths. *USA Today*, A.01.

Morrissey, R. (2004, November 24). NBA: I love, hate this game. *Chicago Tribune*, 1.

Murphy, M. (2000, February 6). Minor matters/as NBA players get younger, minimum-age requirement eyed. *Houston Chronicle*, 18.

Murphy, M. (1996, June 26). NBA becomes a teen dream. *Houston Chronicle*, 1 (sports section).

Mushnick, P. (2004, November 22). "Violent Weekend No Real Surprise." *New York Post*, 076.

Myslenski, S. (1999, May 10). NBA growing up in a hurry: Early departures harm both NBA, college game. *Chicago Tribune*, 1.

Nance, R. (2005, February 25). From high school to NBA, the leap can be too great; teams must decide soon whether to keep 2001 picks. *USA Today*, A.1.

Nance, R. (1999, May 5). Pro game tougher than it looks for underclassmen; time management away from court key to adaptation. *USA Today*, 14.C.

Nance, R. (1996, June 4). Underclassmen say maturity fears overblown. *USA Today*, 12.C.

NBA adopts "business casual" dress code. (2005, October 18). Retrieved October 8, 2008, from http://sports.espn.go.com/nba/news/story?id=2194537

NBA attempts to dress up its image. (2005, October 18). *Nanaimo Daily News*, B.3.

NBA bounces to an edgy hip-hop beat (A discussion). (2004, December). Retrieved August 3, 2005, from http://www.amren.com/mtnews/archives/2004/12/nba_bounces_to.php

NBA can't be NFL. (2006, December 17). Retrieved March 28, 2008, from http://sportsmediawatch.blogspot.com/2006_12_17_archive.html

NBA's cosseted thugs. (2004, November 28). *Providence Journal*, G.04.

NBA culture clash is generation gap. (2004, November 4). Retrieved November 24, 2004, from http://www.blackathlete.net/artman/publish/article_095.shtml

NBA defends age limit policy in letter. (2009, July 20). Retrieved February 18, 2010, from http://sports.espn.go.com/nba/news/story?id=4342058

NBA dress code (n.d.). Retrieved December 27, 2005, from http://www.nba.com/news/player_dress_code_051017.html

NBA's dress code. (2005, October 19). Retrieved August 7, 2006, from http://www.nbadresscode.com/

NBA's dress code. (2005, October 24). *Windsor Star*, A.8.

NBA dress code: NBA dress code policy. (2005, October 17). Retrieved May 18, 2007, from http://www.insidehoops.com/dress-code.shtml

NBA dress code "racist now"???. Retrieved November 4, 2005, from http://www.stormfront.org

NBA's image more than a dress code. —. (2005, October 11). *Toronto Star*, A.23.

NBA Negros [sic] forced to quite wearing their gangbangin clothes. Retrieved November 4, 2005, from http://www.stormfront.org

NBA shows its immaturity: Fight between the Knicks and Nuggets shows a sport gone awry and in need of a major change. (2006, December 19). *Las Vegas Sun*, A.4.

NBA's Stern punishment merited after brawl. (2004, November 26). *Daily Breeze* (Torrance, CA), A.18.

Neumayr, G. (2004, November 23). Rap sheets. *American Spectator*. Retrieved May 1, 2008, from http://www.spectator.org/dsp_article.asp?art_id =7422

Nevius, C.W. (1999, May 20). The young and the restless/college teams are left barren as players jump early to the NBA. *San Francisco Chronicle*, D.1.

Nolan, H. (2004, December 6). When athletes attack: Does brawl bode well for the NBA? *PR Week*, 11.

Norman, G. (2004, November 23). Gangstaball. *National Review*. Retrieved June 5, 2008, from http://www.nationalreview.com/norman/norman 200411230913.asp

Norris, R. (2006, December 22). Carmelo Anthony: New NBA thug? Retrieved March 28, 2008, from http://www.associatedcontent.com/ article/105816/carmelo_anthony_new_nba_thug.html

O'Connor, I. (2005, June 28b). Sometimes kids need to go to work. *USA Today*, C.2.

Olson, L. (2006, December 17). Knick excuses pile on shame: Nitwit Nate has big ego, no clue. *New York Daily News*, 57.

One-size-fits-all dress code draws divergent views. (2005, October 19). Retrieved August 7, 2006, from http://sports.espn.go.com/nba/ news/story?id=2197012

O'Reilly, B. (2006b). Personal story segment: 20th anniversary of MLK, Jr. day. (2006). Retrieved June 11, 2008, from http://www.billoreilly.com/ show?action=viewTVShowByDate&date=20060116

Ostler S. (2005, October 2000). Dress code's naked truth. *San Francisco Chronicle*, D.1. Retrieved May 18, 2007, from http:// www.sfgate.com/cgi-bin/article.cgi?file=/c/a/2005/10/20/SPG54 FB8LG1.DTL&type=printable

Pacers/Pistons Game turns into an ugly fight with fans (A discussion). (2004, November 20). Retrieved October 22, 2007, from http:// tradermike.net/movethecrowd/archives/2004/11/pacers_pistons_game _turns_into_an_ugly_fight_with_fans/

Page, C. (2005, October 26). Whining in NBA about new dress code. *Sentinel and Enterprise*, 1.

Page, C. (2004, November 28). Why don't we call them brawl games. *Chicago Tribune*, 9.

Perace, T. (2005, 26 November). Stepping up their sartorial game. *Globe and Mail*, L.4.

Philips, G. (2005, November 27). The NBA's bling ban: Looking good. *Los Angeles Times*. Retrieved August 7, 2006, from http://www.latimes.com/news/printedition/suncommentary/la-op-nbabling-bling27nov27,1,2923002.story?coll=la-headlines-suncomment

Pitts, L. (2005, October 27). Is NBA dress code racist? Who cares? *Buffalo News*, A.13.

Plaschke, B. (2004, November 21). Stuff happens when the wall comes down. *LosAngeles Times*, D.1.

Plaschke, B. (2000, May 14). Sorry, Jason, but NBA is no place for kids. *Los Angeles Times*, 1.

Povak, T. (2006, December 19). NBA punishes basketball brawlers. *Orlando Sentinel*, D.1.

Powell, S. (2004, November 25). Hip-hop hoops feeding negative stereotypes. *Newsday*, A.95.

Prevenas, N. (2005, April 14). O'Neal plays the race card. Retrieved May 16, 2005, from http://www.sportsfanmagazine.com/sfm/articles.html?id=1451

Purse, J. (2002, November 21). Tale of two stars. *Daily Illini*. Retrieved June 2, 2008, from http://www.illinimedia.com/di/nov02/nov21/sports/stories/sports_column01.shtml

Race and the Knicks/Nuggets fight (a discussion). (2006, December 21). Retrieved March 28, 2008, from http://www.hiphopmusic.com/2006/12/race_and_the_knicksnuggets_fig.html

Rap sheets (Rhetoric question of the day: Why do our athletes behave like criminals (online discussion). (2004, November). Retrieved December 2, 2004, from http://freerepublic.com/focus/f-news/1286455/posts

Ratto, R. (2004, November 19). Plenty of blame to go around. Retrieved November 24, 2004, from http://sports.espn.go.com/nba/columns/story?columnist=ratto_ray&id=1927360

Readers express little sympathy for NBA players. (2004, November 27). *Roanoke Times and World News*, C.2.

Red Eye. (2006, December 19). Deja boo. *Chicago Tribune*, 14.

Redeker, B. (2003, July 30). NBA bad boys: Do basketball players get in trouble more often than other athletes. *ABCnews.com*. Retrieved July 23, 2003, from, http://abcnews.go.com/sections/wnt/US/nba030730_badboys.html

Reed, W. (2003, June 25). The NBA's King James: High school phenom to be first player selected in NBA draft. *Michigan Chronicle*, C.1.

Reese, R. (2005, December 4). NBA dress code: Rebels can learn something from old role models. *Inland Valley Daily Bulletin*, A.15. Retrieved

May 22, 2007, from http://www.csupomona.edu/%7Errreese/ NBADRESS.htm

Reid, J. (2005, April 19). Smith socks it to NBA in protest. *Times-Picayune*, 02.

Reggio, P. (2006, December 20). Racism in the NBA? You don't say. Retrieved Marc 28, 2008, from http://www.phillysportsline.com/ wordpress/archives/838print/

Resler, J. (2004, November 23). NBA brawl a travesty. *Milwaukee Journal Sentinel*, 12.

Resnick, S. (2009, May 7). Ron Artest more than likely will be suspended, but so should Kobe. Retrieved December 8, 2009, from http:// bleacherreport.com/articles/169493–ron-artest-more-than-likely- will-be-suspended-but-so-should-kobe-bryant

Reyes, D. (2005, March 3). NBA, hip-hop merge. Retrieved October 22, 2007, from http://www.dailycampus.com/2.7439/nba-hip-hop- merge-1.1065571

Reynolds, B. (2004, November 23). Shocking brawl a telltale sign of great divide. *Providence Journal*, D.01.

Rhoden, W.C. (2004, November 21a). No innocents in N.B.A in suburban Detroit. *New York Times*, 8.1.

Rhoden, W.C. (2004, November 23b). Now the main event: Stern vs. Hunter. *New York Times*, D.3.

Rhoden, W.C. (1999, July 1). Trying to regain control of a genie way out of the owner's bottle. *New York Times*, D.3.

Robbins, L. (2006, December 18). Anthony punches hole in a rebuilt reputation. *New York Times*, D.1.

Robbins, L. (2004, November 22a). One player barred for season as N.B.A. responds. *New York Times*, A.1.

Robbins, L. (2004, November 21b). N.B.A. bars 4 after a brawl involving fans. *New York Times*, 1.1.

Roberts, S. (2005, December 7). N.B.A. dress code confuses the long and the short of it. *New York Times*. Retrieved December 12, 2005, from http://wwww.nytimes.com

Robinson, D. (2005, October 24). New NBA standards a needed change. *Desert Morning News*, D.1.

Rock, B. (2006, February 17). Fashions get tight in NBA. *Desert Morning News*. Retrieved May 21, 2007, from http://deseretnews.com/ dn/view/0,1249,635185100,00.html

Rodricks, D. (2006, October 1). Race card trumps reason in crime debate. Retrieved May 12, 2008, from http://www.martinomalley.com/news/ 1038/race-card-trumps-reason-in-crime-debate

Rodriguez, C. (2005, November 3). Will NBA's dress code filter down to the street? *Denver Post*, F.01.

Ron Artest plans to auction NBA championship ring for charity. (2010, September 20). Retrieved January 16, 2011 fromhttp://www.usatoday.com/sports/basketball/nba/lakers/2010–09–20–artest-championship-ring-auction_N.htm

Rorrer, R. (2005, October 29). NBA's image mandates a makeover. *News Journal*, 02.D

Rosenberg, M. (2004, November 19). Ron Artest has no business in NBA. *Knight Ridder-Tribune News Service*, 1.

Rovell, D., and Stein, M. (2006, March 31). League would amend uniform code to ban tights. Retrieved May 21, 2007, from http://sports.espn.go.com/nba/news/story?id=2390599

Rovell, D. (2005, October 18). Stern sure players will comply with dress code. Retrieved August 7, 2006, from http://sports.espn.go.com/nba/news/story?id=2195141

Rovell, D. (2003, November 20). Adu could grow soccer's popularity and Nike's wallet. Retrieved June 2, 2008, from http://espn.go.com/sports-business/s/2003/1119/1665998.html

Rutland, G. (2005, October 31). Why the NBA dress code bothers me. *Sacramento Bee*, B.4.

Ryan, B. (2004, November 12). The rap on Artest: He is off-key. *Boston Globe*, E.1.

Ryan, B. (1998, June 25). Youth isn't served by voracious NBA drafting strategy. *Boston Globe*, C.1.

Ryan, J. (1996, May 17). NBA needs improved plan for its rookies. *San Francisco Chronicle*, C1.

Sandoval, G., and Steinberg, D. (2004, May 5). High school stars rushing to NBA: New York's Telfair becomes eighth player to declare for draft this year. *New York Times*, D.01.

Sappenfield, M. (2001, May 22). Straight to the NBA—Without a stop at college. *Christian Science Monitor*, 1.

Schmitz, B. (2006, February 19). Vegas could be dicey for NBA. *Orlando Sentinel*, C.20.

Schrotenboer, B. (2007, April 22). Arresting image. *San Diego Union Tribune*. Retrieved November 7, 2007, from http://www.signonsandiego.com/sports/nfl/20070422–9999–lz1s22arrest.html

Shapiro, M. (24, June 2005). Stern and Hunter find gray area on age limit. Retrieved July 5, 2005, from http://www.cstv.com/sports/m-baskbl/stories/062405aaa.html

Sharp, D. (2006 December 22). NHL would love to feel the NBA's heat. *Detroit Free Press* (*Knight Ridder-Tribune News Service*), 1.

Sharp, D. (2005, October 29). NBA's players unwilling to redress dress code. *Knight Ridder-Tribune News Service*, 1.

Shaw, B. (2001, May 16). NBA has no place limiting draft age. *Plain Dealer*, 1.D.

Sheridan, C. (2006, December 17). Anthony may face stiffest penalty in wake of brawl. Retrieved May 13, 2008, from http://sports.espn.go.com/nba/columns/story?columnist=sheridan_chris&id=2699963

Sheridan, C. (2005, December 7a). Union files grievance over fines for long shorts. Retrieved December 7, 2005, from http://sports.espn.go.com/nba/news/story?id=2251724

Sheridan, C. (2005, April 17b). Hoops all-stars last to avoid NBA age limit? *USA Today*. Retrieved June 2, 2008, from http://www.usatoday.com/sports/preps/basketball/2005–04–17–age-limit-nba_x.htm

Sheridan, C. (2003, August 4). Kobe's true lesson. *SouthCoastToday.com*. Retrieved July 23, 2003, from http://www.southcoasttoday.com/daily/08–03/08–03–03/e10sp176.htm

Shields, D. (2004, May 6). Why not go pro? *New York Times*, A.35.

Shockey, N. (2005, November 11). New NBA dress code elicits controversy. *Falcon*. Retrieved May 18, 2007, from http://www.thefalcononline.com/story/4889

Shum, K. (2005, November 4). Clean up the NBA. *National Post*, A.19.

Simmons, B. (2005, November 3). NBA preview, Part II. Retrieved October 6, 2008, from http://sports.espn.go.com/espn/page2/story?page=simmons/051103

Skolnick, E. (2004, November 26). It's An Athlete . . . Hide! *South Florida Sun–Sentinel*, 3.C.

Sloane, B. (2006, December 23). Letter to editor—More than two sides to fight. *Los Angeles Times*, D.2.

Smith, A. (2004, March 17). Michael McCann interview. Retrieved from http://nbadraft.net/draftbuzz026.asp

Smith, D. (2006, December 2). Players go after the NBA: New ball, zero tolerance on insolence break U.S. labour laws, union declares. *Toronto Star*, E.2.

Smith, E. (2004, November 24). The NBA thugs on parade. *Philadelphia Daily News*, 19.

Smith, J. (2005, December 7). NBA dress code is an acceptable idea. *Phoenix*. Retrieved August 7, 2006, from http://media.www.loyolaphoenix.com/media/storage/paper673/news/2005/12/07/Discourse/Nba-Dresscode.Is.An.Acceptable.Idea-1123448.shtml

Smith, S. (2006, December 20) Ask Sam Smith. *Chicago Tribune*. Retrieved March 28, 2008, from http://chicagosports.chicagotribune.com/sports/basketball/bulls/askthewriter/cs-061220asksamsmith,1,2406687.story?coll=cs-home-headlines

Smith, S, (2005, June 22). New NBA deals ups [sic] age limit, averts lockout. *Atlanta Journal-Constitution*, D.1.

Smith, S. (2004, November 22a). NBA Begins to rehab with harsh penalties: Pacerscrippled as Artest is banned for rest of season. *Chicago Tribune*, 1.

Smith, S. (2004, November 20b). Bulls, NBA knew Artest was a ticking time bomb. *Knight Ridder-Tribune News Service*, 1.

Smith, S.A. (2004, November 12). With Artest, Pacers have to buy his rap, *Philadelphia Inquirer*, D.1.

Sorensen, T. (2006, December 18). NBA has big fight against perception. *Charlotte Observer* (*Knight Ridder-Tribune News Service*), 1.

Soshnick, S. (2005, October 19). NBA order to dress up doesn't mean selling out. Retrieved August 7, 2006, from http://quote.bloomberg. com/apps/news?pid=10000039&refer=columnist_soshnick&sid=aoi7c oZaGVys

Spanberg, E. (2005, June 23). NBA: Why aren't you watching. *Christian Science Monitor*. Retrieved October 7, 2005, from http://www.csmonitor.com/2005/0623/p11s02–alsp.html

Spears, M.J. (2000, June 28a). High school kid or college fan. *Denver Post*, D.01.

Spears, M.J. (2000, May 28b). NBA scouts eye high school stars Garnett, Bryant changedshape of NBA draft. *Denver Post*, C.20.

Spoken word: Spencer Haywood. An interview. Retrieved September 8, 2008, fromhttp://thestartingfive.wordpress.com/2007/05/12/spoken-word-spencer-haywood/

Springer, S. (2005, May 24). Teen angst: NBA grappling with divisive issue of age minimum. *Boston Globe*, F.1.

Starr, M. (2005, October). Duds go out of bounds: Pro basketball's new dress code is just part of a campaign to spruce up the game's tarnished image. *Newsweek*, 146(18), 49.

Starr, M. (2002, December 30). A strong kick for American soccer. *Newsweek*, 70.

Steele, D. (2005, November 20). In the NBA, the focus is on the game. *Sun*, 1.D.

Stein, L. (2005, October 26–November 1). In the game: Is race a factor in new NBA dress code? *Michigan Chronicle*, C.1.

Stein, L. (2004, July 7–July 13a). In the game: Don't believe the hype—High school stars aren't destroying NBA. *Michigan Chronicle*, C.1.

Stein, L. (2004, March 2–March 8b). Young guns: From high school to NBA; league's youth talk of town. *Michigan Chronicle*, C.1.

Stein, M. (2005, October 18). Pacers' Jackson calls ban on chains "racist state-

ment." Retrieved October 19, 2005, from http://sports.espn.
go.com/nba/news/story?id=2197001

Stein, M. (2004, November 20). This isn't doomsday for the NBA.
ESPN.com. Retrieved November 24, 2004, from http://sports.
espn.go.com/nba/columns/story?id=1927536

Stephen Jackson's not happy with the NBA dress code. (2005, October 21).
Girls TalkSports.com. Retrieved September 24, 2006, from
http://www.girlstalksports.com/Basketball/NBA/Stephen-Jack-
son%92s-not-happy-with-the-BA-dress-code-20051021179/

Stern wants NBA age limit raised to 20. (2005, April 13). Retrieved January
10, 2011, from http://sports.espn.go.com/nba/news/story?id=2035132

Stewart, L. (2005, October 21). Barkley fully supports NBA's new dress code.
LosAngeles Times, D.1.

Stop Mike Lupica. (2007, March 29). On Bill Simmons on O.J. Mayo.
Retrieved June 4, 2007, from http://www.stopmikelupica.com/
2007/03/on_bill_simmons_on_oj_mayo.php

Sullivan, J. (2005, June 28). Age restriction spoils NBA's labor deal. *Buffalo
News*, D.1.

Summit to address fracas. (2006, December 20). *Times Union* (Albany), C.5.

Suspensions total 47 games from Knicks-Nuggets fight. (2006, December
18). Retrieved March 28, 2008, from http://sports.espn.go.com/
nba/news/story?id=2701228

Talley Jr., W. (2007, July 29). Enough is enough! When exactly does personal
accountability come into play anymore? Retrieved June 11, 2008, from
http://jacknifedakilla.wordpress.com/2007/07/29/enough-is-enough-
when-exactly-does-personal-accountability-come-into-play-anymore/

Taylor, P. (2005, October 12). Balancing act: Proposed NBA dress code sends
mixed message. *Sports Illustrated*. Retrieved July 8, 2006, from
http://sportsillustrated.cnn.com/2005/writers/phil_taylor/10/12/taylo
r1012/index.html

Taylor, P. (2004, November 22). Slippery slope: Pacers-Pistons fight latest
shot in growing divide between players, fans. *Sports Illustrated*.
Retrieved December 1, 2004, from http://sportsillustrated.cnn.com/
2004/writers/phil_taylor/11/22/artest.fans/

Telander, R. (2007, February 26). Thuggery, lawlessness: Enough is enough.
Chicago Sun-Times, 99.

Telander, R. (2004, November 24). "Dis" mentality the evil behind NBA
brawl. *Chicago Sun-Times*, 150.

Tellem, A. (2001, May 13). Proposed age limit is hollow altruism. *New York
Times*, 8.11.

Temkin, Barry. (1999, May 9). There's no reason to tell Maggette to stay in
school. *Chicago Tribune*, 20.

The new NBA: No bad attitudes. (2006, November 1). Retrieved November

3, 2006, from http://www.sportingnews.com/yourturn/viewtopic. php?t=144476

The answer grows up. (2005, November 5). *Daily News*, 48.

Thomas, E. (2005, November 20). Courting more than just basketball. *Washington Post*, M.05.

Thompson, I. (2004, January 26). Ian Thomsen's fast break. *Sports Illustrated*, 84.

Thompson, J. (2001, May 13). Values of education must be considered. *New York Times*, 8.11.

Thompson, M. (2004, November 1). Hip-hop culture polarizing older white ticket buyers. *Knight Ridder-Tribune News Service*, 1.

Thugs, sports and consequences. (2004, November 23). *Chicago Tribune*, 20.

Trevor Ariza loses shoe, Ron Artest tosses it into the stands. (2009). Retrieved December 8, 2009, from http://www.youtube.com/ watch?v=vu1zMV5j0fo

Vecsey, P. (2006, December 18). Nuggets' Karl also earned ban. *New York Post*, 085.

Vecsey, G. (2006, December 21). As times change, fighting remains part of the game. *New York Times*, D.1.

Ventre, M. (2006, December 18). Two years later, a brawl that's worse. NBC Sports (MSNBC). Retrieved March 28, 2008, from http://nbc-sports.msnbc.com/id/16254683/site/21683474/

Vile conduct a symptom. (2004, November 23). *Augusta Chronicle*, A.04.

Wahl, G. (2003, March 3). Who's next? Freddy Adu. *Sports Illustrated*. Retrieved June 2, 2008, from http://sportsillustrated.cnn.com/si_ online/news/2003/03/03/freddy

Walker, C. (2006, December 18). Anthony's star takes a hit: NBA scoring leader awaits penalty after another "inexcusable" role in brawl. *Baltimore Sun*, 1.D.

Wang, O. (2004, November 19). The throwdown. Retrieved November 24, 2004, from http://www.o-dub.com/weblog/2004/11/throwdown-vibe-awards-fiasco-that.html

Weis, R. (2005, November 5). Embrace the NBA dress code. *American Thinker*. Retrieved May 18, 2007, from http://www.americanthinker. com/2005/11/embrace_the_nba_dress_code.html

Wells, J. (2005, October 21). Dress code: Hit or miss? Retrieved August 7, 2006, from http://www.blackathlete.net/artman/publish/printer_ 1185.shtml

Wharton, D. (1998, June 24). Hoop dreams: Though the NBA, scouts and even his coach aren't believers, Richardson of Poly High in Sun Valley enters today's draft. *Los Angeles Times*, 1.

Wharton, D. (2004, December 24). NBA bounces to an edgy hip-hop beat. *Los Angeles Times*, A.1.

When hoop dreams come true. (1998, April 10). *St. Louis Post-Dispatch*, C.16.

When millionaires attack: Friday's senseless fracas during a basketball game was horrifying and inexcusable. But hardly unexpected. (2004, November 23). Not in this day and age. *Greensboro News Record*, A.12.

Wherry, A. (2004, November 23). Courting disaster. *National Post*, S.3.

Whitaker, L. (2007, February 20). All-star wrap. *Slam*. Retrieved May 12, 2008, from http://slamonline.com/online/2007/02/all-star-wrap/

Whitaker, L. (2006, November 3). Referees gone wild. *Slam*. Retrieved November 3, 2006, from http://www.slamonline.com/online/2006/11/referees-gone-wild/

Whitaker, L. The long and short of it NBA policing of uniform bottoms goes way too far. *Sports Illustrated*. Retrieved May 21, 2007, from http://sportsillustrated.cnn.com/2005/writers/lang_whitaker/12/12/the.links/index.html

Whitlock, J. (2006, November 11). David Sterns rules are strict but necessary. *Knight Ridder-Tribune News Service*, 1.

Whitlock, J. (2005, November 6a). Black NBA players need to realize Stern is on their side. *Kansas City Star*. Retrieved May 15, 2005, from http://www.signonsandiego.com/uniontrib/20051106/news_1s6guest-col.html

Whitlock, J. (2005, April 14b). Stern's decision based on the biz. Retrieved April 14, 2005, from http://sports.espn.go.com/espn/page2/story?page=whitlock/050414

Whitlock, J. (2004, November 21). Fans like pro game, not the players. *Kansas City Star*. Retrieved November 24, 2004, from http://www.findarticles.com/p/articles/mi_kmtkc/is_200411/ai_n8593949

Widening the Waters. (2006, December 21). Retrieved September 8, 2008, from http://freedarko.blogspot.com/2006/12/widening-waters.html

Wilbon, M. (2006, December 19). A hittin' image. *Washington Post*, E.01.

Wilbon, M. (2005, October 15). There's no dressing up bad attitudes. *Washington Post*, E.01.

Wilbon, M. (2004, November 25a). Hip-hop culture contributes to NBA's bad rap. *Washington Post*, D.01.

Wilbon, M. (2004, November 22b). Justice is swift, sure, but perhaps too light. *Washington Post*, D.01.

Wilbon, M. (2004, November 21c). Friday fracas was criminal on every level. *Washington Post*, E.01.

Wilbon, M. (2004, May 6d). The road to the NBA is still filled with potholes. *Washington Post*, D.01.

Wilbon, M. (2002, June 25). For many teams, the NBA draft pool is clear as mud. *Washington Post*, D.01.

Will, G. (2005, November 20). Mentality of entitled fostering bad manners: Cocooned in a world cellphones and iPods, people do not consider others, says George Will. *Toronto Star*, A.17.

Williams, D., and Campbell, B. (1996). Draft lures young: Trend concerns NBA, colleges. *Times-Picayune*, E.1.

Willis, K. (2005, April 16). Old enough to drive? Prep stars too young too deal. *News Journal* (Daytona Beach), 02.D.

Wilstein, S. (2004, November 23a). "Growing Disconnect between fans, players." Retrieved January 6, 2012 from http://nbcsports.msnbc.com/id/6561841-nba/

Wilstein, S. (2004, December 9b). Brawl punishment won't stack up. *Charleston Daily Mail*, 3.B.

Windhorst, B. (2004, November 20). Artest deserves blame for brawl. *Akron Beacon Journal*. Retrieved November 24, 2004, from http://www.ohio.com/mld/becaonjournal

Wise, M. (2005, October 23). Opinions on the NBA dress code far from uniform. *Washington Post*, A01.

Wise, M. (2004, November 22). NBA meltdown provides blame aplenty. *Washington Post*, D.01.

Wise, M. (2002, June 23). Nowadays, the N.B.A. is drafting potential. *Washington Post*, D.01.

Wise, M. (2000, June 30). From Malone to Miles, N.B.A. grows younger. *New York Times*, 8.1.

Wise, M. (2000, January 30). Blinded by talent: Leon Smith struggles to return to the N.B.A. *New York Times*, 8.1.

Wise, M., and Jenkins, S. (2004, November 28). An enigma in the hall of infamy. *Washington Post*, A01.

Wiseman, T. (2004, November 22). Players to blame for brawl in Detroit. *Kentucky Kernel*. Retrieved November 24, 2004, from http://www.kykernel.com/home/index.cfm?event=displayArticle&ustory_id=8e7cba53–4399–4c4a-8ca6–67e5324e7e13

Wolfrum, W. (2007, February 21). Why say "five shot on NBA all-star weekend" instead of "five shot at end of MAGIC Fashion Convention"? Retrieved February 23, 2007, from http://www.williamkwolfrum.com/2007/02/21/why-say-five-shot-on-nba-all-star-weekend-instead-of-five-shot-at-end-of-magic-fashion-convention/

Youth movement in the N.B.A. (2001, June 30). *New York Times*, A.14.

Zero tolerance: No argument here. (2006, December 8). *Washington Post*, C.11.

Zirin, D. (2007, May 7a). An interview with Kevin Cooper: Talking sports from death row. Retrieved May 21, 2007, from http://www.counterpunch.org/zirin05032007.html

Zirin, D. (2006, December 18a). Brawl in the Garden. *Nation*. Retrieved
    March 28, 2008, from http://www.thenation.com/doc/2007
    0101/southpaw

Zirin, D. (2005, April 18). Straight outta high School: Jermaine O'Neal, race,
    and the NBA age limit. Retrieved June 4, 2008, from http://
    www.counterpunch.org/zirin04182005.html

Zirin, D. (2004, November 24, 2004). Fight night in the NBA. Retrieved
    November 24, 2004, from http://www.commondreams.org/views04/
    1122–30.htm

Zirin, D., and Chang, J. (2007, May 8). Hip-hop's E-Z scapegoats. *Nation*.
    Retrieved June 11, 2008, from http://www.thenation.com/doc/2007
    0521/zirin-chang

WORKS CITED: SCHOLARLY DISCOURSE

Abdel-Shehid, G. (2005). *Who da man? Black masculinities and sporting cultures*. Toronto: Canadian Scholars' Press.

Alexander, E. (1994). "Can you be black and look at this?" Reading the Rodney Kingvideo(s). In T. Golden (Ed.), *Black male: Representations of masculinity in contemporary American art* (pp. 91–100). New York: Whitney Museum of American Art.

Alexander, M. (2010). *The new Jim Crow: Mass incarceration in the age ofcolorblindness*. New York: New Press.

Andrews, D.L. (Ed.). (2001a). *Michael Jordan inc: Corporate sport, media culture, and late modern America*. Albany: State University of New York Press.

Andrews, D.L. (2001b). Michael Jordan Matters. In D.L. Andrews (Ed.), *Michael Jordan inc: Corporate sport, media culture, and late modern America* (pp. xiii–xx). Albany: State University of New York Press.

Andrews, D.L. (2001c). The fact(s) of Michael Jordan's blackness: Excavating a floating racial signifier. In D.L. Andrews (Ed.), *Michael Jordan inc: Corporate sport, media culture, and late modern America* (pp. 107–151). Albany: State University of New York Press.

Andrews, D.L., and Jackson, S.J. (Eds.). (2001). *Sports stars: The cultural politics of sporting celebrity*. New York: Routledge.

Andrews, D.L. (2000). Excavating Michael Jordan's blackness. In S. Birrell and M. McDonald (Eds.), *Reading sport: Critical essays on power and representation* (pp. 166–205). Boston: Northeastern University Press.

Andrews, V.L. (1996, December). African American player codes on celebration, taunting, and sportsmanlike conduct. *Journal of African American Studies*, 2(2–3), 57–92.

Ansell, A.E. (1997). *New right, new racism: Race and reaction in the United States*. New York: New York University Press.

Araton, H. (2005a). *Crashing the borders: How basketball won the world and lost its soul at home.* New York: Free Press.

Asante, M.K. (2008). *It's bigger than hip hop: The rise of the post-hip-hop generation.* New York: St. Martin's Press.

Baker, A. (2000). Hoop dreams in black and white: Race and basketball movies. In T. Boyd and K. Shropshire (Eds.), *Basketball Jones: America above the rim* (pp. 215–239). New York: New York University Press.

Baker A., and Boyd, T. (Eds.). (1997). *Out of bounds: Sports, media and the politics of identity.* Bloomington: University of Indiana Press.

Banet-Wiser, S. (1999). Hoop dreams: Professional basketball and the politics of race andgender. *Journal of Sport and Social Issues,* 23(4), 403–420.

Barkley, C., and Wilbon, M. (2005). *Who's afraid of a large black man?* New York: Penguin Press.

Benedict, J. (1997). *Public heroes, private felons: Athletes and crimes against women.* Evanston, IL: Northwestern University Press.

Benedict, J. (1998). Athletes and acquaintance rape, sage series on violence against women. Thousand Oaks, CA: Sage.

Benedict, J. (2004). *Out of bounds: Inside the NBA's culture of rape, violence, and crime.* New York: HarperCollins.

Benedict, J., and Yager, D. *(1998). Pros and cons: The criminals who play the NFL.* New York: Warner Books.

Berlant, L. (1997). *The queen of America goes to Washington city: Essays on sex and citizenship.* Durham, NC: Duke University Press.

Berndt, B. (2003, June 26). Notebook of a prison abolitionist. Retrieved September 8, 2008, from http://www.zmag.org/znet/viewArticle/10211

Bervera, X. (2003). *Reclaiming children from the prison system: The juvenile justice reform Act (Act 1225), state of Louisiana.* Applied Research Center.

Bhabha, H.K. (2000). Race, time and the revision of modernity. In L. Back and J. Solomos, (Eds.), *Theories of race and racism: A reader* (pp. 354–368). New York: Routledge.

Birrell, S., and McDonald, M. (2000). Reading sport, articulating power lines: An introduction. In S. Birrell and M. McDonald (Eds.), *Reading sport: Critical essays on power and representation* (pp. 3–13). Boston: Northeastern University Press.

Birrell, S., and McDonald, M. (1999). "Reading sport critically: A methodology for interrogating power," *Sociology of Sports Journal,* 16(4), 283–300.

Black student college graduation rates inch higher but a large racial gap persists. (2007, Winter). *Journal of Blacks in Higher Education.* Retrieved September 8, 2008, from http://www.jbhe.com/preview/winter07preview.html

Bonilla-Silva, E. (2003). *Racism without racists: Color-blind racism and the persistence of racial inequality in America.* New York: Rowan & Littlefield.

Boyd, T. (2003). *Young, black, rich and famous: The rise of the NBA, the hip hopinvasion and the transformation of American culture.* New York: Doubleday.

Boyd, T. (2000). Mo' money, mo' problems: Keepin it real in the post Jordan era. In T. Boyd and K. Shropshire (Eds.), *Basketball Jones: America above the rim* (pp. 59–67). New York: New York University Press.

Boyd, T. (1997). *Am I black enough for you: Popular culture from the 'hood and beyond.*Bloomington: University of Indiana Press.

Boyd, T., and Shropshire, K. (Eds.). (2000). *Basketball Jones: America above the rim.* New York: New York University Press.

Brooks, S.N. (2009). *Black men can't shoot.* Chicago: University of Chicago Press.

Brown, D. (2000). Sports law history: The Spencer Haywood case. Retrieved June 2, 2008, from http://www.sportslawnews.com/archive/history/SpencerHaywoodcase.htm

Brown, M.K., Carnoy, M., et al. (2003). *Whitewashing race: The myth of a color-blind society.* Berkeley: University of California Press.

Brown, T.N., Jackson, J.S., et al. (2003, May). There's no race on the playing field: Perceptions of racial discrimination among white and black athletes. *Journal of Sport and Social Issues, 27*(2), 162–183.

Camp, J.T. (2009). We know this place: Neoliberal racial regimes and the Katrina circumstance. *American Quarterly, 61*(3), 693–717.

Carey, K. (2003, Fall). *The funding gap: Low-income and minority student still receive fewer dollars in many states.* Retrieved June 5, 2008, from http://www2.edtrust.org/NR/rdonlyres/EE004C0A-D7B8-40A6-8A03-1F26B8228502/0/funding2003.pdf

Cashmore, E. (2001). *The black culture industry.* New York: Routledge.

Carrington, B., and McDonald, I. (2001). Introduce: "Race," sport, and British society. In B.Carrington and I. McDonald (Eds.), *"Race," sport and British society* (pp. 1–26). New York: Routledge.

Cernkovich, S.A., Giordano, P.C., and Rudolph, J. (2000). Race, crime, and the American dream. *Journal of Research in Crime and Delinquency, 37*(2), 131–170.

Chang, J. (2007). *Total chaos: The art and aesthetics of hip-hop.* New York: Basic Civitas Books.

Coker, C., Hampton, D., and Roberts, T. (1994, August). *A hip hop nation divided* (pp. 62–64), 112–115.

Cole, C.L. (2001). Nike's America/America's Michael Jordan. In D.L. Andrews (Ed.), *Michael Jordan inc.: Corporate sport, media culture and late modern America* (pp. 65–71). Albany: State University of New York.

Cole, C.L., and Andrews, D.L. (2001). America's new son: Tiger Woods and America's multiculturalism. In D.L. Andrews and S.J. Jackson (Eds.), *Sports stars: The cultural politics of sporting celebrity* (pp. 70–86). New York: Routledge.

Cole, C.L., and King, S. (1998). Representing black masculinity and urban possibilities: Racism, realism and hoop dreams. In G. Rail (Ed.), *Sport and postmodern times* (pp. 49–86). Albany: State University of New York Press.

Cole, C.L., and Andrews, D.L. (1996). Look—It's NBA show time!: Visions of race in popular imaginary. In N. Denzin (Ed.), *Cultural studies: A research volume* (pp. 141–181, vol. 1). New York: Routledge.

Cole, C.L. (1996). American Jordan: P.L.A.Y, consensus and punishment. *Sociology of Sport Journal*, 13(4), 366–398.

Cole, D. (2000). *No equal justice: Race and class in the American criminal justice system*. New York: New Press.

Collins, P.H. (2006). New commodities, new consumers: Selling blackness in a global marketplace. *Ethnicities*, 6(30), 297–317.

Collins, P.H. (2004). *Black sexual politics: African Americans, gender and the new racism*. New York: Routledge.

Cose, E. (1995). *The rage of a privileged class: Why do prosperous Blacks still have the blues?* New York: Harper Perennial.

Crenshaw, K.W. (2000). Race, reform and retrenchment. In L. Back and J. Solomos (Eds.), *Theories of race and racism: A reader* (pp. 549–560). New York: Routledge.

Crenshaw, K.W. (1997). Color-blind dreams and racial nightmares: Reconfiguring racism in the post–civil rights era. In T. Morrison (Ed.), *Birth of a nation' hood: Gaze, script, and spectacle in the O.J. Simpson Case* (pp. 97–168). New York: Pantheon Books.

Curtis Jr., R. (1998). Racism and rationales: A frame analysis of John Hoberman's Darwin's Athletes. *Social Science Quarterly*, 79(4), 885–891.

Daniels, C. (2007). *Ghetto nation: A journey into the land of bling and the home of the shameless*. New York: Doubleday.

Davis, A.Y. (2003). *Are prisons obsolete?* New York: Open Media Series.

Davis, A.Y. (1998a, Fall). Masked racism: Reflections on the prison industrial complex. *Colorlines*. Retrieved June 2, 2008, from http://www.colorlines.com/article.php?ID=114

Davis, A.Y. (1998b). Race and criminalization: Black Americans and the punishment industry. In Waheema Lubiano (Ed.), *The House that race built* (pp. 264–279). New York: Vintage Books.

Davis, M. (1995, February 20). Hell factories in the field: A prison-industrial complex. *Nation*, 260(7). Retrieved June 2, 2008, from http://www.radicalurbantheory.com/mdavis/hellfactories.html

Davis, R.G. (2008). Locating family: Asian-Canadian historical revisioning in Linda Ohama's "Obaachan's Garden" and Ann Marie Fleming's "The Magical Life of Long Tack Sam." *Journal of Canadian Studies*, 42(1), 1–22.

Denzin, N. (2001). Representing Michael. In D.L. Andrews (Ed.), *Michael Jordan inc.: Corporate sport, media culture and late modern America* (pp. 3–14). Albany: State University of New York Press.

Douglas, D.D. (2005). Venus, Serena, and the Women's Tennis Association: Where and when "race" enters. *Sociology of Sports Journal*, Vol. 22, No. 3, 256–283.

Dyson, M.E. (2007). *Know what I mean? Reflections on hip hop*. New York: Basic Civitas Books.

Dyson, M.E. (2005). *Is Bill Cosby right? Or has the black middle class lost its mind?* New York: Basic Civitas Books.

Dyson, M.E. (2001). Be like Mike? Michael Jordan and the pedagogy of desire. In D.L. Andrews (Ed.), *Michael Jordan inc.: Corporate sport, media culture and late modern America* (pp. 259–268). Albany: State University of New York Press.

Employers' replies to racial names. (2003, September). National Bureau of EconomicResearch. Retrieved May 18, 2007, from http://www.nber.org/digest/sep03/w9873.html

Fanon, F. (2000). The fact of blackness. In Les Back and John Solomos (Eds.), *Theories of race and racism: A reader* (pp. 257–266). New York: Routledge.

Fanon, F. (1991). *Black skin, white masks*. New York: Grove Press.

Farred, G. (2007, spring). The event of the black body at rest: Melee in Motown. *Cultural Critique*, 66, 58–77.

Feagin, J.R. (2010). *The white racial frame: Centuries of racial framing and counter-framing*. New York: Routledge.

Feagin, J., and Sikes, M. (1995). *Living with racism: The black middle-class experience*. Boston: Beacon Press.

Ferber, A. (2007). The construction of black masculinity: White supremacy now and then. *Journal of Sport and Social Issues*, 31(11), 11–24.

Fiorina, M. (2005). *Culture war? The myth of a polarized America*. New York: Longman.

Fiske, John. (1989). *Understanding popular culture*. New York: Routledge.

Foucault, M. (1995). *Discipline and punish: The birth of the prison*. New York: Vintage Books.

Frank, T. (2004). *Whats's the matter with Kansas? How conservatives won the heart ofAmerica.* New York: Metropolitan Books.

Fredrick, B.R. (2007). *This ain't NASCAR: Framing the Pacers-Pistons brawl.* Doctoral Dissertation, School of Journal and Mass Communication, University of Colorado.

Gates, H.L. (1998, June 1). Annals of marketing: Net worth. *New Yorker*, pp. 48–53.

Gates, H.L. (1992). *Loose canons: Notes on the culture wars.* New York: Oxford University Press.

Gillman, S. (1985). *Differences and pathology: Stereotypes of sexuality, race and madness.* Ithaca: Cornell University Press.

Giroux, H. (2003a). Racial injustice and disposable youth in the age of zero tolerance. *Qualitative Studies in Education*, 16(4), July–August, pp. 553–565.

Giroux, H. (2003b). *The abandoned generation: Democracy beyond the culture of fear.* New York: Palgrave Macmillan.

Giroux, H. (2003c). Spectacles of race and pedagogies of denial: Anti-black racist pedagogy under the reign of neoliberalism. *Communication Education*, Vol. 52, No. 3–4, 191–211.

Giroux, H. (1994). *Disturbing pleasures: Learning popular culture.* New York: Routledge.

Gitlin, T. (1995). *Twilight of common dreams: Why America is wracked by culture wars.* New York: Metropolitan.

Goldberg, D.T. (2000). Racial knowledge. In L. Back and J. Solomos (Eds.), *Theories of race and racism: A reader* (pp. 154–180). New York: Routledge.

Goldberg, D.T. (1997). *Racial subjects: Writing on race in America.* New York: Routledge.

Goldberg, D.T. (1993). *Racist culture.* Cambridge: Blackwell.

Gordon, A. (1995). The work of corporate culture: Diversity management. *Social Text*, 44, 3–30.

Gray, H. (2005). *Cultural moves: African Americans and the politics of representation.* Berkeley: University of California Press.

Gray, H. (1995). *Watching race: Television and the struggle for blackness.* Minneapolis: University of Minnesota Press.

Groothuis, P., Hill, J.R., and Perri, T. (2005). Early entry in the NBA draft: The influence of unraveling, human capital, and option value. Working papers from the Department of Economics, Appalachian State University. Retrieved June 2, 2008, from http://econ.appstate.edu/RePEc/pdf/wp0405.pdf

Grossberg, L. (1997). *Bringing it all back home: Essays on cultural studies.* Durham: Duke University Press.

Grossberg, L. (1988). *We gotta get out of this place: Popular conservatism and postmodern Culture.* New York: Routledge.

Guerrero, L. (2011). One nation under a hoop: Race, meritocracy, and messiahs in the NBA. In D. Leonard and C.R. King (Eds.), *Commodified and criminalized: New racism and African Americans in contemporary sports.* Lanham, MD: Rowman & Littlefield.

Hardy. E. (2006). *Blood beats: Vol. 1 demos, remixes & extended versions.* Washington, DC: Redbone Press.

Harrison, C.K. (2001). From Paul Robeson to Althea Gibson to Michael Jordan. In D. L. Andrews (Ed.), *Michael Jordan inc.: Corporate sport, media culture and late modern America* (pp. vii–xii). Albany: State University of New York Press.

Hausman, J.A., and Leonard, G.K. (1997). Superstars in the National Basketball Association: Economic and policy. *Journal of Labor Economics,* 15(4), 586–624.

Heisler, M. (2004) *Madmen's ball: The inside story of the Lakers' dysfunctional dynasties.* New York: Triumph Books.

Hispanic and black high school graduation rates very low. (2004, February 26). Retrieved September 8, 2008, from http://www.parapundit.com/archives/001959.html

Hoberman, J. (1997). *Darwin's athletes: How sport has damaged black America and preserved the myth of race.* Boston: Houghton Mifflin.

hooks, b. (1996). *Reel to real: Race, sex, and class at the movies.* New York: Routledge.

hooks, b. (1992). *Black looks: Race and representation.* Boston: South End Press.

Hopkinson, N., and Moore, N.Y. (2006). *Deconstructing Tyrone: A new look at black masculinity in the hip-hop generation.* New York: Cleis Press.

Hosang, D. (1999, Winter). The economics of the new brutality. *Colorlines.* Retrieved May 8, 2008, from http://www.colorlines.com/article.php?ID=89

Hoechsmann, M. (2001). Just do it: What Michael Jordan has to teach us. In D.L. Andrews (Ed.), *Michael Jordan inc.: Corporate sport, media culture and late modern America* (pp. 269–276). Albany: State University of New York Press.

Hughes, G. (2004). Managing black guys: Representation, corporate culture, and the NBA. *Sociology of Sport Journal,* 21, 163–184.

Hunter, J.D. (1992). *Culture wars: The struggle to define America.* New York: Basic Books.

Hunter, J.D., and Wolfe, A. (2006). *Is there a culture war?: A dialogue on values and American public life.* Washington, DC: Brookings Institute Press.

Jackson, J.L. (2005). *Real black: Adventures in racial sincerity.* Chicago: University of Chicago Press.

Jackson, R. (2006). *Scripting the black masculine body: Identity, discourse, and racial politics in popular media.* New York: State University of New York Press.

Jacoby, R. (1994). *Dogmatic wisdom: How the culture wars divert education and district America.* New York: Doubleday.

James, J. (1999). *Shadowboxing: Representations of black feminist politics.* New York: St. Martin's Press.

James, J. (1996). *Resisting state violence: Radicalism, gender, and race in Americanculture.* Minneapolis: University of Minnesota Press.

Jeffords, S. (1997). *Hard bodies: Hollywood masculinity in the Reagan era.* New Brunswick: Rutgers University Press.

Johnson, A.G. (1997). *Privilege, power, and difference.* New York: McGraw-Hill.

Johnson, L., and Roediger, D. (1997). Hertz, don't it? Becoming colorless and staying black in the crossover. In T. Morrison (Ed.), *Birth of a nation 'hood: Gaze, script and spectacle in the O.J. Simpson case* (pp. 197–240). New York: Random House.

Johnson, T., Boyden, J.E., and Pittz, W. (2001). Racial profiling and punishment in U.S. public schools: How zero tolerance policies and high stakes testing subvert academic excellent and racial equity. Oakland: Applied Research Center, Erase Initiative. Retrieved June 2, 2008, from http://www.arc.org/content/view/235/36/

Judy, R.A.T. (2004). On the question of nigga authenticity. In M. Forman and M.A. Neal (Eds.), *That's the joint: The hip-hop reader* (pp. 105–118). New York: Routledge.

Jung, A. (2008, May/June). Children behind bars for life. *Colorlines.* Retrieved September 8, 2008, from http://www.colorlines.com/printerfriendly. php?ID=293

Kanazawa, M.T., and Funk, J.P. (2001, October). Racial discrimination in professional basketball: Evidence from Nielsen ratings. *Economic Inquiry*, 39(4), 599–608.

Katz, J. (2006). *The macho paradox: Why some men hurt women and how all men can help.* Naperville, IL: Sourcebooks.

Kelley, R.D.G. (2004). Looking for the "real" nigga: Social scientists construct the ghetto. In M. Forman and M.A. Neal (Eds.), *That's the joint: The hip-hop reader* (pp. 119–136). New York: Routledge.

Kelley, R.D.G. (1998). Playing for keeps: Pleasure and profit on the postindustrial playground. In W. Lubiano (Ed.), *The house that race built* (pp. 195–231). New York: Vintage.

Kelley, R.D.G. (1997). *Yo' mama's disfunktional!: Fighting the culture wars in urban America.* Boston: Beacon Press.

Kellner, D. (1995). *Media culture: Cultural studies, identity, and politics between the modern and postmodern.* New York: Routledge.

Keteyian, A., Araton, H., and Dardis, M.F. (1997). *Money players: Days and nights inside the new NBA.* New York: Pocket Books.

King, C.R., and Springwood, C.F. (2005). Body and soul: Physicality, disciplinarity, and the overdetermination of blackness. In D. Hunt (Ed.), *Channeling blackness: Studies in television and race in America* (pp. 185–206). New York: Oxford University Press.

King, C.R., and Springwood, C.F. (2001). *Beyond the cheers: Race as spectacle in college sport.* Albany: State University of New York.

Kitwana, B. (2005). *Why white kids love hip hop: Wangstas, wiggers, wannabes, and the new reality of race in America.* New York: Basic Books.

Lafrance, M., and Rail, G. (2001). Excursions into otherness: Understanding Dennis Rodman and the limits of subversive agency. In D.L. Andrews and S.J. Jackson (Eds.), *Sports stars: The cultural politics of sporting celebrity* (pp. 35–50). New York: Routledge.

Lane, J. (2007). *Under the boards: The cultural revolution in basketball.* New York: Bison Books.

Lapchick, R. (2005, October 24). NBA players should dress up. Retrieved September 25, 2006, from http://sports.espn.go.com/espn/page2/story?page=lapchick/051025

Lapchick, R. (2003a). Crime and athletes: The new racial stereotypes of the 1990's. *Sports Business Journal.* Retrieved September 8, 2008, from http://www.bus.ucf.edu/sport/cgi-bin/site/sitew.cgi?page=/news/articles/article_05.htx

Lapchick, R. (2003b). The Kobe Bryant case: Athletes, violence, stereotypes and the games we play. *Sports Business Journal.* Retrieved May 1, 2008, from http://155.33.32.224/csss/rel.html

Lapchick, R. (2002). *Smashing barriers.* New York: Madison Books.

Leonard, D.J. (2006a). The real color of money: Controlling black bodies in the NBA. *Journal of Sport and Social Issues,* 30(2), 158–179.

Leonard, D.J. (2006b). A world of criminals or a media construction?: Race, gender, celebrity and the athlete/criminal discourse. In A. Raney and J. Bryant (Eds.), *Handbook of Sports Media* (pp. 523–542). Mahwah, NJ: Erlbaum.

Leonard, D.J. (2004). The next M. J. or the next O.J.? Kobe Bryant, race, and the absurdity of colorblind rhetoric. *Journal of Sport and Social Issues,* 28(3), 284–313.

Lewis, A. (2003). *Media representations of rap music: The vilification of hip-hop culture.* Master's Thesis, Communication, Culture, and Technology, Georgetown University.

Males, M., and Macallair, D. (2000). The color of justice: An analysis of juve-
    nile adult court transfers in California. San Francisco: Building Blocks
    for Youth. Retrieved June 2, 2008, from http://www.buildingblocks-
    foryouth.org/colorofjustice/coj.html

Mallory, J.J. (2007, September). Mass incarceration, democracy, and inclu-
    sion. *Socialism and Democracy*, 21(1), 97–122.

Markovitz, J. (2006). Anatomy of a spectacle: Race, gender, and memory in
    the Kobe Bryant rape case. *Sociology of Sport Journal*, 23 (4),
    396–418.

Marriott, D. (2000). *On black men*. New York: New York University Press.

Mauer, M., and the Sentencing Project (2001). *Race to Incarcerate*. New York:
    New Press.

May Buford, R.A. (2008). *Living through the hoop: High school basketball, race,
    and the American Dream*. New York: New York University Press.

McCann, M. (2006). The reckless pursuit of dominion: A situational analysis
    of the NBA and diminishing player autonomy. *Journal of Labor and
    Employment Law*, 8, 819.

McCann, M. (2004). Illegal defense: The irrational economics of banning
    high school players from the NBA draft. Retrieved June 1, 2008,
    http://www.nbadraft.net/illegaldefense/index.html

McClintock. A. (1995). *Imperial leather: Race, gender and sexuality in the colo-
    nial contest*. New York: Routledge.

McDonald, M., and Andrews, D.L. (2001). Michael Jordan: Corporate sport
    and postmodern celebrityhood. In D.L. Andrews and S.J. Jackson
    (Eds.), *Sports stars: The cultural politics of sporting celebrity* (pp. 24–35).
    New York: Routledge.

McDonald, M. (2001). Safe sex symbol? Michael Jordan and the politics of
    representation. In D.L. Andrews (Ed.), *Michael Jordan inc. Corporate
    sport, media culture, and late modern America* (pp. 153–176). Albany:
    State University of New York Press.

McDonald, M. (1996). Horatio Alger with a jump shot: Michael Jordan and
    the American dream. *Iowa Journal of Cultural Studies*, 15, 33–47.

McElya, M. (2001). Trashing the presidency: Race, class and the Clinton/
    Lewinsky affair. In L. Berlant and L. Dugan (Eds.), *Our Monica our-
    selves: The Clinton affair and the national interest* (pp. 156–174). New
    York: New York University Press.

Mc Laughlin, T. (2008). *Give and go: Basketball as a cultural practice*. Albany:
    State University of New York Press.

McNutt, K. (2002). *Hooked on hoops: Understanding black youths' blind devotion
    to basketball*. Chicago: African American Images.

Mercer, K. (1994). *Welcome to the jungle: New positions in black cultural studies*.
    New York: Routledge.

Miller, C. (2004, December 1). Study finds strong link between race, employer response: Calif. researcher finds Arab Americans most likely to face job discrimination. *Michigan Daily*. Retrieved May 18, 2007, from http://media.www.michigandaily.com/media/storage/paper851/news/2004/12/01/News/Study.Finds.Strong.Link.Between.Race.Employer.Response-1427220.shtml

Miller, J. (1997). *Search and destroy: African-American males in the criminal justice system.* New York: Cambridge University Press.

Miller, T., and McHoul, A. (1998). *Popular culture and everyday life.* London: Sage.

Mirpuri, A. (2011). Why can't Kobe pass (the ball)? Race and the NBA in an age of neo-liberalism. In D. Leonard and C.R. King (Eds.), *Commodified and criminalized: New Racism and African Americans in contemporary sports.* Lanham, MD: Rowman & Littlefield.

Moorti, S. (2002). *Color of rape: Gender and race in television's public sphere.* Albany: State University of New York Press.

Neal, M.A. (2006, April 11). A social disaster—(White) male privilege, black respectability, and black women's bodies. Retrieved May 22, 2007, from http://newblackman.blogspot.com/2006/04/social-disaste-voices-from-durham_11.html

Neal, M.A. (2005). *New black man.* New York: Routledge.

Neal, M.A. (2004, November 24). The real nigger show. Retrieved November 24, 2004, from http://www.popmatters.com/features/041124-samboshow.shtml

O'Connor, I. (2005a). *The jump: Sebastian Telfair and the high stakes business of high school ball.* Emmaus, PA: Rodale.

Ogletree, C. (2000). Privileges and immunities for basketball stars and other sports heroes. In T. Boyd and K. Shropshire (Eds.), *Basketball Jones* (pp. 12–26). New York: New York University Press.

Omi, M., and Winant, H. (1994). *Racial formation in the United States: From the 1960s to the 1990s.* New York: Routledge.

O'Reilly, B. (2006a). *Culture warrior.* New York: Broadway Books.

Oriard, M. (2009). *Bowled over: Big-time college football from the sixties to the BCS era.* Chapel Hill: University of North Carolina Press.

Parenti, C. (2000). *Lockdown America: Police and prisons in the age of crisis.* New York: Verso.

Parenti, C. (1997, December). Law and order. *Z Magazine.* Retrieved April 15, 2008, from www.zmag.org/ZMag/articles/dec97Parenti.htm

Patterson, O. (2006, March 26). A poverty of the mind. *New York Times.* Retrieved October 6, 2008, from http://www.nytimes.com/2006/03/26/opinion/26patterson.html?pagewanted=1&ei=5088&en=23bf0dce1434780d&ex=1301029200&partner=rssnyt&emc=rss)

Perry, I. (2005). *Prophets of the hood: Politics and poetics in hip-hop.* Durham, NC: Duke University Press.

Picca, L.H., and Feagin, J.R. (2007). *Two-faced racism: Whites in the backstage and frontstage.* New York: Routledge.

Platt, L. (2003). *Only the strong survive: The odyssey of Allen Iverson.* New York: It Books.

Platt, L. (2002). *New Jack Jocks: Rebels, race, and the American athlete.* Philadelphia: Philadelphia University Press.

Platt, L. (2000). The white shadow. In T. Boyd and K. Shropshire (Eds.), *Basketball Jones: America above the rim* (pp. 68–74). New York: New York University Press.

Pough, G. (2004a). *Check it while I wreck it: Black womanhood, hip-hop culture, and the public sphere.* Boston: Northeastern University Press.

Pough, G. (2004b). Seeds and legacies: Tapping the potential in hip-hop. In M. Forman and M.A. Neal (Eds.), *That's the joint! The hip-hop studies reader* (pp. 283–290). New York: Routledge.

Powell. S. (2007). *Souled out? An evolutionary crossroads for blacks in sport.* Champaign, IL: Human Kinetics.

Praeger, D. (2009). *Marked: Race, crime, and finding work in an era of mass incarceration.* Chicago: University of Chicago Press.

Prashad, V. (2003). *Keeping up with the Dow Joneses.* Cambridge, MA: South End Press.

Proposition 21 Approved by California Voters" (2000, March 9). Retrieved September 8, 2008, from http://www.cyc-net.org/today2000/today000309.html

Rhoden, W.C. (2006). *Forty million dollar slaves: The rise, fall, and redemption of the black athlete.* New York: Crown.

Rodriguez, D. (2007). The meaning of "disaster" under the dominance of white life. In South End Press Collective's (Ed.), *What lies beneath: Katrina, race, and the state of the nation* (pp. 133–156). Boston: South End Press.

Rodriguez, D. (2006). *Forced passages: Imprisoned radical intellectuals and the U.S. prison regime.* Minneapolis: University of Minnesota Press.

Rose, T. (2008). *Hip-hop wars: What we talk about when we talk about hip-hop—And why it matters.* New York: Basic Civitas Books.

Rosenbaum, D. (2003). It doesn't pay to be young in the NBA. Retrieved June 2, 2008, from http://www.uncg.edu/bae/people/rosenbaum/youngnba1.pdf

Russell, K.K. (1998). *The color of crime: Racial hoaxes, white fear, black protectionism, police harassment, and other macroaggressions.* New York: New York University Press.

Saltman, K.J. (2003). Introduction. In K.J. Saltman and D.A. Gabbard (Eds.), *Education as enforcement: The militarization and corporatization of schools*. New York:Routledge.

Sewell Jr., J.I. (2006). *"Don't believe the hype": The construction and export of African American images in hip-hop culture*. Master's thesis, Department of Communication, East Tennessee University.

Sexton, J. (2006). The field of fantasy and the court of appeal: On *Friday Night Lights* and *Coach Carter*. In C.R. King and D.J. Leonard (Eds.), *Visual economies of/in motion: Sport and film* (pp. 103–120). New York: Peter Lang.

Sharpe, E. (Ed.). (1999). *Culture wars and local politics*. Lawrence: University of Kansas Press.

Shropshire, K. (2000). Deconstructing the NBA. In T. Boyd and K. Shropshire (Eds.), *Basketball Jones: America above the rim* (pp. 75–89). New York: New York University Press.

Sine, T. (1995). *Searching for sanity in America's culture wars*. Grand Rapids, MI: Eerdmans.

Skiba, R.J. (2000, August). Zero tolerance, zero evidence: An analysis of school disciplinary practice. Indiana Education Policy Center.

Smith, E. (2007). *Race, sport, and the American Dream*. Durham, NC: Carolina Academic Press.

Smith, E. (2000). Incivility and basketball. In T. Boyd and K. Shropshire (Eds.), *Basketball Jones: America above the rim* (pp. 123–150). New York: New York University Press.

Spencer, N.E. (2004). Sister act VI: Venus and Serena Williams at Indiana Wells: "Sincere fictions" and white racism. *Journal of Sport and Social Issues*, 28(2), 115–135.

Stoler, A. (1997). *Race and education of desire*. Chapel Hill, NC: Duke University Press.

Sullivan, E. (2007). Deprived dignity: Degrading treatment and abusive discipline in New York City and Los Angeles public schools. National Economic and Social Rights Initiative. Retrieved June 5, 2008, from http://www.nesri.org/Deprived%20of%20Dignity%2007.pdf

Teo, P. (2000). Racism in the news: A critical discourse analysis of news reporting in two Australian newspapers. *Discourse and Society*, 11(1), 7–49.

Tompkins, A. (2007, March 14). *College sports and graduation rates*. Retrieved September 8, 2008, from http://www.poynter.org/column.asp?id=2& aid=119780

Tucker, L. (2003, November). Blackballed: Basketball and representations of the black male athlete. *American Behavioral Scientist*, 47(3), 306–328.

Verdugo, R. (2002). Race-ethnicity, social class, and zero-tolerance policies: The cultural and structural wars. *Education and Urban Society*, 35(1), 50–75.

Von Zielbauer, P. (2005, June 17). Race a factor in job offers for ex-convicts. *New York Times*. Retrieved October 8, 2008, from http://www.nytimes.com/2005/06/17/nyregion/17felons.html?_r=1&oref=slogin

X, M., and Haley, A. (1987). *The autobiography of Malcolm X: As told to Alex Haley*. New York: Ballantine Books.

Watkins, S.C. (1998). *Representing: Hip hop culture and the production of black cinema*. Chicago: University of Chicago Press.

West, C. (1999). The new politics of difference. In C. West (Ed.), *The Cornel West reader* (pp. 119–139). New York: Basic Civitas Books.

West, C. (1994). *Race matters*. New York: Vintage Press.

Whertheim, L.J. (2005). *Transition game: How Hoosiers went hip-hop*. New York: Putnam.

Whannel, G. (1998). Individual stars and collective identities in media sport. In M. Roche (Ed.), *Sports, popular culture, and identity* (vol. 5, pp. 23–36). Aachen: Meyer and Meyer Verlag.

Williams, J. (2006). *Enough: The phony leaders, dead-end movements, and culture of failure that are undermining black America—And what we can do about it*. New York: Three Rivers Press.

Williams, P.J. (1997). *Seeing a color-blind future: The paradox of race*. New York: Noonday Press.

Williams, R. (1998). Living at the crossroads: Exploration in race, nationality, sexuality, and gender. In W. Lubiano (Ed.), *The house that race built* (pp. 136–156). New York: Vintage Books.

Wynter, L. (2002). *American skin: Popular culture, big business and the end of white America*. New York: Random House.

Young, L. (2000). Imperial culture. In L. Back and J. Solomos (Eds.), *Theories of race and racism: A reader* (pp. 267–286). New York: Routledge.

Zirin, D. (2007b). *Welcome to the terrordome: The pain, politics, and promise of sports*. Chicago: Haymarket Press.

INDEX

259

SUNY series on Sport, Culture, and Social Relations
CL Cole and Michael A. Messner, editors

Alan M. Klein, *Little Big Men: Bodybuilding Subculture and Gender Construction*

Todd W. Crosset, *Outsiders in the Clubhouse: The World of Women's Professional Golf*

> Winner, North American Society for the Sociology of Sport (NASSS) Book Award

Wanda Ellen Wakefield, *Playing to Win: Sports and the American Military, 1898-1945*

Laurel R. Davis, *The Swimsuit Issue and Sport: Hegemonic Masculinity in Sports Illustrated*

Jim McKay, *Managing Gender: Affirmative Action and Organizational Power in Australian, Canadian, and New Zealand Sport*

Juan-Miguel Fernandez-Balboa (ed.), *Critical Postmodernism in Human Movement, Physical Education, and Sport*

Genevieve Rail (ed.), *Sport and Postmodern Times*

Shona M. Thompson, *Mother's Taxi: Sport and Women's Labor*

Nancy Theberge, *Higher Goals: Women's Ice Hockey and the Politics of Gender*

> Winner, North American Society for the Sociology of Sport (NASSS) Book Award

Helen Jefferson Lenskyj, *Inside the Olympic Industry: Power, Politics, and Activism*

C. Richard King and Charles Fruehling Springwood, *Beyond the Cheers: Race as Spectacle in College Sport*

David L. Andrews (ed.), *Michael Jordan, Inc.: Corporate Sport, Media Culture, and Late Modern America*

Margaret Gatz, Michael A. Messner, and Sandra J. Ball-Rokeach (eds.), *Paradoxes of Youth and Sport*

Helen Jefferson Lenskyj, *The Best Olympics Ever? Social Impacts of Sydney 2000*

Anne Bolin and Jane Granskog (eds.), *Athletic Intruders; Ethnographic Research on Women, Culture, and Exercise*

Ralph C. Wilcox, David L. Andrews, Robert Pitter, and Richard L. Irwin (eds.), *Sporting Dystopias: The Making and Meanings of Urban Sport Cultures*

Robert E. Rinehart and Synthia Sydnor (eds.), *To the Extreme: Alternative Sports, Inside and Out*

Eric Anderson, *In the Game: Gay Athletes and the Cult of Masculinity*

Pirkko Markula (ed.), *Feminist Sport Studies: Sharing Experiences of Joy and Pain*

Michael A. Messner, *Out of Play: Critical Essays on Gender and Sport*

David Nylund, *Beer, Babes, and Balls: Masculinity and Sports Talk Radio*

David Coad, *The Metrosexual: Gender, Sexuality, and Sport*

Murray G. Phillips (ed.), *Deconstructing Sport History: A Postmodern Analysis*

Caroline Joan S. Picart, *From Ballroom to DanceSport: Aesthetics, Athletics, and Body Culture*

Alan Tomlinson and Christopher Young (eds.), *National Identity and Global Sports Events: Culture, Politics, and Spectacle in the Olympics and the Football World Cup*

Helen Jefferson Lenskyj, *Olympic Industry Resistance: Challenging Olympic Power and Propaganda*